Cloud Computing:
A Practical Approach

Anthony T. Velte
Toby J. Velte, Ph.D.
Robert Elsenpeter

Mc
Graw
Hill

New York   Chicago   San Francisco
Lisbon   London   Madrid   Mexico City
Milan   New Delhi   San Juan
Seoul   Singapore   Sydney   Toronto

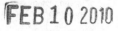

The McGraw-Hill Companies

Cataloging-in-Publication Data is on file with the Library of Congress

McGraw-Hill books are available at special quantity discounts to use as premiums and sales promotions, or for use in corporate training programs. To contact a representative, please e-mail us at bulksales@mcgraw-hill.com.

Cloud Computing: A Practical Approach

1234567890   FGR FGR   019

ISBN   978-0-07-162694-1
MHID   0-07-162694-8

 The pages within this book were printed on paper containing 100% post-consumer fiber.

Sponsoring Editor
Wendy Rinaldi

Editorial Supervisor
Patty Mon

Project Manager
Vipra Fauzdar,
Glyph International

Acquisitions Coordinator
Joya Anthony

Technical Editor
Charles Babcock

Copy Editor
Margaret Berson

Proofreader
Paul Tyler

Indexer
Write Away Indexing
Services

Production Supervisor
Jean Bodeaux

Composition
Glyph International

Illustration
Glyph International

Art Director, Cover
Jeff Weeks

Cover Designer
Jeff Weeks

For Ava Holder—A girl so small who should not have to be so strong, but she is.

—ATV

For Dr. Jon Gottesman—A brilliant mind and great mentor who never loses sight of the big picture.

—TJV

For Bryan Reynolds—a fellow writer and great cousin.

—RCE

About the Authors

Anthony T. Velte, CISSP, CISA, has spent over 20 years in the information systems industry. He is co-founder of Velte Publishing, Inc. and the co-author of more than a dozen books, including the award winning *Green IT: Reduce Your Information System's Environmental Impact While Adding to the Bottom Line* and *Microsoft Virtualization with Hyper-V*. Mr. Velte also works for an industry-leading security software company. He consults with companies large and small, helping them optimize and protect their information systems infrastructures. He can be reached at atv@velte.com.

Toby J. Velte, Ph.D., is an international best-selling author of business technology articles and books. He is co-founder of Velte Publishing, Inc. and the co-author of more than a dozen books, including the award winning *Green IT: Reduce Your Information System's Environmental Impact While Adding to the Bottom Line* and *Microsoft Virtualization with Hyper-V*. Dr. Velte is currently part of Microsoft's North Central practice focused on helping thriving companies with their technology-based initiatives. He works with large organizations to create IT roadmaps that are business focused and practically implemented. He can be reached at tjv@velte.com.

Robert Elsenpeter is an award-winning author and journalist, freelance writer, and author of more than a dozen technology books. He's co-author of the award-winning book *Green IT: Reduce Your Information System's Environmental Impact While Adding to the Bottom Line*. He has a bachelor's degree in Information Technology.

About the Technical Editor

Charles Babcock is former technical editor of Computerworld and technology editor at Interactive Week. He is currently an editor-at-large at Information Week in San Francisco. He has spent 25 years covering various technologies and trends in the computer industry, and holds a bachelor's degree in journalism from Syracuse University.

Contents

Acknowledgments

We were fortunate enough to be able to talk with a lot of very talented people while preparing this book for you. We spoke not only to people who implemented their own cloud solutions, but also those who help develop cloud solutions, as well as officers of several major cloud solution providers.

First, we want to thank Darren Boeck of McNeilus Steel. He told us how he was able to build a virtualized environment for the clients on his network, allowing us to summarize his experiences for you.

We also had the pleasure of speaking again with John Engates, CTO of Rackspace Hosting. He talked with us about Rackspace's cloud computing services and explained their vision of how they see cloud computing as it exists today and how it will continue to evolve.

Steve Fisher, senior vice president of AppExchange at Salesforce.com, was a wonderful resource, talking to us not only about what Salesforce.com brings to the cloud party, but also how businesses are using it and how he sees it evolving.

Ryan Collier, member of Accenture's Citrix XenServer Capability Group, enlightened us about the merits of the Citrix XenServer, as well as how he sees the cloud developing.

Christopher Crowhurst, Vice President of Architecture & BSI at Thomson Reuters, shared his thoughts on cloud computing. He also shared a case study outlining a very forward-thinking implementation of a cloud-based service at Thompson Reuters that was successfully completed back when the words "Cloud Computing" were rarely uttered.

Charles Babcock, our Technical Editor, helped us keep the facts straight and the overall content aligned with your expectations. We appreciate every edit and suggestion and know that it is a better book because of his input.

We also acknowledge the patience and hard work of the people at McGraw-Hill, notably those involved in the process of bringing this book to fruition. Thanks to Wendy Rinaldi, Sponsoring Editor and Editorial Director; Patty Mon, Editorial Supervisor; Jean Bodeaux, Senior Production Supervisor; Vipra Fauzdar, Production Project Manager; Joya Anthony, Acquisitions Coordinator; and Margaret Berson, Copy Editor. You can also flip back a few pages to see the rest of the folks who worked their magic throughout the process of creating this book for you. We acknowledge all of them and appreciate their efforts.

Introduction

Who Should Read This Book

This book is targeted at a broad audience, but in a nutshell–to anyone who wants to learn more about cloud computing. Cloud computing has become a hot topic in recent years, and people at different levels in your organization need to understand cloud computing in different ways.

This book is for anyone who may have recently heard the term "cloud computing" for the first time and needs to know what it is and how it helps them. This book is also for C-level executives, managers, analysts, and all manner of IT professionals. The goals of the book range from just wanting to be able to cut through the hype, to evaluating cloud-based solutions against the time, energy, and expense required to leverage them. We have attempted to fill this book with a broad range of resources and information.

This book explains some of the nuts and bolts of cloud computing and how companies can use cloud computing tools. Not only will the IT department find itself using the cloud to support the organization's objectives, but with properly selected cloud solutions, they will spend less time maintaining servers and clients, running around with patches and service packs, and spend more time on innovative activities that help the organization thrive.

On the front lines, workers may find this book helpful when seeking to understand cloud computing. Moving from a traditional network infrastructure to a cloud solution might be a tough sell for some workers. Understanding the players, the pieces, and why the move is necessary will help with the transition.

What This Book Covers

Cloud computing is the biggest buzz in the computer world these days—maybe too big of a buzz. Cloud computing means different things to different people, and if you are trying to wrap your brain around the topic, asking one question will lead to ten more. This book aims to make the issues more understandable.

Cloud computing is not a small, undeveloped branch of IT. Research firm IDC thinks that cloud computing will reach $42 billion in 2012. Gartner Inc. predicts worldwide cloud-services revenue will rise 21.3 percent in 2009 to $56.3 billion.

Big names that you know are jockeying for position in the cloud. Amazon, for example, offers several cloud sources from its Elastic Compute Cloud (EC2) to its Simple Storage Services (S3), which is part of its Amazon Web Services (AWS). Google has also put a number of applications online. At a basic level they are free, but more robust applications can be accessed with a subscription. Microsoft is betting big with massive new data centers to service millions of cloud users.

For all the stuff you can do on the cloud now, we are really just in the cloud's infancy stage. Think about when the World Wide Web was just picking up in popularity. Every web page had the same HTML look and when frames came along, that was heralded as an innovation. But look where we have come since then. Web pages are exciting, dynamic things that do not look anything like they used to in 1994. We are in that same stage of development with cloud computing. In 10 or 15 years from now, cloud computing is not going to look anything like it does now.

But that does not mean that the cloud of today is not useful. In fact, quite the opposite is true. You can do a lot on the cloud. You can do everything from running applications to storing data off-site. You can run entire operating systems on the cloud. In this book, we will talk about the sorts of things that cloud computing allows you to do.

But for all the usefulness the cloud provides, there are also things you do not want to turn to the cloud for. There are simply some applications that you want to run locally. For instance, mission-critical business processes may best be maintained locally. There is also an issue of security and regulation. Because of government regulations, you simply may not be allowed to store some data on the cloud. This book covers the range of challenges, too.

Security is as much of an issue in the cloud as it is anywhere else. People come to the cloud computing topic from different points of view. Some believe the cloud to be an unsafe place. After all, once you send your data to the cloud, you lose complete control over it and it runs a greater risk of being compromised. But the other side of that coin is that cloud vendors go out of their way to ensure security. Many cloud vendors have teams dedicated to ensuring that their clouds are secure. This only makes sense—all it takes is for one breach to occur before clients start jumping ship. We will talk about security and its cloud considerations in more depth later in this book.

Cloud Computing service providers are those companies that you turn to for cloud services. There are big names like Amazon and Microsoft offering cloud services, and there are smaller companies too. They are all striving to offer cutting-edge, innovative solutions that are compelling enough that you will consider making your move to the cloud. Consider Salesforce.com; it has grown dramatically over the last several years thanks to their widely adopted cloud offerings. We introduce you to a number of cloud computing solutions providers in this book and talk about some innovative partnerships that are helping the cloud evolve.

Part I: Getting Started

Chapter 1: Cloud Computing Basics   This chapter sets the stage to explain what is going on in the world of cloud computing. This chapter explains what cloud computing is, what components comprise a cloud solution, and the different applications you can expect, as well as the cloud's relationship to the Internet. We also talk about cloud infrastructure and how it is built.

Chapter 2: Your Organization and Cloud Computing   Are your organization and its functions suited for the cloud? While the answer might seem like a big "Yes" here, the fact of the matter is that not every business function is suited for the cloud. While you can do an awful lot on the cloud, there are issues you need to consider before making the move. In this chapter we talk about such issues as when you can use a cloud solution, the benefits to your organization (mostly financial, but there are others, too), security issues, regulatory concerns, and limitations. Honestly, the point of this chapter is not to scare you off, but just to present the counterpoint to the issue.

Chapter 3: Cloud Computing with the Titans   Some well-known companies have joined the cloud computing party with their own offerings. While there are hundreds of vendors offering cloud computing solutions, there are some big names like Google, Microsoft, Amazon, Yahoo, and Salesforce.com that have been able to leverage their names, expertise, and client base to build out their cloud computing services. Whether or not you decide to go with one of these companies is a matter of your organization's need and business strategy. We are not pushing these big companies over smaller ones, but wanted to share what prominent names are doing. In this chapter we will look at what the big dogs offer and the direction they would like to take the cloud.

Chapter 4: The Business Case for Going to the Cloud   Why should you consider making a move to the cloud? What is the business benefit for making the move? In this chapter we will talk not only about some of the monetary savings, but some of the operational and organizational benefits you will realize by putting some of your business functions on the cloud. We will give an overview of Platform as a Service (PaaS), Software as a Service (SaaS), and Software plus Services (S+S), as well as some other cloud services that might benefit your organization. We will also talk about deleting your datacenter and what you should get rid of and what you should keep.

Part II: Cloud Computing Technology

Chapter 5: Hardware and Infrastructure   In this chapter we roll up our sleeves and take a closer look at the components used to build your cloud solution. This will include the hardware you will use—mobile clients, thin clients, and fat clients—as well as the security issues surrounding the cloud. We will talk about how you and your vendors can keep your information safe through logging, forensics, and auditing. From there we will talk about the construction of the networks you can use to access your cloud. Finally, we will talk about some of the services that are available to you on the cloud.

Chapter 6: Accessing the Cloud   Access to the cloud can be pretty simple; open a web browser and go to the application's URL. But that said, you can do more than just pop open Internet Explorer or Firefox to get going. In this chapter we will talk about the different platforms you can use, local user interfaces, web applications, and web APIs. We will also talk about some of the most prevalent web browsers out there. While Internet Explorer is the most prevalent browser in the market, it is not the only game in town. We will talk about the merits of Firefox, the Mac's favorite, Safari, and the browser seemingly being groomed for the cloud—Google's Chrome.

Chapter 7: Cloud Storage   One of the areas where the cloud shines is in making your data available, simply by virtue of storing it off-site. Why is this a big deal? Think about the datacenters that were in New Orleans a few years ago. If they had not maintained their data off-site (many, many miles off-site), then it was all lost. And that is true for any disaster. If key data is not stored in a secure location off-site, then you run the risk of losing it all. But it is not just a matter of data security; there are also issues of workers being able to access the data remotely, and being able to use applications that rely on that data in the cloud. In this chapter we will talk about the basics of cloud storage, some providers, security concerns, reliability concerns, advantages, and cautions. We will also look at some providers and talk about the functionality of such services as Amazon Simple Storage Service (S3), Nirvanix, Google Bigtable Datastore, Apple's MobileMe, and Microsoft's Live Mesh.

Chapter 8: Standards It is no shocker that standards make the IT world turn. While cloud computing is still somewhat new, standards exist to make sure that you can work and play well with your vendors. Given the extent to which cloud computing relies on the web, it should be no shock that many of the standards are things like HTTP, HTML, and XMPP. And while we will talk about those standards, we will also delve into the standards that exist for making cloud services, including JSON, SML, REST, and SOAP. We will explain that alphabet soup later in this chapter.

Part III: Cloud Computing at Work

Chapter 9: Software as a Service Software as a Service (SaaS) is, in essence, utilizing an application online. That means you do not need to have the application housed locally on your server or clients. Rather, you access the application through a cloud vendor. In this chapter we will talk about the basics of SaaS: its advantages, software considerations, advantages to vendors, and limitations. From there we will talk about some limitations, and then shift gears to talk about what companies and industries offer in terms of SaaS. While the list is far from comprehensive, we will go below the surface and show you what is out there.

Chapter 10: Software plus Services Going to the cloud is not an all-or-nothing proposal. While you do not need to send all of your applications to the cloud, you also do not need to send an entire application to live solely on the cloud. In the event your connection goes down or there is an outage at the provider, Software plus Services allows you to keep working until everything is back to normal. In this chapter we will discuss the ups and downs of Software plus Services, along with what some vendors are offering. We will also spend a lot of space discussing Microsoft's Software plus Services model, which is a leader in this field.

Chapter 11: Developing Applications Ideally, the vendor you pick will have exactly the application that you want. Within a few minutes you can be up and running. But the fact of the matter is that they might not have exactly what you want. In this case you can build your own applications. In this chapter we will talk about what prominent vendors offer in terms of application development and then we will walk you through the steps of creating your own applications using the Google AppEngine, Salesforce.com's tools, and Microsoft's Cloud OS, Azure.

Chapter 12: Local Clouds and Thin Clients Another approach to the cloud does not involve shipping all your data to a vendor. You can develop a local cloud to offload processing duties from clients to a local server. Virtualization is another increasingly popular trend with offerings from such companies as Microsoft and VMWare. In addition to the server technology that lets you run your clients' software in a centralized location, we will also talk about the thin clients that will find homes on your users' desks. We will also talk about the virtualization efforts that McNeilus Steel underwent to streamline their IT infrastructure.

Chapter 13: Migrating to the Cloud   Getting to the cloud is one thing when you are starting from scratch, but it is another thing completely when you need to migrate existing data. In this chapter we will talk about methods to make the move. We will talk about some services for individuals, mid-size organizations, and enterprises. We will look at some tools to migrate to the cloud and some methodology for making a move.

Chapter 14: Best Practices and the Future of Cloud Computing   Like anything, there is a right way to do something and a wrong way. In order to mitigate your "wrong way" attempts, this chapter talks about best practices for using a cloud computing solution. We will talk about analyzing your service and some tools, as well as the way to find the best vendor for you. We will also talk about the best way to move your data to the cloud. To wrap it all up, we will look into the proverbial crystal ball and talk about how cloud computing is expected to evolve.

Appendix   Cloud computing is so new and so fresh that it is coming with its own terminology that at first seems clever, but the more you hear it without knowing what it means, it becomes very frustrating. In the Appendix, we'll give you a glossary of terms (don't worry, new ones are still popping up all the time—feel free to pencil them in the margins). The Appendix also has a quick reference for some popular cloud computing resources.

Getting Started

Cloud Computing Basics

Cloud computing is everywhere. Pick up any tech magazine or visit almost any IT website or blog and you'll be sure to see talk about cloud computing. The only problem is that not everyone agrees on what it is. Ask ten different professionals what cloud computing is, and you'll get ten different answers. And is cloud computing even worth all the hype? Some people don't think so. In fact, in 2008 Oracle CEO Larry Ellison chastised the whole issue of cloud computing, saying that the term was overused and being applied to everything in the computer world.

"The computer industry is the only industry that is more fashion-driven than women's fashion," he said to a group of Oracle analysts.

So let's talk about what cloud computing is and tighten up our definition and understanding of this implementation.

Cloud Computing Overview

In this first section, we'll talk about what cloud computing is, and how it is developed and deployed. We'll clear up some misconceptions and make sure we all have a common understanding of the topic.

Disambiguation—Just What Is Cloud Computing?

Cloud computing gets its name as a metaphor for the Internet. Typically, the Internet is represented in network diagrams as a cloud, as shown in Figure 1-1. The cloud icon represents "all that other stuff" that makes the network work. It's kind of like "etc." for the rest of the solution map. It also typically means an area of the diagram or solution that is someone else's concern, so why diagram it all out? It's probably this notion that is most applicable to the cloud computing concept.

NOTE *Applications run on hosted servers as a service. We'll define that term later in this chapter, and discuss the different types of "as a service" applications that are prevalent.*

Cloud computing promises to cut operational and capital costs and, more importantly, let IT departments focus on strategic projects instead of keeping the datacenter running.

3

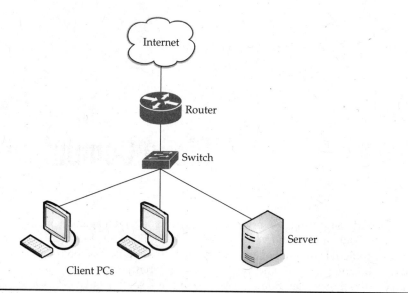

FIGURE 1-1 A cloud is used in network diagrams to depict the Internet.

What Works

But there's more going on under the hood than to simply equate cloud computing to the Internet. In essence, cloud computing is a construct that allows you to access applications that actually reside at a location other than your computer or other Internet-connected device; most often, this will be a distant datacenter. There are many benefits to this. For instance, think about the last time you bought Microsoft Word and installed it on your organization's computers. Either you ran around with a CD- or DVD-ROM and installed it on all the computers, or you set up your software distribution servers to automatically install the application on your machines. And every time Microsoft issued a service pack, you had to go around and install that pack, or you had to set up your software distribution servers to distribute it. Oh, and don't forget the cost of all the licenses. Pete down the hall probably uses Word once a month, but his license cost just as much as everyone else's.

The beauty of cloud computing, as shown in Figure 1-2, is that another company hosts your application (or suite of applications, for that matter). This means that they handle the costs of servers, they manage the software updates, and—depending on how you craft your contract—you pay less for the service.

Don't forget the equipment that you won't need to buy—which will result in fewer capital expenditures—thereby causing the CFO to actually smile when she sees you. By having someone else host the applications, you need not buy the servers nor pay for the electricity to power and cool them.

It's also convenient for telecommuters and traveling remote workers, who can simply log in and use their applications wherever they are.

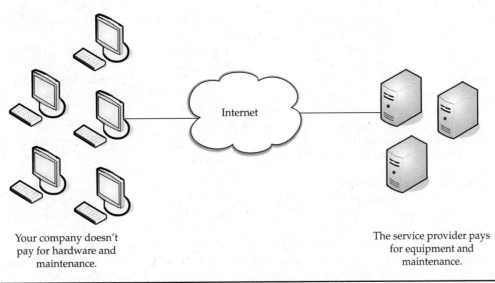

Your company doesn't pay for hardware and maintenance.

The service provider pays for equipment and maintenance.

FIGURE 1-2   With cloud computing, other companies host your applications.

Weak Links

So it all sounds great, right? Not so fast. As with everything in IT, there are pros and cons. Cloud computing is not exempt. Let's take a quick look at a few areas of potential trouble. The following illustration shows potential points of failure.

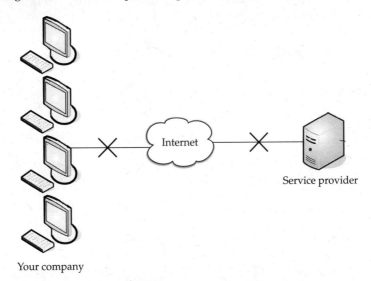

Your company

Service provider

While an Internet outage or problems with your Internet service provider (ISP) are rare, you may not be able to access your applications and do your work. Not that everyone sits in one office much anymore, but if you currently have the application on your own local servers, and all those who access it are not remote, you'd be at least somewhat assured that an Internet outage wouldn't affect your application.

But it isn't your connection to the Internet that can be prone to outages. What if the site you're accessing has problems? It's happened already. In July 2008, Amazon's S3 cloud storage service went down for the second time that year. A lot of applications were hosted by the company and all those services could not be accessed until techs could fix the problem. Some applications were down for eight hours.

Also, there may simply be applications or data that you want located on-site. If you have sensitive or proprietary information, your IT security group may simply mandate that you not store it on someone else's machines.

Application Integration Issues

You might also find that it's more difficult to integrate your applications if they are geographically dispersed. That is, it is easier to manage and access your data if it is nearby, and not under someone else's control.

For instance, if you need two applications to exchange information, it's easier to do if they both reside in the same place. If you have one application in-house and it has to contact another application on the cloud, it becomes far more complicated, and more prone to failure.

Cloud Components

In a simple, topological sense, a cloud computing solution is made up of several elements: clients, the datacenter, and distributed servers. As shown in Figure 1-3, these components make up the three parts of a cloud computing solution.

Each element has a purpose and plays a specific role in delivering a functional cloud-based application, so let's take a closer look.

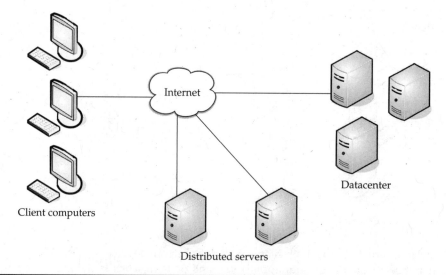

Client computers

Internet

Datacenter

Distributed servers

FIGURE 1-3   Three components make up a cloud computing solution.

Clients

Clients are, in a cloud computing architecture, the exact same things that they are in a plain, old, everyday local area network (LAN). They are, typically, the computers that just sit on your desk. But they might also be laptops, tablet computers, mobile phones, or PDAs—all big drivers for cloud computing because of their mobility.

Anyway, clients are the devices that the end users interact with to manage their information on the cloud. Clients generally fall into three categories:

- **Mobile**   Mobile devices include PDAs or smartphones, like a Blackberry, Windows Mobile Smartphone, or an iPhone.

- **Thin**   Clients are computers that do not have internal hard drives, but rather let the server do all the work, but then display the information.

- **Thick**   This type of client is a regular computer, using a web browser like Firefox or Internet Explorer to connect to the cloud.

Thin clients are becoming an increasingly popular solution, because of their price and effect on the environment. Some benefits to using thin clients include

- **Lower hardware costs**   Thin clients are cheaper than thick clients because they do not contain as much hardware. They also last longer before they need to be upgraded or become obsolete.

- **Lower IT costs**   Thin clients are managed at the server and there are fewer points of failure.

- **Security**   Since the processing takes place on the server and there is no hard drive, there's less chance of malware invading the device. Also, since thin clients don't work without a server, there's less chance of them being physically stolen.

- **Data security**   Since data is stored on the server, there's less chance for data to be lost if the client computer crashes or is stolen.

- **Less power consumption**   Thin clients consume less power than thick clients. This means you'll pay less to power them, and you'll also pay less to air-condition the office.

- **Ease of repair or replacement**   If a thin client dies, it's easy to replace. The box is simply swapped out and the user's desktop returns exactly as it was before the failure.

- **Less noise**   Without a spinning hard drive, less heat is generated and quieter fans can be used on the thin client.

Datacenter

The *datacenter* is the collection of servers where the application to which you subscribe is housed. It could be a large room in the basement of your building or a room full of servers on the other side of the world that you access via the Internet.

A growing trend in the IT world is virtualizing servers. That is, software can be installed allowing multiple instances of virtual servers to be used. In this way, you can have half a dozen virtual servers running on one physical server.

NOTE   *The number of virtual servers that can exist on a physical server depends on the size and speed of the physical server and what applications will be running on the virtual server.*

Distributed Servers

But the servers don't all have to be housed in the same location. Often, servers are in geographically disparate locations. But to you, the cloud subscriber, these servers act as if they're humming away right next to each other.

This gives the service provider more flexibility in options and security. For instance, Amazon has their cloud solution in servers all over the world. If something were to happen at one site, causing a failure, the service would still be accessed through another site. Also, if the cloud needs more hardware, they need not throw more servers in the safe room—they can add them at another site and simply make it part of the cloud.

Infrastructure

Cloud computing isn't a one-size-fits-all affair. There are several different ways the infrastructure can be deployed. The infrastructure will depend on the application and how the provider has chosen to build the cloud solution. This is one of the key advantages for using the cloud. Your needs might be so massive that the number of servers required far exceeds your desire or budget to run those in-house. Alternatively, you may only need a sip of processing power, so you don't want to buy and run a dedicated server for the job. The cloud fits both needs.

Grid Computing

Grid computing is often confused with cloud computing, but they are quite different. Grid computing applies the resources of numerous computers in a network to work on a single problem at the same time. This is usually done to address a scientific or technical problem. A well-known example of this is the Search for Extraterrestrial Intelligence (SETI) @Home project. In this project, people all over the world allow the SETI project to share the unused cycles of their computers to search for signs of intelligence in thousands of hours of recorded radio data. This is shown in Figure 1-4.

Another well-used grid is the World Community Grid—Berkeley Open Infrastructure for Network Computing (BOINC; see www.worldcommunity grid.org). Here you can dedicate as much or as little of your idle CPU processing power as you choose to help conduct protein-folding experiments in an effort to create better and more durable rice crops to feed the world's hungry. I bet you didn't know you could feed the needy with your computer.

Grid computing necessitates the use of software that can divide and then send out pieces of the program to thousands of computers. It can be done throughout the computers of an organization, or it can be done as a form of public collaboration.

Sun Microsystems offers Grid Engine software that allows engineers at companies to pool the computer cycles on up to 80 workstations at a time.

Grid computing is appealing for several reasons:

- It is a cost-effective way to use a given amount of computer resources.
- It is a way to solve problems that need a tremendous amount of computing power.
- The resources of several computers can be shared cooperatively, without one computer managing the other.

So what do grid computing and cloud computing have to do with one another? Not much directly, as they function in fundamentally different ways. In grid computing, a large project is divided among multiple computers to make use of their resources. Cloud computing does just the opposite. It allows multiple smaller applications to run at the same time.

FIGURE 1-4   SETI@Home is a well-known use of grid computing.

Full Virtualization

Full virtualization is a technique in which a complete installation of one machine is run on another. The result is a system in which all software running on the server is within a virtual machine.

Your Company   Service Provider

In a fully virtualized deployment, the software running on the server is displayed on the clients.

NOTE   *Full virtualization dates back to 1967 with IBM's CP-40 research system.*

This sort of deployment allows not only unique applications to run, but also different operating systems.

Virtualization is relevant to cloud computing because it is one of the ways in which you will access services on the cloud. That is, the remote datacenter may be delivering your services in a fully virtualized format.

In order for full virtualization to be possible, it was necessary for specific hardware combinations to be used. It wasn't until 2005 that the introduction of the AMD-Virtualization (AMD-V) and Intel Virtualization Technology (IVT) extensions made it easier to go fully virtualized.

Full virtualization has been successful for several purposes:

- Sharing a computer system among multiple users
- Isolating users from each other and from the control program
- Emulating hardware on another machine

Paravirtualization

Paravirtualization allows multiple operating systems to run on a single hardware device at the same time by more efficiently using system resources, like processors and memory.

In full virtualization, the entire system is emulated (BIOS, drive, and so on), but in paravirtualization, its management module operates with an operating system that has been adjusted to work in a virtual machine. Paravirtualization typically runs better than the full virtualization model, simply because in a fully virtualized deployment, all elements must be emulated.

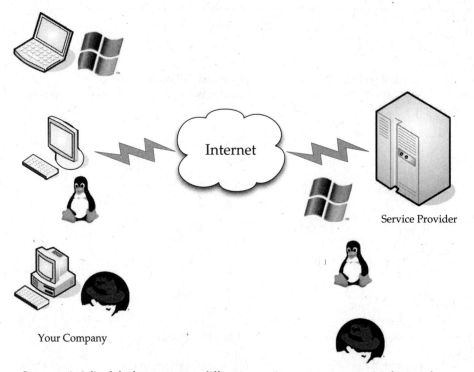

Internet

Service Provider

Your Company

In a paravirtualized deployment, many different operating systems can run simultaneously.

Virtualization Type	Guest Instances	Virtualization Overhead	System Processing Needs	Total
Full Virtualization	5	10% (50% total)	10% (50% total)	100%
Paravirtualization	8	2% (16% total)	10% (50% total)	96%

TABLE 1-1   Processor Power Used in Full Virtualization and Paravirtualization

The trade-off is reduced security and flexibility. For instance, flexibility is reduced because a particular OS or distribution may not be able to work. For example, a new Windows deployment may not be available as a guest OS for the solution. Security can be at risk because the guest OS has more control of the underlying hardware, and there is a risk of impacting the hardware and all the guest systems on the host.

Paravirtualization also allows for better scaling. For example, if a fully virtualized solution requires 10 percent of processor utilization, then five systems are about the most that could be run on a system before performance takes a hit. Paravirtualization requires only 2 percent of processor utilization per guest instance and still leaves 10 percent of the guest OS available. This is illustrated in Table 1-1.

Paravirtualization works best in these sorts of deployments:

- **Disaster recovery**   In the event of a catastrophe, guest instances can be moved to other hardware until the equipment can be repaired.

- **Migration**   Moving to a new system is easier and faster because guest instances can be removed from the underlying hardware.

- **Capacity management**   Because of easier migrations, capacity management is simpler to implement. It is easier to add more processing power or hard drive capacity in a virtualized environment.

Services

The term services in cloud computing is the concept of being able to use reusable, fine-grained components across a vendor's network. This is widely known as "as a service."

Offerings with *as a service* as a suffix include traits like the following:

- Low barriers to entry, making them available to small businesses
- Large scalability
- Multitenancy, which allows resources to be shared by many users
- Device independence, which allows users to access the systems on different hardware

Software as a Service

Software as a Service (SaaS) is the model in which an application is hosted as a service to customers who access it via the Internet. When the software is hosted off-site, the customer doesn't have to maintain it or support it. On the other hand, it is out of the customer's hands when the hosting service decided to change it. The idea is that you use the software out of the box as is and do not need to make a lot of changes or require integration to other systems.

The provider does all the patching and upgrades as well as keeping the infrastructure running.

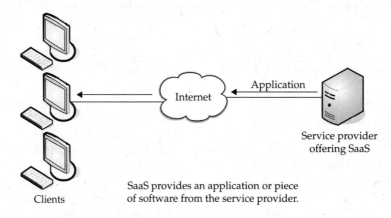

Service provider
offering SaaS

Clients

SaaS provides an application or piece
of software from the service provider.

Costs can be sort of a double-edged sword. On the one hand, costs for accessing the software can be an ongoing thing. Rather than pay for it once and be done with it, the more you use it, the more you'll be billed. On the other hand, in some cases you don't have to pay as much up front and you are only billed based on your use of the application.

For vendors, SaaS has the appeal of providing stronger protection of their intellectual property as well as creating a continuous stream of income.

There are many types of software that lend themselves to the SaaS model. Typically, software that performs a simple task without much need to interact with other systems makes them ideal candidates for SaaS. Customers who are not inclined to perform software development but have need of high-powered applications can also benefit from SaaS. Some of these applications include

- Customer resource management (CRM)
- Video conferencing
- IT service management
- Accounting
- Web analytics
- Web content management

SaaS applications differ from earlier distributed computing solutions in that SaaS was developed specifically to use web tools, like the browser. This makes them web-native. It was also built with a multitenant back end in mind, which enables multiple customers to use an application.

SaaS provides network-based access to commercially available software. Since the software is managed at a central location, customers can access their applications wherever they have web access.

As we'll discuss in the next section—PaaS—SaaS is often used in conjunction with other software. When used as a component of another application, this is known as a *mashup* or a *plugin*.

Benefits   One of the biggest benefits of SaaS is, of course, costing less money than buying the application outright. The service provider can offer cheaper, more reliable applications than organizations can by themselves. Some other benefits include the following:

- **Familiarity with the World Wide Web**   Most workers have access to a computer and know how to use it on the World Wide Web. As such, the learning curve for using external applications can be much smaller.

- **Smaller staff**   IT systems require the overhead of salaries, benefits, insurance, and building space. The ability to farm out applications reduces the need for as much IT staff.

- **Customization**   Older applications were difficult to customize and required tinkering with the code. SaaS applications are much easier to customize and can give an organization exactly what they want.

- **Better marketing**   A provider who had developed an application for a very narrow market might have had problems marketing that application. However, with SaaS, the entire world is open to the providers.

- **Web reliability**   We talked earlier about how the World Wide Web can be seen as a source of failure. And while that is sporadically true, the fact of the matter is that the Web is generally quite reliable.

- **Security**   Secure Sockets Layer (SSL) is widely used and trusted. This allows customers to reach their applications securely without having to employ complex back-end configurations, like virtual private networks (VPNs).

- **More bandwidth**   Bandwidth has increased greatly in recent months and quality of service improvements are helping data flow. This will allow organizations to trust that they can access their applications with low latencies and good speeds.

Obstacles   Like anything, SaaS faces obstacles to its implementation and use. The first is that an organization that has a very specific computational need might not be able to find the application available through SaaS. In that case, they may discover that they need to buy the software and install it on their local machines. That said, companies with unique needs may be able to find some of the components in a SaaS.

There is also an element of "lock-in" with vendors. That is, the customer might pay a provider to use an application, but once they do, they may be unable to port that application to a new vendor. Or, it might be possible to move to a new vendor, but the old vendor might charge a hefty moving fee.

Finally, SaaS also faces challenges from the availability of opensource applications and cheaper hardware. If companies are so inclined, they can put their open source applications on hardware that performs better and costs less than it used to.

Platform as a Service

Following on the heels of SaaS, Platform as a Service (PaaS) is another application delivery model. PaaS supplies all the resources required to build applications and services completely from the Internet, without having to download or install software.

NOTE *PaaS is also known as* cloudware.

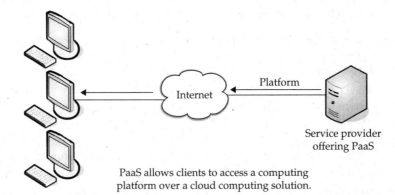

Platform

Internet

Service provider
offering PaaS

PaaS allows clients to access a computing
platform over a cloud computing solution.

PaaS services include application design, development, testing, deployment, and hosting. Other services include team collaboration, web service integration, database integration, security, scalability, storage, state management, and versioning.

A downfall to PaaS is a lack of interoperability and portability among providers. That is, if you create an application with one cloud provider and decide to move to another provider, you may not be able to do so—or you'll have to pay a high price. Also, if the provider goes out of business, your applications and your data will be lost.

NOTE *This was the case with the provider Zimki. The company started in 2006 and by mid-2007 was out of business, causing applications and client data they hosted to be lost.*

PaaS generally offers some support to help the creation of user interfaces, and is normally based on HTML or JavaScript.

Because PaaS is expected to be used by many users simultaneously, it is designed with that sort of use in mind, and generally provides automatic facilities for concurrency management, scalability, failover, and security.

PaaS also supports web development interfaces such as Simple Object Access Protocol (SOAP) and Representational State Transfer (REST), which allow the construction of multiple web services, sometimes called mashups. The interfaces are also able to access databases and reuse services that are within a private network.

PaaS Options   PaaS is found in one of three different types of systems:

- **Add-on development facilities**   These allow existing SaaS applications to be customized. Often, PaaS developers and users are required to purchase subscriptions to the add-on SaaS application.

- **Stand-alone environments**   These environments do not include licensing, technical, or financial dependencies on specific SaaS applications and are used for general developments.

- **Application delivery-only environments**   These environments support hosting-level services, like security and on-demand scalability. They do not include development, debugging, and test capabilities.

Trends Toward Adoption   PaaS faces the same sorts of factors in its adoption as SaaS did, as it is in its early phase. Some other factors influencing adoption include

- The ability of geographically isolated development teams to work together
- The ability to merge web services from multiple sources
- The ability to realize cost savings from using built-in infrastructure services for security, scalability, and failover, rather than having to obtain and test them separately
- The ability to realize cost savings from using higher-level programming abstractions

Hurdles   There are two main obstacles that developers face when considering PaaS.

Because vendors use proprietary services or development languages, some developers are afraid of being locked into a single provider. The vendor may allow the application to be brought to a different provider; however, the costs are typically higher as compared to moving applications between conventional hosts.

Hardware as a Service

Hardware as a Service (HaaS) is the next form of service available in cloud computing. Where SaaS and PaaS are providing applications to customers, HaaS doesn't. It simply offers the hardware so that your organization can put whatever they want onto it.

NOTE *HaaS is sometimes also called Infrastructure as a Service (IaaS).*

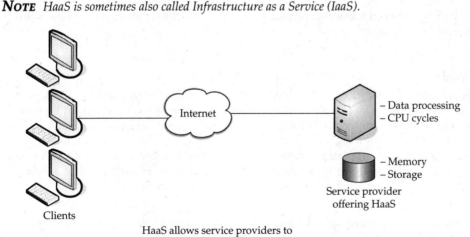

HaaS allows service providers to
rent hardware resources.

Rather than purchase servers, software, racks, and having to pay for the datacenter space for them, the service provider rents those resources.

HaaS allows you to "rent" such resources as

- Server space
- Network equipment
- Memory
- CPU cycles
- Storage space

Additionally, the infrastructure can be dynamically scaled up or down, based on the application resource needs.

Further, multiple tenants can be on the equipment at the same time.

Resources are typically billed based on a utility computing basis, so providers charge by how many resources are consumed.

HaaS involves several pieces:

- **Service level agreements** This is an agreement between the provider and client, guaranteeing a certain level of performance from the system.
- **Computer hardware** These are the components whose resources will be rented out. Service providers often have this set up as a grid for easier scalability.
- **Network** This includes hardware for firewalls, routers, load balancing, and so on.
- **Internet connectivity** This allows clients to access the hardware from their own organizations.
- **Platform virtualization environment** This allows the clients to run the virtual machines they want.
- **Utility computing billing** Typically set up to bill customers based on how many system resources they use.

Applications

So now we get to the question—what does cloud computing actually do? Well, we have applications running on our laptops, servers, phones and the like. Cloud computing either has them too or has the potential to bring them to you. So cloud computing brings you applications, a way of viewing, manipulating, and sharing data. Like their desktop brethren, many "staple" applications exist in cloud computing, but what will differ for you is how you interact with those applications. The most common are storage and database. In this section, we'll take a closer look at storage and database functionality.

NOTE *We'll talk about developing your own interfaces to work with storage and databases in Chapter 6.*

Storage

Somewhat similar to HaaS, one of the uses for cloud computing is simply storage. The benefits are in line with the general benefits of cloud computing—if you lease storage space from a vendor, you are not responsible to buy equipment, pay to run it, and pay to cool it. That's all on the vendor.

But there are different options when it comes down to cloud storage.

Database

Databases (which we will talk more about later in this chapter) are repositories for information with links within the information that help make the data searchable.

Distributed databases, like Amazon's SimpleDB, spread information among physically dispersed hardware. But to the client, the information seems to be located in one place.

The advantages of such a database include the following:

- **Improved availability** If there is a fault in one database system, it will only affect one fragment of the information, not the entire database.

- **Improved performance** Data is located near the site with the greatest demand and the database systems are parallelized, which allows the load to be balanced among the servers.

- **Price** It is less expensive to create a network of smaller computers with the power of one large one.

- **Flexibility** Systems can be changed and modified without harm to the entire database.

Naturally there are disadvantages, including

- **Complexity** Database administrators have extra work to do to maintain the system.

- **Labor costs** With that added complexity comes the need for more workers on the payroll.

- **Security** Database fragments must be secured and so must the sites housing the fragments.

- **Integrity** It may be difficult to maintain the integrity of the database if it is too complex or changes too quickly.

- **Standards** There are currently no standards to convert a centralized database into a cloud solution.

Synchronization

Synchronization, as with Microsoft's Live Mesh or Apple's MobileMe, allows content to be refreshed across multiple devices. For instance, if you have a spreadsheet on your computer and then upload it to the storage service, the next time you check your PDA, that file will be downloaded onto it.

Database Services

Another "as a service" offering that is becoming prevalent in the world of cloud computing is Database as a Service (DaaS). The idea behind DaaS is to avoid the complexity and cost of running your own database.

DaaS offers these benefits:

- **Ease of use**   There are no servers to provision and no redundant systems to worry about. You don't have to worry about buying, installing, and maintaining hardware for the database.

- **Power**   The database isn't housed locally, but that doesn't mean that it is not functional and effective. Depending on your vendor, you can get custom data validation to ensure accurate information. You can create and manage the database with ease.

- **Integration**   The database can be integrated with your other services to provide more value and power. For instance, you can tie it in with calendars, email, and people to make your work more powerful.

- **Management**   Because large databases benefit from constant pruning and optimization, typically there are expensive resources dedicated to this task. With some DaaS offerings, this management can be provided as part of the service for much less expense. The provider will often use offshore labor pools to take advantage of lower labor costs there. So it's possible that you are using the service in Chicago, the physical servers are in Washington state, and the database administrator is in the Philippines.

There are a number of providers out there, but let's take a closer look at two of the biggest players.

MS SQL

Anyone who has worked with databases is no stranger to Microsoft's premier offering, SQL Server. They announced the cloud extension of that tool in the spring of 2008 by introducing Microsoft SQL Server Data Services (SSDS). It is expected to be in a public beta by spring 2009.

SSDS looks very similar to Amazon's SimpleDB, with a straightforward, schema-free data storage, SOAP or REST APIs, and a pay-as-you-go payment system. It is also able to start small and scale larger as needed.

While it looks similar to SimpleDB, it varies greatly. First, one of the main selling points of SSDS is that it integrates with Microsoft's Sync Framework, which is a .NET library for synchronizing dissimilar data sources.

Microsoft wants SSDS to work as a data hub, synchronizing data on multiple devices so they can be accessed offline.

There are three core concepts in SSDS:

- **Authority**   An *authority* is both a billing unit and a collection of containers.

- **Container**   A *container* is a collection of entities and is what you search within.

- **Entity**   An *entity* is a property bag of name and value pairs.

SSDS is based on SQL Server, but it is not a simple retooling of it. Microsoft built it with large-scale deployment in mind.

SSDS is a bit of a twist because it backsteps from being more complex, rather being simple and flexible.

Oracle

In the fall of 2008 Oracle introduced three services to provide database services to cloud users. Customers can license

- Oracle Database 11*g*
- Oracle Fusion Middleware
- Oracle Enterprise Manager

The products are available for use on Amazon Web Services' Elastic Compute Cloud (Amazon EC2). Oracle delivered a set of free Amazon Machine Images (AMIs) to its customers so they could quickly and efficiently deploy Oracle's database solutions.

Developers can take advantage of the provisioning and automated software deployment to rapidly build applications using Oracle's popular development tools such as Oracle Application Express, Oracle JDeveloper, Oracle Enterprise Pack for Eclipse, and Oracle Workshop for WebLogic. Additionally, Oracle Unbreakable Linux Support and AWS Premium Support is available for Oracle Enterprise Linux on EC2, providing seamless customer support.

"Providing choice is the foundation of Oracle's strategy to enable customers to become more productive and lower their IT costs—whether it's choice of hardware, operating system, or on demand computing—extending this to the Cloud environment is a natural evolution," said Robert Shimp, vice president of Oracle Global Technology Business Unit. "We are pleased to partner with Amazon Web Services to provide our customers enterprise-class Cloud solutions, using familiar Oracle software on which their businesses depend."

Additionally, Oracle also introduced a secure cloud-based backup solution. Oracle Secure Backup Cloud Module, based on Oracle's premier tape backup management software, Oracle Secure Backup, enables customers to use the Amazon Simple Storage Service (Amazon S3) as their database backup destination. Cloud-based backups offer reliability and virtually unlimited capacity, available on demand and with no up-front capital expenditure.

The Oracle Secure Backup Cloud Module also enables encrypted data backups to help ensure complete privacy in the cloud environment. It's fully integrated with Oracle Recovery Manager and Oracle Enterprise Manager, providing users with familiar interfaces for cloud-based backups.

For customers with an ongoing need to quickly move very large volumes of data into or out of the AWS cloud, Amazon allows the creation of network peering connections.

Intranets and the Cloud

While your operation is not big as Amazon S3 cloud computing, you can use the same sorts of principles within your organization to develop your IT infrastructure. By setting up thin clients to run applications and services on a local server, rather than on their desktops, you ease the costs of deployment and maintenance, as well as reducing power costs.

NOTE *Ironically, some organizations use cloud computing to deliver their corporate intranet. Intranets are customarily used within an organization and are not accessible publicly. That is, a web server is maintained in-house and company information is maintained on it that others within the organization can access. However, now intranets are being maintained on the cloud. To access the company's private, in-house information, users are having to log on to the intranet by going to a secure public web site.*

In this section we'll talk about the merits of developing your own in-house "cloud" and what is used in its composition.

Components

There are two main components in client/server computing: servers and thin or light clients. The network map in Figure 1-5 shows how they are deployed.

The servers house the applications your organization needs to run, and the thin clients—which do not have hard drives—display the results.

Hypervisor Applications

Applications like VMware or Microsoft's Hyper-V allow you to virtualize your servers so that multiple virtual servers can run on one physical server.

These sorts of solutions provide the tools to supply a virtualized set of hardware to the guest operating system. They also make it possible to install different operating systems on the same machine. For example, you may need Windows Vista to run one application, while another application requires Linux. It's easy to set up the server to run both operating systems.

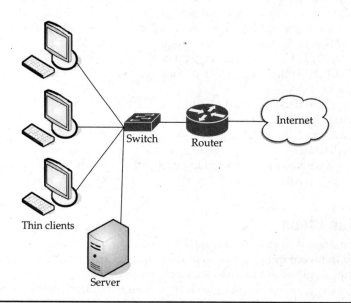

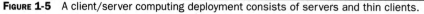

FIGURE 1-5   A client/server computing deployment consists of servers and thin clients.

Thin clients use an application program to communicate with an application server. Most of the processing is done down on the server, and sent back to the client.

There is some debate about where to draw the line when talking about thin clients. Some thin clients require an application program or a web browser to communicate with the server. However, others require no add-on applications at all. This is sort of a discussion of semantics, because the real issue is whether the work is being done on the server and transmitted back to the thin client.

First Movers in the Cloud

There are scores of vendors who offer cloud services. What they have to offer varies based on the vendor and their pricing models are different, as well. Let's take a look at some of the big names in the world of cloud computing and talk, briefly, about what they have to offer.

NOTE *We'll talk about them in greater detail in Chapter 11.*

Cloud computing is a growing field, and there will likely be new players in the market in the foreseeable future. For now, let's look at the names you already know: Amazon, Google, and Microsoft.

Amazon

Amazon was one of the first companies to offer cloud services to the public, and they are very sophisticated. Amazon offers a number of cloud services, including

- **Elastic Compute Cloud (EC2)**   Offers virtual machines and extra CPU cycles for your organization.
- **Simple Storage Service (S3)**   Allows you to store items up to 5GB in size in Amazon's virtual storage service.
- **Simple Queue Service (SQS)**   Allows your machines to talk to each other using this message-passing API.
- **SimpleDB**   A web service for running queries on structured data in real time. This service works in close conjunction with Amazon Simple Storage Service (Amazon S3) and Amazon Elastic Compute Cloud (Amazon EC2), collectively providing the ability to store, process, and query data sets in the cloud.

These services can be difficult to use, because they have to be done through the command line. That said, if you are used to working in a command-line environment, you shouldn't have much trouble using the services.

Amazon's virtual machines are versions of Linux distributions, so those who are experienced with Linux will be right at home. In fact, applications can be written on your own machine and then uploaded to the cloud.

Amazon is the most extensive cloud service to date. You can see more about Amazon's cloud services at http://aws.amazon.com.

Google

In stark contrast to Amazon's offerings is Google's App Engine. On Amazon you get root privileges, but on App Engine, you can't write a file in your own directory. Google removed the file write feature out of Python as a security measure, and to store data you must use Google's database.

Google offers online documents and spreadsheets, and encourages developers to build features for those and other online software, using its Google App Engine. Google reduced the web applications to a core set of features, and built a good framework for delivering them. Google also offers handy debugging features.

Groups and individuals will likely get the most out of App Engine by writing a layer of Python that sits between the user and the database. Look for Google to add more features to add background processing services.

It can be found online at code.google.com/appengine/.

Microsoft

Microsoft's cloud computing solution is called Windows Azure, an operating system that allows organizations to run Windows applications and store files and data using Microsoft's datacenters. It's also offering its Azure Services Platform, which are services that allow developers to establish user identities, manage workflows, synchronize data, and perform other functions as they build software programs on Microsoft's online computing platform.

Key components of Azure Services Platform include

- **Windows Azure**   Provides service hosting and management and low-level scalable storage, computation, and networking.
- **Microsoft SQL Services**   Provides database services and reporting.
- **Microsoft .NET Services**   Provides service-based implementations of .NET Framework concepts such as workflow.
- **Live Services**   Used to share, store, and synchronize documents, photos, and files across PCs, phones, PC applications, and web sites.
- **Microsoft SharePoint Services and Microsoft Dynamics CRM Services**   Used for business content, collaboration, and solution development in the cloud.

Microsoft plans the next version of Office to offer a browser-based option so that users can read and edit documents online as well as offer the ability for users to collaborate using web, mobile, and client versions of Office.

Microsoft is a little late to the cloud party and isn't a leader in cloud computing. That honor goes to Google and Amazon, and more and more companies are offering cloud services, so if Microsoft wants to stay competitive, they're going to have to pick up the pace.

Microsoft's cloud offerings can be found online at www.microsoft.com/azure/default.mspx.

For some, the term "cloud computing" is simply hype. But for others who want to embrace it, cloud computing is a great way for IT professionals to focus less on their datacenters, and more on the work of information technology.

CHAPTER

Your Organization and Cloud Computing

Cloud computing is not a one-size-fits-all affair. Just as the hardware and software configuration you use in your organization is different from that of the company down the street, your cloud computing needs will be different as well.

This chapter will help you understand how your organization can best use cloud computing, and which solutions might be most appropriate for your needs. And while we talk about what cloud computing is good for, we also talk about cloud computing limitations. That is, cloud computing is not perfect, and there are times when you shouldn't turn to it. We'll examine those cases, as well.

When You Can Use Cloud Computing

Whether or not you should use cloud computing depends on a number of factors, including

- Cost/benefit ratio
- Speed of delivery
- How much capacity you will use
- Whether your data is regulated
- Your organization's corporate and IT structure

There may be times when the need you have is a perfect match for cloud computing. But there may also be times when cloud computing is simply not a good match for your needs. In this section we'll take a look at both what you can use clouds for, and when you should steer clear of them.

Scenarios

There are three different major implementations of cloud computing. How organizations are using cloud computing is quite different at a granular level, but the uses generally fall into one of these three solutions.

Compute Clouds

Compute clouds allow access to highly scalable, inexpensive, on-demand computing resources that run the code that they're given. Three examples of compute clouds are

- Amazon's EC2
- Google App Engine
- Berkeley Open Infrastructure for Network Computing (BOINC)

Compute clouds are the most flexible in their offerings and can be used for sundry purposes; it simply depends on the application the user wants to access.

You could close this book right now, sign up for a cloud computing account, and get started right away. These applications are good for any size organization, but large organizations might be at a disadvantage because these applications don't offer the standard management, monitoring, and governance capabilities that these organizations are used to.

Enterprises aren't shut out, however. Amazon offers enterprise-class support and there are emerging sets of cloud offerings like Terremark's Enterprise Cloud, which are meant for enterprise use.

Compute clouds allow you to access applications maintained on a provider's equipment.

Cloud Storage

One of the first cloud offerings was cloud storage and it remains a popular solution. Cloud storage is a big world. There are already in excess of 100 vendors offering cloud storage. This is an ideal solution if you want to maintain files off-site.

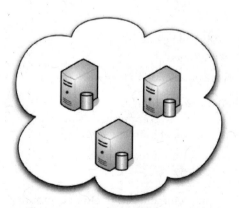

Cloud storage allows you to store your data on a vendor's equipment.

Security and cost are the top issues in this field and vary greatly, depending on the vendor you choose. Currently, Amazon's S3 is the top dog.

NOTE *We'll take a closer look at Amazon and other cloud providers in the next chapter.*

Cloud Applications

Cloud applications differ from compute clouds in that they utilize software applications that rely on cloud infrastructure. Cloud applications are versions of Software as a Service (SaaS) and include such things as web applications that are delivered to users via a browser or application like Microsoft Online Services. These applications offload hosting and IT management to the cloud.

Cloud applications deliver applications that depend
on the infrastructure of the Internet itself.

Cloud applications often eliminate the need to install and run the application on the customer's own computer, thus alleviating the burden of software maintenance, ongoing operation, and support.

Some cloud applications include

- Peer-to-peer computing (like BitTorrent and Skype)
- Web applications (like MySpace or YouTube)
- SaaS (like Google Apps)
- Software plus services (like Microsoft Online Services)

When You Shouldn't Use Cloud Computing

We'd be remiss if we just did the cloud computing cheerleader thing, suggesting you could use it for absolutely everything. The fact of the matter is there are plenty of cases where cloud computing may not be appropriate, for any reason ranging from cost to hardware requirements to simply not needing it.

Minding the Details

If you want to use cloud computing and post data covered by Health Insurance Portability and Accounting Act (HIPAA) on it, you are out of luck. Well, let's rephrase that—if you want to put HIPAA data on a cloud, you shouldn't. That's sensitive healthcare information

	Sarbanes-Oxley	Fair and Accurate Credit Transactions Act of 2003 (FACTA)	HIPAA
Directors and Officers	$1,000,000		
Institution	$5,000,000	$11,000	$50,000 to $250,000
Prison	20 years		1 to 10 years

TABLE 2-1   Potential Penalties If Confidential Data Is Not Protected

and the fact that HIPAA data could commingle on a server with another organization's data will likely get the attention of an observant HIPAA auditor.

Even so, Google and Microsoft are both moving forward on health records services: Microsoft is working on its HealthVault and Google Health promises to be a huge outpouring of private health data online.

While the intent seems well-meaning—to give consumers access to their healthcare data—all it takes is one tiny breach to let sensitive data loose.

If you have data that is regulated—like HIPAA or Sarbanes-Oxley—you are well advised to be very careful in your plans to place data on a cloud. After all, if you have posted a customer's financial data and there's a breach, will they go after the cloud provider, or you?

Oh, and just to add some teeth to what can happen if private data gets out, consider Table 2-1. Table 2-1 illustrates potential penalties if the laws are violated.

It's probably best to avoid a painful fine, flesh-eating lawyers, and possible jail time.

Legislative Issues

An issue of more concern for the sensitivity of private data is that there are laws and policy that allow the government freer access to data on a cloud than on a private server.

For example, the Stored Communications Act allows the FBI access to data without getting a warrant or the owner's consent.

Geopolitical Concerns

It may simply be illegal to post your information on a cloud. If you are in Canada (for instance) and you want to post your data on an American cloud, you're out of luck.

The Canadian government has declared that government IT workers may not use network services that are operating within U.S. borders. The reason is that the Canadian data stored on those servers could be negatively impacted based on the Patriot Act.

Sure, Canada might be the friendly neighbor of the United States to the north, but at this point in time, they have a great policy. All it would take is for the U.S. government to seize a server with foreign data on it, and before you can say "eh," we've got another international incident on our hands.

And the same can be said of clouds operating outside the United States. You probably don't know the laws (if there are any) governing your privacy and protection in a foreign country. All it would take is the Generalissimo and his cadre of willing minions to roll into your provider's office and cart off the server with your data on it.

Hardware Dependencies

If you have an application that requires specific hardware, chips, or drivers, a cloud solution might not be a good fit for you.

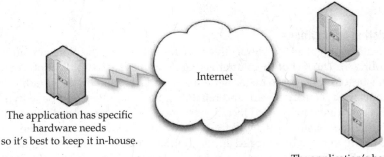

The application has specific
hardware needs
so it's best to keep it in-house.

The application's hardware needs
couldn't be served by the provider.

First, if you have special hardware needs, the chances are lower that the service provider will have the precise hardware you need. That can significantly narrow your options when it comes to shopping around and finding a good deal.

But let's say the planets are in perfect alignment, the provider you like has the hardware you need, and before long you are both humming away. This is all blissful now, but if the provider ever changes chipsets or other critical hardware, you might be out of luck.

Server Control

If your application demands complete control over everything that is running, a cloud solution may not be right for you. If you need detailed control over the amount of memory, CPU, hard drive specs, or interfaces, then the cloud isn't an appropriate match for your application. After all, these are all things managed by the service provider.

NOTE *In some clouds, you are not even allowed root access. If you require advanced levels of access, make sure you understand what your prospective provider will allow.*

Cost

One of the big draws of cloud computing is cost. That is, it tends to be less expensive to run an application on a cloud than to invest in the infrastructure, buy the application outright, and then manage it day to day.

However, over time, it may cost more to pay the cloud subscription than to have simply bought the servers yourself, so it is important to factor in everything from facilities, staff, software, and hardware.

Cost and the way clouds operate are a moving target. Some have suggested that the cloud might bring servers into the client's datacenter. Another school of thought is a concept called *cloud bursting*. In this scenario, on-demand capacity can be provisioned to a cloud.

Lack of Need

Anyone with a grandfather has heard the phrase, "if it ain't broke, don't fix it." And grandpa is right. If your current solution is getting the job done, why tinker with it?

Now, there are certainly cases where cloud computing is advantageous for you. And in those cases, by all means use it. However, if you are just moving applications to the cloud for the fashion of it, take a look at some old pictures of "fashionable" people. You'll realize those polyester leisure suits and mullets may have been fashionable in their day, but not so much now.

Integration with Existing Applications

If you mix oil and water, you get a lava lamp. Given the heading of this section, you already get what we're alluding to. The fact of the matter is that if you have two applications that need to integrate, it's best for one not to be located on-site and a second on the cloud.

It creates problems with security, speed, and reliability. For instance, if you have two databases—one with sensitive data housed locally, and one with nonsensitive data on a cloud—the chances that the sensitive data will find its way to the cloud are very good.

Also, if you are trying to run a high-speed application in-house and you rely on data from the cloud, the application will only run as fast as the cloud will allow. This also leads to questionable reliability. Will data be compromised or damaged from all the flying around it has to do?

Latency Concerns

Since your data and application are located on a series of servers geographically disparate from your own site, it is going to take some time for the data to reach you. This isn't an issue of hours or days—or even minutes. But if you require data instantaneously, the cloud might not be your best option.

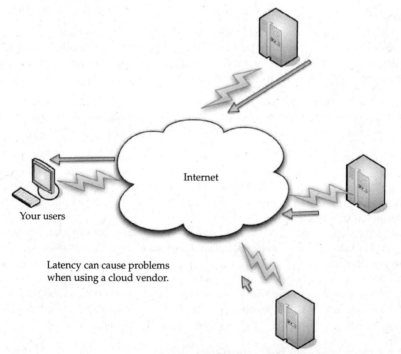

Your users

Internet

Latency can cause problems when using a cloud vendor.

Service provider's distributed servers

There's still travel time involved with your data. Now, it might be the case that a worker can request given data and it comes through in less than a second, and that speed is fine. However, if that same worker needs the data faster than a second, it might not be coming through fast enough.

Throughput Demands

Since cloud computing is generally billed in a utility format, you pay for what you use. That's great and it seems fair, until you deploy applications that use a lot of throughput and costs start to rise. For instance, if you are streaming high-definition video over 100 sources, your costs are going to spike sharply.

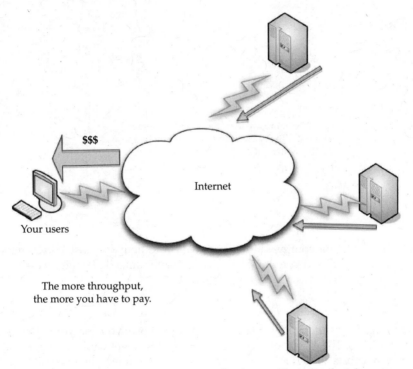

Your users

$$$

Internet

The more throughput,
the more you have to pay.

Service provider's distributed servers

It's best to do the math on these sorts of things. Take into account what a server, power, and all other hardware will cost. Figure in the price of management and associated IT personnel costs and then compare that with what a service provider will charge you. If it's cheaper to buy the server, it might be best to forget about the cloud for now. But even if the cost is the same, you need to ask yourself what business you want to be in.

Benefits

Your organization is going to have different needs from the company next door. However, cloud computing can help you with your IT needs. Let's take a closer look at what cloud computing has to offer your organization.

Scalability

If you are anticipating a huge upswing in computing need (or even if you are surprised by a sudden demand), cloud computing can help you manage. Rather than having to buy, install, and configure new equipment, you can buy additional CPU cycles or storage from a third party.

Since your costs are based on consumption, you likely wouldn't have to pay out as much as if you had to buy the equipment.

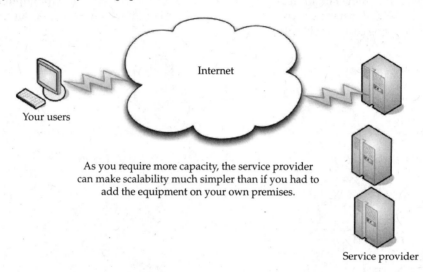

Internet

Your users

As you require more capacity, the service provider
can make scalability much simpler than if you had to
add the equipment on your own premises.

Service provider

Once you have fulfilled your need for additional equipment, you just stop using the cloud provider's services, and you don't have to deal with unneeded equipment. You simply add or subtract based on your organization's need.

Simplicity

Again, not having to buy and configure new equipment allows you and your IT staff to get right to your business. The cloud solution makes it possible to get your application started immediately, and it costs a fraction of what it would cost to implement an on-site solution.

Knowledgeable Vendors

Typically, when new technology becomes popular, there are plenty of vendors who pop up to offer their version of that technology. This isn't always good, because a lot of those vendors tend to offer less than useful technology. By contrast, the first comers to the cloud computing party are actually very reputable companies.

Companies like Amazon, Google, Microsoft, IBM, and Yahoo! have been good vendors because they have offered reliable service, plenty of capacity, and you get some brand familiarity with these well-known names.

More Internal Resources

By shifting your non-mission-critical data needs to a third party, your IT department is freed up to work on important, business-related tasks. You also don't have to add more manpower and training that stem from having to deal with these low-level tasks.

Also, since network outages are a nightmare for the IT staff, this burden is offloaded onto the service provider. True, outages happen, but let Amazon worry about getting the service back online.

When you're looking at service providers, make sure you find someone who offers 24-hour help and support and can respond to emergency situations.

Security

There are plenty of security risks when using a cloud vendor, but reputable companies strive to keep you safe and secure.

NOTE *We'll talk about some security issues later in this chapter.*

Vendors have strict privacy policies and employ stringent security measures, like proven cryptographic methods to authenticate users.

Further, you can always encrypt your data before storing it on a provider's cloud. In some cases, between your encryption and the vendor's security measures, your data may be more secure than if it were stored in-house.

Limitations

There are other cases when cloud computing is not the best solution for your computing needs. This section looks at why certain applications are not the best to be deployed on the cloud. We don't mean to make these cases sound like deal-breakers, but you should be aware of some of the limitations. If you can work around them, that's great, but you should be aware of the issues before getting in too deep.

Your Sensitive Information

We've talked about the concern of storing sensitive information on the cloud, but it can't be understated. Once data leaves your hands and lands in the lap of a service provider, you've lost a layer of control.

What's the Worry?

Let's say a financial planner is using Google Spreadsheets to maintain a list of employee social security numbers. Now the financial planning company isn't the only one who should protect the data from hackers and internal data breaches. In a technical sense, it also becomes Google's problem. However, Google may absolve itself of responsibility in its agreement with you. So, it's no less complicated a task to sort out how sensitive information is genuinely secured. Also, the door is wide open for government investigators to subpoena that information. It has become much easier for the government to get information from third parties than from a privately owned server.

Also, less scrupulous service providers might even share that data with a marketing firm. And other providers may, by way of their agreement with you, be allowed to access and catalog your information and use it in ways you never intended. Again, be absolutely certain you understand fully your agreement with any service provider and that you approve and accept the terms of the agreement.

What's important is that you realize what the provider's policies are governing the management and maintenance of your data. For example, Google's policy states that the company will share data with the government if it has a "good faith belief" that access is necessary to fulfill lawful requests.

NOTE   *In some cases, if providers get "closed" subpoenas, the provider is legally prohibited from telling their customers that data has been given to the government.*

Private data has certainly been released. In 2006, AOL released search terms of 650,000 users to researchers on a public web page. In 2007, Microsoft and Yahoo! released some search data to the U.S. Department of Justice as part of a child pornography case. Obviously, no one wants predators to get away with their crimes, but consider the implication if your data was innocently mixed in with the data that Yahoo! and Microsoft provided the government, and you were wrongly pulled into an investigation.

And in the media we regularly hear about retailers and others losing credit card numbers. In 2007, the British government even misplaced 25 million taxpayer records.

The point is, if you have sensitive or proprietary data, the cloud might not be the safest place for it.

Protect Your Data

That doesn't mean you can't maintain your data on a cloud; you just need to be safe. The best way is to encrypt your data before you send it to a third party. Programs like PGP (www.pgp.com) or open-source TrueCrypt (www.truecrypt.org) can encrypt the file so that only those with a password can access it.

Encrypting your data before it is sent to the service provider ensures that if
the provider's security measures are breached, your data is still secure.

Encrypting your data before sending it out protects it. If someone does get your data, they need the proper credentials or all they get is gibberish.

Of course, that just applies to data you manipulate in-house and then send to the cloud. If you use word-processing files or spreadsheets that are edited online rather than just stored on the Web, then the data, when saved to the cloud, may not be encrypted.

In general, look for paid services, rather than those funded by advertising. Those are most likely to rummage through your data looking to assemble user profiles that can be used for marketing or other purposes. No company can provide you with free tangible goods or services and stay in business for long. They have to make money somehow, right?

When in doubt, always keep your data where you can be most certain it is secure, even if that means keeping it in your own server room until you can develop an alternate solution you know you can trust.

Applications Not Ready

In some cases the applications themselves are not ready to be used on the cloud. They may have little quirks that prevent them from being used to their fullest abilities, or they may not work whatsoever.

First, the application might require a lot of bandwidth to communicate with users. Remember, since cloud computing is paid based on how much you use, it might turn out to be less expensive in the long run to simply house the application locally until it can be rewritten or otherwise modified to operate more efficiently.

The application might also take a lot of effort to integrate with your other applications. If you try to relocate it to a cloud, you may find that the savings are erased by the additional effort required to maintain the integration. In this case it may end up being more cost-effective to continue to host it locally.

If the application has to talk with a database that you have onsite, it may be better to also have the application hosted locally until you can move the entire infrastructure to the cloud. Again, this helps you avoid the service cost of having to transfer to and from the cloud. It's also more efficient, because the application can talk to the database without having to reach out across the network to do so.

Some applications may not be able to communicate securely across the Internet. If they cannot communicate securely or through a tunnel, then your data is at risk. In the event the application cannot communicate securely, you will need to host it locally where you can have other means of security to protect data as it is transported across networks.

Also, since you are displaying the application results on an interface like a web browser, you need to ensure that your application is compatible with a variety of browsers and will operate properly using encryption, like SSL, for some or all of the interaction your user has within the application. If you are unable to display the application's results securely when necessary, then a cloud-based solution will be essentially worthless to you.

If you are relying on applications to be available on the cloud, that may or may not be the case. It depends on whether the developer has created a cloud-friendly version of the application you want. In the event that your application is not ready, you might be out of luck.

But that doesn't mean that you can't still get what you want done. It is still possible to write your own application.

Developing Your Own Applications

Often, the applications you want are already out there. However, it may be the case that you need a very specific application. And in that case, you'll have to commission its development yourself.

Rolling Up Your Sleeves

Developing your own applications can certainly be a problem if you don't know how to program, or if you don't have programmers on staff. In such a case, you'll have to hire a software company (or developer) or be left to use whatever applications the provider offers.

And it isn't just applications that you might need some programming savvy to deploy. If you have a database on the cloud, you'll need some sort of customized interface and some knowledge of Structured Query Language (SQL) to access and manage that data.

This is sort of a minor concern, because chances are good that you have programmers on staff who can pound out what you need in no time. Failing that, you can always hire a firm or a programmer to do it for you. Who you'll need to hire and how much you'll need to invest will depend on the scope of your application.

But There Are Benefits

The fact of the matter is that putting your database needs on a cloud can be very beneficial, in terms of scalability. At some point, your servers are going to have issues if there are too many users trying to access them, and the inherent scalability of cloud-based resources can mitigate that risk.

It is often said that this generation of web services got its start from LAMP. LAMP is a stack of simple, powerful web technologies that power a lot of popular, smaller web sites. LAMP stands for the following popular items:

- **Linux** An open-source operating system
- **Apache** An open-source web server
- **MySQL** An open-source Structured Query Language (SQL) relational database for web servers
- **Perl** A programming language

LAMP is widely used because it is very simple. Because of its ease of use, you can get an application up and running very quickly.

It's not perfect, of course. The first problem is one of scalability.

Scalability issues come from the number of threads and socket connections in the Apache web server. If the server is not properly tuned and a load increases, it can cause problems.

A larger scalability problem comes from MySQL. Relational databases have a hard time growing beyond a certain capacity due to the way they represent information. When you reach that limit, database management becomes more difficult.

You can work around this through a procedure called *data partitioning*. Using this method, you split your data into independent sets, and you can scale indefinitely. But if you can't split your data, then you move to a distributed database, which sends you to a cloud solution.

This is beneficial because the cloud allows you to scale indefinitely; it just means that more servers need to be added. Essentially, you can scale from 1,000 users to 1,000,000 by just adding more servers.

Security Concerns

As with so many other technical choices, security is a two-sided coin in the world of cloud computing—there are pros and there are cons. In this section, let's examine security in the cloud and talk about what's good, and where you need to take extra care.

IDC conducted a survey of 244 IT executives about cloud services. As Figure 2-1 shows, security led the pack of cloud concerns with 74.5 percent.

In order to be successful, vendors will have to take data like this into consideration as they offer up their clouds.

Privacy Concerns with a Third Party

The first and most obvious concern is for privacy considerations. That is, if another party is housing all your data, how do you know that it's safe and secure? You really don't. As a starting point, assume that anything you put on the cloud can be accessed by anyone. There are also concerns because law enforcement has been better able to get at data maintained on a cloud, more so than they are from an organization's servers.

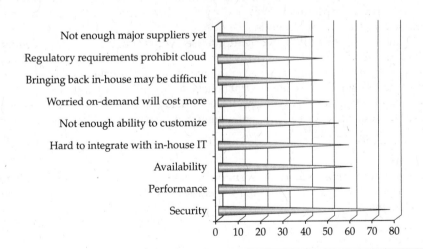

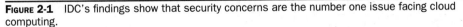

FIGURE 2-1   IDC's findings show that security concerns are the number one issue facing cloud computing.

That doesn't mean that there aren't reputable companies who would never think of compromising your data and who aren't staying on the cutting edge of network security to keep your data safe. In a glass-half-full world, that's what all the companies are doing. But in reality, even if providers are doing their best to secure data, it can still be hacked, and then your sensitive information is at the mercy of whoever broke in.

The best plan of attack is to not perform mission-critical work or work that is highly sensitive on a cloud platform without extensive security controls managed by your organization. If you cannot manage security at that rigorous level, stick to applications that are less critical and therefore better suited for the cloud and more "out of the box" security mechanisms. Remember, nobody can steal critical information that isn't there.

Are They Doing Enough to Secure It?

Before signing on with a reputable vendor, keep in mind, also, that they are doing all they can to protect your data. Now, there is a school of thought that says, in fact, that vendors will be going above and beyond to ensure that your data is secure. This is a simple matter of doing business. If word gets out that they don't protect the data they house, then no one will want to do business with them.

There's also an issue of performance and efficiency. Since you pay as you go, if you spend an inordinate amount of time on CPU cycles using their security tools, you'll go looking to the competition.

Ultimately, while we like to think that they're doing their best, their best simply might not be good enough. There are a lot of ways that their cloud and your data can be compromised.

Hackers

Hackers aren't the nice people that Hollywood has made them out to be. Most aren't just sitting around, drinking Mountain Dew and trying to break into a secure network just because they can. They want something.

There's a lot they can do if they've compromised your data. It ranges from selling your proprietary information to your competition to surreptitiously encrypting your storage until you pay them off. Or they may just erase everything to damage your business and justify the action based on their ideological beliefs. It can and does happen.

Either way, hackers are a real concern for your data managed on a cloud. Because your data is held on someone else's equipment, you may be at the mercy of whatever security measures they support.

Bot Attackers

In a commonly recognized worst-case scenario, attackers use botnets to perform distributed denial of service (DDOS) attacks. In order to get the hackers to stop attacking your network, you face blackmail.

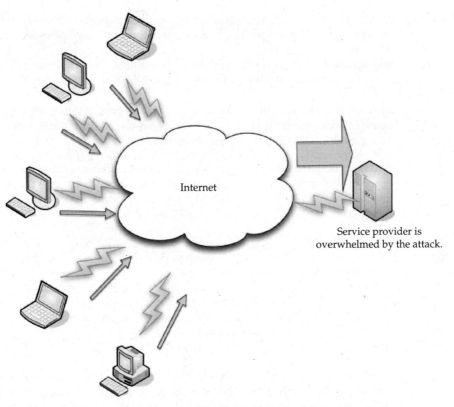

Hackers set up systems to send out distributed denial of service attacks,
bringing the service provider to its knees.

In fact, in Japan, blackmail involving DDOS is on the rise. One major Tokyo firm had to pay 3 million yen (about U.S. $31,000) after the network was brought to a screeching halt by a botnet attack. Because the attack was so dispersed, police have been unable to track down the attackers.

In the world of cloud computing, this is clearly a huge concern. If your data is on the cloud being attacked, who will the ransomers come to for money? Will it be you? Will it be the vendor? And will the ransom even be paid?

Security Benefits

This is not to suggest that your data is unsecure on the cloud. Providers do endeavor to ensure security. Otherwise, word of mouth and repeat business will shrivel up. But the very nature of the cloud lends it to needing some very strong security practices.

Centralized Data

We've talked about the specter of data loss by being in one place. However, there are some good security traits that come with centralizing your data. Just in practice, you make your system more inherently secure.

Reduced Data Loss   More than 12,000 laptops are lost in American airports every year. It's bad enough to lose your data, but it's especially bad for companies who lose proprietary data or other mission-critical information.

Also, how many laptops employ really strong security measures, like whole-disk data encryption? If the laptop can be effectively compromised, the information will be in the hands of the thief.

By maintaining data on the cloud, employing strong access control, and limiting employee downloading to only what they need to perform a task, cloud computing can limit the amount of information that could potentially be lost.

Monitoring   If your data is maintained on a cloud, it is easier to monitor security than have to worry about the security of numerous servers and clients. Of course, the chance that the cloud would be breached puts all the data at risk, but if you are mindful of security and keep up on it, you only have to worry about one location, rather than several.

Instant Swapover

If your data is compromised, while you are conducting your investigation to find the culprits, you can instantly move your data to another machine.

You also don't need to spend the time explaining to your C-level management that the system will be down due to an incident. When you perform the swapover, it's seamless to your users. You don't have to spend hours trying to replicate the data or fix the breach. Abstracting the hardware allows you to do it instantly.

Logging

In the cloud, logging is improved. Logging is usually thought of late in the game, and issues develop with storage space. On a cloud, you don't need to guess how much storage you'll need and you will likely maintain logs from the get-go, if for no other reason than to check your usage.

Also, you can use more advanced logging techniques. For instance, a C2 audit trail can be employed. This is generally rarely used because of the performance hit your network would take. However, in the cloud, you can reach that level of granularity.

Secure Builds

When you developed your own network, you had to buy third-party security software to get the level of protection you want. With a cloud solution, those tools can be bundled in and available to you and you can develop your system with whatever level of security you desire.

Also, you can perform your patches and upgrades offline. As you patch a server image, you can keep it safe offline, and when you are ready to put the virtual machine online, you can conveniently do that.

Finally, the ability to test the impact of your security changes is enhanced. You simply perform and offline-test the version of your production environment. This allows you to make sure the changes you make aren't detrimental to your network before you put it online.

Improved Software Security

Vendors are likely to develop more efficient security software. Since you're charged for your CPU cycles, you're going to notice and squawk if the price is too high. As such, the vendor doesn't want to lose your business and is going to be more inclined to develop more efficient security software. Additionally, the vendor will be likely to look at the entire security setup and tune wherever possible for a more efficient system. They know that the security vendor who delivers the more efficient product will win the game.

Security Testing

SaaS providers don't bill you for all of the security testing they do. It's shared among the cloud users. The end result is that because you are in a pool with others (you never see them, but they are there), you get to realize lower costs for security testing.

This is also the case with PaaS where your developers create their own code, but the cloud code–scanning tools check the code for security weaknesses.

Regulatory Issues

It's rare when we actually want the government in our business. In the case of cloud computing, however, regulation might be exactly what we need. Without some rules in place, it's too easy for service providers to be unsecure or even shifty enough to make off with your data.

No Existing Regulation

Currently there is no existing regulation, but there should be. In September 2008, the United States government took control of Washington Mutual. It was viewed as the greatest bank failure in American history to date. It reminds us that no matter how huge a company is, it can still come tumbling down.

Look at a company like Google, for instance. It's a big one and recently valued at $107 billion. That size and value would seem to make them bulletproof. But WaMu was worth $307 billion when it failed.

While comparing cloud service providers to banks might seem like an apples-to-oranges comparison, it underscores the need for regulation. While banks deal in money, and cloud service providers deal in data, both are of immense value to consumers and organizations alike. The fact that there was some regulation in place (in the form of government-backed insurance) prevented a run on the bank. When WaMu failed, everyone got to keep their money, thanks to the government's insurance. There isn't a third party insuring anyone's cloud data, and if a provider decides to close up shop, then that data can be lost.

Government to the Rescue?

Is it the government's place to regulate cloud computing? As we mentioned, thanks to the Great Depression, we had regulation that protected WaMu's customers' money when the bank failed.

There are two schools of thought on the issue. First, if government can figure out a way to safeguard data—either from loss or theft—any company facing such a loss would applaud the regulation. On the other hand, there are those who think the government should stay out of it and let competition and market forces guide cloud computing.

Who Owns the Data?

There are important questions that government needs to work out. First, who owns the data? Also, should law enforcement agencies have easier access to personal information on cloud data than that stored on a personal computer?

A big problem is that people using cloud services don't understand the privacy and security implications of their online email accounts, their LinkedIn account, their MySpace page, and so forth. While these are popular sites for individuals, they are still considered cloud services and their regulation will affect other cloud services.

So far, U.S. courts have tended to rule that private data stored in the cloud does not have the same level of protection from law enforcement searches than data stored on a personal computer.

A September 2008 report released by the Pew Internet and American Life project reported that 49 percent of U.S. residents who use cloud computing services would be very concerned if the cloud service providers shared files with law enforcement agencies.

These are some of the other cloud computing concerns that were reported:

- Eighty percent said they'd be very concerned if a vendor used their photos and other information in marketing campaigns.

- Sixty-eight percent said they'd be very concerned if the vendor used their personal information to send them personalized ads.

- Sixty-three percent said they'd be very concerned if service providers kept their data after the user deleted it.

Government Procurement

There are also questions about whether government agencies will store their data on the cloud. Procurement regulations will have to change for government agencies to be keen on jumping on the cloud.

The General Services Administration is making a push toward cloud computing, in an effort to reduce the amount of energy their computers consume. Hewlett-Packard and Intel produced a study that shows the federal government spends $480 million per year on electricity to run its computers.

In fact, the GSA is working with a vendor to develop an application that will calculate how much energy government agencies consume.

While this is a responsible, ecologically wise move (not to mention saving millions of taxpayer dollars every year), government agencies may not be moving to the cloud quite so soon. Again, issues of data privacy and ownership of data must still be addressed.

There are pros and cons to using a cloud computing solution. Your organization is a unique animal and there is no one right answer as to whether or not you should use a cloud. However, consider your organization's needs and weigh the pros and cons of whether you should move to the cloud or not.

In the next chapter we'll talk about some of the movers and shakers in the cloud world and take a closer look at what they have to offer.

Cloud Computing with the Titans

There are scores of cloud vendors out there, but it should come as no surprise that some of the biggest names in cloud computing are some of the biggest names in the computer world.

In this chapter we'll take a closer look at some of the cloud computing heavyweights, like Google, Microsoft, Yahoo!, Salesforce.com, IBM, and others. We'll take some time to talk about what they offer, and how they might benefit your own cloud efforts.

Google

There doesn't seem to be a pie that Google doesn't have their fingers in. The cloud is certainly one of Google's biggest business ventures, and they offer a couple of tools to help draw customers to their cloud. In this section, we'll talk about what Google offers.

Google App Engine

Google App Engine enables developers to build their web apps on the same infrastructure that powers Google's own applications.

Features

Leveraging Google App Engine, developers can accomplish the following tasks:

- **Write code once and deploy** Provisioning and configuring multiple machines for web serving and data storage can be expensive and time-consuming. Google App Engine makes it easier to deploy web applications by dynamically providing computing resources as they are needed. Developers write the code, and Google App Engine takes care of the rest.

- **Absorb spikes in traffic** When a web app surges in popularity, the sudden increase in traffic can be overwhelming for applications of all sizes, from startups to large companies that find themselves re-architecting their databases and entire systems several times a year. With automatic replication and load balancing, Google App Engine makes it easier to scale from one user to one million by taking advantage of Bigtable and other components of Google's scalable infrastructure.

- **Easily integrate with other Google services** It's unnecessary and inefficient for developers to write components like authentication and email from scratch for each new application. Developers using Google App Engine can make use of built-in components and Google's broader library of APIs that provide plug-and-play functionality for simple but important features.

"Google has spent years developing infrastructure for scalable web applications," said Pete Koomen, a product manager at Google. "We've brought Gmail and Google search to hundreds of millions of people worldwide, and we've built out a powerful network of datacenters to support those applications. Today we're taking the first step in making this infrastructure available to all developers."

Cost

Google enticed developers by offering the App Engine for free, when it launched, but after a few months slapped on some fees. As of this writing, developers using Google App Engine can expect to pay:

- Free quota to get started: 500MB storage and enough CPU and bandwidth for about 5 million pageviews per month
- $0.10–$0.12 per CPU core-hour
- $0.15–$0.18 per GB-month of storage
- $0.11–$0.13 per GB of outgoing bandwidth
- $0.09–$0.11 per GB of incoming bandwidth

In response to developer feedback, Google App Engine will provide new APIs. The image-manipulation API enables developers to scale, rotate, and crop images on the server. The memcache API is a high-performance caching layer designed to make page rendering faster for developers.

More information about Google App Engine is available at http://code.google.com/appengine/.

Google Web Toolkit

With Google Web Toolkit, developers can develop and debug web applications in the familiar Java programming language, and then deploy them as highly optimized JavaScript. In doing so, developers sidestep common AJAX headaches like browser compatibility and enjoy significant performance and productivity gains. Google Health is one recently launched application to use Google Web Toolkit.

```
/*
 * Copyright 2007 Google Inc.
 *
 * Licensed under the Apache License, Version 2.0 (the "License"); you may not
 * use this file except in compliance with the License. You may obtain a copy of
 * the License at
 *
 * http://www.apache.org/licenses/LICENSE-2.0
 *
 * Unless required by applicable law or agreed to in writing, software
 * distributed under the License is distributed on an "AS IS" BASIS, WITHOUT
 * WARRANTIES OR CONDITIONS OF ANY KIND, either express or implied. See the
 * License for the specific language governing permissions and limitations under
 * the License.
 */
package com.google.gwt.sample.simplexml.client;

import com.google.gwt.core.client.EntryPoint;
import com.google.gwt.http.client.Request;
import com.google.gwt.http.client.RequestBuilder;
import com.google.gwt.http.client.RequestCallback;
import com.google.gwt.http.client.RequestException;
import com.google.gwt.http.client.Response;
import com.google.gwt.user.client.Window;
import com.google.gwt.user.client.ui.FlexTable;
import com.google.gwt.user.client.ui.FlowPanel;
import com.google.gwt.user.client.ui.HTML;
import com.google.gwt.user.client.ui.HTMLTable;
import com.google.gwt.user.client.ui.Label;
import com.google.gwt.user.client.ui.RootPanel;
import com.google.gwt.user.client.ui.TabPanel;
import com.google.gwt.xml.client.Document;
import com.google.gwt.xml.client.Element;
import com.google.gwt.xml.client.Node;
import com.google.gwt.xml.client.NodeList;
import com.google.gwt.xml.client.XMLParser;

/**
 * A very simple XML Example where we take a customer profile and display it on
 * a page.
 */
public class SimpleXML implements EntryPoint {
  private static final String XML_LABEL_STYLE = "xmlLabel";
  private static final String USER_TABLE_LABEL_STYLE = "userTableLabel";
  private static final String USER_TABLE_STYLE = "userTable";
  private static final String NOTES_STYLE = "notes";

  public void onModuleLoad() {
    RequestBuilder requestBuilder = new RequestBuilder(RequestBuilder.GET,
        "customerRecord.xml");

    try {
      requestBuilder.sendRequest(null, new RequestCallback() {
        public void onError(Request request, Throwable exception) {
          requestFailed(exception);
```

Google Web Toolkit includes Java 5 language support so that developers can enjoy using the full capabilities of the Java 5 syntax. These capabilities include Java generics, enumerated types, annotations, auto-boxing, variable parameter lists, and more. The compiler in Google Web Toolkit 1.5 produces faster code than ever, delivering performance gains big enough for end users to notice. Indeed, often the compiler produces faster

JavaScript than a person would write by hand in JavaScript. Google Web Toolkit 1.5 accomplishes this by performing deep inlining, better dead-code elimination, and other forms of enhanced static analysis.

Google Web Toolkit also continues to provide a rich and growing set of libraries that help developers build world-class AJAX, including thoroughly tested, reusable libraries for implementing user interfaces, data structures, client/server communication, internationalization, testing, and accessibility. More information about Google Web Toolkit is available at http://code.google.com/webtoolkit/.

EMC

EMC Corporation is the world leader in products, services, and solutions for information storage and management that help organizations extract value from their information. They have their fingers in all sorts of different cloud computing and virtualization pies.

For example, in early 2009, EMC raised the stakes in its bet that virtualization is going to be the "next big thing" in the world of computing. It introduced its Symmetric V-Max system in April 2009, claiming that it is the first management system to support high-end virtual datacenters.

The system allows customers with vast storage needs to easily manage and expand storage systems without interfering with day-to-day operations. This system allows multiple datacenters to be run as if they were one, making their management much easier and more efficient.

Technologies

But EMC's reach goes far beyond virtualized datacenter management. Their other fields of expertise include

- **Archiving** Creating accessible online archives that offer a reduced operational cost by shrinking backup windows and making restores faster.
- **Backup and recovery** Different tools combine EMC's recovery management offerings, backup technologies, and management strategies to ensure that you have a solid backup and recovery practice.
- **Enterprise content management** Content-enabled solutions help mitigate risk without imposing overly complex technologies on your organization.
- **Intelligent information management** Using various technologies allows organizations to discover, store, and act on information in intelligent ways.
- **IT management** IT management is simplified and its cost reduced through automation, virtualization, and process efficiencies.
- **Replication** Data protection and remote replication technologies provide disaster recovery options.
- **Security** Organizations can deploy products with capabilities for access control, data protection, and auditing.

- **Storage**   Processes and technologies that help manage data and efficiently maintain it.
- **Virtualization**   Products including VMware backup and other EMC virtualization tools improve the management and flexibility for virtual infrastructures.

VMware Acquisition

EMC expanded their virtualization offerings in early 2009 when they acquired Palo Alto–based VMware, Inc., a rapidly growing, privately held software company specializing in industry-standard virtual computing software. EMC acquired VMware in a cash transaction with a final value of approximately US$625 million.

VMware will play a key role in EMC's strategy to help customers lower their costs and simplify their operations by deploying virtualization technologies across their heterogeneous IT infrastructure to create a single pool of available storage and computing resources. VMware's leadership in server virtualization, together with EMC's innovation in storage virtualization, will serve as a strong foundation for next-generation information lifecycle management solutions. Their offerings should be on your radar screens as we move into the future.

EMC will operate VMware as a separate software subsidiary of EMC, headquartered in Palo Alto, California. The VMware name, brand, and products will all be maintained, and VMware employees will remain focused on developing, selling, and servicing VMware's products and solutions.

NetApp

NetApp is an organization that creates storage and data management solutions for their customers. Their goal is to deliver cost efficiency and accelerate business breakthroughs.

In 1992 they introduced the world's first networked storage device. The company continues to introduce new technologies that reduce the costs of IT. NetApp claims they can cut your IT costs in half, use up to 80 percent less storage, hold off on datacenter expansion, and speed up your time to market.

The company grew from an eight-employee startup doing research in a Fry's Electronics store to a US$3 billion powerhouse with more than 130 offices around the world.

Another driver for NetApp is their belief in acting responsibly by protecting and preserving the environment by creating energy-efficient products.

NOTE   *NetApp was listed by* Fortune *as the best company to work for in its annual top 100 list in 2009.*

Offerings

NetApp was one of the first companies in the cloud, offering datacenter consolidation and storage services, as well as virtualization. Their products include a platform OS, storage services, storage security, software management, and protection software.

Their solutions run the gamut from Microsoft SQL Server and SharePoint Services to seismic processing and reservoir development to desktop and server virtualization.

In addition to these services, they also partner with other industry leaders to develop new offerings for NetApp's clients.

Cisco Partnership

NetApp and Cisco are teaming up to provide customers with unified, dynamic datacenter solutions that are based on Cisco's Unified Computing System and NetApp Unified Storage Architecture. Cisco and NetApp are working together to certify the combined solution, and the companies will also collaborate on customer support and marketing activities.

The Cisco Unified Computing System unites compute, network, storage access, and virtualization resources in a cohesive new datacenter architecture. This allows customers to reduce the complexities often associated with datacenter virtualization, lower costs, and improve asset utilization. Through Cisco Validated Design, NetApp will provide flexible and powerful storage solutions for the Cisco Unified Computing System that will be tested for interoperability in virtualized datacenter environments. Customers benefit from the unified storage model across the entire NetApp product portfolio, application integration technologies such as the NetApp SnapManager product suite, and advanced storage efficiency features. As a result, customers can take advantage of NetApp's unique advanced storage efficiency capabilities to drive down raw storage requirements, lower costs, improve utilization in virtualized environments, and simplify administrative tasks. Additionally, NetApp's leadership in Ethernet storage technology complements the Cisco Unified Computing System, which is based on a 10GB per second Unified Fabric that supports Fibre Channel over Ethernet (FCoE).

Cisco and NetApp also plan to collaborate on joint marketing efforts, such as the multicity "Virtualized Dynamic Data Center Roadshow" with VMware and other select solution integration partners. NetApp will also participate in Cisco's Data Center of the Future program. Both of these programs will focus on educating customers about NetApp and Cisco datacenter offerings.

"As more and more customers move to a virtualized infrastructure, they require the necessary storage, compute, and network solutions needed to transition to a truly dynamic data center," said Tom Georgens, president and chief operating officer for NetApp. "Through our long-standing collaboration with Cisco, we are enabling customers to tap deep into the power of their virtualized environment through a unified and scalable platform for a more efficient and streamlined experience."

In March 2009, Cisco announced that NetApp is a participant in Cisco's open ecosystem of partners for the Unified Computing System, which is focused on stimulating innovation, enhancing service delivery, and accelerating the market adoption of Unified Computing. In addition, Cisco and NetApp have a long history of collaboration and many common customers that have deployed Cisco and NetApp technologies and solutions in their datacenters. NetApp supports and resells the Cisco Nexus 5000 and MDS datacenter switching products, and in 2008, Cisco and NetApp announced support for the industry's first native FCoE storage array.

The two companies have also worked together on an Ethernet Unification Center of Excellence, located at NetApp's campus in Research Triangle Park, North Carolina, which was announced in February 2009. The center features Ethernet-based protocols running on a Cisco 10 Gigabit Ethernet backbone.

Microsoft

Microsoft offers a number of cloud services for organizations of any size—from enterprises all the way down to mom-and-pop shops or individuals. A good portion of Microsoft's cloud offerings are cloud variants of products that people already use, so cloud versions aren't that difficult to use.

Azure Services Platform

The cornerstone of Microsoft's offerings is the Azure Services Platform. The Azure Services Platform is a cloud computing and services platform hosted in Microsoft datacenters.

The Azure Services Platform supplies a broad range of functionality to build applications to serve individuals or large enterprises, and everyone in between. The platform offers a cloud operating system and developer tools. Applications can be developed with industry standard protocols like REST and SOAP.

Azure services can be used individually or in conjunction with one another to build new applications or to enhance existing ones. Let's take a closer look at the Azure Services Platform components.

Windows Azure

Windows Azure is a cloud-based operating system that enables the development, hosting, and service management environment for the Azure Services Platform. Windows Azure gives developers an on-demand compute and storage environment that they can use to host, scale, and manage web applications through Microsoft datacenters.

To build applications and services, developers can use the Visual Studio skills they already have. Further, Azure supports existing standards like SOAP, REST, and XML.

Windows Azure can be used to

- Add web service capabilities to existing applications
- Build and modify applications and then move them onto the Web
- Make, test, debug, and distribute web services efficiently and inexpensively
- Reduce the costs of IT management

SQL Services

Microsoft SQL Services extends SQL Server capabilities to the cloud as web-based services. This allows the storage of structured, semistructured, and unstructured data. SQL Services delivers a set of integrated services that allow relational queries, search, reporting, analytics, integration, and synchronization of data. This can be done by mobile users, remote offices, or business partners.

.NET Services

Microsoft .NET Services are a set of Microsoft-hosted, developer-oriented services that provide the components required by many cloud-based and cloud-aware applications.

.NET Services are similar to the .NET Framework, providing high-level class libraries that make development much more robust. .NET Services can help developers focus more on their end product than on building and deploying their own cloud-based infrastructure.

.NET Services are also available to other development technologies through the use of industry-standard protocols, like REST, SOAP, and HTTP.

Live Services

Live Services is a development center and supplier of software development kits for Windows Live and Azure Services platforms. It gives information about getting started with Windows Live services, current documentation and APIs, and samples.

Windows Live

Windows Live is an integrated set of online services that makes it easier and more fun for consumers to communicate and share with others. The new generation of Windows Live includes updated experiences for photo sharing, email, and instant messaging, as well as integration with multiple third-party sites. The release also includes Windows Live Essentials, free downloadable software that enhances consumers' Windows experience by helping them simplify and enjoy digital content scattered across their PC, phone, and on web sites.

NOTE *Windows products with the "Live" moniker are all consumer-oriented, like Xbox Live, for instance. Anything with an "Online" moniker is business-oriented. We'll talk about some of Microsoft's Online offerings later in this section.*

For more information about Windows Live, go to http://www.windowslive.com.

Consumers can create online content and share it in many places across the Web. To help make it simple for Windows Live customers to keep their friends up to date, Microsoft collaborated with companies including Flickr, LinkedIn Corp., Pandora Media Inc., Photobucket Inc., Twitter, WordPress, and Yelp Inc. to integrate activities on third-party sites into Windows Live through a new profile and What's New feed. The new Windows Live also gives consumers the added convenience of having a central place to organize and manage information.

"Think of Windows Live as the single place where people using our e-mail, messaging and photo-sharing services can stay connected," said Chris Jones, corporate vice president of Windows Live Experience Program Management at Microsoft. "Our customers have friends across the Web. They communicate through many unconnected Web services and want access to it all from a single location—without worrying about how it's done. Now, Windows Live takes care of that, with an integrated personal communication service that works across the Web with optimized experiences on the PC and mobile phone."

Extending Live's Reach

The ability for Windows Live customers to add third-party sites to their profiles and have those activities appear in a Windows Live feed across their network was made possible through collaboration with more than 50 leading web companies, including Flickr, LinkedIn, Pandora, Photobucket, Twitter, WordPress, and Yelp, among others. As Windows Live customers share photos, update their profiles, and write reviews, these activities will automatically publish to their Windows Live network.

"Microsoft's Windows Live is an exciting new platform that enables new experiences for both Photobucket and Microsoft users that would not otherwise be possible," said Alex Welch, president of Photobucket. "Online photo sharing is an important part of people's everyday lives and, as the leading stand-alone photo and video-sharing Web site, Photobucket is thrilled to be teaming up with Windows Live to make this experience even easier for users."

In addition to partnering with leading web companies, Microsoft announced alliances with HP and China Telecom Corporation Ltd. to deliver Windows Live services to more people across the globe. HP, the worldwide leader in printing solutions, will distribute Windows Live Photo Gallery with its consumer printers, including Photosmart and Deskjet lines, starting next year. The combined offer provides HP customers with Windows Live Photo Gallery, an end-to-end photo management and printing solution.

"Beginning in 2009, HP will feature Windows Live Photo Gallery and HP Creative Print Projects across the HP Photosmart and HP Deskjet consumer printing portfolios," said Sam Greenblatt, general manager of Core Technologies, Imaging and Printing Group, at HP. "We are pleased to be working with Microsoft to provide an enhanced user experience for our customers. This offering will allow users to print, share, organize and edit a wide array of creative print projects at home, such as photo books, collages, cards and calendars."

Communicating and Collaborating

Windows Live makes it easier for consumers to manage their digital life and keep their life in sync. These are some of the highlights:

- Windows Live provides social features available to all customers, including an updated profile, a "what's new" feed of activities across the network, and web, photo sharing, and on-the-go access from virtually any device with Windows Live SkyDrive. Online storage is increasing from 5GB to 25GB.

- Windows Live Messenger includes more personalization, a "what's new" feed with updates from contacts across the Web, drag-and-drop photo sharing in the conversation window, a Favorites list to designate the most important contacts, and group IM to chat simultaneously with up to 20 people at the same time.

- Windows Live Hotmail was recently upgraded and is now faster and has 80 percent more effective spam filtering compared with previous versions of Hotmail. Upcoming changes include the ability to bring multiple email accounts together, the ability to put multiple email addresses onto almost any device, increased storage, and a revamped calendar that makes it easier to share calendars with others, subscribe to multiple calendars, and use your calendar with Microsoft Outlook.

- Windows Live Groups, a place for groups to collaborate online, includes a shared calendar, shared storage, a shared email address, and shared instant messaging.

All these services work with Windows Live Essentials, a free suite of applications for communication and sharing that also works with leading email, photo, and blogging services worldwide.

Exchange Online

Messaging is a crucial business application, and to help facilitate that in a cloud environment, Microsoft offers Exchange Online.

Microsoft Exchange Online is a Microsoft-hosted enterprise messaging service based on Microsoft Exchange Server 2007. Because it is a cloud service, you and your employees can access messages from anywhere.

Exchange Online servers are geographically dispersed. The service is aimed at easing IT's management duties by removing your need to deploy, configure, monitor, and upgrade on-site email solutions.

Customers using Active Directory can use a synchronization tool to keep the online and local Active Directories in sync. This allows for a mix of users, from on-site users to users traveling and checking in with a mobile device.

These are the key features of the online standard version of the solution:

- A 5GB mailbox (additional storage available for purchase—up to 25GB), shared calendar, contacts, tasks
- Outlook Client Connectivity including Outlook Anywhere
- Outlook Web Access

- Virus/spam filtering via Exchange Hosted Filtering
- Push email for Microsoft Windows Mobile 6.0/6.1 and Exchange ActiveSync 12 devices
- Email synchronization for Nokia E series and N series and iPhone 2.0 (no ActiveSync push)
- Built-in business continuity and disaster recovery capabilities
- Scheduled uptime of 99.9 percent with financially backed service level agreements
- Use of HTTPS to help keep Internet access secure
- Tier 2 support 24/7 (web form and phone based) for IT administrators
- Sign-In Tool for single sign-on capability
- Directory Synchronization Tool to help keep on-premise and online Active Directories in sync
- Coexistence, or the ability for some users to be on mail servers on premises and for some to be online
- Migration Tools to help you move your current mailbox data into the online environment

SharePoint Services

Microsoft offers its SharePoint Services to aid collaboration efforts. SharePoint Services provides communities for team collaboration and makes it easy for users to work together on documents, tasks, contacts, events, and other information. Additionally, team and site managers can coordinate site contents and user activity.

SharePoint sites are made up of Web Parts and Windows ASP.NET-based components. Web Parts are designed to be add-ons to web pages and configured by site administrators and users to create complete page-based applications.

NOTE *SharePoint ships with several ready-to-use Web Parts, but more are expected to be added.*

SharePoint sites are places where teams can participate in discussions, shared document collaboration, and surveys. Site content can be accessed from a web browser and through clients that support web services. Document collaboration controls allow you to check in, check out, and control document versioning.

Microsoft Office System programs use SharePoint site content. A site's collaborative content—like documents, lists, events, and so forth—can be read and edited with Microsoft Office Word. Picture editing is also possible. Microsoft Office Outlook allows SharePoint site event calendars to be viewed side by side with personal calendars.

SharePoint also allows managers to customize the content and layout of sites so that site members can access and work with relevant information. Members' activity can also be monitored and moderated by managers.

SharePoint Services can scale to thousands of sites within an organization. It supports load-balanced web farms and clustered database deployments. For site and serve managers, quotas can be set on storage, sites per server, and users per site. Site usage can be monitored to detect and retire inactive sites.

SharePoint Services servers, sites, and site contents are managed by using a .NET-based object model. Sites can be customized even by nondevelopers by using Microsoft Office FrontPage.

Microsoft Dynamics CRM

Microsoft Dynamics CRM Online is an on-demand customer relationship management service hosted and managed by Microsoft. The Internet service delivers a full suite of marketing, sales, and service capabilities through a web browser or directly into Microsoft Office and Outlook. It provides "instant-on" access to businesses that want a full-featured CRM solution with no IT infrastructure investment or setup required.

"At Microsoft, we're revolutionizing how companies deploy marketing, sales, and service solutions to users within their organization," said Brad Wilson, general manager of Microsoft Dynamics CRM at Microsoft. "Microsoft Dynamics CRM delivers the power of choice to customers, with a familiar and productive user experience and a multitenant platform that enables fast on-premise implementations or 'instant-on' deployments over the Internet."

Microsoft Dynamics CRM Online supplements Microsoft's software plus services strategy for delivering integrated business solutions over the Internet, and it is a part of Microsoft's multibillion-dollar investment in global datacenters. In addition to full access through a zero-footprint browser client, the new service delivers marketing, sales, and service information within a native Microsoft Office experience, integrated with the desktop tools that employees already use every day, enabling businesses to ramp up end-user adoption and productivity rapidly.

Microsoft Dynamics CRM Online is initially packaged in two service offerings:

- Microsoft Dynamics CRM Online Professional delivers a full suite of CRM capabilities with extensive configurability and extensibility options. Businesses get 5GB of data storage, 100 configurable workflows, and 100 custom entities. The Professional edition is priced at US$44 per user per month, with an introductory offer of US$39 per user per month.

- Microsoft Dynamics CRM Online Professional Plus delivers all the capabilities of the Professional version plus offline data synchronization with expanded data storage, workflow, and customization options that give businesses 20GB of data storage, 200 configurable workflows, and 200 custom entities. The Professional Plus edition is priced at US$59 per user per month.

To learn about Microsoft Dynamics CRM and to sign up for the new online service, customers can visit http://crm.dynamics.com.

Amazon

Amazon may be the most widely known cloud vendor. They offer services on many different fronts, from storage to platform to databases. Amazon seems to have their finger in a number of cloud technologies.

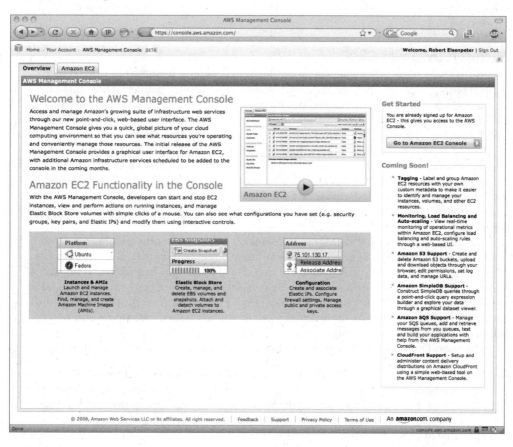

Amazon Elastic Compute Cloud (Amazon EC2)

Amazon Elastic Compute Cloud (Amazon EC2) is a web service that offers resizable compute capacity in the cloud and is designed to make web scaling easier for developers.

Amazon EC2 provides a simple web interface that allows you to obtain and configure capacity with little difficulty. It allows you control of your computing resources. Amazon EC2 cuts the time it takes to obtain and boot new server instances to a few minutes, allowing you to change scale as your needs change.

For instance, Amazon EC2 can run Microsoft Windows Server 2003 and is a way to deploy applications using the Microsoft Web Platform, including ASP.NET, ASP.NET AJAX, Silverlight, and Internet Information Server (IIS).

Amazon EC2 allows you to run Windows-based applications on Amazon's cloud computing platform. This might be web sites, web-service hosting, high-performance computing, data processing, media transcoding, ASP.NET application hosting, or any other application requiring Windows software.

EC2 also supports SQL Server Express and SQL Server Standard and makes those offerings available to customers on an hourly basis.

Amazon SimpleDB

For database services, Amazon offers its Amazon SimpleDB. It provides core database functions of data indexing and querying. This service works closely with Amazon Simple Storage Service (Amazon S3) and Amazon EC2. This provides the ability to store, process, and query data sets in the cloud.

Amazon offers the feature because traditional relational databases require a sizable upfront expense. They are also complex to design and often require the employment of a database administrator. Amazon SimpleDB is—as the name says—simpler. It requires no schema, automatically indexes data, and provides a simple API for storage and access. This makes the process easier to manage and eliminates the administrative burden of data modeling, index maintenance, and performance tuning.

Amazon Simple Storage Service (Amazon S3)

Amazon Simple Storage Service (Amazon S3) is Amazon's storage solution for the Internet. It is designed to make web-scale computing easier for developers.

Amazon S3 utilizes a simple web services interface that can be used to store and retrieve any amount of data from anywhere on the Web. It gives developers access to the same data storage infrastructure that Amazon uses to run its own retail empire.

Amazon CloudFront

Amazon CloudFront is a web service for content delivery. It works in conjunction with other Amazon Web Services to give developers and businesses an easy way to distribute content to clients. Amazon promises low latency, high data transfer speeds, and no commitments.

The service delivers content using a global network of edge locations. Object requests are automatically routed to the nearest edge location, so content is delivered with the best performance possible.

Amazon Simple Queue Service (Amazon SQS)

Amazon Simple Queue Service (Amazon SQS) offers a scalable, hosted queue for storing messages as they travel between computers. Developers can move data between distributed components of their applications that perform different tasks, without losing messages or requiring each component to be always available.

Amazon SQS allows an automated workflow to be created and works closely with Amazon EC2 and other Amazon Web Services.

Amazon SQS exposes Amazon's web-scale messaging infrastructure as a web service. As such, any computer on the Internet can add or read messages without any specially installed software or special firewall configurations. Amazon SQS components can run independently, and need not be on the same network, developed with the same technologies, or running at the same time.

Elastic Block Store

Amazon also launched its Amazon Elastic Block Store (Amazon EBS), a persistent storage feature for the Amazon EC2. Amazon EC2 is an infrastructure service that provides resizable compute capacity in the cloud. With Amazon EBS, storage volumes can be programmatically created, attached to Amazon EC2 instances, and if even more durability is desired, can be backed with a snapshot to the Amazon Simple Storage Service (Amazon S3).

Prior to Amazon EBS, storage within an Amazon EC2 instance was tied to the instance itself so that when the instance was terminated, the data within the instance was lost. With Amazon EBS, users can choose to allocate storage volumes that persist reliably and independently from Amazon EC2 instances. Additionally, for even more durable backups and an easy way to create new volumes, Amazon EBS provides the ability to create point-in-time, consistent snapshots of volumes that are then stored to Amazon S3.

"For over two years, we've focused on delivering a cost-effective, web scale infrastructure to developers, giving them complete flexibility in the kinds of solutions they deliver," said Peter De Santis, general manager of Amazon EC2. "Persistent block storage has been among the top requests of developers using Amazon EC2, and we're excited to deliver Amazon Elastic Block Storage designed specifically for our cloud-based, elastic computing environment."

Amazon EBS is well suited for databases, as well as many other applications that require running a file system or access to raw block-level storage. As Amazon EC2 instances are started and stopped, the information saved in your database or application is preserved in much the same way it is with traditional physical servers.

"ShareThis has received tremendous benefits from working with Amazon Web Services for our leading sharing platform," said Manu Murkerji, senior software developer for ShareThis, a service providing a one-click way to instantly post, tag, and send content via email, instant messaging, and text messaging. "Amazon EBS has enabled us to create large-scale, enterprise-level databases that allow us to run and maintain various, disparate applications. EC2 and EBS together provide a cost-effective, flexible system that allows us to crunch data faster than we had been previously able—giving us a much needed advantage for our business."

"Sun's MySQL is the one of the most popular databases on Amazon EC2. With the introduction of EBS, MySQL users will be able to increase the durability and portability of their database applications deployed in the cloud," said Juan Carlos Soto, vice president of Global Market Development at Sun Microsystems. "With Sun also recently making the OpenSolaris platform available on EC2, Web companies can now access the unique features of the ZFS file system—such as Rollback and 128-bit checksum capabilities—to enable the highest level of data integrity on EC2."

"With the release of Amazon Elastic Block Store, the ability to deploy any application, anywhere, including the cloud is a reality. By providing a persistent and consistent compute environment, both on-premise and in the cloud, Red Hat Enterprise Linux and JBoss EAP on Amazon EC2 will help achieve the vision of the virtual datacenter," said Scott Crenshaw, vice president of Platform Business Unit, Red Hat. "Now with the highly anticipated release of Amazon EBS, our enterprise EC2 customers have the ability to persist virtual machine configuration and application data across instantiations and manage their cloud solutions in as consistent a manner as their on-premise deployments."

Salesforce.com

Salesforce.com made its name with the success of its flagship Salesforce.com automation application. Today, the company has three primary areas of focus:

- **The Sales Cloud**   The popular cloud computing sales application
- **The Service Cloud**   The platform for customer service that lets companies tap into the power of customer conversations no matter where they take place
- **Your Cloud**   Powerful capabilities to develop custom applications on its cloud computing platform, Force.com

The company has made its platform available to other companies as a place to build and deploy their software services. Force.com offers

- A relational database
- User interface options
- Business logic
- Apex, an integrated development environment
- Workflow and approvals engine
- Programmable interface
- Automatic mobile device deployment
- Web services integration
- Reporting and analytics

Using Apex, programmers can test their applications in Force.com's Sandboxes and then offer the finalized code on Salesforce.com's site.

Developers initially used Force.com to create add-ons to the Salesforce CRM, but now it is possible to develop applications that are unrelated to Salesforce.com's offerings. For instance, gaming giant Electronic Arts created an employee-recruiting application on Force.com and software vendor Coda made a general ledger application. Meanwhile, Salesforce.com promotes its own applications, which are used by more than 1.1 million people.

Salesforce.com is into other cloud services, as well. In April 2007 it moved into enterprise content management with Salesforce.com Content. This makes it possible to store, classify, and share information in a manner similar to Microsoft SharePoint.

The company employs a multitenant architecture, similar to Google, Amazon, and eBay. As such, servers and other resources are shared by customers, rather than given to a single account. It allows for better performance, better scalability, better security, and faster innovation through automatic upgrades. Multitenancy also allows apps to be elastic—they can scale up to tens of thousands of users, or down to just a few—always something to consider when moving to cloud-based solutions. As with other providers, upgrades are taken care of by Salesforce.com for their customers, so apps get security and performance enhancements automatically.

Because the company generates all its income based on cloud computing, Salesforce.com is a good bellwether for assessing the growth rate of the application side of cloud computing. Salesforce.com's revenue grew to US$290 million in the quarter ending January 31, 2009—a 34 percent increase year-over-year.

Force.com

Force.com is Salesforce.com's on-demand cloud computing platform—billed by Salesforce.com as the world's first PaaS. Force.com features Visualforce, a technology that makes it much simpler for end customers, developers, and independent software vendors (ISVs) to design almost any type of cloud application for a wide range of uses. The Force.com platform offers global infrastructure and services for database, logic, workflow, integration, user interface, and application exchange.

Visualforce is essentially a framework for creating new interface designs and enables user interactions that can be built and delivered with no software or hardware infrastructure requirements. More on that later in the chapter.

PaaS

Force.com delivers PaaS, a way to create and deploy business apps that allows companies and developers to focus on what their applications do, rather than the software and infrastructure to run them.

The Force.com platform can run multiple applications within the same Salesforce.com instance, allowing all of a company's Salesforce.com applications to share a common security model, data model, and user interface. This is a major benefit found in cloud computing solutions. Add to that an on-demand operating system, the ability to create any database on demand, a workflow engine for managing collaboration between users, and a programming language for building complex logic. A web services API for programmatic access, mash-ups, and integration with other applications and data is another key feature.

Visualforce

As part of the Force.com platform, Visualforce provides the ability to design application user interfaces for practically any experience on any screen. Visualforce uses HTML, AJAX, and Flex, for business applications. Visualforce provides a page-based model, built on standard HTML and web presentation technologies, and is complemented with both a component library for implementing common user interface elements, and a controller model for creating new interactions between those elements.

Visualforce features and capabilities include

- **Pages**   Enables the design definition of an application's user interface.
- **Components**   Provides the ability to create new applications that automatically match the look and feel of Salesforce.com applications or easily customize and extend the Salesforce.com user interface to specific requirements.
- **Logic Controllers**   The controller enables customers to build any user interface behavior.

Salesforce.com CRM

Salesforce.com is a leader in cloud computing customer relationship management (CRM) applications. Its CRM offering consists of the Sales Cloud and the Service Cloud and can be broken down into five core applications:

- **Sales**   Easily the most popular cloud computing sales application, Salesforce.com says that CRM Sales is used by more than 1.1 million customers around the world. Its claim to fame is that it is comprehensive and easy to customize. Its value proposition is that it empowers companies to manage people and processes more effectively, so reps can spend more time selling and less time on administrative tasks.

- **Marketing**   With Salesforce.com CRM Marketing, marketers can put the latest web technologies to work building pipeline while collaborating seamlessly with their sales organization. The application empowers customers to manage multichannel campaigns and provide up-to-date messaging to sales. And since the application is integrated with the Salesforce.com CRM Sales application, the handoff of leads is automated.

- **Service**   The Service Cloud is the new platform for customer service. Companies can tap into the power of customer conversations no matter where they take place. Because it's on the Web, the Service Cloud allows companies to instantly connect to collaborate in real time, share sales information, and follow joint processes. Connecting with partners is made to be as easy as connecting with people on LinkedIn: companies instantly share leads, opportunities, accounts, contacts, and tasks with their partners.

- **Collaboration**   Salesforce.com CRM can help an organization work more efficiently with customers, partners, and employees by allowing them to collaborate among themselves in the cloud. Some of the capabilities include

  - Create and share content in real time using Google Apps and Salesforce.com

  - Track and deliver presentations using Content Library

  - Give your community a voice using Ideas and Facebook

  - Tap into the collective wisdom of the sales team with Genius

- **Analytics**   Force.com offers real-time reporting, calculations, and dashboards so a business is better able to optimize performance, decision making, and resource allocation.

- **Custom Applications**   Custom applications can be quickly created by leveraging one data model, one sharing model, and one user interface.

AppExchange

Launched in 2005, AppExchange is a directory of applications built for Salesforce.com by third-party developers. Users can purchase and add to their Salesforce.com environment. When it launched, AppExchange offered 70 applications. As of September 2008, there were over 750 applications available from over 450 ISVs.

AppExchange allows ISVs to accelerate their time-to-market and extend on-demand success beyond CRM. AppExchange provides an on-demand platform license that includes everything partners need to build and deliver compelling on-demand applications to their customers.

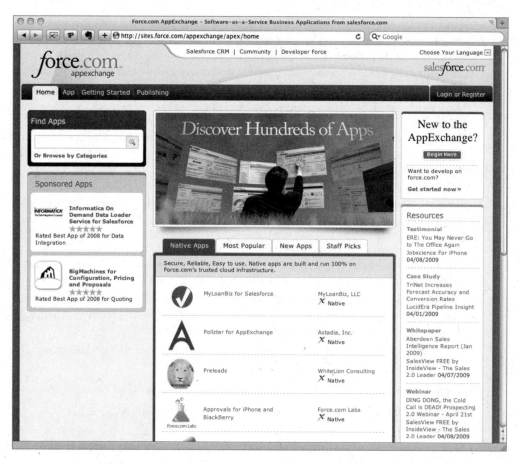

With AppExchange, companies have access to new applications that potentially bring the benefits of Salesforce.com to an entire business, letting them manage and share all of a company's information on demand. Using AppExchange, companies are able to easily add new applications to their existing Salesforce.com deployments.

This allows for the development of applications serving a broad range of business requirements:

- Finance
- Electronic signatures
- Document management
- Project management

- Credit and collections
- Mobile workforce management
- Data cleansing
- Professional services management
- Human resources

A feature called "Get It Now" makes that application instantly available to all subscribers within that customer's Salesforce.com account. Once installed, AppExchange applications will sit alongside their existing on-demand applications, and may be further customized to meet customers' unique business needs.

Applications built for the Force.com platform can run entirely on demand, eliminating the need for developers or partners to create and manage their own datacenter or infrastructure.

Force.com represents a comprehensive suite of development and deployment technologies all available to partners on demand, through their browser. Independent software vendors can jump-start their entry into on-demand computing without risking the initial investment. Salesforce.com expects that developers and business experts around the world will be able to contribute applications to the AppExchange and take advantage of the most compelling community of success in on-demand computing.

IBM

IBM offers cloud computing services to help businesses of all sizes take advantage of this increasingly attractive computing model. IBM is applying its industry-specific consulting expertise and established technology record to offer secure services to companies in public, private, and hybrid cloud models.

Some of their features include

- **Industry-specific business consulting services for cloud computing**   IBM Global Business Services uses an economic model for assessing the total cost of ownership for building private clouds, and/or moving data and applications off-site in a public or hybrid cloud model.
- **Technology consulting, design, and implementation services**   IBM Global Technology Services offers services to help clients install, configure, and deliver cloud computing inside the datacenter.
- **Cloud security**   Spanning IBM Systems, Software, Services and IBM's Research and X-Force arms, this effort is aimed at re-architecting and redesigning technologies and processes, to infuse security and shield against threats and vulnerabilities in the cloud.

Services

IBM's consulting services use economic modeling to assess the total cost of ownership for building and integrating clouds. Initial research indicates that organizations will employ both public and private clouds to achieve business goals, and IBM can help companies find the most effective balance, and manage it all as one integrated strategy.

In addition, cloud technology consulting services are intended to help clients create roadmaps for reconstructing their IT environments, so they can take advantage of cloud computing models to improve operational efficiency, overall carbon posture, and return on investment. With new cloud implementation services, IBM will apply expert-level skills, methods, guidance, and project management techniques to help clients plan, configure, and test the servers, storage, and technologies necessary to support a dynamic technology environment.

"Cloud strategies need to be in line with business strategies," said Willy Chiu, vice president, High Performance on Demand Solutions, IBM. "Over the last year in our 13 cloud computing centers worldwide, we've worked with clients to understand how to help them take advantage of both public and private clouds to get the best economics."

Movement to the Cloud

In addition to consulting services, IBM is helping new clients move into the cloud. One of Houston's largest and fastest-growing human services agencies, Neighborhood Centers serves over 200,000 citizens in southwest Texas and delivers key services including economic development services, citizenship, and immigration services, early childhood development programs, a K–5 charter school, and seniors' programs. The nonprofit organization depends on IBM cloud services to back up server and PC data from distributed environments, and store it in secure off-site locations.

"Neighborhood Centers is dedicated to helping citizens cope with disruption and plan for contingencies in life—as second responders in emergencies we simply cannot afford to be shut down, or slowed down, by a data loss," said Tom Comella, CIO, Neighborhood Centers Inc. "IBM cloud services were critical in our community recovery efforts following Hurricane Ike. Since we experienced no business interruptions in any of our 20 facilities, we were able to focus on bringing the community, our services, and our citizens back online. But the benefits of cloud services reach far beyond disaster recovery. Better data protection— demonstrating that we are good stewards of information—has become a selling point for us in willing contracts."

IBM Research is working directly with clients to create replicable, cloud-delivered, industry-specific services like Lender Business Process Services or Healthcare Process Services, as well as horizontal business services like CRM and supply chain management.

In China, for example, IBM Research is piloting a newly developed cloud computing platform, code-named Project Yun, which is Chinese for "cloud," for companies to access business services, designed to make the selection and implementation of new cloud services as easy as selecting an item from a drop-down menu. With no need for back-end provisioning, the IBM platform stands to cut the time required to deliver new services dramatically. The Yun platform allocates storage, server, and network resources for the customer application with zero human input, achieving top performance, availability, and power utilization.

One of China's largest retailers with more than 10 million customers per day, Wang Fu Jing Department Store has deployed several key cloud services from Project Yun, including a supply chain management solution for its vast network of retail stores to easily share supply chain information and visualize the execution of business-to-business (B2B) processes with thousands of their own small and medium-size business (SMB) suppliers via the cloud.

Security

To ensure the widespread adoption of cloud computing services, IBM initiated a company-wide project to form a unified and comprehensive security architecture for cloud computing environments. The effort—which spans Systems, Software, Services, and IBM's Research and X-Force arms—is aimed at re-architecting and redesigning technologies and processes, to infuse security and shield against threats and vulnerabilities. Security is built into the cloud, not added as an afterthought.

The project incorporates next-generation security and cloud service management technologies, as well as simplified security management and enforcement, offering enterprise customers the same security and compliance guarantees that are equivalent to or better than what they can expect in traditional computing environments.

Built upon IBM's extensive industry security leadership, the project focuses on developing trusted virtual domains, authentication, isolation management, policy and integrity management, and access control technologies designed specifically for cloud computing.

Partnerships

Not everybody is into the cloud for the same reasons. It is clear that Google and Microsoft (and most other providers, to be honest) are trying to make a buck. But not everyone is. In fact, a couple of interesting partnerships are showing how the cloud can be used without seeing money change hands (at least not yet).

Yahoo! Research

Yahoo! takes a different approach to the cloud—while it doesn't offer the same sorts of services as Google and Microsoft, Yahoo! has focused its cloud energies on providing a science that helps improve business processes. Its scientists examine data-driven analysis, high-quality search, algorithms, and economic models. Yahoo! manages large data repositories and researchers mine information from this collection. Yahoo! strives to collaborate with peers from academic and research institutions and provides an academic setting.

Collaboration

Yahoo! and Computational Research Laboratories (CRL) set out in a partnership to research cloud computing. As part of their agreement, CRL will make available to researchers one of the world's top five supercomputers, which has substantially more processors than any supercomputer currently available for cloud computing research.

This effort is the first of its kind in terms of the size and scale of the machine, and the first in making available a supercomputer to academic institutions in India. The Yahoo!/CRL effort is intended to leverage CRL's expertise in high-performance computing and Yahoo!'s technical leadership in Apache Hadoop, an open-source distributed computing project of the Apache Software Foundation, to enable scientists to perform data-intensive computing research on a 14,400-processor supercomputer.

Called the EKA, CRL's supercomputer is ranked the fourth fastest supercomputer in the world—it has 14,400 processors, 28 terabytes of memory, 140 terabytes of disk space, a peak performance of 180 trillion calculations per second (180 teraflops), and sustained computation capacity of 120 teraflops for the LINPACK benchmark. Of the top ten supercomputers in the world, EKA is the only supercomputer funded by the private sector and is available for use on commercial terms. EKA is expected to run the latest version of Hadoop and other state-of-the-art, Yahoo!-supported, open-source distributed computing software such as the Pig parallel programming language developed by Yahoo! Research.

Benefits

"The Tata group has always contributed to scientific research in India, and the EKA will strengthen this cause further in the field of cloud computing. This partnership brings together Yahoo!'s leadership role in the development of Hadoop and CRL's expertise in high performance computing, and will help bridge the gap between traditional supercomputing and cloud computing research in India," said S. Ramadorai, chairman of CRL.

"We are excited to partner with Yahoo! to advance cloud computing research in India as it opens up a new arena of exciting opportunities," said Dr. Gautam Shroff, member of the steering committee of CRL. "We are initiating dialogue with leading Indian academic institutions to collaborate on research using cloud computing."

"We have made our leadership in supporting academic, cloud computing research very concrete by sharing a 4,000-processor supercomputer with computer scientists at Carnegie Mellon University for the last three months. With this supercomputing cluster, researchers were able to analyze hundreds of millions of Web documents and handle two orders of magnitude more data than they previously could," said Ron Brachman, vice president and head of academic relations for Yahoo!. "Launching our cloud computing program internationally with CRL is another significant milestone in creating a global, collaborative research community working to advance the new sciences of the Internet."

SAP and IBM

SAP has also partnered with another large, well-known company—IBM. In their endeavor, SAP is using the cloud to migrate SAP applications live across remote IBM POWER6 systems.

The technology, developed as a part of the European Union–funded Resources and Services Virtualization Without Barriers (RESERVOIR) cloud computing project, is designed to provide companies with a range of cloud computing solutions to meet their specific business needs.

The cloud approach to delivering and consuming IT provides answers to the challenges many businesses face today: the immense complexity of sprawling datacenters, the growing cost of energy, and the need to dynamically adapt the allocation of IT resources to constantly changing workloads and business priorities.

In a technology demonstration, IBM and SAP showed how users can run enterprise applications in the cloud, in particular demonstrating the migration of workloads across physical servers and across datacenters.

"The breakthrough we're showing is that applications can flexibly move across remote physical servers, regardless of location—which makes our work a strong enabling technology for the cloud," explained Dr. Joachim Schaper, vice president of SAP Research. "Specifically, in cloud-scale environments, service providers will need to provide users with access to services across the cloud. Service providers will need to compete on performance and Quality of Service—and so the future cloud will need to support application mobility across disparate datacenters to enhance performance."

"With RESERVOIR, our aim is to provide cloud technologies that will enable energy-efficient, borderless delivery of IT services that are driven by actual demands—with the goal of keeping costs competitive," said Dr. Yaron Wolfsthal, senior manager for system technologies at IBM's Research Lab in Haifa, Israel, where the technology was developed. "The new technology is allowing us to realize the vision of true cloud computing by moving applications across disparate interconnected networks to optimize load balancing across remote servers. When changes in workload occur, the new technology autonomically balances resource utilization and power consumption across remote servers. This is done, for example, by evacuating and turning off underutilized servers (and possibly entire datacenters) when demand drops, and powering on idle servers when load increases."

In their demonstration, the migration of SAP workloads across the cloud is supported by IBM's POWER6 systems, which enable users to run separate applications on different virtual machines, called logical partitions, on the same physical server. The IBM POWER6 system's Live Partition Mobility capability further allows for the movement of a partition from one POWER6-based server to another POWER6-based server in the datacenter with no application downtime, resulting in better system utilization, improved application availability, and energy savings.

The collaborative research relationship between SAP and IBM began in 1999 and has since developed a rich portfolio of research activities. On a quarterly basis, research management and key researchers from both organizations meet to identify topics of mutual interest and to leverage the open collaborative research model, including the EU-sponsored FP7 program, in order to define new project areas that will lead to exciting new research results. Besides cloud computing, key areas of interest are business process management, services science and engineering, model-driven software development, and security and compliance.

RESERVOIR is an IBM-led joint research initiative of 13 European partners to develop technologies that help automate the fluctuating demand for IT resources in a cloud computing environment. The 17M-Euro EU-funded initiative, called RESERVOIR—Resources and Services Virtualization Without Barriers—explores the deployment and management of IT services across different administrative domains, IT platforms, and geographies. This cloud computing project aims to develop technologies to support a service-based online economy, where resources and services are transparently provisioned and managed.

HP, Intel, and Yahoo!

HP, Intel Corporation, and Yahoo! have created a global, multidatacenter, open-source test bed for the advancement of cloud computing research and education. The goal of the initiative is to promote open collaboration among industry, academia, and governments by removing the financial and logistical barriers to research in data-intensive, Internet-scale computing.

Test Bed

The HP, Intel, and Yahoo! Cloud Computing Test Bed provides a globally distributed, Internet-scale testing environment designed to encourage research on the software, datacenter management, and hardware issues associated with cloud computing at a larger scale than ever before. The initiative will also support research into cloud applications and services.

HP, Intel, and Yahoo! have partnered with the Infocomm Development Authority of Singapore (IDA), the University of Illinois at Urbana-Champaign, and the Karlsruhe Institute of Technology (KIT) in Germany to form the research initiative. The partnership with Illinois also includes the National Science Foundation.

The test bed will initially consist of six "centers of excellence" at IDA facilities, the University of Illinois at Urbana-Champaign, the Steinbuch Centre for Computing of the Karlsruhe Institute of Technology, HP Labs, Intel Research, and Yahoo!. Each location will host a cloud computing infrastructure, largely based on HP hardware and Intel processors, and will have 1,000 to 4,000 processor cores capable of supporting the data-intensive research associated with cloud computing. The test bed locations are expected to be fully operational and made accessible to researchers worldwide through a selection process later this year.

The test bed leverages Yahoo!'s technical ability in open-source projects by running Apache Hadoop—an open-source, distributed computing project of the Apache Software Foundation—and other open-source, distributed computing software such as Pig, the parallel programming language developed by Yahoo! Research.

"The HP, Intel, and Yahoo! Cloud Computing Test Bed furthers our commitment to the global, collaborative research community that is advancing the new sciences of the Internet," said Prabhakar Raghavan, head of Yahoo! Research. "With this test bed, not only can researchers test applications at Internet scale, they will also have access to the underlying computing systems to advance understanding of how systems software and hardware function in a cloud environment."

Researchers at HP Labs, the central research arm of HP, will use the test bed to conduct advanced research in the areas of intelligent infrastructure and dynamic cloud services. HP Labs recently sharpened its focus to help HP and its customers capitalize on the industry's shift toward cloud computing, a driving force behind HP's vision of Everything as a Service. With Everything as a Service, devices and services will interact seamlessly through the cloud, and businesses and individuals will use services that anticipate their needs based on location, preferences, calendar, and communities.

"To realize the full potential of cloud computing, the technology industry must think about the cloud as a platform for creating new services and experiences. This requires an entirely new approach to the way we design, deploy, and manage cloud infrastructure and services," said Prith Banerjee, senior vice president of research at HP and director of HP Labs. "The HP, Intel, and Yahoo! Cloud Computing Test Bed lets us tap the brightest minds in the industry, academia and government to drive innovation in this area."

Current platform features such as Data Center Management Interface (DCMI), Node Manager (NM), and virtualization have been designed to improve the manageability and energy efficiency of datacenters. This open, collaborative research effort will give researchers full access to the system's hardware for further innovation of existing and future platform features.

"We are pleased to engage with the academic research community—open collaboration with the academia is in our DNA at Intel Research," said Andrew A. Chien, vice president and director of Intel Research. "Creating large-scale test beds is important because they lower barriers to innovation and provide the opportunity to experiment and learn at scale. Intel's support of Tashi, an open-source cluster management system for cloud computing, and this HP, Intel, Yahoo! Cloud Computing Test Bed are a natural extension of our ongoing, mutually beneficial partnerships with the research community, such as the Universal Parallel Computing Research Centers."

IDA facilitates research in the test bed by providing its users with the computing resources required to develop cloud computing software and applications. IDA will also leverage the test bed and its industry partnerships to train local students and professionals on the technologies and programs associated with cloud computing.

"With the ready and available Internet-scale resources in Singapore to support cloud computer research and development work, we can collaborate with like-minded partners to advance the field," said Khoong Hock Yun, assistant chief executive of the Infrastructure Development Group at the Infocomm Development Authority of Singapore. "Cloud computing is considered by many to be the next paradigm shift in computer technology, and this may be the next 'platform' for innovative ecosystems. Partnerships like this will allow Singapore to leverage this new paradigm for greater economic and social growth."

Deeper into the Cloud

The Cloud Computing Test Bed is the next step in expanding each company's ongoing initiatives in cloud computing. In November 2007, Yahoo! announced the deployment of a supercomputing-class datacenter, called M45, for cloud computing research; Carnegie Mellon University was the first institution to take advantage of this supercomputer.

In 2008, HP announced the formation of its Scalable Computing & Infrastructure Organization (SCI), which includes a dedicated set of resources that provide expertise and spearhead development efforts to build scalable solutions designed for high-performance and cloud computing customers. The company introduced scalable computing offerings including the Intel Xeon-based HP ProLiant BL2x220c G5, the world's first server blade to combine two independent servers in a single blade, and the HP StorageWorks 9100 Extreme Data Storage System (ExDS9100), a highly scalable storage system designed to simplify the management of multiple petabytes. HP also introduced the HP POD (Performance-Optimized Datacenter), an open-architecture, compact, shipped-to-order alternative for deploying IT resources.

IBM and Amazon

IBM also entered into an agreement with Amazon Web Services to deliver IBM's software to clients and developers. The pay-as-you-go model provides clients with access to development and production instances of IBM DB2, Informix Dynamic Server, WebSphere Portal, Lotus Web Content Management, WebSphere sMash, and Novell's SUSE Linux operating system software in the Amazon EC2 environment, providing a comprehensive portfolio of products available on AWS.

Businesses are looking for ways to quickly build, deploy, and take advantage of the flexibility that cloud computing environments can bring. This is challenging for organizations that are constrained by limited resources, technical skills, and capital, as they look to their IT infrastructure to help them gain a competitive advantage. IBM and Amazon Web Services are helping to address these challenges by making it easier for software developers to build solutions based on open standards and backed up by the necessary technical resources to help simplify the process.

IBM is making available new Amazon Machine Images (AMIs) at no charge for development and test purposes, enabling software developers to quickly build preproduction applications based on IBM software within Amazon EC2. The new portfolio will over time extend to include Service Management capabilities from IBM Tivoli software for Amazon EC2 to help clients better control and automate their dynamic infrastructures in the cloud.

Additionally, customers will also be able to run their already-purchased IBM software on Amazon EC2.

"IBM is offering yet another way for our partners and customers to build solutions that can help them meet their business goals," said Dave Mitchell, director of strategy and emerging business, IBM Software Group. "This relationship with Amazon Web Services provides our customers with a new way to use IBM software and broadens our distribution channels."

"We are pleased to be working with IBM to extend this new model for building and deploying applications to companies of all sizes," said Terry Wise, director of business development for Amazon Web Services. "Extending IBM software to the cloud via Amazon EC2 will help even more businesses take advantage of the benefits of the reliable, scalable, and cost efficient infrastructure in the cloud."

We simply don't have the space to write about all the cloud computing players, but this is a sampling of some of the biggest names and their biggest initiatives. In the next chapter we'll talk more about the business case for moving some of your resources to the cloud, which ones to move, and how you can best use the cloud.

The Business Case for Going to the Cloud

Whether or not you move to the cloud depends on your organization, what you need to accomplish, and whether or not the cloud can help you do it. While this book is all about cloud computing (you can tell from the title), we're not telling you that you absolutely should move to the cloud. In fact, there are instances where you should not move to the cloud. But there are also instances when you certainly should add cloud computing to your IT repertoire.

In this chapter we'll talk about how your organization would benefit from a cloud move. We'll also talk about how different cloud services (PaaS, SaaS, and so on) can serve you. We had the opportunity to talk to Steve Fisher, senior vice president of AppExchange at Salesforce.com, about what his company offers and about moving your business's processes to the cloud. We were fortunate enough to get some time with Christopher Crowhurst, VP of Strategic Technology at Thomson Reuters. We talked with him about how businesses can identify viable applications from migration to a cloud-based platform. He also outlined some of the trends he's seeing now, and some he expects to see in the future.

Cloud Computing Services

Your organization can benefit from the cloud in different guises. In this section we'll talk about the different ways your organization can utilize different services as well as how some organizations are doing just that.

Infrastructure as a Service

Let's first talk about Infrastructure as a Service. In this scenario, you're using the cloud provider's machines. Another term for this type of computing is Everything as a Service. That is, you are using a virtualized server and running software on it. One of the most prevalent is Amazon Elastic Compute Cloud (EC2). Another player in the field is GoGrid. In this section we'll take a closer look at both Amazon and GoGrid.

Amazon EC2

As we noted in Chapter 3, Amazon Elastic Compute Cloud (http://aws.amazon.com/ec2) is a web service that provides resizable computing capacity in the cloud. Amazon EC2's simple web service interface allows businesses to obtain and configure capacity with minimal friction. It provides control of computing resources and lets organizations run on Amazon's computing environment.

Amazon EC2 reduces the time required to obtain and boot new server instances to minutes, allowing quick scaling capacity, both up and down, as computing requirements change. Amazon EC2 changes the economics of computing by allowing you to pay only for capacity that you actually use.

"When we launched Amazon EC2 over two years ago, the idea of accessing computing power over the web was still a novel idea. Today a diverse array of businesses drawn by the benefits of cloud computing—cost savings without giving up speed, reliability, flexibility, and performance—are running EC2 for all types of applications," said Peter De Santis, general manager of Amazon EC2. "We've listened closely to our customers for the past two years and worked backward from their requirements, adding important new features such as those we are announcing today—Windows support and a Service Level Agreement."

Eli Lilly and Company is one company that has moved to Amazon EC2 as part of their IT operations. As a part of Lilly's efforts to find new and improved methods to support research, Lilly began using Amazon Web Services (AWS).

"Amazon EC2 has given us the ability to easily spin up tailored computing environments that can quickly and cost-effectively process tremendous amounts of research data," said Dave Powers, associate information consultant at Eli Lilly and Company. "This is a huge step forward in maximizing our results relative to IT spend, and now that Amazon EC2 runs Windows and SQL Server, we have even greater flexibility in the kinds of applications we can build in the AWS cloud."

Windows and SQL Server Support for Amazon EC2   Customers can employ Amazon EC2 running Windows Server or SQL Server with all of the benefits of Amazon EC2. Windows with Amazon EC2 has been a common request of AWS customers since the service launched. Amazon EC2 provides an environment for deploying ASP.NET web sites, high-performance computing clusters, media transcoding solutions, and many other Windows-based applications.

"RenderRocket delivers professional-level rendering power on-demand to 3-D production teams. We launch intensive 3-D rendering jobs for films and TV on Amazon EC2 to take advantage of Amazon's massive compute power. We pay only for the resources we consume, and can expand our use of Amazon EC2 in relation to the growth of our business. Amazon EC2 running Windows Server offers additional opportunities to grow our business by offering Windows-based services to our customers," said Ruben Perez, CEO of RenderRocket.

NOTE   *For more information about Amazon EC2 running Windows or SQL Server, please go to aws.amazon.com/windows.*

Amazon EC2 Service Level Agreement   With over two years of operation Amazon EC2 exited its beta into general availability and offers customers a Service Level Agreement (SLA). The Amazon EC2 SLA guarantees 99.95 percent availability of the service within a region over a trailing 365-day period, or customers are eligible to receive service credits back. The Amazon EC2 SLA is designed to give customers additional confidence that even the most demanding applications will run dependably in the AWS cloud.

Recent Features   In 2009, AWS announced plans for several new features that make managing cloud-based applications easier. Thousands of customers employ the compute power of Amazon EC2 to build scalable and reliable solutions. AWS will deliver additional features that automate customer usage of Amazon EC2 for more cost-efficient consumption of computing power and provide greater visibility into the operational health of an application running in the AWS cloud. These features include

- **Load balancing**   Enables customers to balance incoming requests and distribute traffic across multiple Amazon EC2 compute instances.
- **Auto-scaling**   Automatically grows and shrinks usage of Amazon EC2 compute capacity based on application requirements.
- **Monitoring**   Enables customers to monitor operational metrics of Amazon EC2, providing even better visibility into usage of the AWS cloud.
- **Management Console**   Provides a simple, point-and-click web interface that lets customers manage and access their AWS cloud resources.

NOTE   *For more information about Amazon EC2 and other AWS services, go to http://aws.amazon.com.*

GoGrid

GoGrid is a service provider of Windows and Linux cloud-based server hosting, and offers 32-bit and 64-bit editions of Windows Server 2008 within its cloud computing infrastructure. Parent company ServePath is a Microsoft Gold Certified Partner, and launched Windows Server 2008 dedicated hosting in February of this year.

GoGrid becomes one of the first Infrastructure as a Service (IaaS) providers to offer Windows Server 2008 "in the cloud." The Windows Server 2008 operating system from Microsoft offers increased server stability, manageability, and security over previous versions of Windows Server. As such, interest from Windows Server customers wanting to try it out has been high. GoGrid customers can deploy Windows Server 2008 servers in just a few minutes for as little as 19 cents an hour, with no commitment.

GoGrid enables system administrators to quickly and easily create, deploy, load-balance, and manage Windows and Linux cloud servers within minutes. GoGrid offers what it calls Control in the CloudTM with its web-based Graphical User Interface (GUI) that allows for "point and click" deployment of complex and flexible network infrastructures, which include load balancing and multiple web and database servers, all set up with icons through the GUI.

Initial Windows Server 2008 offerings on GoGrid include both 32-bit and 64-bit preconfigured templates. GoGrid users select the desired operating system and then choose preconfigured templates in order to minimize time to deploy. Preconfigurations include

- Windows Server 2008 Standard with Internet Information Services 7.0 (IIS 7)
- Windows Server 2008 Standard with IIS 7 and SQL Server 2005 Express Edition

- Windows Server 2008 Standard with IIS 7, SQL Server 2005 Express Edition, and ASP.NET

Windows Server 2008 Standard includes Terminal Services Gateway, Remote Desktop Client for Terminal Services, Application Server, Active Directory Domain Services, DHCP Server, DNS Server, and SMTP.

Platform as a Service

Platform as a Service (PaaS) is a way to build applications and have them hosted by the cloud provider. It allows you to deploy applications without having to spend the money to buy the servers on which to house them. In this section we'll take a closer look at companies RightScale and Google. We'll talk about their services, what they offer, and what other companies are getting out of those services.

RightScale

RightScale entered into a strategic product and partnership, broadening its cloud management platform to support emerging clouds from new vendors, including FlexiScale and GoGrid, while continuing its support for Amazon's EC2. RightScale is also working with Rackspace to ensure compatibility with their cloud offerings, including Mosso and CloudFS. RightScale offers an integrated management dashboard, where applications can be deployed once and managed across these and other clouds.

Businesses can take advantage of the nearly infinite scalability of cloud computing by using RightScale to deploy their applications on a supported cloud provider. They gain the capabilities of built-in redundancy, fault tolerance, and geographical distribution of resources—key enterprise demands for cloud providers.

Customers can leverage the RightScale cloud management platform to automatically deploy and manage their web applications—scaling up when traffic demands, and scaling back as appropriate—allowing them to focus on their core business objectives. RightScale's automated system management, prepackaged and reusable components, leading service expertise, and best practices have been proven as best-of-breed, with customers deploying hundreds of thousands of instances on Amazon's EC2.

"Cloud computing is a disruptive force in the business world because it provides pay-as-you-go, on-demand, virtually infinite compute and storage resources that can expand or contract as needed," said Michael Crandell, CEO of RightScale, Inc. "A number of public providers are already adopting cloud architectures—and we also see private enterprise clouds coming on the horizon. Today's announcement of RightScale's partnerships with FlexiScale and GoGrid is an exciting indication of how mid-market and enterprise organizations can really take advantage of multicloud architectures. There will be huge opportunities for application design and deployment—we are at the beginning of a tidal shift in IT infrastructure."

FlexiScale is the only UK-based cloud computing provider and offers a unique infrastructure on demand with 99.99 percent SLA and many special features. For example, each customer gets their own virtual disk so that data is segregated and they can do their own low-level encryption, while virtual network traffic is also segregated to deliver added security. FlexiScale uniquely offers permanent on-demand storage and was the first cloud provider to support Windows. With a strong reputation for customer service, it also enables the creation of custom packages such as golden images.

Tony Lucas, CEO of XCalibre and creator of FlexiScale, commented: "Without this new ability to move swiftly and easily between platforms, customers could feel locked in and much more hesitant to try and use cloud computing. RightScale's partnership initiative is a great example of how having near interoperability between systems will enable customers to be less hesitant of moving to a new technology, which is great for everyone. It means the industry can and will grow quicker than if it was only a handful of individual companies providing distinct services that weren't compatible with each other."

GoGrid offers hosted cloud computing infrastructure that enables system administrators, developers, and IT professionals to create, deploy, and control load-balanced cloud servers and complex hosted virtual server networks. GoGrid also delivers portal-controlled servers for Windows 2003 and 2008 and multiple Linux operating systems, and supports application environments like Ruby on Rails. GoGrid is unique in cloud computing with the availability of 32-bit and 64-bit editions of Windows Server 2008, and was named winner of LinuxWorld 2008 "Best of Show" in August 2008.

"Cloud computing for the enterprise has arrived with the GoGrid and RightScale partnership," said GoGrid CEO, John Keagy. "Corporations now have few excuses not to, and multiple reasons to deploy and manage complex and redundant cloud infrastructures in real-time using the GoGrid, RightScale, and FlexiScale technologies."

Rackspace Hosting provides IT systems and computing-as-a-service to more than 33,000 customers worldwide. Combining RightScale's technologies with Rackspace's focus on Fanatical Support will allow companies to focus more on their business and not spend a disproportionate amount of resources on IT demands.

Salesforce.com

Salesforce.com offers Force.com as its on-demand platform. Force.com features breakthrough Visualforce technology, which allows customers, developers, and ISVs to design any app, for any user, anywhere with the world's first User Interface-as-a-Service. The Force.com platform offers global infrastructure and services for database, logic, workflow, integration, user interface, and application exchange.

"With Force.com, customers, developers and ISVs can choose innovation, not infrastructure," said Marc Benioff, chairman and CEO, Salesforce.com. "Google, Amazon, and Apple have all shown that by revolutionizing a user interface you can revolutionize an industry. With Visualforce we're giving developers the power to revolutionize any interface, and any industry, on demand."

A capability of the Force.com platform, Visualforce provides a framework for creating user experiences, and enables the creation of new interface designs and user interactions to be built and delivered with no software or hardware infrastructure requirements. With Visualforce, developers have control over the look and feel of their Force.com applications enabling wide flexibility in terms of application creation. From a handheld device for a sales rep in the field, to an order-entry kiosk on a manufacturing shop floor, Visualforce enables the creation of new user experiences that can be customized and delivered in real time on any screen.

On Demand   Force.com PaaS provides the building blocks necessary to build business apps, whether they are simple or sophisticated, and automatically deploy them as a service to small teams or entire enterprises. The Force.com platform gives customers the power to run multiple applications within the same Salesforce instance, allowing all of a company's Salesforce applications to share a common security model, data model, and user interface.

The multitenant Force.com platform encompasses a feature set for the creation of business applications such as an on-demand operating system, the ability to create any database on demand, a workflow engine for managing collaboration between users, the Apex Code programming language for building complex logic, the Force.com Web Services API for programmatic access, mashups, and integration with other applications and data, and now Visualforce for a framework to build any user interface.

Delivery   As part of the Force.com platform, Visualforce gives customers the means to design application user interfaces for any experience on any screen. Using the logic and workflow intelligence provided by Apex Code, Visualforce offers the ability to meet the requirements of applications that feature different types of users on a variety of devices. Visualforce uses Internet technology, including HTML, AJAX and Flex, for business applications. Visualforce enables the creation and delivery of any user experience, offering control over an application's design and behavior that is only limited by the imagination.

Visualforce provides a page-based model, built on standard HTML and web presentation technologies, and is complemented with both a component library for implementing common user interface elements, and a controller model for creating new interactions between those elements. As part of the larger Force.com platform, the user experiences created in Visualforce directly leverage the data, logic, and workflow created in the other Force.com features. Visualforce includes the following features and capabilities:

- **Pages**   This capability enables the design definition of an application's user interface. This enables developers to create new pages using standard web technologies including HTML, AJAX, and Flex. Pages allows developers to create any user experience with standard web technologies that will be immediately familiar to any web developer. Visualforce automatically detects a user's device, and gives them the ability to automatically deliver the right experience to the right device.

- **Components**   This provides the ability to create new applications that automatically match the look and feel of Salesforce applications or customize and extend the Salesforce user interface to specific customer and user requirements. Customers can rapidly create a user experience by assembling existing user interface elements. Visualforce provides the means to reuse predefined standard Salesforce and custom-designed UI components.

- **Logic controllers**   The controller enables customers to build any user interface behavior. Customers are able to use Visualforce to quickly create a new look and feel that leverages existing application functionality. Customers can define completely new UI interactions that benefit from Apex Code. The standard controller gives customers the ability to inherit and reuse any standard Salesforce UI behavior like new, edit, and save.

Software as a Service

We touched on Software as a Service (SaaS) a bit in the previous chapter, but let's talk about it in more depth, with a further examination of Salesforce and Google. In essence, SaaS is simply the cloud vendor providing the given piece of software you want to use, on their servers. That is, unlike PaaS in which you developed your own application, SaaS provides the application for you.

The line between SaaS and PaaS gets a little blurry, but the delineation is whether the provider supplies the application (SaaS) or simply provides a mechanism to develop your own applications (PaaS). The gray area becomes even more marked by companies like Google or Salesforce that offer both types of services. For instance, not only can you build an application with Salesforce, but you can also allow others to use the application you developed.

Let's delve a little more deeply into Salesforce and Google.

Google App Engine and Salesforce

Google has partnered with Salesforce to make it easy for companies of all sizes to run their business in the cloud with Salesforce for Google Apps. The combination of the Google Apps suite of productivity applications and the Salesforce suite of Customer Relationship Management (CRM) applications enables businesses to effectively communicate and collaborate without any hardware or software to download, install, or maintain. Salesforce for Google Apps also leverages the Force.com Platform and Google's open APIs, opening up even more development opportunities for developers and partners.

NOTE *Salesforce's senior vice president of AppExchange, Steve Fisher, talks about their company and the business case for moving your organization to the cloud later in this chapter.*

"Google and Salesforce.com have always had similar models and philosophies about delivering innovations made possible by the Internet," said Eric Schmidt, CEO of Google. "Salesforce.com was a pioneer in Software-as-a-Service and a year ago we joined them in this mission to bring the benefits of cloud computing to businesses of all types. Together, we are making more applications and services available online so customers can focus on building their core business rather than the applications that support it."

"Salesforce.com is thrilled to be offering Google Apps integrated with our Salesforce applications and Force.com Platform-as-a-Service to the millions of businesses looking to manage their entire office in the cloud," said Marc Benioff, chairman and CEO of Salesforce .com. "The combination of our leading CRM applications and Google's business productivity applications pushes forward the transformation of the industry to cloud computing. The end of software is here."

Salesforce for Google Apps Salesforce for Google Apps is a combination of essential applications for business productivity (email, calendaring, documents, spreadsheets, presentations, instant messaging) and CRM (sales, marketing, service and support, partners) that enables an entirely new way for business professionals to communicate, collaborate, and work together in real time over the Web. Salesforce for Google Apps offers a complete way for businesses to harness the power of cloud computing without the cost and complexity of managing hardware or software infrastructure. The following features are included in Salesforce for Google Apps:

- **Salesforce and Gmail** Businesses can now easily send, receive, and store email communication, keeping a complete record of customer interactions for better sales execution and improved customer satisfaction.

- **Salesforce and Google Docs**   Create, manage, and share online Google Documents, Google Spreadsheets, and Google Presentations within your sales organization, marketing group, or support team for instant collaboration.

- **Salesforce and Google Talk**   Instantly communicate with colleagues or customers from Salesforce and optionally attach Google Talk conversations to customer or prospect records stored in Salesforce.

- **Salesforce and Google Calendar**   Expose sales tasks and marketing campaigns from Salesforce on Google Calendar. Built by Appirio, this application is one example of a new category of partner extensions to Salesforce for Google Apps.

"While Salesforce.com has always enabled us to work easily with client desktop productivity tools, we love that we now have the freedom to run our office in the cloud," said Prasan Vyas of UST Global.

Force.com and Google Platform   Salesforce.com and Google's alliance has created the world's largest cloud computing platform for building and running applications. The Force.com Platform-as-a-Service encompasses a feature set for the creation of business applications and Google's open APIs enable integration and extension of the applications in Google Apps. The integration of the two creates opportunities for developers and partners to build and run business applications that help customers run their entire business smarter in the cloud. Applications like sales quote generation and business forecasting are now easy to build and test, and can be deployed by customers with just a few clicks via the AppExchange.

Appirio and Astadia are the first companies to take advantage of these new development opportunities made possible through the Google and Salesforce.com partnership. Each company has developed several applications that enhance Salesforce for Google Apps, and all of these applications are available in a created AppExchange category, Google Apps, at http://www.salesforce.com/appexchange.

Google

Google offers a host of applications that businesses can use immediately, as well as a platform on which to make your own, business-specific apps.

Much of a business's data is stored on user desktops, laptops, or removable USB drives. Google promotes their SaaS offerings as a way to secure your sensitive data by taking USB and user disk drives out of the equation. As such, users can access their data from the office, a remote office, at home, or on the road. Further, Google promises 99.9 percent uptime.

Google operates on one of the largest networks of distributed datacenters, and they strive for data security. They say their controls, processes, and policies that protect your data undergo an SAS 70 Type II audit. Security falls under three main topics:

- **People**   Google employs a full-time information security team, which includes experts in information, application, and network security. This team handles the company's perimeter defense systems, security review processes, and customized security plans.

- **Process**   Each Google application is built with security in mind. Applications are constantly reviewed for security as part of their Secure Code development process. The application development environment is also restricted and monitored for an additional layer of security. External security audits are also routinely conducted.

- **Technology**   Google Apps data is divided between multiple servers and disks, which makes it impossible to read, if someone were to breach a lone server. Also, the way in which the Google servers are built makes it possible to rapidly distribute updates and configuration changes.

Software plus Services

Microsoft's take on SaaS is slightly different with their Software plus Services (sometimes they shorten it to S+S). In this model, typical SaaS is bolstered with software running locally. That is, you run some software on-site and reach out to the cloud for additional services. This provides the flexibility of using a cloud provider, and also the reliability of having data stored on-site, as well.

Microsoft's Business Productivity Online Suite, part of Microsoft Online Services, is available for trial to businesses of all sizes in 19 countries. In addition, Microsoft offers its Microsoft Office Communications Online, for instant messaging and presence, and the Business Productivity Online Deskless Worker Suite, an email, calendaring, and collaboration service for the occasional user.

"These services open up new possibilities for businesses to control costs while continuing to enhance the productivity of their employees," said Stephen Elop, president of the Microsoft Business Division. "Customers can save between 10 percent and 50 percent in IT-related expenditures as a result of deploying Microsoft Online Services."

The worldwide availability of the Deskless Worker Suite offers customers an email and collaboration solution for occasional users. By providing this subscription service, Microsoft wants the Deskless Worker Suite to make it possible for organizations to give all employees access to the same messaging and collaboration systems. In organizations that have deployed email, more than 40 percent of employees do not have email.

"GlaxoSmithKline has more than 100,000 employees, hundreds of business partners, and locations around the world, so effective collaboration is critical to our business," said Bill Louv, CIO, GlaxoSmithKline. "We have chosen Microsoft Online Services because it promises to deliver a simple intuitive Information Workplace that should not only add value to the company through simplification, but provide an improved user experience and ultimately create a more productive GSK."

How Those Applications Help Your Business

Cloud computing offers a number of benefits that your organization can realize. There's a reason cloud computing is the latest "big" thing in the world of computing. It helps your organization on a number of levels, not the least of which is the bottom line. In this section, let's talk a little bit about why a move to the cloud helps your organization.

Operational Benefits

There are benefits to the way you operate. You can change business processes (for the better) by moving some applications and storage to the cloud. The following are some of the operational benefits:

- **Reduced cost**   Since technology is paid incrementally, your organization saves money in the long run.

- **Increased storage**   You can store more data on the cloud than on a private network. Plus, if you need more it's easy enough to get that extra storage.

- **Automation**   Your IT staff no longer needs to worry that an application is up to date—that's the provider's job. And they know they have to keep it up to date or they'll start losing customers.

- **Flexibility**   You have more flexibility with a cloud solution. Applications can be tested and deployed with ease, and if it turns out that a given application isn't getting the job done, you can switch to another.

- **Better mobility**   Users can access the cloud from anywhere with an Internet connection. This is ideal for road warriors or telecommuters—or someone who needs to access the system after hours.

- **Better use of IT staff**   IT staff no longer has to worry about server updates and other computing issues. They can focus on duties that matter, rather than being maintenance staff.

Economic Benefits

Where the rubber really meets the road is when you consider the economic benefits of something. And with cloud computing, cost is a huge factor. But it isn't just in equipment savings; it is realized throughout the organization. These are some benefits to consider:

- **People**   We hate to suggest that anyone lose their job, but the honest-to-goodness truth (we're sorry) is that by moving to the cloud, you'll rely on fewer staffers. By having fewer staff members, you can look at your team and decide if such-and-such a person is necessary. Is he or she bringing something to the organization? Are their core competencies something you still need? If not, this gives you an opportunity to find the best people to remain on staff.

- **Hardware**   With the exception of very large enterprises or governments, major cloud suppliers can purchase hardware, networking equipment, bandwidth, and so forth, much cheaper than a "regular" business. That means if you need more storage, it's just a matter of upping your subscription costs with your provider, instead of buying new equipment. If you need more computational cycles, you needn't buy more servers; rather you just buy more from your cloud provider.

- **Pay as you go**   Think of cloud computing like leasing a car. Instead of buying the car outright, you pay a smaller amount each month. It's the same with cloud computing—you just pay for what you use. But, also like leasing a car, at the end of the lease you don't own the car. That might be a good thing—the car may be a piece of junk, and in the case of a purchased server, it's sure to be obsolete.

- **Time to market**   One of the greatest benefits of the cloud is the ability to get apps up and running in a fraction of the time you would need in a conventional scenario. Let's take a closer look at that and see how getting an application online faster saves you money. Before the cloud, launching a startup meant using either an underpowered or inflexible host or an overpriced self-host. The former was a bad option, because it was inflexible. The latter cost a lot of money: You had to find a host, configure the machine, ship the machine, and manage the machine. With a cloud, you can spin up a new instance in seconds.

Tips for Evaluating SaaS

Before employing a SaaS solution, there are factors to consider. You should evaluate not only the SaaS provider and its service, but also what your organization wants from SaaS. Be sure the following factors are present as you evaluate your SaaS provider:

- **Time to value**   As we mentioned earlier, one of the great benefits of using cloud services is the ability to shorten the time it takes to get a new system or application up and running. Unlike traditional software that might require complex installation, configuration, administration, and maintenance, SaaS only requires a browser. This allows you to get up and running much more quickly than by using traditional software.

- **Trial period**   Most SaaS providers offer a 30-day trial of their service. This usually doesn't happen with traditional software—and certainly you wouldn't move everyone en masse to the trial. However, you can try out the SaaS vendor's offering and if it feels like a good fit, you can start making the move.

NOTE *Be wary of vendors who don't offer a free trial. It's no skin off the vendor's nose to let you try their services for a while. In fact, if a vendor doesn't offer a free trial, it might be indicative of other problems within their organization.*

- **Low entry costs**   Another appeal of SaaS is the low cost to get started using it. Rather than laying out an enormous amount of money, you can get started relatively inexpensively. Using an SaaS solution is much less expensive than rolling out a complex software deployment across your organization.

- **Service**   In SaaS, the vendor serves the customer. That is, the vendor becomes your IT department—at least for the applications they're hosting. This means that your own, in-house IT department doesn't have to buy hardware, install and configure software, or maintain it. That's all on your SaaS vendor. And if the vendor isn't responsive to your needs, pack up your toys and move to a different service. It is in the vendor's best interests to keep you and other customers happy.

- **Wiser investment**   SaaS offers a less risky option than traditional software installed locally. Rather than spend a lot of money up front, your organization will pay for the software as it is used. Also, there is no long-term financial commitment. The monetary risk is greatly lessened in an SaaS environment.

- **Security**   Earlier in this book we talked about the security concerns with going to the cloud. We mentioned those issues for the sake of completeness, but in reality it is in your vendor's best interests to keep you as secure as possible. Most SaaS vendors understand that application data must be backed up often and that security is a top concern. Your local IT department has a lot going on and might not be able to spend as much time as they would like on safety and security. Since the cloud vendor wants to keep customers safe and secure, they will have staff dedicated to ensuring that your data is safe.

- **Your voice**   When's the last time you made a suggestion for a change in Microsoft Word and Redmond listened? We're not just picking on Microsoft here. The fact of the matter is that customers of traditionally installed software have very little ability to influence the development of new product features. But your SaaS vendor wants to keep you happy so that you will not jump ship for another provider. As such, they will listen to your wants and respond. Because you will have a closer relationship, you have a greater ability to influence the product and its features.

- **Reduced capital expense**   Using an SaaS provider eliminates the need for buying hardware and software. This not only makes your CFO happy, but it makes it faster to get approval for a project when the need to buy hardware is taken out of the equation.

- **Meet short-term needs**   Quite often organizations experience busy times, or they launch a new product, a new office opens, or something else occurs that requires more computational power. Rather than buy new hardware to deal with your capacity needs, an SaaS provider can instantly expand and offer you more resources. And when you're done, you scale back what you are using. The best part is that once you're done paying for those additional resources, you go back to paying for what you need.

Staffing Benefits

There are a number of benefits the people in your organization will realize when you shift some applications to the cloud. For the most part their lives should be easier with the ease and convenience cloud computing offers. Not only do your workers benefit, but there are also benefits in being a cloud provider.

For the Consumer

The consumer benefits from cloud computing in a number of ways, for example:

- **No software installation or maintenance**   That means no more 1,000-page planning and implementation guides.

- **Shorter deployment time**   It takes only a few minutes to spin up a new server, rather than the months it would normally take to plan, prepare, test, and deploy.

- **Worldwide availability**   By using a cloud, your users can access data and applications from anywhere they have Internet access.

- **Service Level Agreement (SLA) adherence**   If you have an SLA, then you're guaranteed that level of service. And if you report any bugs, the vendor will fix them, but you don't have to hassle with the patch yourself—it'll likely be done in a way that is transparent to you.

- **Upgrades**   The provider wants to keep you happy, so it's in their best interests to ensure the application is constantly improved. With SaaS this can be in the guise of small changes that you don't see that add up over time, rather than getting a monstrous patch that costs you time and money to implement.

- **Make life easier on your IT staff**   SaaS offloads a lot of the maintenance duties onto your cloud provider so that your IT staff can focus on improving the day-to-day technical operations of your company, rather than being called to fix some piece of software that isn't playing well with the others on the network.

- **More money**   Your organization saves money by using a cloud vendor, both in operational costs and the IT budget. This is money that can be added to your bottom line or redistributed to other departments to boost productivity.

For the Provider

The goal of this book is to highlight the pros and cons of cloud computing, especially as they pertain to you, the (potential) cloud customer. However, there is benefit to the cloud providers as well, and it isn't just money. Here are some of the ways that cloud computing is a plus for the provider:

- **Operating environment**   The provider owns their domain. They aren't just sending technicians to fix or customize software because it doesn't fit on a client's unique (or antique) infrastructure. The provider has the control to optimize an infrastructure to their specific SaaS needs.

- **Predictable revenue stream**   Because customers will be paying a subscription for their cloud use, it is easy to get a handle on forecasting revenues.

- **Study use**   The provider is able to study how their SaaS is used and is then able to give customers more of what they want. This isn't possible if software is housed on customers' networks.

- **Small, regular upgrades**   This isn't just a benefit for customers, but the providers, as well. The provider's development teams can focus on fixing bugs with incremental patch rollouts, rather than saving them for one, monstrous rollout.

- **Customer relationship management**   Providers also must develop strong relationships with their customers. Since they are providing a subscription-based service, it is important to keep customers happy, rather than try to score the next big deal. While it is important to keep customers coming in, it is just as important to keep existing customers happy.

Deleting Your Datacenter

When you move to the cloud, you won't need to maintain some things on-site. But what and when you delete it is a complicated issue. Certainly, you can back up the data and file it away on some DVDs somewhere, but that's just a snapshot in time of your organization. As you continue to use the cloud, your data will evolve and change.

In this section we'll talk about the issue of deleting your datacenter, when you can do it, and some best practices for doing it.

What You Can Delete

Desktop applications are one of the areas perfect for a move to the cloud. What drives such a move is the lower costs for both large and small companies. Moving to the cloud allows companies to realize the benefits of economies of scale that come with managing several desktops. Those who specialize in desktop management are going to get the best economies of scale.

It should come as no shock that desktop management is pretty low on the IT staff's list of desirable jobs. In fact, in large enterprises down to the home user, the least pleasurable thing to do is update operating systems, patch applications, or set firewall rules.

A key component in making desktops cloud capable and helping client virtualization go mainstream is the introduction of so-called bare metal hypervisors for clients. These hypervisors allow the desktop to run locally without network access to take advantage of the Pac's computing power, rather than just relying on the server.

What You Should Keep

As we have noted time and again, security might be an issue for you. Are you really comfortable moving mission-critical or sensitive information to the cloud? If you are happy with your vendor's security measures, then you should have no problems moving sensitive data to the cloud. But that's only if you are absolutely satisfied with their security measures. If you have even a glimmer of doubt, it's not worth the sleepless nights, worrying about the potential for compromised information.

You should also keep large files and things like media on-site. If you are storing more than you access online, you get a bigger bill from the vendor each month. Better to let those infrequently accessed files sit on a local drive than to pay the vendor bill each month.

Steps

Does your vendor have a solid disaster recovery plan in place? This is important because, obviously, you don't want to lose important data. Having downtime is one thing—losing important data is something else. When you talk to potential vendors, be sure to ask about disaster recovery, and if you aren't satisfied with their safeguards, move to the next candidate.

There are a lot of reasons to make a move to the cloud, but inevitably cost is the way that companies get into the cloud. However, once they're there, convenience and reliability is what will keep them. Having the vendor to rely on for hardware maintenance is a huge bit of convenience. For instance, all you need to do is call up a web browser and make adjustments to the amount of processing power, memory, and disk space each virtual server gets. You can tune your network to the precise configuration you need, without having to pop in new blades or add additional machines.

AppZero

AppZero provides a set of tools for creating Virtual Application Appliances (VAAs). This approach to provisioning and deploying applications on physical or virtual servers running anywhere is designed for the cloud environment and for movement of server applications and datacenter to cloud, hosting environment, or cloud to cloud. VAAs package a server application with all of its dependencies, but no operating system component (zero OS). AppZero's first public demonstration of its VAA technology showed a live production application provisioned in seconds on an Amazon EC2 cloud, and moved in less than one minute to a GoGrid cloud computing environment.

Designed for instant server-based application provisioning and deployment, VAAs enable an application to run wherever the business requires without the licensing issues that inclusion of an operating system introduces—VAAs contain zero OS. AppZero VAAs work with applications across all tiers: web servers, application servers, and database servers. Enterprise middleware from Microsoft, Oracle, IBM, and open-source servers like MySQL as well as in-house developed applications can all be easily transformed into VAAs without changing any code.

AppZero VAAs encapsulate applications at a level above the operating system, turning server applications into discrete objects that run protected from other applications and the underlying operating systems. In a virtual environment such as VMware, Xen, and Microsoft Hyper-V, AppZero drives higher server consolidation ratios by provisioning applications to virtual machines with almost no overhead. VAAs significantly reduce VM sprawl and speed the time to get an application up and running. AppZero VAAs also simplify the use of existing configuration and server provisioning solutions, such as HP-Opsware and BMC's Bladelogic, allowing these systems to manage server applications as discrete objects.

AppZero's VAA toolset runs on Windows, Solaris, and Linux and includes three tools: the AppZero Creator for building a VAA; the AppZero Director, a runtime system; and AppZero Administrator for administering a VAA.

Salesforce.com

Salesforce.com offers SaaS with a host of different applications, many of which are created and shared by other Salesforce customers. Steve Fisher, senior vice president of AppExchange at Salesforce.com, talked about his company as well as the best way for companies considering a move to the cloud to get the most out of their move.

Fisher emphasizes the differences between Salesforce and other cloud vendors.

"We have a different take on the cloud than Amazon or Google," noted Fisher. "Maybe it's because we started with applications. But for whatever reason, we all offer something different."

The chief difference is in what the vendors supply and how they supply it.

"Amazon has Linux boxes, we offer different applications," observed Fisher. "If you're a business that wants to use an application, that's where we shine."

Salesforce has the good fortune to have a broad variety of customers, existing in different industries and having different needs.

"You look at our customer base and it's every company, every size, and every location," said Fisher.

He notes that the company has one product that serves companies of all sizes. For instance, they serve 30,000 users at Dell, while some other companies may only have 25 users.

"We have customers in every industry," added Fisher.

There doesn't seem to be one app that everyone uses or is more prevalent than others. Salesforce sees customers using different applications.

"We have customers with applications all over the board," said Fisher. "Anything from project management to financials, to recruiting."

Fisher sees the cloud expanding. The system is scalable and secure, and as more people join, it gives the cloud more credence and legitimacy.

"We don't see the technical barriers," said Fisher.

Why It's Good for Business

Working on the cloud comes with great advantages, and Fisher noted several.

"Obviously, the lower upfront cost is huge," said Fisher.

A great advantage is that it drives the vendor to keep the customer happy.

"Because the vendor is running the applications, they're constantly tuned and improved on," said Fisher.

In a multitenant environment, the vendor can see what and how users are taking advantage of applications and can make changes based on their observations.

"That's not typical in the traditional model," said Fisher.

Getting started is especially easy, especially when compared to traditional deployments.

"The ability to get started is there," observed Fisher. "You don't have to buy software. It's so much easier than deploying conventional software."

But cost—as it is for so many other business concerns—is where the rubber meets the road.

"The biggest value, if you think of the traditional model, is you don't need to ship the upgrade, test it, and rewrite code," said Fisher. "You can upgrade everything at once and it's seamless."

Best Business Practices

So what's the best way for a company to move to the cloud? After researching vendor companies, Fisher advises asking for a free trial.

"You can go to Salesforce.com and get a free trial," said Fisher. "In fact, I would demand a free trial whoever you decide to use."

Pilot it first with a single department.

"Try it at a small level first," advised Fisher. "Have a division or a department try it first. Bring on 25 to 100 users to test it out."

But Fisher warns not to jump to the cloud if you don't need to. Don't follow trends or do it just because the other guy is doing it.

"Only do it if there is a need," said Fisher. "Don't do it just to do it."

Once you are on the cloud, don't expect to have a static experience. Your applications and how you use them will evolve.

"Have the mindset of it being a gradual iteration," said Fisher. "Expect that things will change."

Another benefit is the ability to really get what an organization wants out of an application.

"Traditional software is hard to customize," observed Fisher. "You can really mold [cloud applications] as you go."

But is any company 100 percent in the cloud?

"I know of two companies that have that agenda, certainly there are more," said Fisher. "But we certainly believe that'll be the future."

Fisher compares cloud computing with electrical utilities. Very few organizations rely on their own generators for power, with electricity delivered by power companies. Fisher believes one day all computing will be done on the cloud. But it'll take time.

"The electric grid has had 120 years," said Fisher. "We're only a couple years into cloud computing."

Concludes Fisher, "We're orders of magnitude away from where we were five years ago. You can only imagine where we'll be in five or ten years from now."

Thomson Reuters

Thomson Reuters is a company that provides information to a wide range of clients—lawyers, accountants, scientists, reporters, and a host of others. For the most part, they have nothing in common but the need to get information. Providing that information is what Thomson Reuters is all about. Thomson Reuters calls itself "the world's leading provider of 'intelligent information' for businesses and professionals." To live up to that billing, they need to do more than simply deliver search engine results, a lot more. They pull distributed information together; they analyze the information first to ensure it is what the customer wants; and they provide methods of data delivery and retrieval that help their customers get what they want.

Their Cloud Use

Thomson Reuters wanted to give its customers a better, more intelligent way to search for information than they were providing at the time. Their solution was to adopt a Microsoft Software-plus-Services solution. They integrated Microsoft Live Search with their own search engines and databases. When information is requested, both Live Search and Thomson Reuters's databases are scanned for the information, and Thomson Reuters analyzes the results to return the best information to the client.

Thomson Web outlined its requirements for teaming with an existing web search engine provider:

- The company needed an engine that could return results in 200 milliseconds. This gave Thomson Reuters time to apply business logic to make the results more meaningful.

- The engine also needed to accept hundreds of thousands of search requests from a single IP address—theirs—without it being seen as a Denial of Service attack.

The system works this way:

1. A customer accesses the Thomson Reuters information service, which can be a web application or a Windows-based application.

2. Once a search is initiated, that request is passed to the Thomson Reuters intranet to the Thomson Reuters Web Plus service layer.

3. The service layer begins two actions concurrently: It applies its custom business logic to the request, culling relevant information from it.

4. The service layer returns the information to the client.

Using the Cloud

Thomson Reuters is a company making good use of cloud computing solutions. Christopher Crowhurst, VP of Strategic Technology, talked about how he's seeing the cloud shaping up and how companies can best take advantage of the opportunities.

He sees different types of businesses on the cloud—not just a single type.

"The (infrastructure) cloud due to its on-demand nature is allowing rapid development of novel business propositions in ways that previously would not have been economic, as such people are able to build massively scalable architectures in the cloud without the investment that pre-cloud development required," said Crowhurst. "When platforms like MySpace were first created, their builders had no idea how quickly the usage would explode. This resulted in them having to scale out rapidly. Many war stories of instability and overloading have been told about these explosive growth platforms during their infancy. Arguably, if the cloud had existed as an option for them to exploit they would have responded far quicker with lower investment."

Web 2.0 has proven to go hand-in-hand with cloud computing. Because of the flexibility of the cloud, these types of web sites have a better chance of success.

"Social Network site growth—as with many other business models—is highly unpredictable. This unpredictable growth lends itself to a fast provisioning cloud model," noted Crowhurst. "Other examples of great cloud opportunities are those that may need large storage or database infrastructure; think Flickr as an example. It would now be a lot easier to recreate these social sites (Facebook, MySpace, Flickr, Twitter, etc.) in the cloud and be in a position to respond to growth on demand."

Cloud Computing and Web 2.0

Crowhurst likens social networking sites to sites like Yahoo and Google, in terms of their resource demand.

"Arguably, MySpace and Facebook—like Hotmail, Live Search, Yahoo and Google—are now application clouds in their own right. Their sheer scale, the massive compute platform they reside upon is an application on-demand, which is another definition of cloud computing," observed Crowhurst. "It is interesting that all of these applications are funded through advertising revenue. The relationship between massive scale, massive user populations results in large multimillion—if not billion—page view counts that enable the micro transactions of advertising revenue to add up to the vast incomes we now see reported by these companies.

"Salesforce.com and other business applications are another category of on-demand computing in the cloud. These models are mainly focused around business process automation, user access based pricing and individual business process customization. Substantial proportions of these companies' revenue comes from the customization and integration of their cloud platforms into the customer's applications and back office systems."

Applications and the Cloud

When it comes to what type of application is best suited for the cloud, Crowhurst didn't identify a type of program (like a word processor), although he recognizes the architecture of such applications.

"Stateless architectures are far more tolerant of massively scaled out infrastructure without needing custom state management software development," said Crowhurst.

"Additionally, stateless architectures can survive hardware failure very cleanly. Cloud's relatively low SLA and unknown quality of infrastructure require applications to be designed for survivability of data and transactions. Going beyond the basic architecture, I think the decision is more one of business model and growth predictability; the less predictable the demand for the application, the more likely the cloud will be a good place to start. Also a major factor will be the funding level required to start. Cloud development can be done at a lower cost initially than dedicated infrastructure buildouts."

To get started on the cloud, he recommends businesses start with business systems clouds, like hosted email services and collaboration suites.

"The cost of entry for most companies is relatively comparable with the cost of traditional upgrades, such as upgrading Microsoft Exchange to 2010," said Crowhurst. "Companies should look at the economics of these transition times as opportunities to 'outsource' the infrastructure problem and reap the rewards of the scale that these solutions can provide them."

Another buzzword in the world of computing these days is "virtualization." And it is simply that—virtualization—that can help a business move to the cloud.

"Current server infrastructure clouds are mostly hosted virtualized environments," he observed. "Businesses should start developing applications designed to run within virtual machines; they should become comfortable with the agility created by being able to spin up and down VMs on demand and adapt their application architectures to allow for this."

Getting Started

Starting small is another recommendation.

"From a business systems perspective, branch offices present opportunities to take small segments of a business off traditional infrastructure," said Crowhurst. "Most hosted email systems, for example, offer the ability to have a mix of hosted and cloud environments enabling a gentle transition."

But moving to the cloud is not always a clean, easy experience—especially for a business that has never done it before. But he hasn't seen any common mistakes being made repeatedly.

"I think that, due to the cloud still being in its infancy, I am not yet seeing a trend in mistakes," observed Crowhurst. "Factors that vary between cloud and traditional hosted infrastructure include bandwidth utilization and service levels, for example. Bandwidth between the cloud, your own data centers and your staffs' desktops can become the bottleneck for moving large datasets for batch processing. This is obviously less critical in transactional processing scenarios. This becomes noticeable in cloud email systems. Simply compare the time taken to upload a large document or image to Hotmail or Gmail and compare it with the ease of emailing using your local Exchange server."

Be Realistic

SLAs are important to have in place, but Crowhurst doesn't see them as being greatly binding, and they tend to be something that is not easily acted upon.

"Service levels are now being defined for cloud infrastructure, but generally your recourse is minimal (a refund of hosting fees as an example)," he said. "You are unlikely to be able to recover lost revenue for example. Also, when hosting your own infrastructure, you get to decide how to maintain it, how to ensure it is resilient and robust. In the cloud you don't. It's a matter of buyer beware. That said, many commercial clouds are maintaining high uptimes."

And while most companies have nothing in the cloud, Crowhurst has seen many companies that have fully embraced the cloud. And other companies are embracing cloud technology to help mitigate costs.

"Many smaller startup technology companies are completely in the cloud," he noted. "I am also seeing a trend for companies to be moving their staff to thin client, low performance, desktop PCs, as more companies opt for office productivity solutions like Google Docs, and hosted Office solutions. I expect this trend to continue due to the substantial cost to corporations of maintaining the equipment and desktop software environments for distributed employees. Soon I anticipate companies no longer supplying employees with laptops, but expecting them to provide their own and simply using browser and other remote application access technologies to hosted office productivity and business process applications."

In this chapter we talked about how different cloud vendors offer their services and how your business can utilize those services. We also looked at some businesses that have already decided to make the move and talked about how your business can make a successful move. In the next chapter we'll talk about the hardware and infrastructure that are involved in a cloud computing solution.

PART

Cloud Computing Technology

Hardware and Infrastructure

In order to get the most out of your cloud computing solution, it's important to have the right hardware and infrastructure in place. In this chapter we'll talk about what equipment you need on your end and how it should be configured for the best interaction with your cloud.

Clients

Ultimately, the clients on your end users' desks are how you will interact with the cloud. In this section we'll talk about the different types of clients and how they can be configured to communicate with the cloud. We'll also talk about some security measures and how you can keep your data safe on the cloud.

There are different types of clients that can link to the cloud, and each one offers a different way for you to interact with your data and applications. Depending on your organization and its needs, you may find yourself using any combination of these devices. How you interact with your data based on these clients will be a combination of factors—what your needs are, and the benefits and limitations of these client types.

Mobile

Mobile clients run the gamut from laptops to PDAs and smartphones, like an iPhone or BlackBerry. You're not likely to utilize a particularly robust application on a PDA or smartphone, but laptop users can connect to the cloud and access applications just as if they were sitting at their desk.

Mobile clients, of course, have security and speed concerns. Because the clients will be connecting to the cloud from various locations that may not have an optimized connection, as in a hotel, you can't expect the speed that a desk-bound client will achieve. But not all applications need speedy connections, and mobile users probably aren't inputting gigabytes worth of data into a database. Further, since you can create your own applications in the cloud, they can be crafted with a mobile client in mind. While a mobile user won't put tons of information into a database, an application can still be developed to let them access it.

Security is a major concern, but it's a two-sided issue. On the one hand, it's easier to lose or misplace a laptop, and whatever information is on it could be compromised. On the other hand, if data is maintained on the cloud and the user only has select files on his or her laptop, if the laptop were to be stolen, only a minimal set of data would be compromised.

Thin

Thin clients, as we've mentioned before, are client computers that have no hard drives, no DVD-ROM drives, and simply display what's on the server.

Thins may have a role in your organization, but likely only if you have an in-house cloud. Of course, it depends on what applications and services you're accessing on the cloud. If a client only needs to access cloud-based services or is accessing a virtualized server, then thin clients are a great option. They're less expensive than thick clients, are much less expensive to maintain, and use less energy.

There's also a high level of security, because no data is stored on the thin client. All the data resides in your datacenter or on the cloud, so the risk of a physical breach is small.

NOTE *We talk more about building your own in-house cloud in Chapter 12.*

Thick

Chances are that thick clients are the clients you already use and are likely to use to connect to applications in the cloud. You likely already have applications installed on your end users' machines. While you can offload some of your applications to the cloud, chances are there are still going to be some mission-critical applications that simply need to stay in-house.

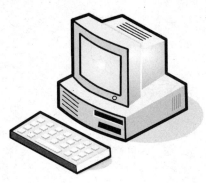

These machines can certainly still connect to a virtualized server, and if you don't want to spend any more money for clients, just use the machines that you already have. Thick clients are good choices if users need to maintain files on their own machines or run programs that don't exist on the cloud.

Security-wise, thick clients are more vulnerable to attack than thins. Since data is stored on the machine's hard drive, if the machine is stolen then the data could be compromised. There's also an issue of reliability. If a thin client fails, all it takes is for another thin to get plugged in and the user's work environment is right there. If a thick client fails, whatever data is stored on the machine, including the operating system and all the configuration settings, is lost and a new computer will have to be configured for the user.

Security

Security is the number one issue when it comes to cloud computing, and that only makes sense. Since a third party stores your data, you don't know what's going on with it. It's easy to worry about the security risks of a cloud solution, but let's not overlook the inherent security benefits, as well.

PART II

Data Leakage

The biggest benefit is the centralization of data. Organizations have an issue with asset protection, in no small part because of data being stored in numerous places, like laptops and the desktop.

Thick clients are apt to download files and maintain them on the hard drive, and there are plenty of laptops out there with nonencrypted files. Using thin clients creates a better chance for centralized data storage. As such, there's less chance for data leakage.

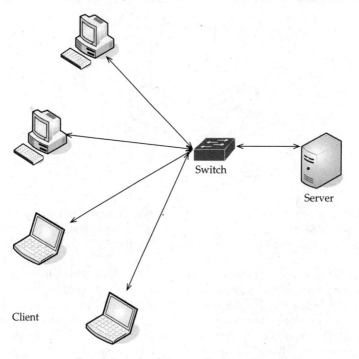

Data store on local server with clients that store data
has more opportunity for data leakage than clients
that maintain no permanent storage.

Centralization also provides the opportunity for better monitoring. That data is in one place makes it easier to check in on your data and see that everything is okay.

Offloading Work

Another security benefit isn't so much a technology, but the fact that you don't have to do it yourself. It's up to the cloud provider to provide adequate security. After all, can your organization afford 24/7 IT security staffing? The fact of the matter is that your cloud provider might offer more security features than you had before.

The fact that so many clients are paying allows cloud providers to have beefier security, simply because of the economy of scale involved. That is, there are many paying clients so the provider is able to do more, because there is more money in the pot. Plus it's to the provider's benefit to offer more, because they want to get a good reputation.

Logging

Logging is also improved. It's something that, in-house, usually gets the short end of the stick. But in the virtualized world of cloud computing, providers can add as much memory as they need to extend logging.

Forensics

If there is a breach, the cloud provider can respond to the incident with less downtime than if you had to investigate the breach locally. It is easy to build a forensic server online, and it costs almost nothing until it comes into use.

If there is a problem, the virtual machine can be cloned for easy offline analysis.

Further, many companies don't have a dedicated in-house incident response team. If there is a problem, IT staff have to quickly figure out their new job of taking the server down, quickly investigating, and getting it back online for minimal production downtime.

Development

Even more good news is that security vendors aren't in the dark about this whole cloud thing. They are actively developing products that can apply to virtual machines and the cloud.

Security vendors also have a unique opportunity in the cloud. Since it's new ground, there are new opportunities for the vendors who are open-minded enough to imagine them.

Auditing

As an IT professional, you already know the headache of securing your own local network. But when you send your data to the cloud, a whole new set of issues arise. This is largely because your data is being stored on someone else's equipment.

Compliance

The same security issues that your organization deals with are the sorts of issues that SaaS providers face—securing the network, hardware issues, applications, and data. But compliance adds another level of headache. Regulations like Sarbanes-Oxley (SOX), Gramm-Leach-Bliley (GLBA), and HIPAA, and industry standards like the Payment Card Industry Data Security Standard (PCI DSS) make things particularly challenging.

Prior to SaaS, compliance could be managed by a few tasks:

- Identify users and access privileges
- Identify sensitive data
- Identify where it's located
- Identify how it is encrypted
- Document this for auditors and regulators

SaaS makes these steps even more complicated. If you store compliance-sensitive data with an SaaS provider, it is difficult to know where the data is being stored. It could be on the provider's equipment, or it could even be on the equipment of one of the provider's partners.

SaaS brings with it a number of regulations, including PCI DSS. Within PCI DSS are regulations for service providers. Requirement 12.8 of PCI mandates that service providers be compliant and contractually acknowledge their responsibility for protecting credit card data.

The PCI DSS Appendix A goes into even more depth laying out rules and regulations.

The PCI Appendix A

Requirement A.1 of Appendix A has four subprovisions that regulate how data is maintained by a service provider. Let's take a closer look at this appendix.

Requirement A.1.1—Unauthorized Exposure   The first subsection requires that each client of the provider only has access to their own data. The important question to ask is how the SaaS provider's system architecture prevents the unauthorized exposure of data to other subscribers using the same service.

Appendix A.1.1 of PCI Requirement 12.8 mandates
that no entity other than your organization be able to view your data.

Since cloud providers are in the business of having as many clients as they can get, that means your data could be sitting on a server with another client's data—maybe even your competitor's.

Appendix A.1.2—Credential Management   This section of Appendix A requires that access controls be held by the service provider and that the controls only allow the client to be able to access that data and to protect the data from others. Either the provider can maintain those controls or maintenance can be done by connecting to the client's access management system. If the SaaS provider handles access controls, the authentication credentials are stored on the provider's servers. While providers generally claim this method is safe and secure, use extra caution. If there is a breach at the provider, then not only could your data be compromised, but also your authentication credentials. Further, if the provider handles the authentication, you must keep careful control of user accounts. If a user leaves your organization, their credentials need to be revoked, and that's easier to do in-house by your own IT staff than by relying on a service provider.

The best method is to have a direct connection with the company's directory services, like Active Directory or LDAP for authentication to the SaaS. Many SaaS vendors offer this service.

Appendix A.1.3—Logging   Logging and audit trails are covered by Appendix A.1.3. This is also mandated by Requirement 10 of PCI. Logs and audit trails are used for investigating incidents.

Appendix A.1.4—Reporting   The final relevant portion of the Appendix is Appendix A.1.4. In this section, service providers must "provide for timely forensic investigation" if there is a breach.

The SaaS provider's logs are internal and most likely not accessible by clients, so monitoring is nearly impossible. Access to logs is required for PCI compliance, and auditors or regulators may request access to them. As such, you should be sure to negotiate access to the provider's logs as part of your service agreement.

Web Application Breaches   Because service providers use so many web connections, they should be asked about the security of their web applications. This should include whether they follow Open Web Application Security Project (OWASP) guidelines for secure application development. This is similar to Requirement 6.5 of PCI, which requires compliance with OWASP coding procedures.

When dealing with a provider, you should seek out those who are able (willing) to talk about how they handle breaches among their staff as well as where data is stored. Given the wide range of server deployment, your data could be sitting on a server in Brazil, Germany, or Thailand. This harkens back to the jurisdictional issues we discussed in Chapter 2, but it also adds compliance and legal issues in different countries.

VPNs

With applications being moved to the cloud, it makes it possible for each and every worker to be a telecommuter. Thus, the organization doesn't have to lease as much space, pay as much for utilities, and those stupid holiday parties can be eliminated.

True, your organization might not lend itself to telecommuting simply by the work you do, or maybe you like those holiday parties and warm bodies in chairs. But the more applications get offloaded to the cloud, the fewer things you have to worry about in-house.

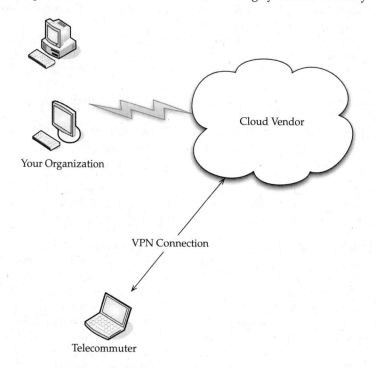

Also, there is certainly more to your datacenter than web applications. You have file storage, email, productivity applications, and anything else that doesn't lend itself to being web-based.

But in any event, whether your employees access the cloud across the public Internet or from your office, you need a secure remote access solution, like an SSL VPN.

What SSL Is   An SSL VPN (Secure Sockets Layer virtual private network) is a VPN that can be used with a standard web browser. As compared to the traditional IPsec (Internet Protocol Security) VPN, an SSL VPN does not require you to install specialized client software on end users' computers.

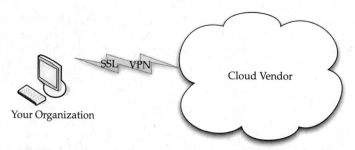

SSL VPNs use an established protocol to connect to the cloud securely.

SSL is a protocol for managing the security of message transmission on the Internet. SSL is included as part of popular web browsers and most web server products. It employs a public and private key encryption system from RSA.

NOTE *You might also hear SSL VPNs referred to as TLS VPNs. This is because Transport Layer Security (TLS) is a refinement of SSL and is replacing it.*

An SSL VPN cloud computing connection between your data center and the cloud provider secures your data without a lot of the Public Key Infrastructure (PKI) overhead that comes from an IPsec-based VPN solution.

Most SSL VPN gateways provide an on-demand client, so there's very little management overhead on the client side and it's easy for the end user to use.

Better Security Practices   An SSL VPN also makes sure that end users are compliant with your organization's security policies through the use of endpoint security. Those measures include

- Requiring antivirus software to be running
- Verifying that OS patches have been installed
- Checking to see if malware or bots are running

The SSL VPN is a great security solution because it secures access to your applications in a simple, inexpensive, and efficient way. And if you were so inclined, you can offer your employees more chance to telecommute.

Key Management

With your data stored off-site, there's certainly opportunity for your data to be compromised. Your applications, compute cycles, and storage are not under your direct control, so while cloud vendors aspire to keep your data safe, you can never really be 100 percent sure that it's not at risk.

Add to that the possibility that there may just be an accident that causes your data to be seen by others. Further, when you are done with data and try to purge it, there's no guarantee that it will be eradicated. That's because many cloud services simply do not erase freed storage and some do not even initialize storage when they assign it to you. And in the event of a hardware or software failure, some cloud providers may not destroy data on failed machines.

Additionally, it's not just the cloud provider who might be at fault if your data gets out. There are also concerns stemming from man-in-the-middle attacks.

The point here is not to scare you away from cloud computing, but to remind you that safeguards must be taken and the tough questions asked. And in this case, it's imperative that you cryptographically authenticate remote services and servers.

This is accomplished through client and server certificates that let you know you are connecting securely to your cloud assets.

Remote services must also be cryptographically protected. You use an authorization infrastructure, like Kerberos, to ensure that you are properly authenticated.

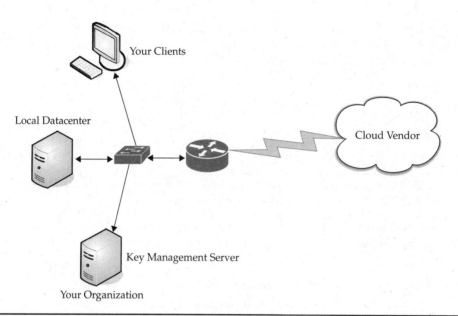

FIGURE 5-1 Cloud computing key management diagram

With cloud storage, be sure to protect it cryptographically as well. This includes encrypting the data you store and ensuring that data is set up to be destroyed when the storage key is destroyed.

This process will make your data more secure, but it also requires a lot of keys. Consider the network diagram in Figure 5-1.

Obviously this doesn't show every element of your network, but you'll notice a key management server, which is critical to have to keep track of all your keys. Keys on the server include

- Transport keys
- Authentication keys
- Authorization tokens
- File encryption keys
- Hardware storage keys
- Revocation keys
- Certificates

Network

We've talked about accessing the cloud via the Internet, and that is the case, in a general sort of way. In order for the cloud to deliver its best resources, there are differing levels of connectivity needed.

Research firm Gartner identified four different levels in a June 2008 study.

In the study, Gartner notes that different organizations require different things from the cloud, and as such they will have to connect in different ways. What works for one organization might not necessarily be the best means of connectivity for another.

NOTE *Gartner also notes that one organization doesn't need to lock into one solution. They might have one, two, three, or all four connectivity types, based on their need.*

Basic Public Internet

The first option is the pipe most of us have coming into our office or homes. The public Internet is the most basic choice for cloud connectivity.

This is the type of access that you buy from an Internet service provider (ISP) and connect with via broadband or dial-up, based on your location.

NOTE *Cloud computing over a dial-up connection is difficult to do, but depending on the location of your site or a remote site, it may be all you have. We'll talk about it later in this chapter.*

But "basic public Internet" is just that—basic. There are no extras like Transmission Control Protocol (TCP) acceleration, advanced compression, or application-specific optimization.

This model has the following advantages:

- There's a large audience. Anyone with Internet access can use this solution.
- It's highly fault tolerant.
- Many provider options are available.
- Secure Sockets Layer (SSL)–based, Hypertext Transport Protocol Over Secure Sockets Layer (HTTPS), encrypted access provides confidentiality.
- It's cost-effective.

It also has the following disadvantages:

- Lack of end-to-end quality of service (QoS), thus making end-to-end service-level agreements (SLAs) difficult to reach.
- Probability of poor response over high-latency connections. This is worsened by protocol inefficiencies in TCP, HTTP, and web services.
- Downtime that might be out of your control (cable cuts, problems at the ISP, and so forth).

Utilizing this method, organizations should consider subscribing with multiple ISPs, and cloud providers should also get bandwidth from multiple sources. Ideally, the client would get bandwidth from one of the same ISPs as the vendor. This aids in speed, reliability, and a better chance of success with an SLA.

The Accelerated Internet

Employing advanced application delivery features on top of your Internet connection can benefit both the service provider and the client. Cloud improvement can increase by 20 percent to 50 percent by offloading network-related functions from the server.

SSL termination and TCP connection management remove a significant amount of processing from the front-line servers. Additionally, dynamic caching, compression, and prefetching results in better than a 50 percent performance increase for end users.

Some providers offering this service include

- AT&T Hosting
- Citrix NetScaler
- F5's WebAccelerator

This method is mostly oriented toward the cloud service provider, but in the end it benefits the end user. Organizations opting for this method of connectivity should look at SLAs and monthly bandwidth charges, rather than worry about what acceleration methods the service provider is adding.

At the cloud, this method of acceleration requires the installation of a server-side appliance. At the end user, it normally requires the installation of a downloadable client.

NOTE *While this is an acceleration of the basic public Internet option, it does not address any of its network connectivity issues.*

Optimized Internet Overlay

An optimized Internet overlay approach allows customers to access the cloud via the public Internet, but enhancement occurs on the provider's cloud. Enhancements at these points of presence (POP) include

- Optimized real-time routing. This helps avoid slowdowns, helping to make SLAs easier to attain.
- An SSL session can be stopped so that protocols and payload can be optimized and re-encrypted.
- Some of the application logic can reside on the POP. This allows for better scalability, fault tolerance, and response time, usually in excess of 80 percent.
- Content that is frequently accessed can be delivered from local caches.

Disadvantages of this method include

- It is costlier than public Internet connectivity, sometimes as much as four times as much.
- There is a strong vendor lock-in if the application is distributed into the carrier's network.

Site-to-Site VPN

The fourth option is to connect to the service provider directly using a private wide area network (WAN) (normally an MPLS/VPN connection). This setup allows confidentiality, guaranteed bandwidth, and SLAs for availability, latency, and packet loss. MPLS can also scale to meet changing bandwidth needs, and QoS can also be written into the SLAs.

On the downside, private WANs are not normally more reliable than Internet connections, especially redundant connections to multiple ISPs.

Table 5-1 compares all four connections.

Cloud Providers

Cloud providers that use services dispersed across the cloud need a robust connection method. Private tunnels make sure that bandwidth, latency, and loss aren't as likely to affect performance. Plus, encryption and strong authentication offer another benefit.

Cloud providers that are growing might face big costs as network bandwidth charges increase. This traffic is from traffic both to and from clients as well as traffic among provider sites. Big providers, like Google, are able to sidestep these charges by building their own WANs with multiple peering points with major ISPs. Unfortunately, most cloud providers aren't able to do this. Smaller providers can use WAN optimization controllers (WOCs) to reduce bandwidth requirements by up to 80 percent.

Connection Method	Description	Examples of Use
Basic public internet	Anyone can use it Fault tolerant Multiple providers Cost-effective Performance issues for globally delivered applications	Consumer applications Advertising supported services Applications where "best effort" service is sufficient
Accelerated internet	Improved end-user performance Inconsistent performance, based on provider and ISP configuration Low cost	Best for cost-sensitive service where improved response times and bandwidth are necessary
Optimized overlay	Consistent performance Ability to have strong SLAs Expensive Limited provider options Provider risk	Business-critical applications that require SLAs delivering promised response times and bandwidth
Site-to-site VPN	Ability to have strong SLAs Site-specific delivery Consistent performance Lowest latency Limited reach	Business-critical applications, including server-to-server traffic

TABLE 5-1   Features of Connectivity Options

Performance can be improved and bandwidth charges reduced if providers use asymmetrical optimization. This requires an appliance at the provider and a client applet. This can reduce response time by up to 70 percent and bandwidth requirements by up to 80 percent. The benefit is that additional equipment is not needed at client sites.

Cloud Consumers

Large companies can build their own scalable distributed IT infrastructure in which datacenters are connected with their own private fiber optic connections. This depends on distance, bandwidth requirements, and—of course—their budgets. This infrastructure starts to look like a cloud computing service.

Clients located at major sites normally access applications over the corporate WAN. For smaller offices or mobile workers, VPN connections across optimized and accelerated Internet services provide a more robust solution. VPN tunnels across the Internet are best as a primary link only when high performance is not crucial.

Pipe Size

Bandwidth is, simply put, the transmission speed or throughput of your connection to the Internet. But, measuring bandwidth can be difficult, since the lowest point of bandwidth between your computer and the site you're looking at is what your speed is at that moment.

There are three factors that are simply out of your control when it comes to how much bandwidth you need:

- The Internet bandwidth between your organization and the cloud
- The round-trip time between your organization and the cloud
- The response time of the cloud

Upstream/Downstream

Another factor to consider is whether it is okay for the transfers to be symmetric or asymmetric. If your connection with the cloud is symmetric, then that means you are sending and receiving data at the same rate. If your connection is asymmetric, then data is sent from your organization at a slower rate than you're receiving it.

Be cognizant of how fast data is able to be sent
in addition to how fast you are able to receive data.

For instance, ADSL connections send and receive data at different rates. The "A" in ADSL stands for asymmetric. Depending on what service we're talking about, data can be received at 1.5Mbps while it is sent at 750Mbps.

Your organization is likely connecting to its ISP using something more robust than DSL, and in most cases those connections are symmetrical.

Consider also that the Internet changes from one moment to the next in ways that are impossible to predict. Data moves through different routers and network appliances, so your speed will vary from time to time. It may not be noticeable, but it does fluctuate. As such, even though you're paying for a T1 line, don't call the phone company to complain right away—there's always a delay somewhere.

The best rule of thumb is that if you are consistently measuring 85 percent of your nominal bandwidth, then you're doing okay.

Perform an Internet connection test several times a day. Try it first thing in the morning, at lunchtime, and close to the end of business. Generally speaking, bandwidth measurement at 7 A.M. will give better results than in the evening.

How Much Do We Need?

This can be a complex question, based on what you'll be doing on the cloud. What you have to do is figure out how much data will be moving in and out of the cloud at any given time, and then decide how big of a pipe you need to move that data.

Chances are good that you have a beefy enough Internet connection to make cloud computing viable. However, realize that the more you do on the cloud, the more demand will be placed on your Internet connection. If you do not have enough capacity, then everyone will experience a slowdown.

Take the time to figure out how much capacity you'll use, and make sure you have enough resources to accommodate that need. If not, you are likely to have another expense that you hadn't planned on, in the guise of a faster Internet connection.

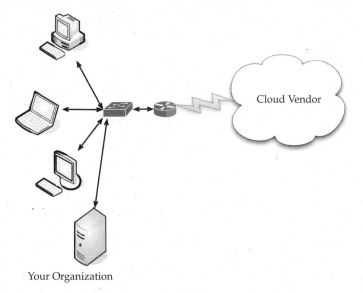

Your Organization

Figure out how much capacity all your clients will use when accessing the cloud, and ensure you have a big enough pipe to accommodate that need.

It's important to secure an SLA that meets your bandwidth requirements. This not only ensures that you are getting the speed that you need, but if the ISP fails to meet those levels, there can be some sort of remediation in it for you.

Redundancy

When formulating your cloud infrastructure, be sure to consider the issue of reliability and uptime and ask your service provider to configure your computing infrastructure for redundancy and failover.

In your LAN, redundancy used to mean that another server or two were added to the datacenter in case there was a problem. These days with virtualization, redundancy might mean a virtual server being cloned onto the same device, or all the virtual servers of one machine being cloned onto a second physical server.

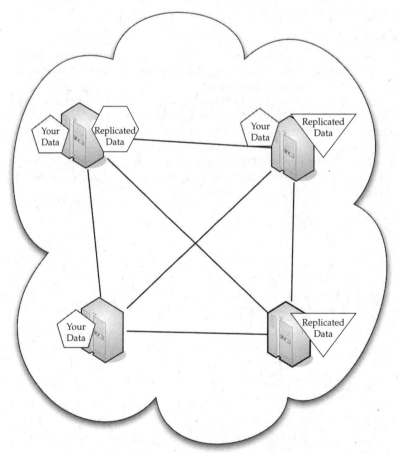

The cloud vendor is likely to have your data
and its redundant clone in geographically dispersed locations.

It becomes more complex in the cloud. While you may think of your server being hosted at the datacenter of your cloud provider, it's not as easy to nail down. Parts of your data may be housed in one location and other parts scattered throughout the country (possibly even the world). And when the provider adds a redundant system, again the data is scattered throughout their cloud. So it's not an issue of the service provider wheeling in a new server to provide redundant services. Rather, they simply reallocate resources to give you a redundant system.

NOTE   *This is one of the selling points for cloud computing—the fact that failover and redundancy are inherent parts of the architecture. However, it's best to ask about these features and make sure they are included.*

Services

There are different services you will need to run, depending on your cloud provider and what your organization does. Also, these services will likely affect how your cloud infrastructure is deployed.

Identity

No matter where an application runs—in-house or on the cloud—it needs to know about its users. To accomplish this, the application asks for a digital identity—a set of bytes—to describe the user. Based on this information, the application can determine who the user is and what he or she is allowed to do.

In-house applications rely on services like Active Directory to provide this information. Clouds, however, have to use their own identity services. For instance, if you sign on to Amazon cloud services, you have to sign on using an Amazon-defined identity. Google's App Engine requires a Google account, and Windows uses Windows Live ID for use with Microsoft's cloud applications.

Identity services need not be proprietary. OpenID is an open, decentralized, single sign-on standard that allows users to log in to many services using the same digital identity.

An OpenID is in the form of a uniform resource locator (URL) and does not rely on a central authority to authenticate a user's identity. Since a specific type of authentication is not required, nonstandard forms of authentication may be used, including smart cards, biometric, or passwords. An OpenID registration is shown in Figure 5-2.

OpenID authentication is used by many organizations, including:

- Google
- IBM
- Microsoft
- Yahoo!

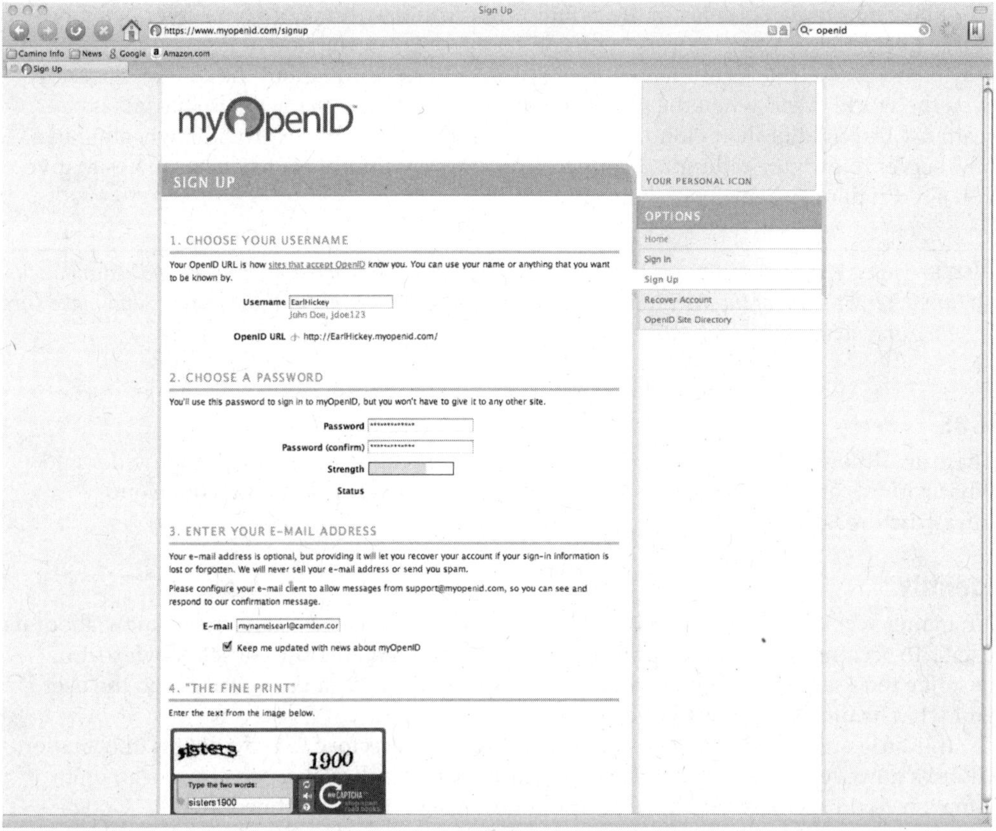

FIGURE 5-2 . OpenID is a means to keep login information consistent across several sites.

Integration

Applications talking among themselves have become highly common. Vendors come up with all sorts of on-premises infrastructure services to accomplish it. These range from technologies like message queues to complex integration servers.

Integration is also on the cloud and technologies are being developed for that use, as well. For example, Amazon's Simple Queue Service (SQS) provides a way for applications to exchange messages via queues in the cloud.

SQS replicates messages across several queues, so an application reading from a queue may not see all messages from all queues on a given request. SQS also doesn't guarantee in-order delivery. These sound like shortcomings, but in fact it's these simplifications that make SQS more scalable, but it also means that developers must use SQS differently from on-premises messaging.

Another example of cloud-based integration is BizTalk Services. Instead of using queuing, BizTalk Services utilizes a relay service in the cloud, allowing applications to communicate through firewalls. Since cloud-based integration requires communicating through different organizations, the ability to tunnel through firewalls is an important problem to solve.

BizTalk Services also utilizes simplified workflow support with a way for applications to register the services it exposes, and then lets those services be invoked by other applications.

Integration services in the cloud is going to gain in prominence as it becomes more and more important, especially given how important it is in-house.

Mapping

Maps are becoming more and more popular in web applications. For instance, hotel and restaurant web sites show their locations on their web sites and allow visitors to enter their addresses to get customized directions.

But the guy who developed the web site likely didn't have the time or money (not to mention the interest) to make his own mapping database. Enough organizations want this functionality, however, so it is offered as a cloud application.

Such services as Google Maps and Microsoft's Virtual Earth provide this cloud-based function, allowing developers to embed maps in web pages.

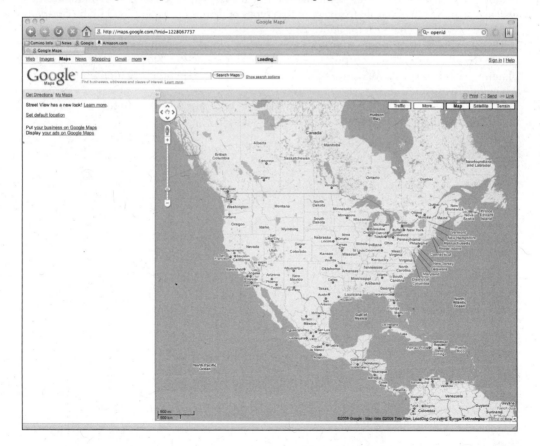

These services are really just additions to existing web sites.

Payments

Another cloud service that you might want to plan for and configure your hardware appropriately for is payments. Depending on your organization, you may or may not want to accept online payments from customers. Luckily, there is no lack of ways to get paid online.

You can simply sign up with a service to accept credit cards, or you can go the route of PayPal. With an online payment service, customers can send money directly to your organization.

Search

The ability to embed search options in a web site is certainly nothing new, but it is a rich feature that you might want to employ in your own web or application development.

Microsoft's Live Search allows on-site and cloud applications to submit searches and then get the results back.

Searchability is limited only to the organization and what it does. For instance, a company might develop an application that does both. For instance, let's say a company has a database of movie information. By typing in the name of the movie, you can search its own database as well as a search of the Internet to give you two types of results—what's stored in the company database as well as what's on the entire Web.

If you were to use a single computer to access the cloud, the requirements are pretty minimal—all you need is a computer and an Internet connection. However, when you start planning cloud solutions for your organization, you need to spend more time figuring out which hardware and infrastructure is best for you.

In the next chapter we'll talk about how you can use your newly configured network to access the cloud and about how your clients are set up.

Accessing the Cloud

How you will interact with your cloud will depend on many factors, not the least of which is the provider you use. There are a number of development tools that allow you to build your applications and several browser options that you can use to access those applications.

In this chapter we'll take a closer look at the tools you can use to connect with the cloud so you can realize which tools will work best for your organization and your particular needs.

Platforms

A platform is how a cloud computing environment is delivered to you. In this section we'll take a closer look at how the cloud can be produced and presented to you.

Web Application Framework

A web application framework is used to support the development of dynamic web sites, web applications, and web services. The point of a framework is to reduce the overhead that comes with common activities in web development. For instance, frameworks provide libraries that are already written so the developer doesn't have to reinvent the wheel every time a web site is developed.

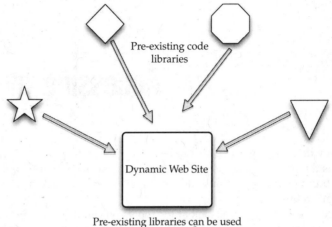

Pre-existing libraries can be used
to create web applications.

Early in the Web's life, hypertext was mostly hand-coded Hypertext Markup Language (HTML) that was published on Web servers. If a published page needed to be changed, it had to be done by the page's author. As the Web grew up, it became more dynamic with the addition of the Common Gateway Interface (CGI). This allowed external applications to interface with web servers.

AJAX

Asynchronous JavaScript and XML (AJAX) is a group of web development techniques used for creating interactive web applications. By using AJAX, web applications can retrieve data from the server asynchronously. Because it is being done in the background, it won't interfere with the display and behavior of the current page.

Technologies   AJAX is a term that represents a wide range of web technologies that can be used to help web applications communicate with a server, but without interfering with the current state of that page. AJAX refers to these technologies:

- Extensible Hypertext Markup Language (XHTML) and Cascading Style Sheets (CSS) for presentation
- The Document Object Model for dynamic display of and interaction with data
- XML and Extensible Style Sheet Language Transformations (XSLT) for the interchange and manipulation of data, respectively
- The XMLHttpRequest object for asynchronous communication
- JavaScript to bring these technologies together

AJAX continues to evolve. For instance, while JavaScript claims a place in the acronym for AJAX, it is not the only client-side language that can be used for developing an AJAX application. Languages like VBScript can be used, as well. Further, XML is not required for data exchange. JavaScript Object Notation (JSON) is a widely used alternative. HTML and plain text can also be used.

Pros and Cons   AJAX does some things right, but struggles with others. Among its advantages are the following capabilities:

- Often, multiple pages on a web site contain the same information. If those pages were coded by hand, the same content would have to be written into each and every page. AJAX allows a web application to simply retrieve new information and adjust how the content is presented. This is very efficient and reduces the amount of bandwidth consumed and reduces load times.

- Using asynchronous requests allows the client's web browser to be more interactive and respond quickly to user inputs. The user may even perceive the application to be faster.

- Connections to the server are reduced, because scripts and style sheets need only be downloaded once.

Disadvantages to AJAX include

- Dynamically created web pages do not show up in the browser's history engine, so clicking on the Back button would not re-create the last seen page.

- It is difficult to bookmark a dynamically created web page.

- If a browser does not support AJAX or if JavaScript is disabled, AJAX functionality cannot be used.

- There is no standards body behind AJAX, so there is no widely adopted best practice to test AJAX applications.

Python Django

Django is an open-source web application framework written in Python. Originally it was created to manage news sites for The World Company and released publicly under a BSD license in July 2005. In June 2008 it was announced that the Django Software Foundation will be the authority for Django.

NOTE *Django was named for jazz guitarist Django Reinhardt.*

Django was developed to ease the creation of database-driven web sites and uses reusability of components. Django utilizes the principle of DRY (Don't Repeat Yourself). It also uses an administrative CRUD (create, read, update, and delete) interface that is dynamically generated.

Included in the core framework are

- A lightweight, stand-alone web server for development and testing
- A caching framework, which can use any of several cache methods
- An internal dispatcher system that allows an application's components to communicate using predefined signals
- An internationalization system that translates Django's components into multiple languages
- A scheme for extending the capabilities of the template engine

---

NOTE *The Google App Engine includes Django.*

There is a free Django book, released under the GNU Free Document License, which tells more about the framework. It was published in December 2007 and can be found at http://www.djangobook.com.

Web Hosting Service

You will need a web hosting service that will allow you to store your data and applications. This is what we think of when the term "cloud provider" is used. This is the organization that will host your data.

Some web hosting services include Amazon Elastic Compute Cloud and Mosso.

Amazon Elastic Compute Cloud

Amazon Elastic Compute Cloud (http://aws.amazon.com/ec2) is a web service that provides resizable compute capacity in the cloud. Amazon EC2's web service interface allows you to obtain and configure capacity with minimal friction.

It provides complete control of your computing resources and lets you run on Amazon's computing environment. Amazon EC2 reduces the time required to obtain and boot new server instances to minutes, allowing you to quickly scale capacity, both up and down, as a client's computing requirements change. Amazon EC2 changes the economics of computing by allowing you to pay only for capacity that you actually use.

EC2 uses Xen virtualization. Each virtual machine, called an instance, is a virtual private server and can be one of three sizes: small, large, or extra large. Instances are sized based on EC2 Compute Units, which is the equivalent CPU capacity of physical hardware.

One EC2 Compute Unit equals a 1.0–1.2GHz 2007 Opteron or 2007 Xeon processor. The available instance sizes are shown in Table 6-1.

The service initially offered Sun Microsystems OpenSolaris and Solaris Express Community Edition. In October 2008, EC2 added the Linux and Windows Server 2003 operating systems to its offerings.

Mosso

Mosso is the home of The Hosting Cloud and CloudFS, providing enterprise-grade hosting and storage services. Mosso provides an easily managed interface so that developers, designers, and IT managers can deploy reliable web applications quickly and easily as well as a high-performance cloud-based storage service.

Instance Size	Small	Large	Extra Large	High CPU–Medium	High CPU–Extra Large
EC2 Compute Units	1	4	8	5 (two virtual cores with 2.5 Compute Units each)	20
Memory	1.7GB	7.5GB	15GB	1.7GB	7GB
Storage	160GB	850GB	1,690GB	350GB	1,690GB
Platform	32-bit	64-bit	64-bit	32-bit	64-bit

TABLE 6-1 Amazon Elastic Compute Cloud Sizes

Founded by two Rackspace employees, The Hosting Cloud is built upon a cross-platform, clustered-computing architecture. For more information, visit www.mosso.com. There are three components to Mosso's offering:

- **Cloud Sites** Advertised as "the fastest way to put sites on the cloud"; runs Windows or Linux applications across hundreds of servers.

- **Cloud Files** Provides unlimited online storage for media (examples include backups, video files, user content), which is served out via Limelight Networks' Content Delivery Network.

- **Cloud Servers** Able to deploy from one to hundreds of cloud servers instantly and creates advanced, high-availability architectures.

Proprietary Methods

In addition to the widely used standards (like AJAX and Django), individual companies offer their own, proprietary methods to connect to the cloud. Microsoft and Force.com are two examples of companies that have designed their own infrastructure for connecting to the cloud.

Azure

The Azure Services Platform is Microsoft's cloud solution that spans from the cloud to the enterprise datacenter. Further, it delivers content across the PC, web, and phone.

The platform combines cloud-based developer capabilities with storage, computational, and networking infrastructure services, all hosted on servers operating within Microsoft's global datacenter network. This provides developers with the ability to deploy applications in the cloud or on-premises and enables experiences across a broad range of business and consumer scenarios.

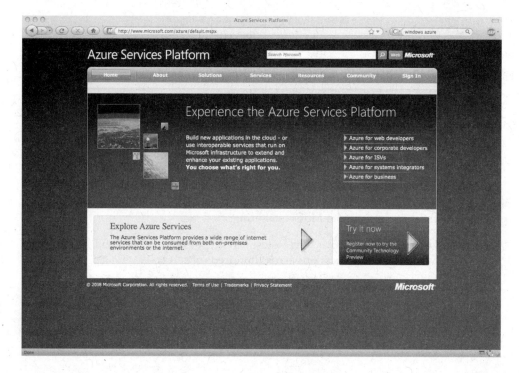

The Azure Services Platform provides developers with the ability to create applications while taking advantage of their existing skills, tools, and technologies such as the Microsoft .NET Framework and Visual Studio.

Developers also can choose from a broad range of commercial or open-source development tools and technologies, and access the Azure Services Platform using a variety of common Internet standards including HTTP, representational state transfer (REST), and Atom Publishing Protocol (AtomPub).

Key components of the Azure Services Platform include the following:

- Windows Azure for service hosting and management, low-level scalable storage, computation, and networking

- Microsoft SQL Services for a wide range of database services and reporting

- Microsoft .NET Services, which are service-based implementations of familiar .NET Framework concepts such as workflow and access control

- Live Services for a consistent way for users to store, share, and synchronize documents, photos, files, and information across their PCs, phones, PC applications, and web sites

- Microsoft SharePoint Services and Microsoft Dynamics CRM Services for business content, collaboration, and rapid solution development in the cloud

As a key part of their cloud offering, Microsoft has built datacenters to deliver online services. Microsoft has opened major datacenters in Quincy, Washington, and San Antonio, Texas, with additional centers scheduled to open in Chicago and in Dublin, Ireland.

Force.com

Force.com, a PaaS from Salesforce.com, is another way to create and deploy business applications. By replacing the complexity of software platforms with a complete, scalable service, Force.com provides developers a fast path to turn ideas into business impact.

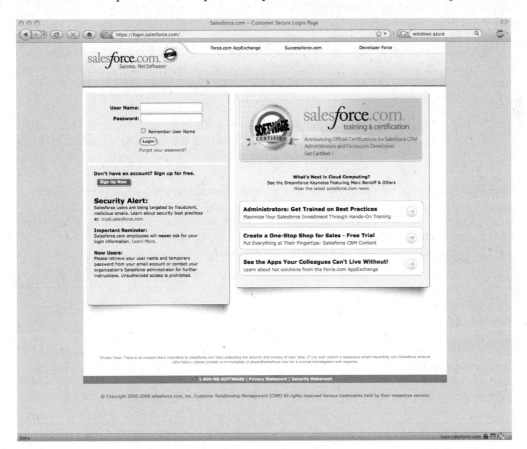

Force.com Features   Force.com PaaS provides the building blocks necessary to build any kind of business application, and automatically deploy them as a service to small teams or entire enterprises. The Force.com platform gives customers the ability to run multiple applications within the same Salesforce.com instance, allowing all of a company's Salesforce.com applications to share a common security model, data model, and user interface.

The multitenant Force.com platform encompasses a complete feature set for the creation of business applications such as an on-demand operating system, the ability to create any database on demand, a workflow engine for managing collaboration between users, the Apex Code programming language for building complex logic, the Force.com Web Services API for programmatic access, mashups, and integration with other applications and data, and now Visualforce for a framework to build any user interface.

Visualforce   As part of the Force.com platform, Visualforce gives customers the ability to design application user interfaces for any experience on any screen. Using the logic and workflow intelligence provided by Apex Code, Visualforce offers the flexibility to meet the requirements of applications that feature many different types of users on a variety of devices. Visualforce uses HTML, AJAX, and Flex for business applications. Visualforce enables the creation and delivery of any user experience, offering control over an application's design and behavior.

Visualforce provides a page-based model, built on standard HTML and web presentation technologies, and is complemented with both a component library for implementing common user interface elements and a controller model for creating new interactions between those elements. Visualforce features and capabilities include

- **Pages**   Enables the design definition of an application's user interface. This enables developers to create new pages using standard web technologies including HTML, AJAX, and Flex. Pages allows developers to create any user experience with standard web technologies.

- **Components**   Provides the ability to create new applications that automatically match the look and feel of Salesforce applications or easily customize and extend the Salesforce user interface to specific customer and user requirements. Customers can create a user experience by assembling existing user interface elements.

- **Logic Controllers**   Enables customers to build any user interface behavior. Customers can use Visualforce to quickly create a new look and feel that leverages existing application functionality. The standard controller gives customers the ability to inherit and reuse any standard Salesforce UI behavior like new, edit, and save.

Web Applications

If you are going to use applications on the cloud, there are many to choose from. Much of your decision-making process will come down to your provider and what they offer. In this section we'll talk about the choices you have in existing cloud applications.

NOTE *In the next section we'll talk about the tools you can use to build your own applications if what you want isn't already available.*

Your Choices

You have tons of options when it comes to finding online applications. Your provider may have a stable of premade applications that you can use. For instance, Google offers a slew of applications geared toward productivity. We'll talk about some of those applications in a bit, but what if your provider doesn't offer an application that you want?

It may be that someone else has already created the application and it's simply a matter of using what they have created. For example, we talked about Force.com earlier in this chapter. Force.com allows you and others to create your own apps and then make them available for others to use.

If you don't see an application that you want, ask your service provider—they may have it offline somewhere—or they can point you to it.

Sample Applications

Different companies offer different things, but for the sake of understanding the market, let's take a closer look at cloud giant Google and their offerings. They have a slate of apps that are targeted right toward your enterprise. Following this link (http://www.google .com/apps/intl/en/business/index.html) will take you to their apps.

Google Apps, launched as a free service in August 2006, is a suite of applications that includes

- Gmail webmail services
- Google Calendar shared calendaring
- Google Talk instant messaging and Voice Over IP
- Start Page for creating a customizable home page on a specific domain

More than 100,000 small businesses and hundreds of universities now use the service.

"So much of business now relies on people being able to communicate and collaborate effectively," said Gregory Simpson, CTO for General Electric Company. "GE is interested in evaluating Google Apps for the easy access it provides to a suite of web applications, and the way these applications can help people work together. Given its consumer experience, Google has a natural advantage in understanding how people interact together over the web."

Google also offers a premium service called Google Apps Premier Edition. Google Apps Premier Edition has the following unique features:

- **Per-user storage of 10GBs**   Offers about 100 times the storage of the average corporate mailbox, eliminating the need to frequently delete email.

- **APIs for business integration**   APIs for data migration, user provisioning, single sign-on, and mail gateways enable businesses to further customize the service for unique environments.

- **Uptime of 99.9 percent**   Service Level Agreements for high availability of Gmail, with Google monitoring and crediting customers if service levels are not met.

- **Support for critical issues 24/7**   Includes extended business hours telephone support for administrators.

- **Advertising optional**   Advertising is turned off by default, but businesses can choose to include Google's relevant target-based ads if desired.

- **Low fee**   Simple and affordable annual fee (US$50 per user account per year) makes it practical to offer these applications to everyone in the organization.

In addition to Gmail, Google Calendar, Google Talk and Start Page, all editions of Google Apps also include

- **Google Docs and Spreadsheets**   With this addition, teams can collaborate on documents and spreadsheets without the need to email documents back and forth. Multiple employees can securely work on a document at the same time. All revisions are recorded for editing, and administrative controls allow organizations to define limits on document sharing.

- **Gmail for mobile devices on BlackBerry**   Gmail for mobile devices provides the same Gmail experience—such as search, conversation view, and synchronization with desktop version—on BlackBerry handheld devices for users of Google Apps. Gmail for mobile devices joins a list of other mobile options for Google Apps and BlackBerry users that already includes a Google Talk client and a variety of calendar sync tools.

- **Application-level control**   Allows administrators to adapt services to business policies, such as sharing of calendars or documents outside of the company.

To provide more options and value to customers of Google Apps Premier Edition, Google Enterprise Professional partners like Avaya and Postini are developing a variety of solutions based on Google's APIs, including email gateways, enhanced security, Google Calendar synchronization, and third-party integration with Google Talk, as well as offering deployment, migration, and additional support services.

Google-hosted applications are available in many languages, such as French, Italian, German, Spanish, Chinese, Japanese, and Korean. You can find more information at http://www.google.com/.

Web APIs

You are likely to use APIs when building your apps. There are a number of different APIs out there, and which one you use will depend on your (or your programmers') skills and which company you use for cloud services. Different cloud providers use different APIs.

What Are APIs?

An application programming interface (API) is a set of programming instructions and standards for accessing a web-based program. Software companies release their APIs to the public so that other software developers can design products that are powered by its service.

For example, Amazon released its own API so that web site developers could more easily access information maintained at the Amazon web site. By using Amazon's API, a third-party web site can directly link to products on the Amazon site.

APIs allow one program to speak with another. They are not user interfaces. Using APIs, programs can speak to each other without the user having to be involved. For instance, when you buy something at Amazon and enter your credit card information, Amazon uses an API to send your credit card information to a remote application that verifies whether your information is correct. As a user, all you saw was the place to enter your credit card information, but behind the scenes, APIs were getting the job done.

An API works in between two pieces of software to exchange information.

An API is similar to Software as a Service (SaaS), because software developers don't have to start from scratch every time they write a program. Rather than build one program that does everything (email, billing tracking, and so forth), the application can farm out those duties to other applications that do it better.

How APIs Work

An API is (as the acronym says) an interface that defines the way in which two things will communicate. With APIs, the calls back and forth are managed by web services. Web services are a collection of standards including XML, the programming language that allows applications to communicate over the Internet. XML is a general-purpose markup language. It describes structured data in a way that both humans and computers can read and write.

The API is a piece of software code written as a series of XML messages, like the one for the Google Maps API shown here:

```
<script type="text/javascript"
src="http://www.google.com/jsapi?key=ABCDEFG"></script>
<script type="text/javascript">
  google.load("maps", "2.x");

  // Call this function when the page has been loaded
  function initialize() {
    var map = new google.maps.Map2(document.getElementById("map"));
    map.setCenter(new google.maps.LatLng(37.4419, -122.1419), 13);
  }
  google.setOnLoadCallback(initialize);
</script>
```

Your programmers can use APIs by programming new or existing applications to generate the right XML messages to utilize remote applications. For instance, if you wanted to archive emails on the cloud, you could use an API to automatically send emails from your inboxes to the cloud archive.

Companies that release their API usually do so as part of a larger software development kit (SDK) that includes the API, programming tools, and documentation.

APIs and web services are invisible to your users as they access the cloud. Their whole purpose is to run silently in the background, doing the job for which they were created.

XML isn't the only standard that makes APIs work. Other standards include

- **SOAP (Simple Object Access Protocol)** SOAP encodes XML messages so that they can be received and understood by any operating system over any type of network protocol.

- **UDDI (Universal Description, Discovery, and Integration)** UDDI is an XML-based directory that allows businesses to list themselves, find each other, and collaborate using web services.

- **WSDL (Web Services Description Language)** WSDL is the SOAP of UDDI. WSDL is the XML-based language that businesses use to describe their services in the UDDI.

API Creators

There are many different APIs you can use to link your organization with your cloud applications. Whatever you need is probably already out there—you just need to do a little looking. But failing that, you might have to create your own APIs.

Google Gadgets

Google Gadgets are a desktop search application that enables users to search their email, files, web history, and chats. Called Google Desktop Search, this new application makes it possible for users to find information on their computers as fast and easily as they can search the Web with Google.

NOTE *You could create a Google Gadget that interfaces with your cloud data.*

The Google Gadgets API is composed of three languages:

- **XML** This is the language you use to write gadget specifications. A gadget is just an XML file, placed on the Web somewhere where Google can find it. The XML file contains the instructions on how to process and render the gadget. The XML file can contain all the data, or it can have reference URLs where the data can be found.

- **HTML** HTML is the markup language used to format the pages on the web. It is generally responsible for the static portions of your web pages. HTL and XML look similar, but HTML is used to format web documents, whereas XML is used to describe structured data.

- **JavaScript** JavaScript is the scripting language you can use to add dynamic behavior to your gadgets.

Google Desktop Search is a lightweight, free, downloadable application that brings Google search to information on your computer. The application operates locally on the user's computer, where it provides the following capabilities:

- **System-wide search** Users can search across their email and a wide range of files and information such as email in Microsoft Outlook and Outlook Express; files in Microsoft Word, Microsoft Excel, Microsoft PowerPoint, and text; web site history in Internet Explorer; and instant message chats in AOL Instant Messenger.

- **High search speed** Google.com can search billions of web pages in a fraction of a second. Google Desktop Search is built with the same technology, and it can search a single hard drive in even less time.

- **Easy access to desktop results via Google.com** Google Desktop Search enables users to search both their computer and the Web simultaneously. When users search through Google.com (either from the home page or the Google Toolbar), Google Desktop Search runs the same search in parallel on the user's computer. If Google Desktop Search finds relevant results, those results are added to the Google.com search results page. This means that users don't need to decide before they search whether to search the Web or their computer.

- **Dynamic results** Unlike traditional computer search software that updates once a day, Google Desktop Search updates continuously for most file types. When a user downloads a new email in Outlook, for example, it can be found within seconds using Google Desktop Search.

Google Desktop Search is available at http://desktop.google.com.

Google Data APIs

The Google Data APIs provide a simple standard protocol for reading and writing data on the Web. They encompass a broad range of business functions that can be used to link your applications within and outside of the cloud.

Description These REST-style APIs are based on the Atom Publishing Protocol (AtomPub), and use the Atom syndication format to represent data and HTTP to handle communication. The Google Data APIs include

- Google Apps APIs
- Google Base Data API
- Blogger Data API
- Google Book Search Data API
- Google Calendar Data API
- Google Code Search Data API
- Google Contacts Data API
- Google Documents List Data API
- Google Finance Portfolio Data API
- Google Health Data API
- Google Notebook Data API
- Picasa Web Albums Data API
- Google Spreadsheets Data API
- Webmaster Tools Data API
- YouTube Data API

Partnership   Salesforce.com partnered with Google, making it easier for developers to create applications for cloud computing. The Force.com Toolkit for Google Data APIs provides a set of tools and services to allow developers to take advantage of Google Data APIs, a common set of standard APIs for interacting with data in Google services, within their applications and projects on Force.com.

The APIs are freely available at http://developer.force.com/ and http://code.google.com/p/apex-google-data/.

The alliance between Salesforce.com and Google gives developers a multicloud computing platform for building and running applications. The Force.com PaaS and Google's open APIs and technologies enable the creation of powerful applications delivered on the Web.

Additionally, the Force.com Toolkit for Google Data APIs creates new opportunities for developers and ISVs to extend the widely adopted Salesforce for Google Apps. The toolkit gives developers and partners the ability to create business applications that extend Salesforce for Google Apps as well as build entirely new applications to help customers run their business in the cloud.

GoGrid

GoGrid's API is a web service that allows developers to control their interaction with GoGrid's cloud hosting infrastructure. The GoGrid API provides two-way communication for controlling GoGrid's control panel functionality. Typical uses for the API include

- Auto-scaling network servers
- Listing assigned public and private IP addresses
- Deleting servers
- Listing billing details

GoGrid's REST-like API Query interface is designed for individuals who want to programmatically control their cloud hosting infrastructure over the Internet.

The GoGrid API requires you to be a GoGrid customer and to have technical knowledge and programming skills. The GoGrid API supports these languages:

- Java
- PHP
- Python
- Ruby

Apex

The Apex Web Services API is one of the world's most widely used enterprise web services, handling more than 50 percent of Salesforce.com's 3.7 billion service transactions.

The Apex Web Services API makes it possible to access and manage complex data relationships—such as a set of information about an account, all the products they have bought, and all of their contacts—in a single request. This capability, analogous to database JOIN functionality, enhances both the speed and simplicity of integrations, and will be unique to the Apex API.

Development Platform   Apex is a development platform for building Software as a Service (SaaS) applications on top of Salesforce.com's customer relationship management (CRM) functionality. By using Apex, developers can access Salesforce.com's back-end database and client-server interfaces to create SaaS applications. This API allows developers to use common SaaS components, like web widgets or a multitenant database, without the need to develop much of the infrastructure traditionally associated behind SaaS programs.

The Apex platforms consist of three tools:

- **Apex Builder**   An on-demand component allowing easy drag-and-drop customization with a limited set of features.

- **Apex API**   A method of retrieving raw data from Salesforce.com's servers. The API is used by programs that are external to Salesforce.com, like Java applications that need access to information on a client's Salesforce.com account.

- **Apex Code**   A programming language that is executed on Salesforce.com's servers. The Apex Code offers flexibility in developing by using the Apex API while reducing the number of calls between the client and server.

Sample Code   The following is an example of an Apex API. The code defines a system that prevents duplicate records, based on email address, from being entered into the system.

```
trigger blockDuplicates_tgr on Lead bulk(before insert, before update) {
    /*
     * begin by building a map which stores the (unique) list of leads
     * being inserted/updated, using email address as the key.
     */
    Map<String, Lead> leadMap = new Map<String, Lead>();
    for (Lead lead : System.Trigger.new) {
        if (lead.Email != null) { // skip null emails
            /* for inserts OR
             * updates where the email address is changing
             * check to see if the email is a duplicate of another in
             * this batch, if unique, add this lead to the leadMap
             */
            if  ( System.Trigger.isInsert ||
                    (System.Trigger.isUpdate &&
                    lead.Email !=
                        System.Trigger.oldMap.get(lead.Id).Email)) {

                if (leadMap.containsKey(lead.Email)) {
                    lead.Email.addError('Another new lead has the
                        same email address.');
                } else {
                    leadMap.put(lead.Email, lead);
                }
            }
        }
    }

    /* Using the lead map, make a single database query,
     * find all the leads in the database that have the same email address
```

```
 * as any of the leads being inserted/updated.
 */
for (Lead lead : [select Email from Lead where Email IN
    :leadMap.KeySet()]) {
        Lead newLead = leadMap.get(lead.Email);
        newLead.Email.addError('A lead with this email address already
            exists.');
    }
}
```

Web Browsers

To connect to the cloud, most likely you and your users will utilize a web browser. Which one should you use? Well, that's really up to you. Browsers tend to be mostly the same, but with some subtle functional differences. There might be cases when you cannot use anything but Microsoft's Internet Explorer, but for the most part you should be able to use any browser you want.

Internet Explorer enjoys the highest market share of browser usage—69.77 percent (according to a December 2008 study released by the web metrics firm Net Applications). You can attribute that dominance to the fact that Internet Explorer is included with Windows, the dominant operating system in the world.

But you don't have to use Internet Explorer if you don't want to. As the chart in Figure 6-1 shows, there are other options out there, just not as widely used. Mozilla's Firefox accounts for 20.78 percent, Apple's Safari represents 7.13 percent, while Google Chrome accounts for less than 1 percent of the market at .98 percent. The remaining almost 2 percent of browsers include products like Camino, Opera, and others. Of course these numbers are moving targets, but the market shares have been more or less the same over the months.

Market Share

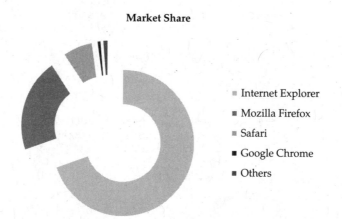

- Internet Explorer
- Mozilla Firefox
- Safari
- Google Chrome
- Others

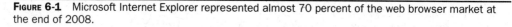

FIGURE 6-1 Microsoft Internet Explorer represented almost 70 percent of the web browser market at the end of 2008.

In this section we'll talk about the top browsers in the market: Internet Explorer, Firefox, and Safari. Although it only accounts for less than 1 percent of the market, we're also going to talk about Google Chrome, mainly because it has been developed as a cloud computing tool.

Internet Explorer

Windows Internet Explorer 8 for Windows Vista, XP, and Windows 7 is the latest version of the popular web browser.

IE 8 Features

Internet Explorer 8 delivered a new look and enhanced capabilities that made everyday tasks—such as searching, browsing multiple sites, and printing—simple and fast.

The big change in IE 8 is its rendering modes. The progressive evolution of the Web has necessitated that browsers such as Internet Explorer include multiple content-rendering modes—both supporting strict interpretation of certain web standards and also supporting behaviors designed to maintain compatibility with existing web sites. Web site designers generally have the ability to specify which mode they are designing for; in the absence of specific instructions from a web site, browsers are preset to use one of the modes by default.

Internet Explorer 8 has been designed to include three rendering modes:

- One that reflects Microsoft's implementation of current web standards
- A second reflecting Microsoft's implementation of web standards at the time of the release of Internet Explorer 7 in 2006
- A third based on rendering methods dating back to the early Web

The newest rendering mode is forward-looking and preferred by web designers, while the others are present to enable compatibility with the myriad sites across the Web that are currently optimized for previous versions of Internet Explorer.

Figure 6-2 shows an example of Internet Explorer 8.

While Internet Explorer 8 includes important end-user advancements, it was also designed with developers and IT managers in mind. Microsoft engineered Internet Explorer 8 for compatibility with existing web sites by adhering to some of the most important standards for web site development.

Internet Explorer 8 also features improved manageability for enterprises through the enhanced support of Active Directory Group Policy, which enables IT managers to easily deploy and centrally manage the browser on each of the desktops in their network.

Firefox

In June 2008 Mozilla released Firefox 3, a major update to its popular, free, open-source web browser. Firefox 3 is the culmination of three years of efforts from thousands of developers, security experts, localization and support communities, and testers from around the globe.

Available in approximately 50 languages, Firefox 3 is two to three times faster than its predecessor and offers more than 15,000 improvements, including the revolutionary smart location bar, malware protection, and extensive under-the-hood work to improve the speed and performance of the browser.

FIGURE 6-2   Microsoft's Internet Explorer 8 is the most current version of the popular web browser.

"We're really proud of Firefox 3 and it just shows what a committed, energized global community can do when they work together," said John Lilly, CEO of Mozilla.

User Experience

The enhancements to Firefox 3 include the new Firefox 3 smart location bar, affectionately known as the "Awesome Bar." It learns as people use it, adapting to user preferences and offering better-fitting matches over time.

The Firefox 3 Library archives browsing history, bookmarks, and tags, where they can be easily searched and organized. One-click bookmarking and tagging make it easy to remember, search, and organize web sites. The new full-page zoom displays any part of a web page, up close and readable, in seconds. Figure 6-3 shows a sample Firefox 3 screen.

FIGURE 6-3 Firefox 3 was released in August 2008, and runs two to three times faster than its predecessor.

Firefox Performance

Firefox 3 is built on top of the Gecko 1.9 platform, resulting in a safer, easier-to-use, and more personal product. Firefox 3 uses less memory while it's running than previous releases, and its redesigned page rendering and layout engine means that users see web pages two to three times faster than with Firefox 2.

Security

Firefox 3 raises the bar for security. The new malware and phishing protection helps protect from viruses, worms, trojans, and spyware to keep people safe on the Web. Firefox 3's one-click site ID information allows users to verify that a site is what it claims to be. Mozilla's open-source process leverages the experience of thousands of security experts around the globe.

Customization

Firefox 3 lets users customize their browser with more than 5,000 add-ons. Firefox add-ons allow users to manage tasks like participating in online auctions, uploading digital photos, seeing the weather forecasts, and listening to music, all from the convenience of the browser. The new Add-ons Manager helps users to find and install add-ons directly from the browser.

For more information about Mozilla Firefox 3 and how it delivers an easier, faster, and safer online experience, visit http://www.mozilla.com/firefox/features.

Mozilla Firefox 3 is available now for Windows, Linux, and Mac OS X operating systems as a free download from http://www.getfirefox.com.

NOTE *The release of Firefox 3 kicked off Download Day, the Mozilla community's grassroots campaign to set a brand new Guinness World Record for the greatest number of software downloads in 24 hours. From 18:16 UTC on June 17, 2008 to 18:16 UTC on June 18, 2008, 8,002,530 copies of Firefox 3 were downloaded.*

Safari

Apple claims that Safari 3.1 is the world's fastest web browser for Mac and Windows PCs, loading web pages 1.9 times faster than Internet Explorer 7 and 1.7 times faster than Firefox 2.

Safari also runs JavaScript up to six times faster than other browsers, and is the first browser to support the latest innovative web standards needed to deliver the next generation of highly interactive Web 2.0 experiences. Safari 3.1 is available as a free download at www.apple.com/safari for both Mac OS X and Windows.

Safari is shown in Figure 6-4.

"Safari 3.1 for Mac and Windows is blazingly fast, easy to use and features an elegant user interface," said Philip Schiller, Apple's senior vice president of Worldwide Product Marketing. "And best of all, Safari supports the latest audio, video and animation standards for an industry-leading Web 2.0 experience."

Safari Performance

Safari features an intuitive browsing experience with drag-and-drop bookmarks, easy-to-organize tabs, an integrated Find capability that shows the number of matches in a page, and a built-in RSS reader to quickly scan the latest news and information.

Safari 3.1 is the first browser to support the new video and audio tags in HTML 5 and the first to support CSS Animations. Safari also supports CSS Web Fonts, giving designers limitless choices of fonts to create stunning new web sites.

System Requirements

Safari 3.1 for Mac OS X requires Mac OS X Leopard or Mac OS X Tiger version 10.4.11 and a minimum of 256MB of memory and is designed to run on any Intel-based Mac or a Mac with a PowerPC G5, G4, or G3 processor and built-in FireWire.

Safari 3.1 for Windows requires Windows XP or Windows Vista, a minimum of 256MB of memory, and a system with at least a 500MHz Intel Pentium processor.

Chrome

Chrome is Google's foray into the open-source browser market. In the early days of the Internet, web pages were frequently little more than text. But today the Web has evolved into a powerful platform that enables users to collaborate with friends and colleagues through email and other web applications, edit documents, watch videos, listen to music, manage finances, and much more. Google Chrome was built for today's Web and for the applications of tomorrow.

FIGURE 6-4 Safari is the number three most popular web browser and is available for both Mac and PC platforms.

"We think of the browser as the window to the web—it's a tool for users to interact with the web sites and applications they care about, and it's important that we don't get in the way of that experience," said Sundar Pichai, vice president of product management, Google Inc. "Just like the classic Google homepage, Google Chrome has a simple user interface with a sophisticated core to enable the modern web."

A screen of Chrome's open-source sibling, Chromium, is shown in Figure 6-5.

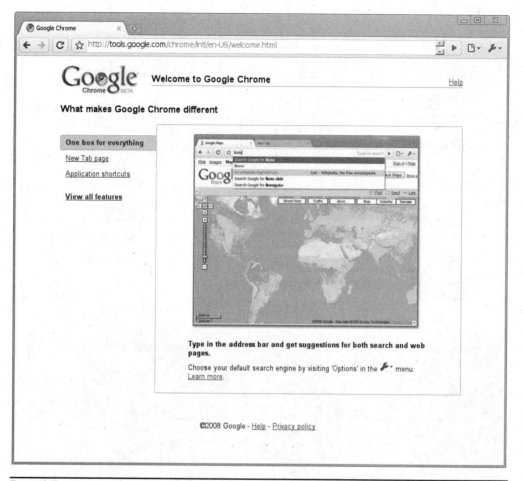

Figure 6-5   Chromium is an open-source derivation of the Google Chrome web browser.

Chrome Features

Google Chrome was designed to make it easy for users to search and navigate the Web for the content they're looking for. Features include

- A combined search and address bar quickly takes users where they want to go.

- When users open a new tab in Google Chrome, they'll see a page that includes snapshots of their most-visited sites, recent searches, and bookmarks, making it easier to navigate the Web.

- Each browser tab operates as a separate process; by isolating tabs, if one tab crashes or misbehaves, others remain stable and responsive, and users can continue working without having to restart Google Chrome.

Google also built a new JavaScript engine, V8, which not only speeds up today's web applications, but enables a whole new class of web applications that couldn't exist on today's browsers.

Open Source

"While we see this as a fundamental shift in the way people think about browsers, we realize that we couldn't have created Google Chrome on our own," said Linus Upson, director of engineering, Google Inc. "Google Chrome was built upon other open source projects that are making significant contributions to browser technology and have helped to spur competition and innovation."

To further advance the openness of the Web, Google Chrome is being released as an open-source project under the name Chromium. The intent is that Google will help make future browsers better by contributing the underlying technology in Google Chrome to the market, while continuing to develop additional features.

Chrome Cloud

There's a lot of buzz around Chrome being a great tool for cloud computing. It extends the cloud into your organization's computer, and vice versa. This is mainly because of the power of the V8 JavaScript engine and built-in Google Gear.

Google Gears are also open source, and they enable powerful web applications by adding new features to the web browser. Major API components to Gears include

- A database module that can store data locally
- A WorkerPool module that provides parallel execution of JavaScript code
- A LocalServer module that caches and serves application resources (like HTML, JavaScript, images, and so on)
- A Desktop module that lets web applications interact more naturally with the desktop
- A Geolocation module that lets web applications detect the geographical location of their users

It is believed that Chrome will allow desktop and web applications to merge, putting everything into the cloud so that you won't even have to think about both terms. Chrome is an application virtual machine for both on and offline web applications.

Google Chrome can be downloaded at www.google.com/chrome. Google Chrome for Mac and Linux users is still in the works. For more information on the open-source project, Chromium, visit www.chromium.org.

There are a number of ways to connect to the cloud. The way you opt to do so will depend on a number of factors including your or your programmers' skills, which computing platform you use, and what your vendor offers.

In the next chapter we'll take a closer look at cloud storage, what you can do, and how you can get started.

7

CHAPTER

Cloud Storage

Cloud storage involves exactly what the name suggests—storing your data with a cloud service provider rather than on a local system. As with other cloud services, you access the data stored on the cloud via an Internet link.

NOTE *Even though data is stored and accessed remotely, you can maintain data both locally and on the cloud as a measure of safety and redundancy. We'll talk about that more later.*

In this chapter we'll talk more about the specifics of cloud storage, what it's used for, when you don't want to use it, and some security issues. We'll also highlight some popular cloud vendors and discuss what they offer.

Overview

Cloud storage has a number of advantages over traditional data storage. If you store your data on a cloud, you can get at it from any location that has Internet access. This makes it especially appealing to road warriors. Workers don't need to use the same computer to access data nor do they have to carry around physical storage devices. Also, if your organization has branch offices, they can all access the data from the cloud provider.

The Basics

There are hundreds of different cloud storage systems, and some are very specific in what they do. Some are niche-oriented and store just email or digital pictures, while others store any type of data. Some providers are small, while others are huge and fill an entire warehouse.

NOTE *One of Google's datacenters in Oregon is the size of a football field and houses thousands of servers.*

At the most rudimentary level, a cloud storage system just needs one data server connected to the Internet. A subscriber copies files to the server over the Internet, which then records the data. When a client wants to retrieve the data, he or she accesses the data server with a web-based interface, and the server then either sends the files back to the client or allows the client to access and manipulate the data itself.

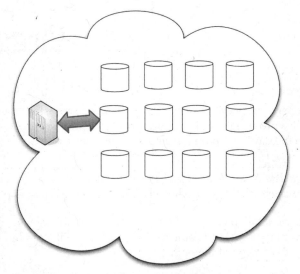

A cloud service provider can simply add more commodity
hard drives to increase the organization's capacity.

More typically, however, cloud storage systems utilize dozens or hundreds of data servers. Because servers require maintenance or repair, it is necessary to store the saved data on multiple machines, providing redundancy. Without that redundancy, cloud storage systems couldn't assure clients that they could access their information at any given time. Most systems store the same data on servers using different power supplies. That way, clients can still access their data even if a power supply fails.

Many clients use cloud storage not because they've run out of room locally, but for safety. If something happens to their building, then they haven't lost all their data.

Storage as a Service

The term Storage as a Service (another Software as a Service, or SaaS, acronym) means that a third-party provider rents space on their storage to end users who lack the budget or capital budget to pay for it on their own. It is also ideal when technical personnel are not available or have inadequate knowledge to implement and maintain that storage infrastructure.

Storage service providers are nothing new, but given the complexity of current backup, replication, and disaster recovery needs, the service has become popular, especially among small and medium-sized businesses.

The biggest advantage to SaaS is cost savings. Storage is rented from the provider using a cost-per-gigabyte-stored or cost-per-data-transferred model. The end user doesn't have to pay for infrastructure; they simply pay for how much they transfer and save on the provider's servers.

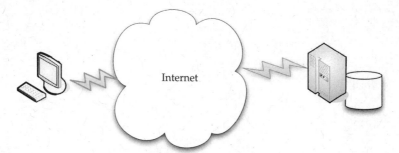

Clients rent storage capacity from cloud storage vendors.

A customer uses client software to specify the backup set and then transfers data across a WAN. When data loss occurs, the customer can retrieve the lost data from the service provider.

NOTE *In some cases, the provider can copy the data onto DVDs and ship them to the client.*

Providers

As we noted earlier, there are hundreds of cloud storage providers on the Web, and more seem to be added each day. Not only are there general-purpose storage providers, but there are some that are very specialized in what they store. We'll look more closely at some big players later, but here are some examples of specialized cloud providers:

- Google Docs (shown in Figure 7-1) allows users to upload documents, spreadsheets, and presentations to Google's data servers. Those files can then be edited using a Google application.

- Web email providers like Gmail, Hotmail, and Yahoo! Mail store email messages on their own servers. Users can access their email from computers and other devices connected to the Internet.

- Flickr and Picasa host millions of digital photographs. Users can create their own online photo albums.

- YouTube hosts millions of user-uploaded video files.

- Hostmonster and GoDaddy store files and data for many client web sites.

- Facebook and MySpace are social networking sites and allow members to post pictures and other content. That content is stored on the company's servers.

- MediaMax and Strongspace offer storage space for any kind of digital data.

Many of these services are provided for free, but others charge you per stored gigabyte and by how much information is transferred to and from the cloud. As more and more providers offer their services, prices have tended to drop, and some companies offer a certain amount for free.

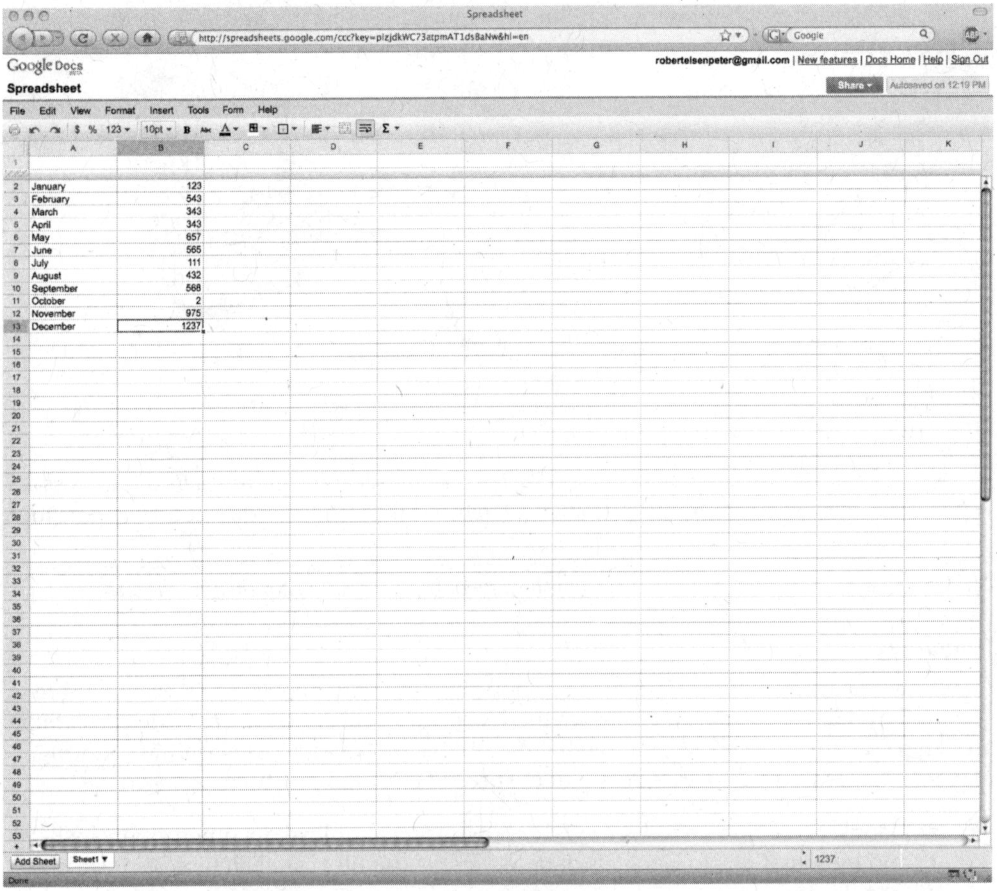

Figure 7-1 Google Docs provides an online suite of office applications, allowing you to store your documents on Google's cloud.

Security

To secure data, most systems use a combination of techniques:

- **Encryption** A complex algorithm is used to encode information. To decode the encrypted files, a user needs the encryption key. While it's possible to crack encrypted information, it's very difficult and most hackers don't have access to the amount of computer processing power they would need to crack the code.

- **Authentication processes** This requires a user to create a name and password.

- **Authorization practices** The client lists the people who are authorized to access information stored on the cloud system. Many corporations have multiple levels of authorization. For example, a front-line employee might have limited access to data stored on the cloud and the head of the IT department might have complete and free access to everything.

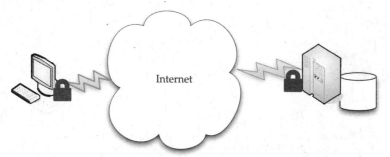

Encryption and authentication are two security measures
you can use to keep your data safe on a cloud storage provider.

But even with these measures in place, there are still concerns that data stored on a remote system is vulnerable. There is always the concern that a hacker will find a way into the secure system and access the data.

Also, a disgruntled employee could alter or destroy the data using his or her own access credentials.

Reliability

The other concern is reliability. If a cloud storage system is unreliable, it becomes a liability. No one wants to save data on an unstable system, nor would they trust a company that is financially unstable.

Most cloud storage providers try to address the reliability concern through redundancy, but the possibility still exists that the system could crash and leave clients with no way to access their saved data.

Reputation is important to cloud storage providers. If there is a perception that the provider is unreliable, they won't have many clients. And if they are unreliable, they won't be around long, as there are so many players in the market.

Advantages

Cloud storage is becoming an increasingly attractive solution for organizations. That's because with cloud storage, data resides on the Web, located across storage systems rather than at a designated corporate hosting site. Cloud storage providers balance server loads and move data among various datacenters, ensuring that information is stored close—and thereby available quickly—to where it is used.

Storing data on the cloud is advantageous, because it allows you to protect your data in case there's a disaster. You may have backup files of your critical information, but if there is a fire or a hurricane wipes out your organization, having the backups stored locally doesn't help.

Having your data stored off-site can be the difference between closing your door for good or being down for a few days or weeks.

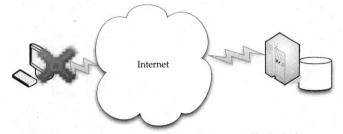

If there is a catastrophe at your organization, having your files backed up
at a cloud storage provider means you won't have lost all your data.

Which storage vendor to go with can be a complex issue, and how your technology interacts with the cloud can be complex. For instance, some products are agent-based, and the application automatically transfers information to the cloud via FTP. But others employ a web front end, and the user has to select local files on their computer to transmit.

Amazon S3 is the best-known storage solution, but other vendors might be better for large enterprises. For instance, those who offer service level agreements and direct access to customer support are critical for a business moving storage to a service provider.

Cautions

A mixed approach might be the best way to embrace the cloud, since cloud storage is still immature. That is, don't commit everything to the cloud, but use it for a few, noncritical purposes.

Large enterprises might have difficulty with vendors like Google or Amazon, because they are forced to rewrite solutions for their applications and there is a lack of portability. A vendor like 3tera, however, supports applications developed in LAMP, Solaris, Java, or Windows.NET.

The biggest deal-breakers when it comes to cloud storage seem to be price and reliability. This is where you have to vet your vendor to ensure you're getting a good deal with quality service. One mistake on your vendor's part could mean irretrievable data.

A lot of companies take the "appetizer" approach, testing one or two services to see how well they mesh with their existing IT systems. It's important to make sure the services will provide what you need before you commit too much to the cloud.

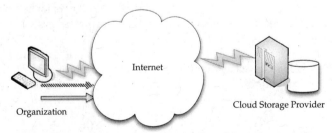

Many companies test out a cloud storage vendor with
one or two services before committing too much to them.
This "appetizer" approach ensures the provider can give you what you want.

Legal issues are also important. For instance, if you have copyrighted material—like music or video—that you want to maintain on the cloud, such an option might not be possible for licensing reasons.

Also, keep in mind the accountability of your storage provider. Vendors offer different assurances with the maintenance of data. They may offer the service, but make sure you know exactly what your vendor will or will not do in case of data loss or compromise.

The best solution is to have multiple redundant systems: local and offsite backup; sync and archive.

Outages

Further, organizations have to be cognizant of the inherent danger of storing their data on the Internet. Amazon S3, for example, dealt with a massive outage in February 2008. The result was numerous client applications going offline. Amazon reports that they have responded to the problem, adding capacity to the authentication system blamed for the problem. They also note that no data was lost, because they store multiple copies of every object in several locations.

The point remains, however, that clients were not able to access their data as they had intended, and so you need to use caution when deciding to pursue a cloud option.

Theft

You should also keep in mind that your data could be stolen or viewed by those who are not authorized to see it. Whenever your data is let out of your own datacenter, you risk trouble from a security point of view.

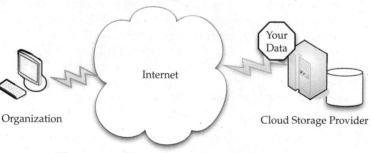

Whenever you let your data out of your organization,
you give up a measure of security.

Also, because storage providers put everything into one pot, so to speak, your company's data could be stored next to a competitor's, and the risk of your competition seeing your proprietary information is real.

If you do store your data on the cloud, make sure you're encrypting data and securing data transit with technologies like SSL.

Is Cloud Storage for Me?

As with so many of the cloud technologies we've discussed, figuring out whether your organization is cloud storage–friendly or not really comes down to your organization and what you want to do on the cloud.

For instance, if you are sending data using SSL (and you should), do you trust your programmers? The simple mistake of not including "s" in HTTPS transfers can put your files at risk.

You should also think about how much latency you are willing to tolerate. If you want to stream video from your cloud store, you might be out of luck if you face latency problems.

Cloud Storage Providers

In this section we're going to talk about some of the cloud providers out there. This list is not meant to be comprehensive—there's no way it could be. There are hundreds of them and new players every day. This is simply a listing of what some of the big players in the game have to offer, and you can use it as a starting guide to determine if their services match your needs.

Amazon and Nirvanix are the current industry top dogs, but many others are in the field, including some well-known names. Google is ready to launch its own cloud storage solution called GDrive. EMC is readying a storage solution, and IBM already has a number of cloud storage options called Blue Cloud.

Amazon Simple Storage Service (S3)

The best-known cloud storage service is Amazon's Simple Storage Service (S3), which launched in 2006. Amazon S3 is designed to make web-scale computing easier for developers. Amazon S3 provides a simple web services interface that can be used to store and retrieve any amount of data, at any time, from anywhere on the Web. It gives any developer access to the same highly scalable data storage infrastructure that Amazon uses to run its own global network of web sites. The service aims to maximize benefits of scale and to pass those benefits on to developers.

Amazon S3 is intentionally built with a minimal feature set that includes the following functionality:

- Write, read, and delete objects containing from 1 byte to 5 gigabytes of data each. The number of objects that can be stored is unlimited.
- Each object is stored and retrieved via a unique developer-assigned key.
- Objects can be made private or public, and rights can be assigned to specific users.
- Uses standards-based REST and SOAP interfaces designed to work with any Internet-development toolkit.

Design Requirements

Amazon built S3 to fulfill the following design requirements:

- **Scalable**   Amazon S3 can scale in terms of storage, request rate, and users to support an unlimited number of web-scale applications.

- **Reliable**   Store data durably, with 99.99 percent availability. Amazon says it does not allow any downtime.

- **Fast**   Amazon S3 was designed to be fast enough to support high-performance applications. Server-side latency must be insignificant relative to Internet latency. Any performance bottlenecks can be fixed by simply adding nodes to the system.

- **Inexpensive**   Amazon S3 is built from inexpensive commodity hardware components. As a result, frequent node failure is the norm and must not affect the overall system. It must be hardware-agnostic, so that savings can be captured as Amazon continues to drive down infrastructure costs.

- **Simple**   Building highly scalable, reliable, fast, and inexpensive storage is difficult. Doing so in a way that makes it easy to use for any application anywhere is more difficult. Amazon S3 must do both.

A forcing function for the design was that a single Amazon S3 distributed system must support the needs of both internal Amazon applications and external developers of any application. This means that it must be fast and reliable enough to run Amazon.com's web sites, while flexible enough that any developer can use it for any data storage need.

Design Principles
Amazon used the following principles of distributed system design to meet Amazon S3 requirements:

- **Decentralization**   It uses fully decentralized techniques to remove scaling bottlenecks and single points of failure.

- **Autonomy**   The system is designed such that individual components can make decisions based on local information.

- **Local responsibility**   Each individual component is responsible for achieving its consistency; this is never the burden of its peers.

- **Controlled concurrency**   Operations are designed such that no or limited concurrency control is required.

- **Failure toleration**   The system considers the failure of components to be a normal mode of operation and continues operation with no or minimal interruption.

- **Controlled parallelism**   Abstractions used in the system are of such granularity that parallelism can be used to improve performance and robustness of recovery or the introduction of new nodes.

- **Small, well-understood building blocks**   Do not try to provide a single service that does everything for everyone, but instead build small components that can be used as building blocks for other services.

- **Symmetry**   Nodes in the system are identical in terms of functionality, and require no or minimal node-specific configuration to function.

- **Simplicity**   The system should be made as simple as possible, but no simpler.

How S3 Works

Amazon keeps its lips pretty tight about how S3 works, but according to Amazon, S3's design aims to provide scalability, high availability, and low latency at commodity costs.

S3 stores arbitrary objects at up to 5GB in size, and each is accompanied by up to 2KB of metadata. Objects are organized by *buckets*. Each bucket is owned by an AWS account and the buckets are identified by a unique, user-assigned key.

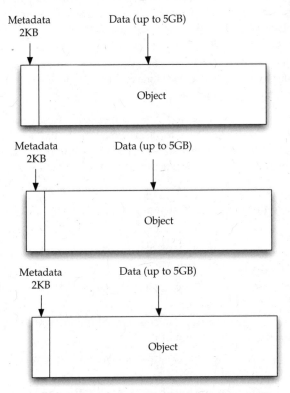

Multiple objects are stored in buckets in Amazon S3.

Buckets and objects are created, listed, and retrieved using either a REST-style or SOAP interface. Objects can also be retrieved using the HTTP GET interface or via BitTorrent. An access control list restricts who can access the data in each bucket.

Bucket names and keys are formulated so that they can be accessed using HTTP.

Requests are authorized using an access control list associated with each bucket and object, for instance:

```
http://s3.amazonaws.com/examplebucket/examplekey
http://examplebucket.s3.amazonaws.com/examplekey
```

The Amazon AWS Authentication tools allow the bucket owner to create an authenticated URL with a set amount of time that the URL will be valid. For instance, you could create a link to your data on the cloud, give that link to someone else, and they could access your data for an amount of time you predetermine, be it 10 minutes or 10 hours.

Bucket items can also be accessed via a BitTorrent feed, enabling S3 to act as a seed for the client. Buckets can also be set up to save HTTP log information to another bucket. This information can be used for later data mining.

"Amazon S3 is based on the idea that quality Internet-based storage should be taken for granted," said Andy Jassy, vice president of Amazon Web Services. "It helps free developers from worrying about where they are going to store data, whether it will be safe and secure, if it will be available when they need it, the costs associated with server maintenance, or whether they have enough storage available. Amazon S3 enables developers to focus on innovating with data, rather than figuring out how to store it."

S3 lets developers pay only for what they consume, and there is no minimum fee. Developers pay just $0.15 per gigabyte of storage per month and $0.20 per gigabyte of data transferred. This might not seem like a lot of money but storing 1TB would be $1800 per year alone, whereas an internal 1TB drive these days costs about $100 to own outright. So it's really not so much about the cost of storage as it is about the total cost to serve. What are your internal costs to serve 1TB of data to your users?

Early S3 Applications

The science team at the University of California Berkeley responsible for NASA's "Stardust@Home" project (http://stardustathome.ssl.berkeley.edu/) is using Amazon S3 to store and deliver the 60 million images that represent the data collected from their dust particle aerogel experiment. These images will be delivered to 100,000 volunteers around the world who scan the images looking for dust particles from comet Wild2.

"We quickly ran into challenges when we started the project using our own infrastructure," said Andrew Westphal, project director of Stardust@Home. "Using Amazon S3 has allowed us to proceed without having to worry about building out the massive storage infrastructure we realized that we needed to successfully complete the project. The fact that Amazon S3 is an Internet-connected storage service is particularly useful to us as we expect the data examination phase of the project to take only a few months. We can quickly ramp up and back down again without a huge investment."

Nirvanix

Nirvanix uses custom-developed software and file system technologies running on Intel storage servers at six locations on both coasts of the United States. They continue to grow, and expect to add dozens more server locations.

SDN Features

Nirvanix Storage Delivery Network (SDN) turns a standard 1U server into an infinite-capacity network attached storage (NAS) file accessible by popular applications and immediately integrates into an organization's existing archive and backup processes.

"Up until recently, cloud storage has primarily served as an on-tap back end for application developers," said Adam Couture, principal analyst at Gartner. "Today, we're starting to see enterprises begin to consider cloud storage as a low-cost storage tier for selective applications such as backup and archiving."

Nirvanix has built a global cluster of storage nodes collectively referred to as the Storage Delivery Network (SDN), powered by the Nirvanix Internet Media File System (IMFS). The SDN intelligently stores, delivers, and processes storage requests in the best network location, providing the best user experience in the marketplace. With the ability to store multiple file copies in multiple geographic nodes, the SDN enables unparalleled data availability for developers, businesses, and enterprises.

The Nirvanix CloudNAS for Linux mounts the Nirvanix Storage Delivery Network as a virtual drive that can be accessed via NFS, CIFS, or FTP. After installation, storage administrators can apply standard file, directory, or access permissions, and users on the network can then access the Nirvanix-mapped drive from their existing applications or storage processes. Additionally, storage administrators get access to the robust Nirvanix SDN functionality such as automated policy-based file replication, single global namespace that scales to petabytes, and storage of secure, encrypted data on one or more of Nirvanix's globally clustered storage nodes.

Benefits of CloudNAS

The benefits of cloud network attached storage (CloudNAS) include

- Cost savings of 80–90 percent over managing traditional storage solutions
- Elimination of large capital expenditures while enabling 100 percent storage utilization
- Encrypted offsite storage that integrates into existing archive and backup processes
- Built-in data disaster recovery and automated data replication on up to three geographically dispersed storage nodes for a 100 percent SLA
- Immediate availability to data in seconds, versus hours or days on offline tape

Nirvanix CloudNAS is aimed at companies that maintain repositories of archival, backup, or unstructured data that requires long-term, secure storage, or organizations that use automated processes to transfer files to mapped drives. Example use cases include long-term archiving of data leveraging an established backup/archival solution; departments using a centralized, shared data repository; disk-to-disk-to-cloud replacing tape for archival of data; and simple backup of all computers within a department.

Availability and Pricing

CloudNAS is free to use for companies who have a 2TB or greater contract with Nirvanix and optional 24/7 support is offered at $200 per month per server. Companies who don't have a Nirvanix account can take part in "Experience Nirvanix Now." The trial allows you to have unlimited use of any of Nirvanix's tools including CloudNAS and up to 50GB for 15 days, risk free.

For more information on CloudNAS, visit www.nirvanix.com/ExperienceNirvanix.aspx.

Google Bigtable Datastore

In cloud computing, it's important to have a database that is capable of handling numerous users on an on-demand basis. To serve that market, Google introduced its Bigtable. Google started working on it in 2004 and finally went public with it in April 2008.

Bigtable was developed with very high speed, flexibility, and extremely high scalability in mind. A Bigtable database can be petabytes in size and span thousands of distributed servers.

Bigtable is available to developers as part of the Google App Engine, their cloud computing platform.

How Bigtable Works

Bigtable is a complex offering that is not easy to understand. If you have trouble sleeping, they offer a very technical explanation at http://labs.google.com/papers/bigtable-osdi06.pdf. But in a nutshell, here's how it works.

NOTE *Developers who want to understand the technical details of Bigtable are encouraged to read the white paper so they can get the most out of it.*

Google describes Bigtable as a fast and extremely scalable DBMS. This allows Bigtable to scale across thousands of commodity servers that can collectively store petabytes of data.

Each table in Bigtable is a multidimensional sparse map. That is, the table is made up of rows and columns, and each cell has a timestamp. Multiple versions of a cell can exist, each with a different timestamp. With this stamping, you can select certain versions of a web page, or delete cells that are older than a given date and time.

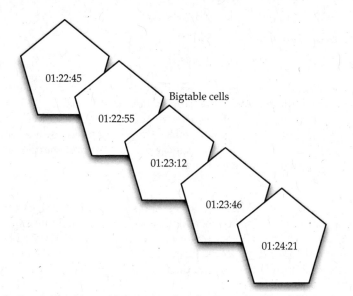

In Google Bigtable, multiple copies of a cell exist, each with a different timestamp.

Because the tables are so large, Bigtable splits them at row boundaries and saves them as tablets. Each tablet is about 200MB, and each server houses 100 tablets. Given this, data from a database is likely to be stored in many different servers—maybe not even in the same geographic location.

This architecture also allows for load balancing. If one table is getting a lot of queries, it can remove other tablets or move the busy table to another machine that is not as busy. Also, if a machine fails, since the tablet is spread to different machines, users may not even notice the outage.

When a machine fills up, it compresses some tablets using a Google-proprietary technique. On a minor scale, only a few tablets are compressed. On a large scale, entire tablets are compressed, freeing more drive space.

Bigtable tablet locations are stored in cells, and looking them up is a three-tiered system. Clients point to the META0 table. META0 then keeps track of many tables on META1 that contain the locations of the tablets. Both META0 and META1 make use of prefetching and caching to minimize system bottlenecks.

Issues

While Bigtable is a robust tool, developers have been cautious about using it. Because it is a proprietary system, they get locked into Google. That is also the case with Amazon's Web Services and other cloud providers.

On the other hand, Google App Engine and Bigtable are affordable, costing about the same as Amazon's S3.

Costs are as follows:

- $0.10–$0.12 per CPU core-hour
- $0.15–$0.18 per GB-month of storage
- $0.11–$0.13 per GB of outgoing bandwidth
- $0.09–$0.11 per GB of incoming bandwidth

MobileMe

MobileMe is Apple's solution that delivers push email, push contacts, and push calendars from the MobileMe service in the cloud to native applications on iPhone, iPod touch, Macs, and PCs. MobileMe also provides a suite of ad-free web applications that deliver a desktop-like experience through any modern browser. MobileMe applications (www.me.com) include Mail, Contacts, and Calendar, as well as Gallery for viewing and sharing photos and iDisk for storing and exchanging documents online.

MobileMe Features

With a MobileMe email account, all folders, messages, and status indicators look identical whether checking email on iPhone, iPod touch, a Mac, or a PC. New email messages are pushed instantly to iPhone over the cellular network or Wi-Fi, removing the need to manually check email and wait for downloads. Push also keeps contacts and calendars continuously up to date so changes made on one device are automatically pushed up to the cloud and down to other devices.

Push works with the native applications on iPhone and iPod touch, Microsoft Outlook for the PC, and Mac OS X applications, Mail, Address Book, and iCal, as well as the MobileMe web application suite.

MobileMe web applications provide a desktop-like experience that allows users to drag and drop, click and drag, and even use keyboard shortcuts. MobileMe provides anywhere access to Mail, Contacts, and Calendar, with a unified interface that allows users to switch between applications with a single click, and Gallery makes it easy to share photos on the Web in stunning quality. Gallery users can upload, rearrange, rotate, and title photos from any browser; post photos directly from an iPhone; allow visitors to download print-quality images; and contribute photos to an album. MobileMe iDisk lets users store and manage files online with drag-and-drop filing and makes it easy to share documents too large to email by automatically sending an email with a link for downloading the file. MobileMe includes 20GB of online storage that can be used for email, contacts, calendar, photos, movies, and documents.

Pricing and Requirements

MobileMe is a subscription-based service with 20GB of storage for US$99 per year for individuals and US$149 for a Family Pack, which includes one master account with 20GB of storage and four Family Member accounts with 5GB of storage each. A free, 60-day MobileMe trial at www.apple.com/mobileme and current Mac members will be automatically upgraded to MobileMe accounts. MobileMe subscribers can purchase an additional 20GB of storage for US$49 or 40GB of storage for US$99 annually.

Using an iPhone or iPod touch with MobileMe requires iPhone 2.0 software and iTunes 7.7 or later. For use with a Mac, MobileMe requires Mac OS X Tiger 10.4.11 or the latest version of Mac OS X Leopard. For a PC, MobileMe requires Windows Vista or Windows XP Home or Professional (SP2), and Microsoft Outlook 2003 or later is recommended. MobileMe is accessible on the Web via Safari 3, Internet Explorer 7, and Firefox 2 or later.

Live Mesh

Live Mesh is Microsoft's "software-plus-services" platform and experience that enables PCs and other devices to be aware of each other through the Internet, enabling individuals and organizations to manage, access, and share their files and applications seamlessly on the Web and across their world of devices. Live Mesh has the following components:

- A platform that defines and models a user's digital relationships among devices, data, applications, and people—made available to developers through an open data model and protocols.

- A cloud service providing an implementation of the platform hosted in Microsoft datacenters.

- Software, a client implementation of the platform that enables local applications to run offline and interact seamlessly with the cloud.

- A platform experience that exposes the key benefits of the platform for bringing together a user's devices, files and applications, and social graph, with news feeds across all of these.

Microsoft promises an open data model, and developers will be able to help Live Mesh grow through the development of additional applications and services.

Of similar importance are Microsoft's plans to make Live Mesh compatible with various systems.

The Live Mesh software, called Mesh Operating Environment (MOE), is available for

- Windows XP
- Windows Vista
- Windows Mobile
- Mac OS X

The software is used to create and manage the synchronization relationships between devices and data. Live Mesh also incorporates a cloud component, called Live Desktop. This is an online storage service that allows synchronized folders to be accessible via a web site.

It also includes remote desktop software called Live Mesh Remote Desktop, which can be used to remotely connect and manage any of the devices in the synchronization relationship. Live Mesh Remote Desktop allows you to control your devices from the Live Mesh application, as well as from any other PC connected to the Internet.

Live Framework
For developers, there is a development component consisting of a protocol and APIs known as Live Framework.

NOTE *Live Framework was formerly known as MeshFX.*

Live Framework is a REST-based API for accessing the Live Mesh services over HTTP. Live Framework differs from MOE in that MOE simply lets folders be shared. The Live Framework APIs can be used to share any data item between devices that recognize the data.

The API encapsulates the data into a Mesh Object, which is the synchronization unit of Live Mesh. It is then tracked for changes and synchronization.

A Mesh Object consists of data feeds, which can be represented in Atom, RSS, JSON, or XML.

The MOE software also creates Mesh Objects for each Live Mesh folder so they can be synchronized.

Like cloud computing itself, cloud storage takes its fair share of knocks for being used as a trendy term. If the term is used too often, it could wind up referring to any type of Internet-accessible storage. Organizations should think of cloud computing as scalable IT capabilities that are delivered to external customers using the Web.

Standards are one of the things that make the IT world go around. And with cloud computing, there are a number of standards that ensures everyone works and plays together nicely. We'll take a closer look at those standards in the next chapter.

8

CHAPTER

Standards

Standards make the World Wide Web go around, and by extension, they are important to cloud computing. Standards are what make it possible to connect to the cloud and what make it possible to develop and deliver content.

In this chapter we'll look at the prevalent standards that make cloud computing possible, and also the sorts of standards that are used to develop applications on the cloud.

Application

A cloud application is the software architecture that the cloud uses to eliminate the need to install and run on the client computer. There are many applications that can run, but there needs to be a standard way to connect between the client and the cloud. In this section we'll take a closer look at the protocols that are used to manage connections between both parties.

Communication

Computers need a common way to speak with one another. Think of it like talking on the telephone to someone who doesn't speak English and you don't speak their language. There's no way to achieve a common understanding. You may be able to guess a word here or there, but for the most part, the conversation won't work. Computers can't even guess a common word, so without a language in common, that communication won't happen.

HTTP

To get a web page from your cloud provider, you'll likely be using the Hypertext Transfer Protocol (HTTP) as the computing mechanism to transfer data between the cloud and your organization.

HTTP is a stateless protocol. This is beneficial because hosts do not need to retain information about users between requests, but this forces web developers to use alternative methods for maintaining users' states. For example, when a host needs to customize the content of a web site for a user, the web application must be written to track the user's progress from page to page. The most common method for solving this problem is sending and receiving cookies.

HTTP is the language that the cloud and your computers use to communicate. This language isn't hard to understand, and you've probably seen it before. Say your browser wants to get a given web page. The browser initiates it by "saying"

```
GET/HTTP/1.0
Host: www.velte.com
```

The server responds with

```
HTTP/1.0 200 OK
Content-Type: text/html
<head>
<title>Thank you for visiting Velte Publishing. </title>
```

{The rest of the Velte Publishing web page appears here}

```
</body>
```

Let's break down this very simple example and understand what each line is telling us.

The first line of the browser's request, GET/HTTP/1.0, tells us that the browser wants to see the site's home page and that it is using version 1.0 of HTTP. The second line, Host: www.velte.com, says which web site the browser wants to see.

NOTE *It's necessary to add the web site name because many web sites share the same IP address on the Internet and are hosted by a single server. The Host: line was added a few years after HTTP was initially released, to allow for this behavior.*

The first line of the server's reply, HTTP/1.0 200 OK, is the server letting the browser know that it also speaks HTTP 1.0 and that the request was successful. If the page did not exist, the response would have been HTTP/1.0 404 Not Found. The second line in the server's response, Content-Type: text/html, lets that browser know that it is about to receive the web page. This is how the browser can understand what to do with the data that it's about to receive. If this line were Content-Type:image/jpg, then the browser would know that it would be receiving a JPG image file.

HTTP 1.1   This example used HTTP 1.0, but current browsers use 1.1. The request and response would include a bit more information, but the differences are not distinct enough to go into. The example we just used is perfectly valid and would still return the proper results.

The primary difference between the two is that originally, web browsers made separate HTTP requests like this for each page, each image, and every other component on the page. Using HTTP 1.1, a browser and server can negotiate to leave the connection open and transfer all the page's components without hanging up and opening new sessions.

Requests   HTTP defines eight methods to describe how the desired action is to be performed on the server. What this server presents—whether pre-existing data or dynamically generated data—depends on the implementation of the server. Table 8-1 lists the different requests that can be made.

HTTP is the most common way you will connect your browsers with the cloud. A protocol that is brewing is the XMPP.

Request	Description
HEAD	Asks for the response identical to the one that would correspond to a GET request, but without the response body. This is good for retrieving metainformation in the response headers, but without transporting the entire content.
GET	Requests information from a server.
POST	Submits data to be processed to the server. The data is included in the body of the request. The result of the request might be the creation of the resource or updating the existing resource.
PUT	Uploads a representation of the resource.
DELETE	Deletes the specified resource.
TRACE	Echoes the request back to the browser so that the client can see which servers are adding or changing in the request.
OPTIONS	Returns HTTP methods that the server supports for the given URL. This can be used to check the functionality of a web server.
CONNECT	Converts the request connection to a transparent TCP/IP tunnel. It's usually used to facilitate SSL-encrypted communication through an unencrypted HTTP proxy.

TABLE 8-1   The Different Requests in HTTP

XMPP

The Extensible Messaging and Presence Protocol (XMPP) is being talked about as the next big thing for cloud computing. The problem is that current cloud services—including SOAP and other HTTP-based protocols—are all one-way information exchanges. This means that clouds do not operate in real time and might have difficulties clearing a firewall. XMPP allows for two-way communication and eliminates polling.

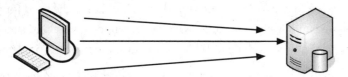

HTTP requires multiple polling events to update status from the web browser.

XMPP maintains a connection between the client and the web server.

XMPP (also known as Jabber) is a protocol that Google, Apple, AOL, IBM, and LiveJournal have all signed on with. But with so many big names already adopting XMPP, why hasn't this change been broader, and why aren't clouds, especially, using this?

The Problem with Polling   When you wanted to sync services between two servers, the most common means was to have the client ping the host at regular intervals. This is known as *polling*. This is generally how we check our email. Every so often, we ping our email server to see if we got any new messages. It's also how the APIs for most web services work.

The web site High Scalability reported in 2008 that Twitter was reporting an average of 200 to 300 connections per second, with spikes that rose as high as 800 requests per second. And at one point, during the Macworld keynote, the service went down because of so many polls.

Some companies are trying to address the polling problem with existing protocols, but it is difficult. Salesforce.com tries to do this by sending notifications back to your web service to avoid polling. That's difficult for developers, and your firewall has to be configured to allow the messages back through.

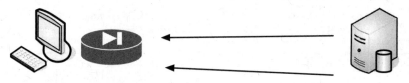

Responses to polling requests
might be blocked by your organization's firewall.

Not Ready   XMPP's biggest problem is that it's not HTTP. There's a thought that anything new needs to be based on existing web standards, and while HTTP serves well, it's not perfect, especially for cloud computing.

XMPP was developed for instant messaging and presence, and it is widely used in those circles. It includes the following features:

- XMPP allows for easy two-way communication, eliminating the need for polling.
- It is XML-based and easily extensible, which makes it ideal for cloud services.
- It is efficient and able to scale to millions of concurrent users on a single service.

XMPP will gain in prevalence, but hopefully cloud vendors will make the move sooner rather than later.

Security

Securing your cloud sessions is especially important as security is one of the top reasons businesses are reluctant to join the cloud. Securing your cloud sessions can be accomplished via encryption and authentication. The most prevalent means of web encryption comes standard on every browser. Authentication is another matter, with several options open to you.

In this section we'll talk about the widely used Secure Sockets Layer (SSL) for encryption, and one means of authentication, OpenID.

SSL

The last time you bought something from your favorite online retailer, you passed along your credit card information, probably using Secure Sockets Layer (SSL).

SSL is the standard security technology for establishing an encrypted link between a web server and browser. This ensures that data passed between the browser and the web server stays private.

To create an SSL connection on a web server requires an SSL certificate. When your cloud provider starts an SSL session, they are prompted to complete a number of questions about the identity of their company and web site. The cloud provider's computers then generate two cryptographic keys—a public key and a private key.

The public key does not need to be secret and is placed into a Certificate Signing Request (CSR). This is a file that contains your details. You then submit the CSR. During the SSL certificate application process, the certification authority will validate your details and issue an SSL certificate, containing your details, allowing you to use SSL. The cloud provider will then match your issued SSL certificate to your private key. Your web browser will be able to establish an encrypted link between your computer and the cloud provider.

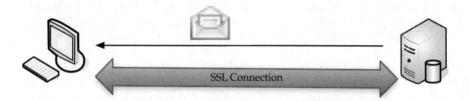

1. The browser checks the web site's certificate to ensure that the site you are connecting to is the real site and not someone else intercepting and spoofing the site.
2. The browser and web site decide on what type of encryption to use.
3. The browser and server send each other unique codes to use when encrypting information to be sent.
4. The browser and server use the encryption to start talking.
5. The browser shows the encrypting icon, and web pages are passed as secured.

This is a fairly streamlined process, and operates in the background. The only difference you are likely to see is that the page takes a little longer to load because of all the behind-the-scenes certificate passing.

Normally, the SSL certificate will contain your cloud provider's domain name, company name, address, city, state, and country. It will also contain the expiration date of the certificate and details of the certification authority responsible for issuing the certificate.

When a browser tries to connect securely to the cloud, it will retrieve the site's SSL certificate and check that it has not expired and that it is being used by the web site for which it was issued. It also checks to see if the certificate was issued by an authority that the browser trusts. If it fails any of these checks, the browser lets the user know that the site is not secured by SSL.

OpenID

We talked about OpenID back in Chapter 2. OpenID is an open-source solution for the problem of needing a unique username and password for access to different web sites, thus making your life simpler.

This allows you to choose the OpenID provider that best meets your need and that you trust. Also, OpenID can stay with you no matter which provider you move to. Best of all, OpenID is free. This is good for businesses, because it means a lower cost for password and account management.

OpenID is still in the adoption phase and is becoming more popular as big names like AOL, Microsoft, Sun, and Novell begin to accept and provide OpenIDs. OpenID is a product of the open-source community to solve problems that were not easily solvable by existing technology. OpenID is a lightweight way to authenticate users, using the same technology that is used to identify web sites. Anyone can be an OpenID user or provider for free.

The OpenID Foundation was formed to assist the open-source model and act as the technology's source of support.

PCI DSS

Payment Card Industry Data Security Standards (PCI DSS) requirement 2.2.1 is a nebulous area for many, especially as it relates to cloud computing. The requirement states that an organization can "implement only one primary function per server." But does that mean one *physical* server?

The short answer is "no." You can have multiple systems that are virtualized; you just have to ensure that they are segmented and isolated from each other.

Virtualization is an emerging technology, and technology changes everything. In the past, copyright law was written to prevent you from making copies of movies and music. At the time, no one dreamed that there would be a day when copyrighted materials could be saved on a computer or an iPod. Now the copyright laws are written in such a way that all the bases are covered, no matter what technology throws at them. Expect PCI DSS rules to be changed as well.

Client

When your clients connect to the cloud, they need to run certain software on their machines, and most often it'll be a web browser, or a similarly equipped application. Web browsers use a number of ways to store and display data, like the widely known Hypertext Markup Language (HTML). In this section we'll talk about the different means to store and display information.

HTML

Since so much of cloud computing is based on connecting via the World Wide Web, it's important to talk about the main standard to communicate data—HTML.

HTML is under constant revision to improve its usability and functionality. W3C is the organization that is charged with designing and maintaining the language. When you click on a link in a web page, you are accessing HTML code in the form of a hyperlink, which then takes you to another page.

How HTML Works

HTML is a series of short codes typed into a text file by the author or created by web page design software. These short codes are called *tags*. The text is then saved as an HTML file and viewed through a browser, like Internet Explorer or Mozilla Firefox. The browser reads the file and translates the text into the form the author wanted you to see.

Writing HTML can be done using a number of methods, with either a simple text editor or a powerful graphical editor.

Tags

Tags are what separate normal text from HTML code. You've likely seen them as the words between <angle brackets>. Tags are what allow things like tables and images to appear in a web page. Different tags perform different functions. The tags don't appear when you view the page through a browser, but they affect how the browser behaves. For instance:

```
<b>This text will appear in bold.</b> But this text won't.
```

In this example, the <b> tags were wrapped around some text, which will appear bold when viewed through an ordinary web browser.

Cascading Style Sheets in HTML

Cascading Style Sheets (CSS) are used to control how pages are presented, and make pages more accessible. Basic special effects and interaction are provided by JavaScript, which adds a lot of power to basic HTML.

Dynamic HTML

Dynamic HTML (DHTML) is not a new specification of HTML, but rather a different way of looking at and controlling the standard HTML codes and commands. When a regular HTML page loads, it will not change until another request comes to the server. DHTML gives you more control over the HTML elements, allowing them to change without returning to the web server.

There are four parts to DHTML:

- Document Object Model (DOM)
- Scripts
- Cascading Style Sheets (CSS)
- XHTML

DOM

The Document Object Model (DOM) is what allows you to access your web page and make changes with DHTML. The DOM specifies every part of a web page, and provides consistent naming conventions, allowing you to access your web pages and change their properties.

Scripts

The most common scripting languages in DHTML are JavaScript and ActiveX. Scripts are used to control the objects specified in the DOM.

Cascading Style Sheets in DHTML

CSS is used in DHTML to control the look and feel of the web page. Style sheets list the colors and fonts of text, the background colors and images, and the placement of objects on the page. Using scripting and the DOM, you can change the style of various elements.

XHTML

DHTML web pages are actually written in XHTML or HTML 4.x. DHTML is also used to build the elements for the CSS and the DOM to work on. There is nothing unique about XHTML for DHTML. But it is important to have valid XHTML, because there are more things working from it than just the browser.

DHTML Features

DHTML has four main features:

- Changing the tags and properties
- Real-time positioning
- Dynamic fonts
- Data binding

Changing the Tags and Properties   One of the most common uses of DHTML is changing the qualities of an HTML tag, depending on an event outside of the browser (such as a mouse click, a time, and so forth). You can use this to preload information onto a page, but not display it until the user clicks a specific link.

Real-Time Positioning   Real-time positioning allows objects, images, and text to move around the web page. Normally, this is used for interactive games, but it is a feature you may program into your cloud pages on the basis of organizational need.

Dynamic Fonts   Dynamic fonts are a Netscape-only feature. Netscape developed this to avoid the problem designers had with not knowing which fonts would be on a reader's system. Fonts are encoded and downloaded with the page so that the page always looks the way the designer intended.

Data Binding   Data binding is an Internet Explorer–only feature. Microsoft developed the feature to allow easier access to databases and web sites. It is similar to using CGI to access a database, but uses an ActiveX control to function.

JavaScript

Basic HTML does only basic stuff. It's when you use JavaScript to write functions that are embedded in the HTML pages and interact with the DOM that you start adding pizzazz and specific user-entered data that adds functionality to your web pages.

Here are some examples of the uses of JavaScript:

- Opening or popping up new windows, and having control of the size and attributes of the window (whether to include menus, toolbars, and so on).
- Validating web form input values to ensure that they will be accepted before submitting them to the server.
- Changing images as the cursor rolls over them.

JavaScript is a scripting language used for client-side web development. JavaScript was influenced by many languages and was designed to look like Java but be easier for non-programmers to work with. Although JavaScript is best known for its use in web sites, it is also being used to enable scripting access to objects embedded in other applications.

In spite of its name, JavaScript has very little to do with the Java programming language, although both use the common C syntax and JavaScript uses many Java names and naming conventions. To a Java programmer, JavaScript would appear to be a "lite" version of the Java programming language. The name comes from a marketing agreement between Sun and Netscape in exchange for Netscape bundling Sun's Java Runtime with the then-dominant browser.

JavaScript runs locally on a user's browser rather than on the server, so it responds quickly to user actions. Further, JavaScript code can detect user action, which HTML cannot, like sensing individual keystrokes.

The most common host environment for JavaScript is the web browser. Web browsers use the public API to create host objects, which are responsible for reflecting the DOM into JavaScript. A JavaScript web server would house the host objects representing an HTTP request and response, then a JavaScript program could manipulate the data to dynamically generate a web page.

The following is a sample JavaScript program:

```
<!DOCTYPE HTML PUBLIC "-//W3C//DTD HTML 4.01//EN"
"http://www.w3.org/TR/html4/strict.dtd">
<html>
  <head><title>simple page</title></head>
  <body>
    <script type="text/javascript">
      document.write('Hello World!');
    </script>
    <noscript>
      <p>Your browser either does not support JavaScript, or you have
          JavaScript turned off.</p>
    </noscript>
  </body>
</html>
```

Infrastructure

Infrastructure is a way to deliver virtualization to your cloud computing solution. We talked about virtualization before, both across the Internet (having your machines running on a remote server and displayed at your organization) and locally (having your clients' sessions run on a local server and displayed at their desktops).

In this section we'll talk about how virtualization—a fairly new computing solution—is being standardized and how major players are working and playing together to make it come together.

Virtualization

Whenever something new happens in the world of computing, competitors duke it out to have their implementation be the standard. Virtualization is somewhat different, and major players worked together to develop a standard.

In a virtualized environment, applications run
on a server and are displayed on the client.
The server can be local or on the other side of the cloud.

VMware, AMD, BEA Systems, BMC Software, Broadcom, Cisco, Computer Associates International, Dell, Emulex, HP, IBM, Intel, Mellanox, Novell, QLogic, and Red Hat all worked together to advance open virtualization standards.

VMware says that it will provide its partners with access to VMware ESX Server source code and interfaces under a new program called VMware Community Source. This program is designed to help partners influence the direction of VMware ESX Server through a collaborative development model and shared governance process.

"Virtualization is gaining widespread adoption due to its indisputable customer benefits. It is an area rich in opportunities and the ecosystem will develop most fully with open standards. VMware is thus taking our industry-leading products, opening up the APIs and providing shared governance and source access to them," said Diane Greene, president of VMware. "We look forward to this next phase of increased partner collaboration and believe it is the best possible way to give customers the ability to realize the full potential of the x86 virtualization layer."

These initiatives are intended to benefit end users by

- **Expanding virtualization solutions**   The availability of open-standard virtualization interfaces and the collaborative nature of VMware Community Source are intended to accelerate the availability of new virtualization solutions.

- **Expanded interoperability and supportability**   Standard interfaces for hypervisors are expected to enable interoperability for customers with heterogeneous virtualized environments.

- **Accelerated availability of new virtualization-aware technologies**   Vendors across the technology stack can optimize existing technologies and introduce new technologies for running in virtual environments.

Open Hypervisor Standards

Hypervisors are the foundational component of virtual infrastructure and enable computer system partitioning. An open-standard hypervisor framework can benefit customers by enabling innovation across an ecosystem of interoperable virtualization vendors and solutions.

As an initial step, VMware contributed an existing framework of interfaces, called Virtual Machine Hypervisor Interfaces (VMHI), based on its virtualization products to facilitate the development of these standards in an industry-neutral manner. Consistent adoption of open interfaces is expected to facilitate interoperability and supportability across heterogeneous virtualized environments.

Collaboration around open hypervisor standards is expected to focus on the following areas of interoperability and performance optimization for virtualized environments:

- Cross-platform frameworks that govern the standardized operation and management of stand-alone virtual machine environments as well as highly dynamic, data center-scale deployment of virtualized systems

- Cooperative virtualization APIs between hypervisors and guest operating systems

- Virtual machine formats that enable virtual machine migration and recovery across platforms

Community Source

The Community Source program provides industry partners with an opportunity to access VMware ESX Server source code under a royalty-free license. Partners can contribute shared code or create binary modules to spur and extend interoperable and integrated virtualization solutions. The idea is to combine the best of both the traditional commercial and open-source development models. Community members can participate and influence the governance of VMware ESX Server through an architecture board. This approach will help drive open collaboration while still preserving the ability of partners to build differentiated, intellectual property–protected solutions.

For customers, the VMware Community Source program is expected to yield a richer and broader set of partner solutions that are well integrated with VMware virtual infrastructure products. For partners, the source access and development model allows them to efficiently deliver complementary solutions or differentiated product capabilities around the VMware ESX Server code base.

"More than ever standards are critical to innovation in enterprise infrastructures. Red Hat applauds the efforts of technology partners like VMware who are working to establish open, standards-based solutions," said Paul Cormier, executive vice president of engineering at Red Hat. "We are pleased to work with VMware, partners and the community to offer customers virtualization as a key component of their open source architectures."

OVF

As the result of VMware and its industry partners' efforts, a standard has already been developed called the Open Virtualization Format (OVF). OVF describes how virtual appliances can be packaged in a vendor-neutral format to be run on any hypervisor. It is a platform-independent, extensible, and open specification for the packaging and distribution of virtual appliances composed of one or more virtual machines.

OVF gives customers and developers the choice to select any hypervisor based on price, preference, or functionality, and it prevents vendor lock-in. This standard packaging and distribution format for virtual appliances will be important in accelerating the adoption of virtual appliances.

As part of their efforts to work with other vendors, VMware developed a standard with these features:

- Optimized for distribution
  - Enables the portability and distribution of virtual appliances
  - Supports industry-standard content verification and integrity checking
  - Provides a basic scheme for the management of software licensing
- A simple, automated user experience
  - Enables a robust and user-friendly approach to streamlining the installation process
  - Validates the entire package and confidently determines whether each virtual machine should be installed
  - Verifies compatibility with the local virtual hardware
- Portable virtual machine packaging
  - Enables platform-specific enhancements to be captured
  - Supports the full range of virtual hard disk formats used for virtual machines today, and is extensible to deal with future formats that are developed
  - Captures virtual machine properties concisely and accurately
- Vendor and platform independent
  - Does not rely on the use of a specific host platform, virtualization platform, or guest operating system
- Extensible
  - Designed to be extended as the industry moves forward with virtual appliance technology
- Localizable
  - Supports user-visible descriptions in multiple locales
  - Supports localization of the interactive processes during installation of an appliance
  - Allows a single packaged appliance to serve multiple market opportunities

It seems logical that VMware would take the lead in the development of the standard, as they are one of the most dominant forces in the world of virtualization. It is also encouraging that they opened their own code to partners to make the standard a true industry-developed standard.

Service

A *web service*, as defined by the World Wide Web Consortium (W3C), "is a software system designed to support interoperable machine-to-machine interaction over a network" that may be accessed by other cloud computing components. Web services are often web APIs that can be accessed over a network, like the Internet, and executed on a remote system that hosts the requested services.

In this section we'll talk about some of the popular web services, like REST, SOAP, and JSON.

Data

Data can be stirred and served up with a number of mechanisms; two of the most popular are JSON and XML. Both are based on leading industry standards—HTML and JavaScript— to help deliver and present data.

JSON

JSON is short for JavaScript Object Notation and is a lightweight computer data interchange format. It is used for transmitting structured data over a network connection in a process called *serialization*. It is often used as an alternative to XML.

JSON Basics   JSON is based on a subset of JavaScript and is normally used with that language. However, JSON is considered to be a language-independent format, and code for parsing and generating JSON data is available for several programming languages.

This makes it a good replacement for XML when JavaScript is involved with the exchange of data, like AJAX.

NOTE *www.json.org provides a number of listing JSON bindings, based on language.*

In December 2005 Yahoo! began offering some of its web services in JSON, and Google followed suit in December 2006.

XML vs. JSON   JSON should be used instead of XML when JavaScript is sending or receiving data. The reason for this is that when you use XML in JavaScript, you have to write scripts or use libraries to handle the DOM objects to extract the data you need. However, in JSON, the object is already an object, so no extra work needs to be done.

This reduces the amount of overhead, CPU use, and the amount of code you or your programmers have to write.

Example   The following is a sample JSON representation of an object describing a person:

```
{
    "firstName": "Johnny",
    "lastName": "Johnson",
    "address": {
        "streetAddress": "123 Main Street",
        "city": "Minneapolis",
        "state": "MN",
        "postalCode": 55102
    },
    "phoneNumbers": [
        "612 555-9871",
        "952 555-1598"
    ]
}
```

The object contains the person's first and last name, street address, city, state, and an array with telephone numbers in it.

XML

Extensible Markup Language (XML) is a standard, self-describing way of encoding text and data so that content can be accessed with very little human interaction and exchanged across a wide variety of hardware, operating systems, and applications.

XML provides a standardized way to represent text and data in a format that can be used across platforms. It can also be used with a wide range of development tools and utilities.

XML Basics   XML is very similar to HTML (both are based on the SGML language, which has been a standard since 1986), so those who already know HTML will find it easy to pick up XML. That said, there are two major differences between the two:

- **Separation of form and content**   HTML uses tags to define the appearance of text, while XML tags define the structure and the content of the data. Individual applications will be specified by the application or associated style sheet.

- **XML is extensible**   Tags can be defined by the developer for specific application, while HTML's tags are defined by W3C.

Functionality   XML makes database use much easier for your organization. Relational database systems cannot meet all the demands of electronic business because they process data independently from its context. They are also unable to handle rich data, like audio, video, or nested data structures, which are common in cloud environments.

Traditional databases are usually retrofitted to deal with XML, but the conversion process is prone to error and there's a lot of overhead, especially with greater transaction rates and document complexity.

XML databases smooth out this process because they store XML natively in structured, hierarchical form. Queries can be resolved much more quickly because there is no need to map the XML data tree to relational database tables.

Other benefits of XML include

- **Self-describing data**   XML does not require relational schemata, file description tables, external data type definitions, and so forth. Also, while HTML only ensures the correct presentation of the data, XML also guarantees that the data is usable.

- **Database integration**   XML documents can contain any type of data—from text and numbers to multimedia objects to active formats like Java.

- **No reprogramming if modifications are made**   Documents and web sites can be changed with XSL Style Sheets, without having to reprogram the data.

- **One-server view of data**   XML is exceptionally ideal for cloud computing, because data spread across multiple servers looks as if it is stored on one server.

- **Open and extensible**   XML's structure allows you to add other elements if you need them. You can easily adapt your system as your business changes.

- **Future-proof**   The W3C has endorsed XML as an industry standard, and it is supported by all leading software providers. It's already become industry standard in fields like healthcare.

- **Contains machine-readable context information**   Tags, attributes, and element structure provide the context for interpreting the meaning of content, which opens up possibilities for development.

- **Content vs. presentation**   XML tags describe the meaning of the object, not its presentation. That is, XML describes the look and feel of a document, and the application presents it as described.

Web Services

Web services describe how data is transferred from the cloud to the client. We've mentioned the content of this section in Chapter 7, but let's take a look under the hood and see how REST and SOAP work, and which would be best for your cloud needs.

REST

Representational state transfer (REST) is a way of getting information content from a web site by reading a designated web page that contains an XML file that describes and includes the desired content.

For instance, REST could be used by your cloud provider to provide updated subscription information. Every so often, the provider could prepare a web page that includes content and XML statements that are described in the code. Subscribers only need to know the uniform resource locator (URL) for the page where the XML file is located, read it with a web browser, understand the content using XML information, and display it appropriately.

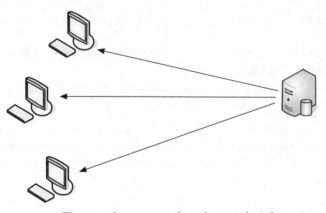

Clients send a request to the web server for information,
using the same URL. The web site has updated its content,
and uses REST to send the information back to the clients.

REST was developed in a PhD dissertation by Roy Fielding, and he calls it an "architectural style." He says REST exploits existing technology and protocols of the Web including HTTP and XML.

REST is similar in function to the Simple Object Access Protocol (SOAP), but is easier to use. SOAP requires writing or using a data server program and a client program (to request the data). However, SOAP offers more capability.

For instance, if you were to provide syndicated content from your cloud to subscribing web sites, those subscribers might need to use SOAP, which allows greater program interaction between the client and the server.

REST uses the same publishing approach that many sites use with RDF Site Summary (RSS). RSS uses the Resource Description Framework (RDF), which is a standard way to describe a web site.

Resources   An important component in REST is the existence of resources. Resources are sources of specific information and each one is referenced by a global identifier, like a URL in HTTP. To manipulate these resources, network components communicate via a standard interface (like HTTP) and exchange representations of the resources (for instance, the actual documents conveying the information).

For instance, a resource, which is a triangle, might be described as a polygon with three sides of equal length. It may also combine three points that are connected in a comma-separated list.

Benefits   REST offers the following benefits:

- It gives better response time and reduced server load due to its support for the caching of representations.
- Server scalability is improved by reducing the need to maintain session state.
- A single browser can access any application and any resource, so less client-side software needs to be written.
- A separate resource discovery mechanism is not needed, due to the use of hyperlinks in representations.
- Better long-term compatibility and evolvability characteristics exist than in RPC. This is due to:
  - The ability of documents, like HTML, to evolve with both forward- and backward-compatibility.
  - Resources can add support for new content types as they are defined, without eliminating support for older content types.

A benefit when using RESTful applications on the cloud is that REST allows users to bookmark specific queries and allows those queries to be sent to others via email or instant messaging. This "representation" of a path or entry point into an application becomes very portable.

SOAP

Simple Object Access Protocol (SOAP) is a way for a program running in one kind of operating system (such as Windows Vista) to communicate with a program in the same or another kind of an operating system (such as Linux) by using HTTP and XML as the tools to exchange information.

Procedure Calls   Often, remote procedure calls (RPC) are used between objects like DCOM or COBRA, but HTTP was not designed for this use. RPC is a compatibility problem, because firewall and proxy servers will block this type of traffic.

Because web protocols already are installed and available for use by the major operating systems, HTTP and XML provide an easy solution to the problem of how programs running under different operating systems in a network can communicate with each other.

SOAP describes exactly how to encode an HTTP header and an XML file so that a program on one computer can call a program in another computer and pass it information. It also explains how a called program can return a response.

NOTE *SOAP was developed by Microsoft, DevelopMentor, and Userland Software.*

One of the advantages of SOAP is that program calls are more likely to get through firewalls that normally screen out requests for those applications. Because HTTP requests are normally allowed through firewalls, programs using SOAP can communicate with programs anywhere.

Sample   When you look at the following SOAP example, you can see how it is based on HTTP. In fact, the first line in the request is nearly identical to a standard HTTP request. Here is the request fully written out:

```
POST /InStock HTTP/1.1
Host: www.example.org
Content-Type: application/soap+xml; charset=utf-8
Content-Length: nnn

<?xml version="1.0"?>
<soap:Envelope
xmlns:soap="http://www.w3.org/2001/12/soap-envelope"
soap:encodingStyle="http://www.w3.org/2001/12/soap-encoding">

  <soap:Body xmlns:m="http://www.example.org/stock">
    <m:GetStockPrice>
      <m:StockName>IBM</m:StockName>
    </m:GetStockPrice>
  </soap:Body>
</soap:Envelope>
```

And like a standard HTTP response, a SOAP response follows the similar format. Here is a sample SOAP response:

```
HTTP/1.1 200 OK
Content-Type: application/soap+xml; charset=utf-8
Content-Length: nnn

<?xml version="1.0"?>
<soap:Envelope
xmlns:soap="http://www.w3.org/2001/12/soap-envelope"
soap:encodingStyle="http://www.w3.org/2001/12/soap-encoding">

  <soap:Body xmlns:m="http://www.example.org/stock">
    <m:GetStockPriceResponse>
      <m:Price>34.5</m:Price>
    </m:GetStockPriceResponse>
  </soap:Body>

</soap:Envelope>
```

PART II

Standards are extremely important, and something that we take for granted these days. For instance, it's nothing for us to email Microsoft Word documents back and forth and expect them to work on our computers. But before .doc and .txt files were standardized, it wasn't uncommon for files created on different computers to be unreadable.

In this chapter we talked about the standards you're likely to come across while you're working on your cloud solution and how they work. In the next chapter we'll take a closer look at Software as a Service (SaaS) and how it shapes the way the cloud functions.

Cloud Computing at Work

PART III

Software as a Service

Software as a Service (SaaS) is what traditionally comes to mind when we think of cloud computing (if any part of cloud computing can be considered traditional). In SaaS, an application is hosted by a service provider and then accessed via the World Wide Web by a client. In this chapter we'll look under the hood of SaaS and examine the pros and cons of it. We will also talk about how specific vendors are offering SaaS, and then how SaaS exists in different industries.

Overview

SaaS (Software as a Service) is an application hosted on a remote server and accessed through the Internet.

SaaS Application Delivered to Client

World Wide Web

Client

Vendor offering SaaS application

An easy way to think of SaaS is the web-based email service offered by such companies as Microsoft (Hotmail), Google (Gmail), and Yahoo! (Yahoo Mail). Each mail service meets the basic criteria: the vendor (Microsoft, Yahoo, and so on) hosts all of the programs and data in a central location, providing end users with access to the data and software, which is accessed across the World Wide Web.

Email is stored by the vendor, and accessed by the client.

This is a simple explanation of SaaS, but the same architecture can be applied to a broad variety of applications, used either by businesses or individual end users.

SaaS can be divided into two major categories:

- **Line of business services**   These are business solutions offered to companies and enterprises. They are sold via a subscription service. Applications covered under this category include business processes, like supply-chain management applications, customer relations applications, and similar business-oriented tools.

- **Customer-oriented services**   These services are offered to the general public on a subscription basis. More often than not, however, they are offered for free and supported by advertising. Examples in this category include the aforementioned web mail services, online gaming, and consumer banking, among others.

Advantages

There are definite advantages to your organization pursuing SaaS, for example:

- There's a faster time to value and improved productivity, when compared to the long implementation cycles and failure rate of enterprise software.

- There are lower software licensing costs.

- SaaS offerings feature the biggest cost savings over installed software by eliminating the need for enterprises to install and maintain hardware, pay labor costs, and maintain the applications.

- SaaS can be used to avoid the custom development cycles to get applications to the organization quickly.

- SaaS vendors typically have very meticulous security audits.

- Many SaaS vendors have the capabilities to let customers comply with Sarbanes-Oxley Section 404, Generally Accepted Accounting Principles (GAAP), Financial Accounting Standards Board (FASB), US Securities and Exchange Commission (SEC), and American Institute of Certified Public Accountants (AICPA) regulations.

- SaaS vendors allow companies to have the most current version of an application as possible. This allows the organization to spend their development dollars on new innovation in their industry, rather than supporting old versions of applications.

Software Considerations

Using the existing software paradigm, the user purchases a software package and license by paying a one-time fee. The software then becomes the property of the user who bought it. Support and updates are provided by the vendor under the terms of the license agreement. This can be costly if you are installing a new application on hundreds or thousands of computers.

SaaS, on the other hand, has no licensing. Rather than buying the application, you pay for it through the use of a subscription, and you only pay for what you use. If you stop using the application, you stop paying.

You only pay for the applications when you use them.

Additionally, the software is not installed on the user's computer. Think back to the Hotmail example earlier. You access your Hotmail inbox via your web browser.

It may sound as if SaaS is only useful for small to medium-sized businesses. Not so. In 2005 Salesforce.com signed a deal with Merrill-Lynch for 25,000 subscriptions.

Vendor Advantages

The advantages flow both ways. Not only does the end user benefit, but so does the vendor. (Of course, they're in the business to make money, so there is at least that benefit.)

And financial benefit is the top one—vendors get a constant stream of income, often what is more than the traditional software licensing setup. Additionally, through SaaS, vendors can fend off piracy concerns and unlicensed use of software.

Vendors also benefit more as more subscribers come online. They have a huge investment in physical space, hardware, technology staff, and process development. The more these resources are used to capacity, the more the provider can clear as margin.

Limitations

While the preceding pages have presented a "glass-half-full image" of SaaS, naturally there are some downsides. Happily, a lot of these hurdles can be easy to clear and are being overcome.

Technical obstacles to SaaS have included an effective, multitenant architecture. This has become less and less of a problem due to virtualization, but designing an application to efficiently deliver it to thousands of customers via the Internet is hard work.

Another problem is that software companies are being asked to become service companies, and the two don't necessarily mesh well. They tend to have a corporate culture that is dominated by engineering innovation and a license-sales mindset. These are fine traits to have if you're writing programs and applications, but it's not the best when you're called upon for customer service. Further, a business model that is built on selling licensed software does not easily transform into a subscription model very cleanly.

Not only does the vendor face challenges, but so does the customer. While some applications are ideal for SaaS, others are not good to use employing an SaaS model. For example, Business Intelligence (BI) is tough to translate to a traditional SaaS approach. The data schemes and transactions are usually very complex, and the customer's configuration requirements vary from customer to customer. The application requires intensive processing, so it is not attractive to the vendor to provide the burden needed for this high-CPU infrastructure. Also, considering the bandwidth cost and network performance for the transfer of BI data, it gets very expensive very fast. But as SaaS providers become more sophisticated in the customization of their offerings, BI will also flourish because organizations will not want to keep the expertise or hardware around to successfully run their own BI operations.

Driving Forces

Some would argue that SaaS is popular because of the popularity of cloud computing. In fact, there are a number of issues that are driving more cloud vendors to offer SaaS and more clients to sign on. Let's take a look at why SaaS is driven as much as it is.

Popularity

SaaS has become big buzz in the already buzzy issue of cloud computing. SaaS is becoming trendy, thanks to a number of factors. But there are solid reasons—other than hype—that make it so popular.

Software Vendors Love it

A couple of years ago, there were plenty of vendors who had nothing nice to say about SaaS. But the pendulum has swung the other way, and more and more vendors are on board for SaaS. Now, even big guns like SAP and Oracle have joined the ranks of SaaS developers. In addition to the big names, there are hundreds of smaller developers cranking out SaaS offerings.

You can expect even more SaaS applications to be made available in the months and years to come.

Enterprises Love it

SaaS can be deployed both internally and externally. External use is especially appealing to IT professionals, because it takes work off their shoulders. They are able to focus more on their work, which one would hope is to generate a competitive advantage in their marketplace, rather than on simply maintaining servers and responding when servers fail.

That said, IT professionals might enjoy developing their own SaaS applications to be used internally. If they are able to offload their work to the cloud, it gives them the opportunity to focus on creating their own complementary internal SaaS tools.

Not only that, but more and more companies are being drawn to SaaS to answer their application needs.

Plenty of SaaS Platforms

There are many SaaS platforms out there, and they grow each month. For example, Oracle is developing its own SaaS platform while Microsoft is working to make their own applications SaaS-ready. As SaaS becomes more and more popular, more vendors are going to be forced to make their platforms SaaS-friendly for SaaS-based applications.

Another reason SaaS platforms will continue to grow is because of the interest in Green IT and the efforts to move toward virtualized infrastructure. That means clients are likely to move toward SaaS platforms so they can reduce the number of servers they power and cool.

Virtualization Benefits

Virtualization makes it easy to move to an SaaS system. One of the main reasons is that it is easier for independent software vendors (ISVs) to adopt SaaS is the growth of virtualization.

The growing popularity of some SaaS vendors using Amazon's EC2 cloud platform and the overall popularity of virtualized platforms help with the development of SaaS.

SaaS and SOA

A service-oriented architecture (SOA) is one in which IT supports the business processes that cover current and emerging requirements to run the business end-to-end. This ranges from electronic data interchange (EDI) to online auctions.

By updating older technologies—like Internet-enabling EDI-based systems—companies can make their IT systems available to internal or external customers.

SOA unifies business processes by structuring large applications as a collection of smaller modules known as "services." SOA presents a design framework for realizing rapid and low-cost system development and improving total system quality.

SaaS and SOA are quite similar; what they have in common is that they use a services model.

Economic Impact

As of this writing, we're in the midst of a recession and that poses a problem for SaaS vendors. However, many industry observers think conventional ISVs will have a tougher time than SaaS vendors.

InfoWorld in its "top underreported stories of 2007" blamed SaaS for pricing pressures that ISVs would face in the coming year. The subscription-based payment model of SaaS makes it more appealing in these tough times.

According to Goldman Sachs: "The ability to quickly and easily turn on new applications with a significantly lower initial cost of ownership makes SaaS an attractive offering for small- and mid-sized businesses, significantly expanding the market for software applications. More broadly, and including enterprises, these benefits are likely to be key in a slower economic environment where purchasers of software may be increasingly skeptical of significant upfront investments which we anticipate to characterize 2008."

Company Offerings

There are dozens of companies offering SaaS. There are a lot of fish in the SaaS pond, and in this section we'll take a closer look at some of the bigger fish. They are all companies that you've heard of—like Microsoft and IBM, for instance—and they all want their own slice of the SaaS pie.

Intuit

QuickBooks has been around for years as a conventional application for tracking business accounting. With the addition of QuickBooks online, accounting has moved to the cloud.

QuickBooks Overview

QuickBooks Online (www.qboe.com) gives small business owners the ability to access their financial data whether they are at work, home, or on the road. Intuit Inc. says the offering also gives users a high level of security because data is stored on firewall-protected servers and protected via automatic data backups. There is also no need to hassle with technology—software upgrades are included at no extra charge.

For companies that are growing, QuickBooks Online Plus offers advanced features such as automatic billing and time tracking, as well as the ability to share information with employees in multiple locations. QuickBooks Online features include

- The ability to access financial data anytime and from anywhere. QuickBooks Online is accessible to users 24 hours a day, seven days a week.

- Automated online banking. Download bank and credit card transactions automatically every night, so it's easy to keep data up to date.

- Reliable automatic data backup. Financial data is automatically backed up every day and is stored on Intuit's firewall-protected servers, which are monitored to keep critical business information safe and secure. QuickBooks Online also supports 128-bit Secure Sockets Layer (SSL) encryption.

- No software to buy, install, or maintain and no network required. The software is hosted online, so small business users never have to worry about installing new software or upgrades. QuickBooks Online remembers customer, product, and vendor information, so users don't have to re-enter data.

- Easy accounts receivable and accounts payable. Invoice customers and track customer payments. Create an invoice with the click of a button. Apply specific credits to invoices or apply a single-customer payment to multiple jobs or invoices. Receive bills and enter them into QuickBooks Online with the expected due date.

- Write and print checks. Enter information in the onscreen check form and print checks.

iPhone and BlackBerry Capabilities

Additionally, Intuit Inc. offers both iPhone and BlackBerry integration with QuickBooks Online, the leading web-based small business accounting software.

With the iPhone and BlackBerry upgrade, the more than 130,000 small businesses that subscribe to QuickBooks Online can manage their business anywhere—with or without a computer. These early versions of web-based mobile applications are part of Intuit's

Connected Services strategy to help entrepreneurs connect to their data when and where they need it.

Available on IntuitLabs.com, these iPhone and BlackBerry applications help QuickBooks Online users get an up-to-date view of their finances by

- Checking current bank and credit card balances
- Tracking who owes them money and whom they owe
- Finding vendor and customer contact info with addresses via Google Maps
- Running balance sheet and profit and loss reports

"A growing number of small businesses are looking to mobile technology to run their business," said Rick Jensen, senior vice president of Intuit's Small Business Division. "Our goal with these new mobile services is to give QuickBooks Online users the edge they need to compete and manage their busy lives by keeping tabs on their business even when they are out of the office."

The iPhone and BlackBerry web-based applications for QuickBooks Online are part of IntuitLabs.com, a site where customers are encouraged to try Intuit's early concept releases and contribute to the innovation process by providing feedback. The site includes applications that address several important customer problems in a range of categories for consumers and small businesses.

More information on QuickBooks Online on the iPhone and BlackBerry is available at www.intuitlabs.com/apps/category/mobile/. QuickBooks Online is available starting at $9.95 per month at www.qboe.com. The iPhone and BlackBerry applications are free to QuickBooks Online users.

Google

Google's SaaS offerings include Google Apps and Google Apps Premier Edition. The Premier Edition includes hosted services for communication and collaboration designed for businesses of all sizes. Google Apps Premier Edition is available for US$50 per user account per year, and includes phone support, additional storage, and a new set of administration and business integration capabilities.

Google Apps, launched as a free service in August 2006, is a suite of applications that includes Gmail webmail services, Google Calendar shared calendaring, Google Talk instant messaging and Voice over IP, and the Start Page feature for creating a customizable home page on a specific domain. More than 100,000 small businesses and hundreds of universities use the service. Google Apps Premier Edition now joins Google Apps Standard Edition and Google Apps Education Edition, both of which will continue to be offered for free to organizations.

Google also offers Google Docs and Spreadsheets for all levels of Google Apps. Additionally, Google Apps supports Gmail for mobile on BlackBerry handheld devices.

"Businesses are looking for applications that are simple and intuitive for employees, but also offer the security, reliability, and manageability their organizations require," said Dave Girouard, vice president and general manager, Google Enterprise. "With Google Apps, our customers can tap into an unprecedented stream of technology and innovation at a fraction of the cost of traditional installed solutions."

Google Apps Premier Edition has the following unique features:

- **Per-user storage of 10GBs**　Offers about 100 times the storage of the average corporate mailbox.

- **APIs for business integration**　APIs for data migration, user provisioning, single sign-on, and mail gateways enable businesses to further customize the service for unique environments.

- **Uptime of 99.9 percent**　Service level agreements for high availability of Gmail, with Google monitoring and crediting customers if service levels are not met.

- **Advertising optional**　Advertising is turned off by default, but businesses can choose to include Google's relevant target-based ads if desired.

- **Low fee**　Simple annual fee of $50 per user account per year makes it practical to offer these applications to select users in the organization.

In addition to Gmail, Google Calendar, Google Talk, and Start Page, all editions of Google Apps now include

- **Google Docs and Spreadsheets**　Teams can collaborate on documents and spreadsheets without the need to email documents back and forth. Multiple employees can securely work on a document at the same time. All revisions are recorded for editing, and administrative controls allow organizations to define limits on document sharing.

- **Gmail for mobile devices on BlackBerry**　Gmail for mobile devices provides the same Gmail experience—such as search, conversation view, and synchronization with desktop version—on BlackBerry handheld devices for users of Google Apps. Gmail for mobile devices joins a list of other mobile options for Google Apps and BlackBerry users that already includes a Google Talk client and a variety of calendar sync tools.

- **Application-level control**　Allows administrators to adapt services to business policies, such as sharing of calendars or documents outside of the company.

NOTE *Google also offers development tools for offline viewing of online documents. We talk about Google Gears in more depth in Chapter 11.*

Microsoft

Microsoft offers SaaS in a number of forms. One that is particularly appealing to small businesses is Microsoft Office Live Small Business. You can find it at http://www .smallbusiness.officelive.com.

Microsoft Office Live Small Business offers features including Store Manager, an e-commerce tool to help small businesses easily sell products on their own web site and on eBay; and E-mail Marketing beta, to make sending email newsletters and promotions simple and affordable.

Small businesses that sign up will receive a set of tools and features for free, including

- Web hosting
- Rich site-design capabilities
- Numerous productivity applications
- Contact management software for performing basic customer relationship management (CRM)
- Custom domain name registration with 100 business email accounts (custom domains are free for the first year).
- This release is also compatible with the Firefox 2.0 web browser, making the service accessible on both Macs and PCs.

Microsoft's efforts in this arena are offering their own web site to businesses. They observe that despite consumers' growing tendency to search for products and services online, about half of the small businesses in the United States with fewer than 10 employees do not have a web site.

"Today having a professional Web site is as essential to running a small business as having business cards," said Baris Cetinok, director of product management and marketing for Microsoft Office Live Small Business. "By making it simple and affordable to develop and maintain a Web site, and offering user-friendly sales and marketing features, Office Live Small Business provides a one-stop shop to help small businesses easily take, promote and manage their businesses online."

Cetinok also points out that once small businesses have a web site, they do not always take advantage of online marketing techniques to drive traffic and sales. "We design our features specifically with the needs of small businesses in mind," Cetinok said. "Our Store Manager e-commerce tool, our email marketing feature, and the updated adManager search marketing tool are user-friendly and low cost, and work together."

While it is designed to be an easy "do-it-yourself" service, Office Live Small Business also provides customers with access to designers and developers with helpful "do-it-for-me" solutions. From web designers who can produce sophisticated web sites to developers who create custom applications for specific industry verticals and much more, third-party partners can help Office Live Small Business customers get the most from the service.

The following features are available in Microsoft Office Live Small Business:

- Store Manager is a hosted e-commerce service that enables users to easily sell products on their own web site and on eBay.

- Custom domain name and business email is available to all customers for free for one year. Private domain name registration is included to help customers protect their contact information from spammers. Business email now includes 100 company-branded accounts, each with 5GB of storage.

- Web design capabilities, including the ability to customize the entire page, as well as the header, footer, navigation, page layouts, and more.

- Support for Firefox 2.0 means Office Live Small Business tools and features are now compatible with Macs.

- A simplified sign-up process allows small business owners to get started quickly. Users do not have to choose a domain name at sign-up or enter their credit card information.

- Domain flexibility allows businesses to obtain their domain name through any provider and redirect it to Office Live Small Business. In addition, customers may purchase additional domain names.

- Synchronization with Microsoft Office Outlook provides customers with access to vital business information such as their Office Live Small Business email, contacts, and calendars, both online and offline.

- E-mail Marketing beta enables users to stay connected to current customers and introduce themselves to new ones by sending regular email newsletters, promotions, and updates.

- Contact Manager is the foundation of customer marketing. The improved user interface enables customers to find and add contacts more efficiently.

- The adManager search marketing tool is now easier to use and allows users to advertise across multiple sites and search engines, including MSN, Live Search, Ask.com, Excite.com, and Lycos.com.

Business applications are included free to all customers. Two of the most popular applications—Team Workspace and Document Manager—are automatically provisioned. Customers can activate any of the more than 20 others, such as Project Manager.

Reports include reporting for Store Manager, adManager, and E-mail Marketing. Home page gadgets include additional gadgets such as a Reports gadget that shows users at a glance the number of unique visitors and page views for the current week and the previous two weeks.

IBM

Big Blue—IBM—offers its own SaaS solution under the name "Blue Cloud." Blue Cloud is a series of cloud computing offerings that will allow corporate datacenters to operate more like the Internet by enabling computing across a distributed, globally accessible fabric of resources, rather than on local machines or remote server farms.

Blue Cloud is based on open-standards and open-source software supported by IBM software, systems technology, and services. IBM's Blue Cloud development is supported by more than 200 IBM Internet-scale researchers worldwide and targets clients who want to explore the extreme scale of cloud computing infrastructures.

IBM is collaborating on cloud computing initiatives with select corporations, universities, Internet-based enterprises, and government agencies, including the Vietnamese Ministry of Science and Technology.

IBM's first Blue Cloud offerings were available to customers in the spring of 2008, supporting systems with Power and x86 processors. IBM also offered a System z "mainframe" cloud environment in 2008, taking advantage of the very large number of virtual machines supported by System z.

Blue Cloud—based on IBM's Almaden Research Center cloud infrastructure—includes Xen and PowerVM virtualized Linux operating system images and Hadoop parallel workload scheduling. Blue Cloud is supported by IBM Tivoli software, which manages servers to ensure optimal performance based on demand. This includes software that is capable of instantly provisioning resources across multiple servers. Tivoli monitoring checks the health of the provisioned servers and makes sure they meet service level agreements.

"Blue Cloud will help our customers quickly establish a cloud computing environment to test and prototype Web 2.0 applications within their enterprise environment," said Rod Adkins, senior vice president, Development and Manufacturing for IBM Systems and Technology Group. "Over time, this approach could help IT managers dramatically reduce the complexities and costs of managing scale-out infrastructures whose demands fluctuate."

IBM developed Blue Cloud to help clients take advantage of cloud computing, including the ability of cloud applications to integrate with their existing IT infrastructure via SOA-based web services. Blue Cloud will particularly focus on the breakthroughs required in IT management simplification to ensure security, privacy, and reliability, as well as high utilization and efficiency. Cloud computing is targeted for existing workloads and emerging massively scalable, data-intensive workloads.

On November 13, 2007, IBM and the Vietnamese Ministry of Science and Technology (MoST) announced an open-innovation pilot program that would run on a cloud computing infrastructure.

"The Vietnam Information for Science and Technology Advance Innovation Portal (VIP), created with IBM, will help provide Vietnamese communities and residents a dynamic, rich content source and foster innovation among the citizens, communities and government organizations," said Dr. Tran Quoc Thang, Vice Minister of MoST. "VIP will be based on IBM's enterprise Web 2.0 Innovation Factory solution and made available to universities and research institutions through the cloud infrastructure at IBM's Almaden Research Center."

The Blue Cloud concept grew out of work that IBM did in support of its own software innovators with an IBM innovation portal called the Technology Adoption Program. IBM developers can request that computing resources be provisioned with software to test and conduct trials on their innovations with IBM employees through the program.

"By providing a dynamic infrastructure environment to IBM innovators over the past several months, we gained valuable experience with cloud computing technologies," said Dr. Willy Chiu, vice president of the IBM High Performance on Demand Solutions team. "Our customers have expressed strong interest in deploying a similar solution when we speak with them about how much time we can save innovators in obtaining the hardware and software resources they need to bring their solutions to market."

Industries

But it isn't just the big names like Amazon and Microsoft offering general SaaS. Different industries have their own players that offer unique, industry-specific SaaS applications. In this section, we take a closer look at some of those industries and the players within them.

Healthcare

While it seems risky to have health files on the cloud, two prominent systems provide the security for such a solution. Both Microsoft's HealthVault and AdvancedMD offer cloud solutions for the healthcare industry.

HealthVault

Microsoft launched its Microsoft HealthVault, a software and services platform aimed at helping people better manage their health information. The company says its vision is for ways in which HealthVault can bring the health and technology industries together to create new applications, services, and connected devices that help people manage and monitor their personal health information, including weight loss and disease management, such as for diabetes. HealthVault is shown in Figure 9-1.

"People are concerned to find themselves at the center of the healthcare ecosystem today because they must navigate a complex web of disconnected interactions between providers, hospitals, insurance companies and even government agencies," said Peter Neupert, corporate vice president of the Health Solutions Group at Microsoft. "Our focus is simple: to empower people to lead healthy lives. The launch of HealthVault makes it possible for people to collect their private health information on their terms and for companies across the health industry to deliver compatible tools and services built on the HealthVault platform."

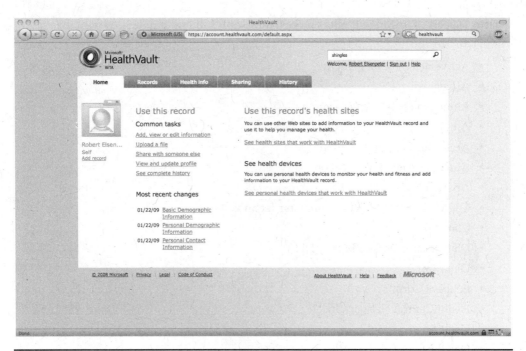

FIGURE 9-1   HealthVault allows users to manage their healthcare data.

Microsoft also offers HealthVault Search, a vertical health search tool designed to work with the platform. Integrated with Live Search and accessible on the HealthVault web site, this health-specific search engine organizes the most relevant online health content, allowing people to refine searches faster and with more accuracy, and eventually connect them with HealthVault-compatible solutions.

Privacy   Privacy is obviously a major concern, especially when health records are at stake. HealthVault was created in cooperation with privacy advocates, security experts, and healthcare organizations. HealthVault was designed and built to enhance privacy while providing people with the control they expect and require.

"Microsoft is the first major technology company to engage with the bipartisan Coalition for Patient Privacy in a serious way. The privacy protections built into HealthVault reflect the privacy principles of the Coalition. HealthVault prohibits onward transfer of data without explicit informed consent; its contractual obligations with advertisers require protection of any data transferred from the platform; its privacy policy is simple and easy to understand," said Dr. Deborah Peel, founder of the Patient Privacy Rights Foundation. "That means consumers finally have a trusted place to store their personal health information that will not be data-mined, because they alone control it. Microsoft's use of strong privacy principles including the principles of the Coalition, its ongoing relationship with consumer advocates, and its commitment to independent third-party audits set a new standard for privacy protections in health information technology."

Industry Support   HealthVault offers more than 40 applications and devices from the following organizations:

- ActiveHealth Management
- Allscripts
- American Diabetes Association
- American Heart Association
- American Lung Association
- American Stroke Association
- Aperion Companies
- CapMed, a division of Bio-Imaging Technologies Inc.
- Claricode
- Diabetes Prevention Source (DPS)
- Diet.com
- Eclipsys Corp.
- HealthCentral Network Inc.
- HealthMedia Inc.
- Healthphone Solutions Ltd.
- Healthways
- Healthy Circles LLC
- Home Diagnostics Inc.
- iMedica Corp.
- Kryptiq Corp.
- LifeScan Inc., a Johnson and Johnson company
- LiveHealthier
- Matria Healthcare Inc.
- Medem Inc.
- MedHelp
- Medical Informatics Engineering (MIE)
- Medifast Inc.
- MEDSEEK
- Medstar Health
- Microlife USA Inc.
- NewYork-Presbyterian Hospital
- NexCura, a Thomson Healthcare Business
- NextGen Healthcare Information Systems Inc.

- NoMoreClipboard.com
- OMRON Healthcare Inc.
- Peaksware LLC
- Physicians Wellness Network
- Podfitness
- Polar
- PureWellness
- Sound Health Solutions Inc.
- StayWell, a MediMedia company
- Texas Instruments Inc.
- US Wellness Inc.
- Vital Data Technology
- Whole Health Management
- WorldDoc Inc.

With a new platform provided by Microsoft based on compatible Internet and healthcare technology standards, organizations can spend development time working to connect a range of applications and devices. Instead, they can deliver solutions to consumers that focus on care delivery, giving HealthVault the potential to greatly enhance the quality and value of healthcare information technology across the ecosystem.

Development   Developers interested in building their own HealthVault-based solutions can download the HealthVault software development kit at http://msdn.microsoft.com/healthvault. The HealthVault platform is available to people for free at http://www.healthvault.com.

AdvancedMD

Another popular healthcare SaaS is AdvancedMD. It is a medical billing software company providing a medical billing software product for physician office and billing office management.

Thousands of medical office users and healthcare providers use AdvancedMD's medical software every day. And according to the company, each year, some 98 percent of their active medical clients renew their service.

AdvancedMD's medical billing and practice management software is 100 percent web-based, meaning it can be used at any time, anywhere one can get on the Internet. In the early stages of the company's product development, Microsoft, in conjunction with their initial efforts to enter the healthcare market, aided the company development effort by providing significant resources to ensure that the very latest web-based technologies were utilized. This early help from Microsoft allowed the company to provide a full-featured, efficient solution at a low total cost of ownership. AdvancedMD continues today as a Microsoft corporate partner and Healthcare user group member.

AdvancedMD Medical Billing Software, Inc. is a privately held company with headquarters located in Salt Lake City, Utah.

Collaboration—WebEx

There are dozens of different collaboration applications on the market, and a big name in cloud collaboration is WebEx. WebEx was acquired by Cisco Systems in 2007. The WebEx collaboration suite consists of five applications, each designed for specific collaborative business processes. The suite consists of five components:

- WebEx Meeting Center
- WebEx Event Center
- WebEx Sales Center
- WebEx Training Center
- WebEx Support Center

NOTE *You can download a free trial at www.webex.com/go/Fall2007Release.*

The platform provides network-based recording (NBR) capabilities for web conferencing, allowing hosts to record sessions and create valuable libraries of archived meetings, events, seminars, and support sessions. WebEx differs from traditional desktop-based recording by offering network-based recording, optimized to allow on-demand streaming and downloading of archived sessions.

Administrators can configure WebEx NBR to automatically capture all meeting content, including chat, presentations, and audio and video data. WebEx NBR can be easily customized to archive files on a company's write-once read-many (WORM)–compliant storage network. Content is recorded in a highly secure format, optimized for scalable storage, and customers can customize the solution's administrative settings to meet their specific retention polices.

"Just as TiVo revolutionized home entertainment and made recording and sharing your favorite shows easy for consumers, WebEx NBR will make recording and sharing information easier for business users," said Gary Griffiths, president of products and operations, WebEx. "WebEx Fall 2007 extends our reach beyond the actual meeting with new features for collaboration before, after and outside the meeting."

With more than 100 usability features across the suite, WebEx Fall 2007 streamlines meeting attendance. Automatic form completion and attendee profiles with preferred telephone numbers make joining meetings faster. In addition, asynchronous collaboration capabilities improve attendee participation between meetings, whether it is through a customized sales portal in the WebEx Sales Center or an enhanced post-event survey for WebEx Event Center.

Construction—CMiC

CMiC offers its construction software solutions for the architectural, engineering, and construction industry. CMiC's offering—CMiC Emerging—provides general contractors who have revenues under $250 million with SaaS applications specifically designed to help achieve growth, improve productivity, and enhance efficiency.

"Emerging companies in the past have relied on either basic spreadsheet and database applications, or point solutions that don't provide the efficiencies that an integrated software solution can," said Bassem Hamdy, vice president, Solutions, CMiC.

"Operating as a SaaS, CMiC Emerging allows contractors who don't have the technical resources to use the same robust financial and project management capabilities enjoyed by some of the biggest and best AEC companies in North America."

CMiC Emerging is divided into three sections to better suit companies at different stages of development. The first level, Getting Started, is intended for smaller contractors, and includes financial and project management applications, human resources, and document management. The next level, On The Grow, adds more applications, including CMiC CRM. The third stage is Emerging and includes CMiC Collaboration and CMiC Imaging and Workflow.

"The main focus for growing contractors is completing projects," said Hamdy, "not running and maintaining software. CMiC Emerging gives contractors the tools to compete with larger contractors without having to dedicate large amounts of IT resources. Being scalable, CMiC Emerging is the last software solution a contractor will ever need. With all mission critical information in one database, CMiC Emerging is the solution for contractors looking for breakthrough improvements in productivity and growth."

Retail—Epicor

Epicor Software Corporation offers its Retail SaaS solution for retailers.

The SaaS application gives small and medium specialty and department store retailers a delivery method that reduces capital investment and implementation requirements.

Epicor's integrated Retail SaaS solution is a pay-as-you-go model that consists of merchandising, allocation, replenishment, business intelligence, POS, sales audit, and CRM. Epicor SaaS is deployed on IBM's SurePOS 700 series hardware. SaaS services include hosting of all applications on secure redundant servers; the procurement and management of wide area networks; helpdesk support; system maintenance, including data security and backups; disaster recovery; and ongoing updates and upgrades to the latest Epicor software releases.

In 2008, research group Gartner noted that, "In 2009, SaaS delivery models will see a 25 percent increase in adoption by retailers." The same report notes, according to a Gartner survey of more than 110 retailers conducted in third-quarter 2008: "Twenty-two percent of retailers stated that they had implemented or were in the process of implementing a SaaS application."

IBM Partnership

An example of their smart integrated technology is IBM's Remote Management Agent (RMA) which, together with Epicor Retail POS software, provides retailers with the ability to remotely monitor, configure, and track hardware, software, and applications in one store or multiple store locations, from a central point, as well as perform asset tracking, and diagnostic and problem determination down to the device level. RMA delivers business benefits to retailers with proactive support and monitoring of in-store hardware and infrastructure that will ensure greater system uptime and enable a more enhanced customer shopping experience.

"Our Retail SaaS offering is a true end-to-end retail solution," said David Henning, executive vice president and general manager for Epicor Retail. "We are the leading provider that offers a complete integrated retail solution with a full range of support services that leverages our extensive in-house expertise from development to deployment through training. Our SaaS solution enables retailers to leverage a trusted and proven solution, delivering everything a retailer needs."

Clients

In business since 1963, The Paper Store is a family-owned and operated Specialty Gift Store chain of 23 stores in New England. The company contracted for the Epicor Retail SaaS solution to provide an updated technology framework to support its growing retail operations.

"We conducted an extensive search for a comprehensive integrated retail solution," said Tim Walsh, director of IT, The Paper Store. "We were very excited to find that the Epicor Retail SaaS solution offered us the same strong functionality that Tier 1 retailers had access to, but without all the heavy overhead from a deployment, management and cost perspective."

Epicor Retail solutions are used by hundreds of retailers. Their solutions leverage Microsoft .NET technology to improve business operations and meet the evolving merchandise and service expectations of today's cross-channel shoppers.

Banking—OpenChannel

OpenChannel's SaaS offerings provide options for implementing online banking and bill payment functionality across multiple channels, including mobile devices. Utilizing web services, financial institutions can customize presentations to meet the needs of their customers and differentiate online capabilities. Fully hosted by CheckFree or used as part of hybrid model integrated into existing environments, this solution supports value-based routing/payment preference and cross sell/upsell services.

CheckFree's OpenChannel provides a range of options for implementing online banking and bill payment functionality across multiple channels. Utilizing industry-standard web services, financial institutions can customize the presentation of online banking and bill payment functionality to meet the unique needs of their customers and differentiate their online capabilities.

USAA, a Fortune 200 diversified financial services company, leveraged CheckFree's OpenChannel strategy and the CheckFree Builder suite of open web services components to customize its online banking and bill payment user experience and streamline navigation to better serve its 6 million members.

"USAA's global membership relies extensively on usaa.com, so we place a premium on making our services as accessible and easy to use as possible through the online channel," said Jeff Dennes, executive director, USAA. "CheckFree OpenChannel gives us the control and flexibility we need to enhance the user experience, improve integration across the site, and deliver a full range of online and mobile banking functionality to our members."

CheckFree's deployment options enable financial institutions to integrate online banking, electronic billing, and payment, and selected value-added services into an end-to-end solution that can either be fully hosted by CheckFree or used as individual components as part of a hybrid model that they can integrate into their existing environments.

Leveraging the same web services that push electronic banking and bill payment functionality to a financial institution's online channel, CheckFree can also enable access to these services across multiple channels, including mobile devices, ATMs, kiosk, teller stations, and contact centers.

"The online channel is a growing priority for financial institutions as they seek to optimize customer loyalty, retention and profitability," said Alex Hart, executive vice president and general manager, CheckFree Electronic Banking Services. "CheckFree OpenChannel brings together the industry's best online banking and bill payment capabilities with an extremely flexible approach to integrating, implementing and managing world class financial management solutions across a diverse range of devices, channels and platforms."

"As online financial services evolves, the integration and management of new, compelling services into the legacy environment threatens to bring more complexity, preventing banks from maximizing the return on investment through an optimal customer experience," said James Van Dyke, president and founder of Javelin Strategy and Research. "As a result, open and flexible system approaches for integrating diverse electronic financial content and services becomes more important for helping financial institutions keep up with the rapid pace of new technology services, such as more interactive bills and statements, and online money management capabilities, converging content from lines of business and much more."

Financial institutions can use the OpenChannel strategy to take advantage of new capabilities, such as

- **Electronic bill payment integration**   Industry-standard web services can enable financial institutions to quickly implement a wide range of online banking and electronic bill payment functionality through a user interface that they control while leveraging their existing technologies.

- **Value-based routing/payment preference**   The OpenChannel strategy enables financial institutions to deliver premium content, such as data-fed electronic bills, and additional capabilities such as expedited payments and card-based payments. In addition, CheckFree plans to expand the processing window to approximately 10 P.M. Eastern time to enable even more payments to be processed by the next business day.

- **Security**   The OpenChannel strategy is designed to enable CheckFree FraudNet, a fraud detection and case management system, to be delivered as part of a service-based model. Utilizing web services, a financial institution can leverage the power and intelligence of CheckFree's bill payment network by sending payments to CheckFree for scoring. Those payments that fail to meet the financial institution's risk threshold could then be proactively stopped before they are processed.

- **Cross-sell and upsell services**   OpenChannel enables financial institutions to leverage the rich data in their CheckFree payment warehouse as well as data from other sources to analyze consumer behavior for their specific customer segments, and to plan and execute targeted marketing campaigns aimed at improving online banking and bill payment adoption and usage.

- **Mobile banking and payments**   Through web services, CheckFree enables banks and credit unions to offer customers the convenience of banking and paying bills using their mobile devices. OpenChannel provides the flexibility to support a wide range of technologies, including micro-browser wireless application protocol (WAP), short message service (SMS) text messaging, and device-resident applications. Some financial institutions will choose one of these technologies, while others may use a combination of approaches to support different online banking and bill payment functionality, such as paying bills, checking account balances or payment histories, transferring funds, or receiving alerts.

SaaS comes in all shapes and forms and is used by a broad variety of industries. If you are looking for a specific application, chances are good that it is out there. If not, you can be patient and wait for it to be developed, or you can roll your sleeves up and make it yourself using Platform as a Service (PaaS). We'll talk more about PaaS in the next chapter.

Software plus Services

U p to this point we have talked about organizational IT design in absolute terms—either you store your applications and data locally, or you employ a cloud solution. We didn't talk about any middle ground. It certainly would be nice to have the flexibility to mix and match, to use the best of both worlds in a way that better suits your requirements. The good news is that you can have it your way.

The answer is Software plus Services. In this architecture, you maintain some software on-site, which accesses data stored on the cloud. This is especially good for remote workers, road warriors, telecommuters, and anyone else who needs to be away from the corporate datacenter.

NOTE *Microsoft seems to use the phrasing Software + Services inconsistently, as they also use the more common Software plus Services. We're going to go with the more prevalent Software plus Services, just so we don't sound as if Steve Ballmer owns us, though we'd save typing by just going to the + key.*

In this chapter we'll talk about the ups and downs of Software plus Services, and we'll spend some extra time looking at Microsoft's solution, which employs an in-depth use of Software plus Services.

Overview

In a nutshell, Software plus Services takes the notion of Software as a Service (SaaS) to complement packaged software. Here are some of the ways in which it can help your organization:

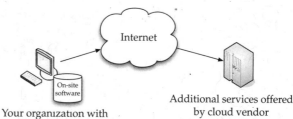

Your organization with
locally hosted software

Additional services offered
by cloud vendor

With Software plus Services,
locally hosted software is supplemented
by cloud offerings.

- **User experience** Browsers have limitations as to just how rich the user experience can be. Combining client software that provides the features you want with the ability of the Internet to deliver those experiences gives you the best of both worlds.

- **Working offline** Not having to always work online gives you the flexibility to do your work, but without the limitations of the system being unusable. By connecting occasionally and synching data, you get a good solution for road warriors and telecommuters who don't have the same bandwidth or can't always be connected.

- **Privacy worries** No matter how you use the cloud, privacy is a major concern. With Software plus Services, you can keep the most sensitive data housed on-site, while less sensitive data can be moved to the cloud.

- **Marketing** Software plus Services gives vendors a chance to keep their names in front of clients. Since it's so easy to move from vendor to vendor, providing a part-software/part-Internet solution makes it easier to sell your product to a client.

- **Power** More efficiency is realized by running software locally and synching to the cloud as needed.

- **Flexibility** Vendors can offer software in different sizes and shapes—whether on-site or hosted. This gives customers an opportunity to have the right-sized solution.

As with anything, there are good reasons to use Software plus Services, but also downsides. Let's talk about those issues.

Pros

In Earl's company, software is installed on the datacenter servers and on the client PCs. Earl and his staff spend a healthy portion of their time maintaining equipment and installing patches and updates. But for all the headache of managing their own datacenter and clients, the software is always available (unless a piece of equipment happens to go down) and under their control. This is a tough model for telecommuters or workers who leave the office and work remotely. They can certainly dial in via a virtual private network, but that adds another element of hassle for Earl and his IT staff.

Joy's company makes extensive use of the cloud. They maintain all their applications and data on the cloud. This is great for them, because it eases the headaches of managing a datacenter, and they really only pay for what they use. This is also a good model for workers who have to work remotely—they just need access to an Internet connection and they can do their work. But, unfortunately, if their link to the cloud is out or if vendor equipment goes down, then Joy's workers can't get their work done.

Software plus Services is the happy middle ground between the two architectures that Darnell and his organization use. While data is maintained on the cloud, software is still maintained at the client's location. The software is smaller and sleeker than a full-scale deployment, but if the connection to the cloud is down or the cloud vendor has problems, then Darnell isn't totally out of luck. Software plus Services periodically checks the cloud and updates local software with current information, also sending changed information back to the cloud. If the connection does go down, the software will have the most recently updated information and work can still continue.

Cons

So what are the downsides of Software plus Services? The main one is cost. If you don't use as much of the services portion of the model, then you won't pay as much. However, if you are using it heavily, it might make more financial sense to house the servers locally. For instance, if you outsource your email to a cloud vendor, you could be paying quite a lot, whereas you would pay a fraction if you just bought a server and installed it locally.

Second is Quality of Service (QoS). This, of course, depends on your cloud vendor and is something you should address in a service level agreement before committing, but your ability to access data might be at risk if there are so many clients using your vendor's equipment. Unless your vendor is especially responsible, you run the risk of slow response times and possibly even failure.

The last downside is a big mental hurdle for a lot of people: simple fear. If you have your data stored on a cloud somewhere, is it really safe? Is it really secure? Social networking site Facebook came under fire in early 2009 when they issued a terms of service adjustment saying, in essence, "We own whatever you put up here." Site members got understandably annoyed, fought back, and Facebook backed down.

"As people share more information on services like Facebook, a new relationship is created between Internet companies and the people they serve," founder Mark Zuckerberg said in a statement. "The past week reminded us that users feel a real sense of ownership over Facebook itself, not just the information they share."

While Facebook flinched, other vendors might not be so amenable—or as open. It underscores the notion that once data leaves your company's datacenter, it is open to others' eyes.

Vendors

A little later in this chapter we'll drill down into some vendor-specific solutions, but let's take a 20,000-foot aerial view of some of the Software plus Services offerings that prevalent companies have.

- **Microsoft** Microsoft offers Dynamics CRM, Microsoft Outlook, Windows Azure, and Azure Services Platform. Windows Azure is a collection of cloud-based services, including Live Framework, .NET Services, SQL Services, CRM Services, SharePoint Services, and Windows Azure Foundation Services for compute, storage, and management.

- **Adobe** Adobe Integrated Runtime (AIR) brings Flash, ActionScript, and MXML/Flex to the PC. Using AIR, vendors can build desktop applications that access the cloud.

- **Salesforce.com**   Salesforce.com's AppExchange is a set of APIs that vendors can use to create desktop applications to access salesforce data and run on the desktop of an end user.

- **Apple**   Apple offers a number of cloud-enabled features for its iPhone/iPod touch. Not only does it come with an integrated Safari web browser, but they also offer a software developer's kit (SDK) that allows software to be created for the iPhone/iPod touch. Vendors can build their own applications, and on-the-go users can access cloud offerings with those applications.

- **Google**   Google's mobile platform is called "Android" and helps vendors build software for mobile phones. Google also offers its Google Apps and the Google Chrome browser, which also installs Google Gears software on the desktop. This allows offline and online solutions.

- **WeatherBug**   An API from api.weatherbug.com (an example of its use is shown on an iPod touch in Figure 10-1) is a set of APIs that vendors can use to create applications that utilize current weather data.

- **DiCentral's DiIntegrator EDI Solution**   DiIntegrator is an application enabling users to perform supply chain functions related to electronic data interchange (EDI) and order fulfillment. Trading partners are connected within DiCentral's infrastructure.

Figure 10-1   WeatherBug takes weather information stored on the Internet and displays it, depending on how the API is created.

Mobile Device Integration

A key component of Software plus Services is the ability to work in the cloud from a mobile device. But what do you need to put on the cloud? It really depends on your organization.

There are a number of free applications that you can use on the cloud. Take, for instance, Google's free apps. You can start a document at your PC and then share it with others or continue working on it on your mobile device. The same document is shown (in Figure 10-2) on a desktop computer, and (in Figure 10-3) on a mobile device.

This is a simplistic example, but it shows how you can use the cloud to your advantage, especially with mobile users.

NOTE *This is the gray area in cloud computing. You could consider the aforementioned example as both SaaS and Software plus Services. We use it as an example of Software plus Services because you need a web browser to use it, but by the same token, you need a browser to use SaaS. As we said: gray area.*

Your needs might be more proprietary, however. Rather than using Microsoft Live or Google Docs to collaborate on documents, maybe your company needs a special application in service vehicles. In such cases, you simply need to turn to a service like Force.com and see if anyone has already created the application you need. If not, assign your programmers to the problem. Google Android is one way to keep your programmers busy.

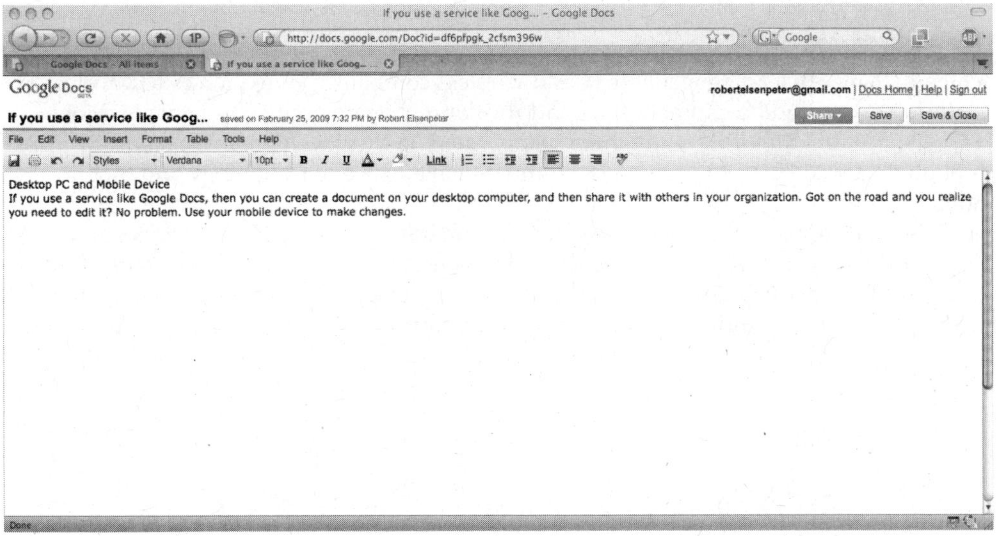

FIGURE 10-2   It's easy enough to create a document with Google's Docs.

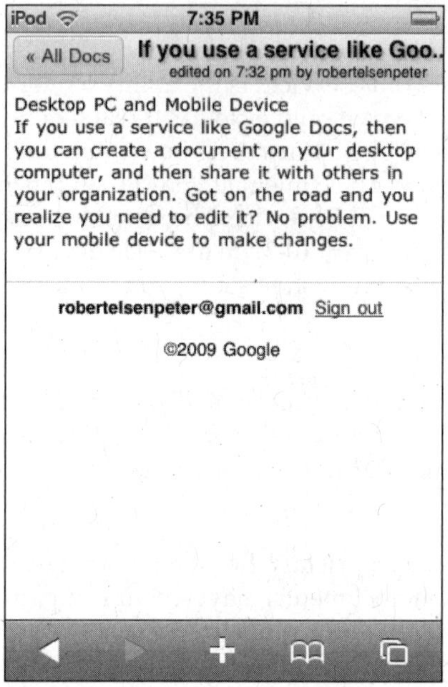

FIGURE 10-3   You can edit your documents on a mobile device, if you so choose.

Google Android

A broad alliance of leading technology and wireless companies joined forces to develop Android, an open and comprehensive platform for mobile devices. Google Inc., T-Mobile, HTC, Qualcomm, Motorola, and others collaborated on the development of Android through the Open Handset Alliance, a multinational alliance of technology and mobile industry leaders.

This alliance shares a common goal of fostering innovation on mobile devices and giving consumers a chance to experience performance improvements over existing mobile platforms. By providing developers with a new level of openness that enables them to work more collaboratively, Android accelerates the pace at which new mobile services are made available to consumers.

```
    ○○○                        AndroidManifest.xml
   ◄   ►       AndroidManifest.xml   ⬥
 1  <?xml version="1.0" encoding="utf-8"?>
 2  <!-- Copyright (C) 2007 The Android Open Source Project
 3
 4      Licensed under the Apache License, Version 2.0 (the "License");
 5      you may not use this file except in compliance with the License.
 6      You may obtain a copy of the License at
 7
 8          http://www.apache.org/licenses/LICENSE-2.0
 9
10      Unless required by applicable law or agreed to in writing, software
11      distributed under the License is distributed on an "AS IS" BASIS,
12      WITHOUT WARRANTIES OR CONDITIONS OF ANY KIND, either express or implied.
13      See the License for the specific language governing permissions and
14      limitations under the License.
15  -->
16
17  <!-- This file describes the code in the SkeletonApp package, which is
18      used by the system to determine how to start your application and
19      integrate it with the rest of the system.  -->
20
21  <!-- Declare the contents of this Android application.  The namespace
22      attribute brings in the Android platform namespace, and the package
23      supplies a unique name for the application.  When writing your
24      own application, the package name must be changed from "com.example.*"
25      to come from a domain that you own or have control over. -->
26  <manifest xmlns:android="http://schemas.android.com/apk/res/android"
27      package="com.example.android.skeletonapp">
28
29      <!-- This package contains an application...  The 'label' is the name
30          to display to the user for the overall application, and provides
31          a default label for all following components.  The syntax here is a
32          reference to one of our string resources.-->
33      <application android:label="@string/skeleton_app">
34
35          <!-- An Activity in the application - this is something the user
36              can launch and interact with.  The "name" attribute is the
37              name of the class within your package that implements this
38              activity. -->
39          <activity android:name="SkeletonActivity">
40
41              <!-- An IntentFilter tells the system when it should use your
42                  activity.  This allows the user to get to your activity
43                  without someone having to explicitly know to launch your
44                  class "com.example1.android.skeletonapp.SkeletonActivity". -->
45              <intent-filter>
46                  <!-- The MAIN action describes a main entry point into an
47                      activity, without any associated data. -->
48                  <action android:name="android.intent.action.MAIN" />
49
50                  <!-- This places this activity into the main app list. -->
51                  <category android:name="android.intent.category.LAUNCHER" />
52              </intent-filter>
53
54          </activity>
55
56      </application>
57
58  </manifest>
59
```

PART III

With nearly 3 billion users worldwide, the mobile phone has become the most personal and ubiquitous communications device. However, the lack of a collaborative effort has made it a challenge for developers, wireless operators, and handset manufacturers to respond as quickly as possible to the ever-changing needs of savvy mobile consumers. Through Android, developers, wireless operators, and handset manufacturers will be better positioned to bring to market innovative new products faster and at a much lower cost. The end result is a mobile platform enabling wireless operators and manufacturers to give their customers better, more personal, and more flexible mobile experiences.

Thirty-four companies have formed the Open Handset Alliance, which aims to develop technologies that will significantly lower the cost of developing and distributing mobile devices and services. The Android platform is the first step in this direction—a fully integrated mobile "software stack" that consists of an operating system, middleware, and user-friendly interface and applications.

The Android platform is available under one of the most progressive, developer-friendly open-source licenses, which gives mobile operators and device manufacturers significant freedom and flexibility to design products.

Android holds the promise of benefits for consumers, developers, and manufacturers of mobile services and devices. Handset manufacturers and wireless operators will be free to customize Android in order to bring to market innovative new products faster and at a much lower cost. Developers will have access to handset capabilities and tools that will enable them to build compelling and user-friendly services, bringing the Internet developer model to the mobile space. And consumers worldwide will have access to less expensive mobile devices that feature more compelling services, rich Internet applications, and easier-to-use interfaces—ultimately creating a superior mobile experience.

An Open Solution

"This partnership helps unleash the potential of mobile technology for billions of users around the world. A fresh approach to fostering innovation in the mobile industry will help shape a new computing environment that will change the way people access and share information in the future," said Google chairman and CEO Eric Schmidt.

"As a founding member of the Open Handset Alliance, T-Mobile is committed to innovation and fostering an open platform for wireless services to meet the rapidly evolving and emerging needs of wireless customers," said René Obermann, CEO, Deutsche Telekom, parent company of T-Mobile. "Google has been an established partner for T-Mobile's groundbreaking approach to bring the mobile open Internet to the mass market. We see the Android platform as an exciting opportunity to launch robust wireless Internet and Web 2.0 services for T-Mobile customers in the US and Europe in 2008."

"The convergence of the wireless and Internet industries is creating new partnerships, evolving business models and driving innovation," said Dr. Paul E. Jacobs, CEO of Qualcomm. "We are extremely pleased to be participating in the Open Handset Alliance, whose mission is to help build the leading open-source application platform for 3G networks. The proliferation of open-standards-based handsets will provide an exciting new opportunity to create compelling services and devices. As a result, we are committing research and development resources to enable the Android platform and to create the best always-connected consumer experience on our chipsets."

"Motorola has long been an advocate of open software for mobile platforms. We're excited to continue this support by joining Google and others in the announcement of the Open Handset Alliance and Android platform. Motorola plans to leverage the Android platform to enable seamless, connected services and rich consumer experiences in future Motorola products," said Ed Zander, chairman and CEO of Motorola, Inc.

Open Handset Alliance Founding Members

Members of the Open Handset Alliance include

- Aplix (www.aplixcorp.com)
- Ascender Corporation (www.ascendercorp.com)
- Audience (www.audience.com)
- Broadcom (www.broadcom.com)
- China Mobile (www.chinamobile.com)
- eBay (www.ebay.com)
- Esmertec (www.esmertec.com)
- Google (www.google.com)
- HTC (www.htc.com)
- Intel (www.intel.com)
- KDDI (www.kddi.com)
- LivingImage (www.livingimage.jp)
- LG (www.lge.com)
- Marvell (www.marvell.com)
- Motorola (www.motorola.com)
- NMS Communications (www.nmscommunications.com)
- Noser (www.noser.com)
- NTT DoCoMo Inc. (www.nttdocomo.com)
- Nuance (www.nuance.com)
- Nvidia (www.nvidia.com)
- PacketVideo (www.packetvideo.com)
- Qualcomm (www.qualcomm.com)
- Samsung (www.samsung.com)
- SiRF (www.sirf.com)
- SkyPop (www.skypop.com)
- SONiVOX (www.sonivoxrocks.com)
- Sprint Nextel (www.sprint.com)
- Synaptics (www.synaptics.com)

PART III

- TAT - The Astonishing Tribe (www.tat.se)
- Telecom Italia (www.telecomitalia.com)
- Telefónica (www.telefonica.es)
- Texas Instruments (www.ti.com)
- T-Mobile (www.t-mobile.com)
- Wind River (www.windriver.com)

For more information about the Open Handset Alliance, visit the web site at www.openhandsetalliance.com.

Providers

But while Software plus Services is a good match for mobile users, telecommuters, and others on the go, there is still value for deskbound users. Applications can be developed by your organization or your vendor, depending on what your vendor offers or what you need.

Let's look at some development solutions you might consider when creating your own Software plus Services deployments.

Adobe AIR

Adobe Systems offers its Adobe Integrated Runtime (AIR), formerly code-named Apollo. Adobe AIR is a cross-operating-system application runtime that allows developers to use HTML/CSS, AJAX, Adobe Flash, and Adobe Flex to extend rich Internet applications (RIAs) to the desktop. New features in Adobe AIR include an embedded local database, PDF support, enhanced capabilities for JavaScript developers, and deeper integration with Adobe Flex. Adobe AIR and the Adobe AIR Software Developer's Kit (SDK) can be downloaded for free from www.adobe.com/go/air.

RIA

Adobe AIR, along with Adobe Flex, are cornerstones of Adobe's RIA platform, which enables developers and designers to create and deliver rich, dynamic, branded content and applications across all major operating systems. Key elements of Adobe AIR are open source, including the WebKit HTML engine, the ActionScript Virtual Machine (Tamarin project), and SQLite local database functionality. Additionally, Adobe also offers Adobe Flex as open source. By embracing open-source technologies and offering prerelease versions of software, Adobe enables developers worldwide to participate in the growth of the industry's most advanced platform for building cross-operating-system RIAs.

"Adobe AIR represents a new medium, as the best of the Web and the best of the desktop come together," said Kevin Lynch, senior vice president and chief software architect at Adobe. "Adobe AIR expands the universe of possibilities for Web developers who can now deliver a new generation of applications that work across operating systems and both inside and outside the browser, bridging the gap between the Web and the personal computer."

Adobe AIR allows developers to incorporate PDF by leveraging Adobe Reader 8.1 functionality. Users will be able to view and interact with PDF documents within Adobe AIR applications similarly to how they interact with a PDF in the browser today. New capabilities such as support for transparent HTML windows, drag-and-drop support, and complete access to Adobe AIR and Flash APIs allow AJAX developers to create engaging desktop applications. Developers building Adobe AIR applications can use the AJAX frameworks of their choice, and the latest version of WebKit incorporated into Adobe AIR provides more components than were previously available in Apollo.

Tools

The embedded, cross-platform, open-source SQLite local database was one of the most requested features from the Apollo release. It requires no extra setup while providing large data capacity and full text search, enabling web developers who traditionally rely on a database for storage to easily build desktop applications without changing existing techniques. Additionally, a tool is now available on Adobe Labs for Dreamweaver CS3 that enables Dreamweaver projects to be delivered as Adobe AIR applications.

"Ajax developers have helped define Web 2.0 by making Web applications more interactive and usable," said Ben Galbraith, co-founder of Ajaxian. "Adobe AIR allows Ajax developers to use their skills to take Web 2.0 to the desktop—without requiring them to learn a whole new set of skills. By exposing rich desktop and Flash functionality to Ajax developers as another set of JavaScript APIs, Adobe AIR opens up a whole new world of possibilities."

"Salesforce.com is excited about the promise Adobe AIR shows for our developer community," said Parker Harris, cofounder and EVP, Technology, Salesforce.com. "Developers who build on-demand business applications with the Salesforce Platform can already use Adobe Flex to add rich user interfaces to their solutions, and now with Adobe AIR they can be further extended with the persistent desktop functionality and interactivity AIR enables, making on-demand business applications more compelling than ever."

Apple iPhone SDK

For its popular iPhone and iPod touch devices, Apple offers its iPhone Software Development Kit (SDK) as well as enterprise features such as support for Microsoft Exchange ActiveSync to provide secure, over-the-air push email, contacts, and calendars as well as remote wipe, and the addition of Cisco IPsec VPN for encrypted access to private corporate networks.

"We're excited about creating a vibrant third-party developer community with potentially thousands of native applications for iPhone and iPod touch," said Steve Jobs, Apple's CEO. "iPhone's enterprise features combined with its revolutionary Multi-Touch user interface and advanced software architecture provide the best user experience and the most advanced software platform ever for a mobile device."

The iPhone SDK provides developers with a rich set of application programming interfaces (APIs) and tools to create applications for iPhone and iPod touch. Currently, anyone can download the beta iPhone SDK for free and run the iPhone Simulator on their Mac. Apple also introduced its new iPhone Developer Program, giving developers everything they need to create native applications, and the new App Store, a way for developers to wirelessly deliver their applications to iPhone and iPod touch users.

With the iPhone SDK, third-party developers are able to build native applications for the iPhone with a rich set of APIs, including programming interfaces for Core OS, Core Services, Media, and Cocoa Touch technologies. The iPhone SDK allows developers to create applications that leverage the iPhone's multitouch user interface, animation technology, large storage, built-in three-axis accelerometer, and geographical location technology to deliver innovative mobile applications.

Leverage

Apple has licensed Exchange ActiveSync from Microsoft and is building it right into the iPhone, so that iPhone will connect out-of-the-box to Microsoft Exchange Servers 2003 and 2007 for secure over-the-air push email, contacts, calendars, and global address lists. Built-in Exchange ActiveSync support also enables security features such as remote wipe, password policies, and auto-discovery.

The iPhone software supports Cisco IPsec VPN to ensure the highest level of IP-based encryption available for transmission of sensitive corporate data, as well as the ability to authenticate using digital certificates or password-based, multifactor authentication. The addition of WPA2 Enterprise with 802.1x authentication enables enterprise customers to deploy iPhone and iPod touch with the latest standards for protection of Wi-Fi networks.

The iPhone software provides a configuration utility that allows IT administrators to easily and quickly set up many iPhones, including password policies, VPN setting, installing certificates, email server settings, and more. Once the configuration is defined, it can be easily and securely delivered via web link or email to the user. To install, all the user has to do is authenticate with a user ID or password, download the configuration, and click Install. Once the software has been installed, the user will have access to all their corporate IT services.

App Store

The iPhone software contains the App Store, an application that lets users browse, search, purchase, and wirelessly download third-party applications directly onto their iPhone or iPod touch. The App Store enables developers to reach every iPhone and iPod touch user. Developers set the price for their applications—including free—and retain 70 percent of all sales revenues. Users can download free applications at no charge to either the user or developer, or purchase priced applications with just one click. Enterprise customers can create a secure, private page on the App Store accessible only by their employees.

Apple handles all credit card, web hosting, infrastructure, and DRM costs associated with offering applications on the App Store. Third-party iPhone and iPod touch applications must be approved by Apple and will be available exclusively through the App Store.

The iPhone SDK provides a way to create innovative applications for the iPhone and iPod touch. In addition to the rich set of iPhone OS APIs, the iPhone SDK also provides advanced tools for creating native iPhone and iPod touch applications including: Xcode for source code editing, project management, and graphical debugging; Interface Builder with drag-and-drop interface creation and live preview; Instruments to monitor and optimize iPhone application performance in real time; and the iPhone Simulator to run and debug applications.

Apple's iPhone Developer Program offers the ability to get code onto iPhones for testing. The Standard Program costs US$99 per year and gives members an iPhone SDK and development tools; access to prerelease iPhone software; technical support; the ability to get code onto iPhones for testing; and distribution of applications via the new App Store. The Enterprise Program costs US$299 per year.

In addition to these iPhone network and security features, the iPhone software provides several new Mail features such as the ability to view PowerPoint attachments, in addition to Word and Excel, as well as the ability to mass delete and move email messages.

Microsoft Online

Microsoft hit the gas especially hard with its own Software plus Services offerings, integrating some of its most popular and prevalent offerings, like Exchange. Not only does Microsoft's Software plus Services offering allow a functional way to serve your organization, but it also provides a means to function on the cloud in a way that you are probably already used to with your in-house computers.

Hybrid Model

With Microsoft services like Exchange Online, SharePoint Online, and CRM 4.0, organizations big and small have more choices in how they access and manage enterprise-class software—from entirely web-based, to entirely on-premise solutions, and anywhere in between. Having a variety of solutions to choose from gives customers the mobility and flexibility they need to meet constantly evolving business needs. To meet this demand, Microsoft is moving toward a hybrid strategy of Software plus Services, the goal of which is to empower customers and partners with richer applications, more choices, and greater opportunity through a combination of on-premise software, partner-hosted software, and Microsoft-hosted software.

As part of this strategy, Microsoft expanded its Microsoft Online Services—which includes Exchange Online and SharePoint Online—to organizations of all sizes. With services like Microsoft Online Services and Microsoft Dynamics CRM 4.0, organizations will have the flexibility required to address their business needs.

Partnership

The shift toward delivery models that combine on-premise software with hosted services is part of a continuum that will grow over time, with a focus on how hybrid solutions can empower customers with richer applications and more choices, and provide partners of all sizes with greater business opportunities. To help partners understand how they can benefit from Microsoft's Software plus Services strategy, Microsoft created a partner opportunity framework that maps the three main delivery models—on-premise, partner-hosted, and Microsoft-hosted. This framework helps partners to define, understand, and capitalize on the full range of business opportunities that are enabled by a Software plus Services strategy.

"In contrast to an online-only services approach, Microsoft supports the entire spectrum of software delivery. This is a unique competitive advantage that allows us to create new customer opportunities for a broad range of partners," said Allison L. Watson, corporate vice president, Microsoft Worldwide Partner Group. "We are working closely with partners of all types—whether it's systems integrators, hosters, web designers, advertisers and publishers, system builders, retailers, independent software vendors and finally value-added resellers and distributors—to drive clear guidelines for engagement, ranging from service delivery and monetization to the partner's business model and marketplace velocity."

Exchange Online and SharePoint Online

Exchange Online and SharePoint Online are two examples of how partners can extend their reach, grow their revenues, and increase the number to sales in a Microsoft-hosted scenario. In September 2007, Microsoft initially announced the worldwide availability of Microsoft Online Services—which includes Exchange Online, SharePoint Online, Office Communications Online, and Office Live Meeting—to organizations with more than 5,000 users.

The extension of these services to small and mid-sized businesses is appealing to partners in the managed services space because they see it as an opportunity to deliver additional services and customer value on top of Microsoft-hosted Exchange Online or SharePoint Online. Microsoft Online Services opens the door for partners to deliver reliable business services such as desktop and mobile email, calendaring and contacts, instant messaging, audio and video conferencing, and shared workspaces—all of which will help increase their revenue stream and grow their businesses.

Ceryx Inc., a messaging solution and Hosted Exchange provider with locations in Toronto, Canada, and New York, sees this announcement as another example of how Microsoft is collaborating with partners to create more business opportunities.

"Our experience working with Microsoft has demonstrated that the partner channel is very important to them," says Gus Harsfai, CEO and president of Ceryx Inc. An 18-year veteran of the hosted services space, Ceryx is excited to leverage Microsoft's innovation and brand to reach new customers and deliver greater value.

Microsoft partners can leverage Microsoft-hosted solutions to speed the deployment of Exchange and Office SharePoint in customer organizations, freeing them to focus on migration, customization, integration, and other services.

For Evolve Partners Inc., a leading provider of information technology solutions and services based in Anaheim, California, the focus of their business is delivering managed services to customers, so the announcement of Microsoft Online Services ties closely to their own services strategy. Supporting both on-premise and hosted solutions, Evolve Partners understands the efficiencies and added value that hosted solutions can provide. "Nine out of ten times we spend one to two weeks just prepping a customer's existing software to support a traditional on-premise solution," said Tim Acker, Evolve Partners president and COO. "With hosted services, we're able to get up and running immediately, and that shows value to the customer."

Evolve Partners also sees the flexibility that Microsoft Online Services provides as having helped them generate add-on revenue by reaching new customers or expand their existing customer base. "We've seen customers want an offsite, rent-as-you-go type option," shared Acker. "So we see this actually accelerating a number of opportunities in our pipeline."

Because Microsoft manages the deployment and maintenance of Exchange Online and SharePoint Online, partners can leverage that time and cost savings to have deeper conversations with customers about their business needs and fill the role of trusted advisor. For this very reason, Courtesy Computers, a managed network services provider in Fort Lauderdale, Florida, outsources its hosting business so it can focus on the various needs of its customers, and leverage these conversations with customers as an opportunity to deliver greater value and generate more revenue.

"Hosted solutions provide an affordable way for small businesses to get up and running and are a great foot in the door for partners to support them," said Tim Woodcock, president and CEO of Courtesy Computers. "The potential for add-on services, additional training, and a high level of support provides us with great business opportunities whether it is right now or down the road."

Microsoft Online Services helps partners to deliver greater value to customers and grow their own businesses profitably.

"With the release of Exchange Online and SharePoint Online, Microsoft will be closer to the hosting community than it's ever been," says Ceryx's Harsfai. "We see this as an opportunity to continue delivering tailored solutions, but to a broader market segment, faster and at a lower cost."

Microsoft Dynamics CRM 4.0

Microsoft Online Services isn't the only opportunity for partners in the Software plus Services space. Microsoft Dynamics CRM 4.0, released in December of 2007, also provides a key aspect of Microsoft's Software plus Services strategy. The unique advantages of the new Microsoft Dynamics CRM 4.0, which can be delivered on-premise or on-demand as a hosted solution, make Microsoft Dynamics CRM an option for solution providers who want to rapidly offer a solution that meets customer needs and maximizes their potential to grow their own business through additional services.

Partners such as Axonom, a provider of vertical modules for high-tech, multichannel manufacturers and distributors for Microsoft CRM based in Minneapolis, Minnesota, clearly see business opportunities through a Software plus Services model.

"Customers are looking for choice," said Mike Belongie, vice president of sales for Axonom. "They want flexibility in how their software is delivered. Being able to provide our CRM solutions on-premise or through a hosted model helps us to deliver greater value to customers, and that's ultimately helping us to grow our business."

Flexibility

Microsoft's Software plus Services strategy includes the best of on-premise software combined with the best of hosted services, bridging this continuum to allow for a range of superior options in customer choice and business opportunities for partners. This blended approach is designed to deliver the best of both worlds, with the goal of empowering customers and partners with richer applications, more choices, and greater opportunity. Microsoft partners play a critical role in delivering that value to customers.

Partnership

As part of its Software plus Services strategy, Microsoft has partnered with a number of other organizations to deliver their products and services. In 2008 the Microsoft Worldwide Partner Conference started with the announcement of a new pricing and partner model for Microsoft Online Services, a key component of its Software plus Services initiative. Additional announcements focused on its overall investment in delivering innovation and creating partner opportunities.

"Partners have always been at the core of Microsoft's business model, and that will never change," said Allison L. Watson, corporate vice president of the Worldwide Partner Group at Microsoft. "We are excited to announce new business models for our Online offerings, which will drive opportunity and profitability for our partners, while delivering incredible value and choice for customers."

Business Model

During the opening keynote address, Stephen Elop, president of the Microsoft Business Division, announced the pricing and partner model for two new suites of subscription services as part of the Microsoft Online Services family, which delivers software as a subscription service managed from a Microsoft datacenter and sold by partners. With Microsoft Online Services, customers have the option to access messaging, collaborations and communications software over the Internet. These services will be sold as a suite or as stand-alone products with prices starting as low as US$3 per month.

"Our vision is that everything you can do with our onsite servers, you will be able to do with our online services," Elop said. "For partners, it's about the differentiated value they can deliver on top of our services, as well as providing them with an ongoing revenue stream. There is incredible partner opportunity at every level—integration, migration, customization, consulting services and managed services. Microsoft Online Services provides stability and an opportunity to create long-term customer relationships."

Under the business model, partners selling the two suites will receive 12 percent of the first-year contract value with a recurring revenue stream of 6 percent of the subscription fee every year for the life of the customer contract.

To help partners get the guidance for discovery, enrollment, and activation of the two suites, a program called Quickstart for Microsoft Online Services was announced. Any partner can take advantage of the new business model, and hosting partners that already participate in models like this will have expanded opportunities to offer choice and flexibility to their customers for online services of all types.

NOTE *You can find more information about Quickstart at http://www.quickstartonlineservices.com.*

Resources

Building on the success of its Early Access program involving 200 partners, and the general availability of Microsoft Dynamics CRM Online, Microsoft offers a program expansion and readiness tool:

- The Microsoft Partner Program will provide discounts to qualified partners in the U.S. and Canada for use of Microsoft Dynamics CRM Online in their own organizations. The discounted price is US$19 per user per month.

- The Microsoft Dynamics CRM ISV SaaS Readiness tool extends Microsoft's Innovate On program, helping ISVs evolve their on-premise solutions into on-demand services.

Opportunities

In addition to significant new Software plus Services to support customer and partner choice and flexibility, Microsoft also offers a spectrum of new partner opportunities: across the fast-growing unified communications platform; the range of opportunities for Microsoft Windows and small businesses; a new Mobile Readiness program to help partners take advantage of the burgeoning mobility space; and new licensing and financing programs to help partners improve their customers' purchasing experience with more flexible, predictable, and manageable options.

Unified Communications

Microsoft has also seen broad adoption of its unified communications platform and products, including Microsoft Office Communications Server 2007, Microsoft Office Communicator 2007, and Microsoft Exchange Server 2007. Microsoft Office Communications Server alone has experienced triple-digit business growth over the past couple of years, is licensed to 35 percent of Fortune 500 companies, and partners are recognizing the opportunity:

- More than 150 partners have achieved the Voice specialization.

- More than 2,500 partner companies have achieved the Unified Communications Solutions competency.

- More than 90 companies have joined the Notes Transition Partner Program to assist businesses that are migrating to the Microsoft platform.

As part of Microsoft's unified communications approach, Microsoft subsidiary Tellme Networks Inc. launched a new partner strategy for enterprise contact center partners that allows Tellme to scale its business and bring improved speech-enabled solutions to enterprise customers. As a first step, Tellme and SpeechCycle Inc. announced an alliance where SpeechCycle will use Tellme's platform for on-demand speech applications. Additional information can be found at http://www.tellme.com/business.

PART III

Mobility Opportunities

Microsoft's SMB customers have reported that among network devices, smartphones will constitute their largest growth area in the next five years. To help reseller partners prepare for this, Microsoft's Mobile Communications Business offers its Mobile Readiness Program, which will address resellers with four components:

- The Get Mobile Ready initiative offers Microsoft consulting to small and midsize resellers.

- The Try and Buy initiative deploys Microsoft mobility solutions within resellers to create SMB mobility experts around the globe and help partners showcase the technology in action.

- The Microsoft Partner Program Mobility Competency is a full-scale resource to train and certify resellers that are ready to take the next step in mobility.

- Microsoft distributors worldwide offer solutions to help resellers provide their SMB customers with a ready-made package of mobility offerings at a competitive price.

Active Directory

Starting with Windows 2000, Microsoft added a key component to its flagship operating system—Active Directory. Active Directory is a Microsoft directory service, and it is used to provision, store, and manage users, groups, passwords, and contacts, among other objects. Further, it is the basis for the global address list (GAL) that Outlook clients use.

It is key not only in your organization's Microsoft network, but it is also necessary to use it as part of an Exchange Online deployment. In order to use it with Exchange Online, there are two scenarios:

- The organization has no corporate Active Directory, and all users, mailboxes, distribution groups, and so on are managed through a web-based management console.

- The organization does have a corporate Active Directory and has integrated the corporate and Exchange directories using synchronization tools.

To configure Active Directory with Exchange Online, you want to use the Microsoft Online Services Directory Synchronization Tool. You should also configure Active Directory User attributes if you want to use User Login User Principal Names (UPNs) for the sake of consistency with the on-site Active Directory environment.

For instance, an on-site Active Directory using the domain name of compuglobalmegaware .com has users with a login of *user*@compuglobalmegaware. There is no Exchange messaging environment within this Active Directory, but user objects have their MAIL attribute configured, so they are set to have email. In a non-Exchange AD environment, DirSync must be used to create new Microsoft Online Users.

To make a replica of your on-site Active Directory environment with the Microsoft Online environment, follow these steps:

1. Create a Microsoft Online Service Domain name. Use the same name as your on-site company (like compuglobalmegaware.com).

2. Verify the Microsoft Online Service Domain name. This proves that you have ownership and allows a Microsoft Online Services administrator to create new users for this domain. It also provides a means to add SMTP addresses for existing users.

3. Set this domain name as default. As new users are created, their accounts and email address will use this domain.

4. Modify the on-site Active Directory User object's MAIL attribute with an email address that was previously created and verified (for instance, *user*@compuglobalmegaware.com)

5. Run the Microsoft Online Services Directory Synchronization Tool. This replicates all mail and mailbox-enabled users and groups into the Microsoft Online Company.

In this chapter we took a look at Software plus Services, and noted the ways you can develop your own software to work with cloud offerings. However, we barely scratched the surface. In the next chapter we'll take a closer look at how you can develop your own applications and some of the different options for doing so.

PART III

CHAPTER

Developing Applications

Chances are good that the application you need to work on the cloud has already been created; it's just a matter of finding and subscribing to it. But if you can't find the application you're looking for, you can make your own, and you wouldn't be alone in your endeavor. A 2009 survey from Evans Data shows that 40 percent of surveyed developers working on open-source projects plan to deliver their applications as web services offerings using cloud providers.

In this chapter we'll talk about some of the different cloud offerings out there. Varying levels of intricacy and functionality are available. For instance, you can write an app and host it on the Google App Engine in a few minutes (we'll show you how later in this chapter), while other clouds are more complex, but offer more features. Some clouds cater to specific needs, like Intuit's QuickBase, which allows you to develop financial-based cloud apps. Let's start by looking at some different development platforms and talk about their strengths and weaknesses.

Google

If you want to get an app on the cloud, the Google App Engine is the perfect tool to use to make this dream become reality. In essence, you write a bit of code in Python, tweak some HTML code, and then you've got your app built, and it only takes a few minutes.

NOTE *It takes a few minutes for a simple, basic app. It'll take longer if you have something more complex in mind. Your mileage may vary.*

Best of all, you don't have to worry about buying servers, load balancers, or DNS tables—Google handles all the heavy lifting for you. There are a number of points that need to be considered when writing an app for the cloud.

Having knowledge of Python certainly helps, but it isn't a deal-breaker, because Python is a lot like other scripting languages. A seasoned programmer should be able to pick it up with some ease, and there are certainly plenty of resources—either paper-and-glue books or web sites—that can help.

Java is very prevalent on the cloud. It is a very robust scripting tool and one that programmers know well. But its complexity is probably hurting it more than helping.

On average, hosting for Java applications begins around US$10 per month, while Python services start at around US$2 per month.

Other Python advantages include the open-source nature of Python and the fact that the language's creator—Guido van Rossum—works at Google. Google was able to tweak the language slightly so that dangerous operations are not allowed, like writing to the file system. This prevents robust uploading services and spawn subthreads. Your app has to be pretty efficient, because App Engine will kill any thread that takes too long to run.

NOTE *Google built this in by design, given the fact that new programmers are likely to screw up and make an app that falls into an endless loop. It also means that App Engine is better for the front ends of databases that don't have to do a lot of independent thinking or computation.*

App Engine is akin to a data store. It won't do the complex things that Oracle will allow. The database is integrated well with Python, but only allows basic search and store functions that you would need to tuck away users' information. Data objects are set up in Python, and then you use the save method and all the data disappears into the cloud where instances of the app can find it.

Python looks a lot like SQL, but with a different syntax. That means that you can't use any of the millions of already scripted SQL tools to generate reports or produce graphs. Also, App Engine doesn't store joins, which will break some of the code written for traditional databases.

Google App Engine isn't perfect. The documentation mentions web services and Asynchronous JavaScript and XML (AJAX), but there isn't much support for them.

Payment

Google is charging when applications exceed certain limits. For instance, Google says that you can only get "200 million megacycles of CPU per day." This can be a little frightening, because Google can skew the number in odd ways that are beyond your control. Further, you could see resources being used up as the database stores information on more than one server. That means that if one server starts asking for information, interserver traffic can slow everything down, and if two users are trying to get at the same data at the same time, access can become slow and expensive. On the plus side, App Engine will bring up new servers when demand rises.

As with other cloud offerings, you are at Google's mercy. Looking at the terms and conditions, you can see that Google has the power to do whatever they want with your creation. Lock-in can be a problem, but at least it is somewhat offset by the open-source nature of the scripting language. Since Python is open source, you can take your toys and leave if you want.

App Engine is best for simple applications that plan on staying simple. The cloud can scale the application as needed, but if you have dreams of making your application big, Google might not be the best option.

Also, since the cloud is somewhat new territory, Google says it reserves the right to "pre-screen, review, flag, filter, modify, refuse or remove any or all Content from the Service." It's still early to tell, but given that amount of control, if there is a copyright infraction, will Google work with the developer, or just wipe the developer's account from their servers?

There are plenty of competitors in the cloud. Amazon has its own cloud, but it takes a different approach, giving the user an empty Linux shell. That offers more flexibility, but the handholding isn't there as it is on Google. It might take longer to place an application on Amazon's Elastic Compute Cloud, but it offers richer APIs, including web services for REST and SOAP queries.

Force.com and Google

Salesforce.com struck up a strategic alliance with Google with the availability of Force.com for Google App Engine. Force.com for Google App Engine is a set of tools and services to enable developer success with application development in the cloud. The offering brings together Force.com and Google App Engine, enabling the creation of entirely new web and business applications. Force.com for Google App Engine builds on the relationship between Salesforce.com and Google, spanning philanthropy, business applications, social networks, and cloud computing.

"We have an open vision for cloud computing," said Marc Benioff, chairman and CEO, Salesforce.com. "Developers now can take advantage of the easy to use and rapidly scalable cloud computing infrastructures from Google and Salesforce.com to build and deliver powerful business applications."

"At Google, as at Salesforce.com, we are committed to enabling developer success with cloud computing," said Tom Stocky, director of product management at Google. "Bringing together Google App Engine and Force.com will foster the creation of new Web applications and further demonstrate the power of the Web as a platform."

Force.com for Google App Engine provides a set of tools and services meant to foster the creation of new kinds of web and business applications built and delivered entirely in the cloud. Instead of managing and maintaining their own client/server infrastructure, developers can use cloud computing infrastructure from Google and Salesforce.com to build, run, and deliver new applications on the Web. Web applications developed on App Engine are easy to build, easy to maintain, and easy to scale as traffic and data storage needs grow. App Engine offers a developer community and libraries to power consumer-oriented interactive web applications.

Similarly, Force.com provides developers a complete environment to quickly build business applications that run on Salesforce.com's trusted global infrastructure. Now, consumer-oriented web applications built on App Engine can leverage enterprise data stored in Force.com.

For end users of these applications, the integration of Force.com and Google App Engine means that applications can be powered by both systems.

Using Force.com for Google App Engine, developers can build applications that span both Salesforce.com and Google's cloud computing platforms, and take advantage of the sum of their features as desired. Force.com for Google App Engine provides:

- A means to leverage Python in a scalable cloud environment and interact directly with database, workflow, and logic capabilities in Force.com.

- Force.com for Google App Engine enables the creation of Python libraries that, when placed on Google App Engine, allow App Engine apps to read and write to Force.com using the Force.com API.

- App Engine developers get access to Force.com services and capabilities including mobile, analytics, security and sharing models, user authentication, multilanguage and currency support, and more.

"In times like these, companies are asking for ways they can take advantage of the low-cost and low-risk benefits of cloud computing for their enterprise application development projects," said Narinder Singh, CMO, Appirio, a leading Salesforce.com and Google Enterprise partner. "Force.com for Google App Engine brings together the leaders in cloud computing to help address those needs and allows corporate IT to easily scale up or down to meet changing business conditions."

The companies have been working together to advance philanthropic causes as well as the benefits of cloud computing for developers and customers. Beginning in 2003 with joint work around the creation of Google.org, the alliance has been extended to work together on mashups, Salesforce for Google AdWords, Group Edition featuring Google AdWords, OpenSocial, Salesforce for Google Apps, Force.com for Google Data APIs, and now Force.com for Google App Engine.

More than 5,000 Salesforce.com customers are using Google Apps, and more than 10,000 are using Salesforce for Google AdWords. And five of the top ten most popular applications on the Force.com AppExchange marketplace come from Google-related partners.

Force.com for Google App Engine helps developers create new web and business applications that leverage the capabilities of App Engine, at the same time allowing access to Force.com data and APIs from directly within App Engine projects and applications. Force.com for App Engine includes

- Getting started guide
- Python library documentation
- Examples showing Python code accessing Force.com
- Testing harness for the provided library
- Wiki FAQ page on developer.force.com with best practices and latest tips and tricks

Google Gears

Another development tool that Google offers is Google Gears, an open-source technology for creating offline web applications. This browser extension was made available in its early stages so that the development community could test its capabilities and limitations and help Google improve upon it. Google's long-term hope is that Google Gears can help the industry as a whole move toward a single standard for offline capabilities that all developers can use.

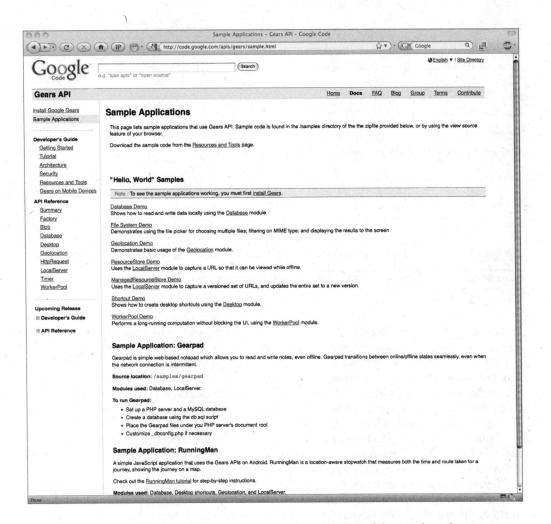

Google Gears addresses a major user concern: availability of data and applications when there's no Internet connection available, or when a connection is slow or unreliable. As application developers and users alike want to do more on the Web—whether it's email or CRM or photo editing—enhancements that make the browser environment itself more powerful are increasingly important.

"With Google Gears we're tackling a key limitation of the browser in order to make it a stronger platform for deploying all types of applications and enabling a better user experience in the cloud," said Eric Schmidt, CEO of Google. "We believe strongly in the power of the community to stretch this new technology to the limits of what's possible and ultimately emerge with an open standard that benefits everyone."

Google offers Google Gears as a free, fully open-source technology in order to help every web application, not just Google applications. As an example of what is possible, the Google Reader feed reader (http://reader.google.com) is available with Gears-enabled offline capabilities.

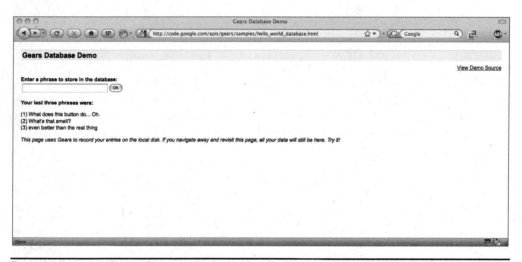

FIGURE 11-1   In this Google Gears application, some searched phrases are maintained on the local machine.

Google intends to work closely with all members of the web community to converge upon a standard so developers have one consistent API for offline functionality.

"We're very excited to be collaborating with Google to move the industry forward to a standard cross-platform, cross-browser local storage capability," said Kevin Lynch, senior vice president and chief software architect at Adobe. "The Gears API will also be available in Apollo, which enables web applications to run on the desktop, providing developers with consistent offline and local database solutions."

"This announcement is a significant step forward for web applications," said Brendan Eich, CTO at Mozilla Corporation. "We're pleased to see Google working with open source and open standards bodies on offline web applications."

"Opera and Google share the common goal of making Web applications richer and more robust," said Håkon Wium Lie, CTO, Opera Software. "Developers have long desired the functionality and flexibility Google Gears can offer browsers. Because Opera has always prioritized giving our users what they want, we're excited to work with Google to extend the reach and power of Web applications."

Google Gears builds on the Web's existing programming model by introducing new JavaScript APIs for sophisticated data storage, application caching, and multithreading features. With these APIs, developers can bring offline capabilities to even their most complex web applications. Google Gears works with all major browsers on all major platforms: Windows, Mac, and Linux. A sample of Google Gears in use is shown in Figure 11-1.

Google Gears is available at http://gears.google.com.

Microsoft

Microsoft's Azure Services Platform is a tool provided for developers who want to write applications that are going to run partially or entirely in a remote datacenter.

The Azure Services Platform (Azure) is an Internet-scale cloud services platform hosted in Microsoft datacenters, which provides an operating system and a set of developer services that can be used individually or together. Azure can be used to build new applications to run from the cloud or to enhance existing applications with cloud-based capabilities, and it forms the foundation of all Microsoft's cloud offerings. Its open architecture gives developers the choice to build web applications, applications running on connected devices, PCs, servers, or hybrid solutions offering the best of online and on-premises. Some of the applications available on the Azure cloud are shown in Figure 11-2.

Azure allows developers to quickly create applications running in the cloud by using their existing skills with the Microsoft Visual Studio development environment and the Microsoft .NET Framework. In addition to managing code languages supported by .NET, Microsoft plans more support for additional programming languages and development environments.

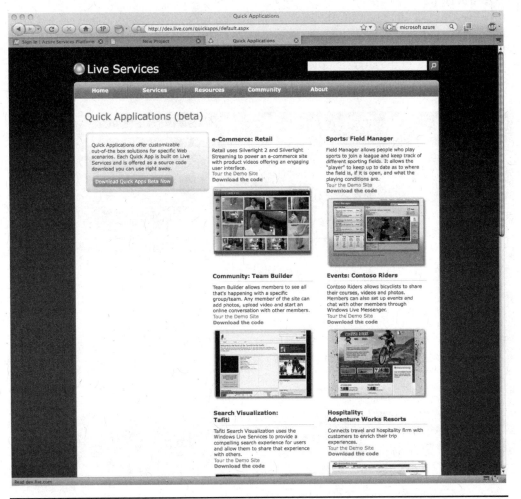

FIGURE 11-2   Microsoft's Azure offers a number of applications that you can use right away.

Infrastructure management is automated with a platform that is designed for high availability and dynamic scaling to match usage needs with the option of a pay-as-you-go pricing model. Azure provides an open, standards-based, and interoperable environment with support for multiple Internet protocols, including HTTP, REST, SOAP, and XML.

Microsoft also offers cloud applications ready for consumption by customers such as Windows Live, Microsoft Dynamics, and other Microsoft Online Services for business such as Microsoft Exchange Online and SharePoint Online. The Azure Services Platform lets developers provide their own unique customer offerings by offering the foundational components of compute, storage, and building block services to author and compose applications in the cloud.

Azure utilizes several other Microsoft services as part of its platform, known as the Live Mesh platform.

Live Services

Live Services is a set of building blocks within the Azure Services Platform that is used to handle user data and application resources. Live Services provides developers with a way to build social applications and experiences across a range of digital devices that can connect with one of the largest audiences on the Web.

Microsoft SQL Services

Microsoft SQL Services enhances the capabilities of Microsoft SQL Server into the cloud as a web-based, distributed relational database. It provides web services that enable relational queries, search, and data synchronization with mobile users, remote offices, and business partners. It can store and retrieve structured, semistructured, and unstructured data.

Microsoft .NET Services

Microsoft .NET Services is a tool for developing loosely coupled cloud-based applications. .NET Services includes access control to help secure applications, a service bus for communicating across applications and services, and hosted workflow execution. These hosted services allow the creation of applications that span from on-premises environments to the cloud.

Microsoft SharePoint Services and Dynamics CRM Services

Microsoft SharePoint Services and Dynamics CRM Services are used to allow developers to collaborate and build strong customer relationships. Using tools like Visual Studio, developers can build applications that utilize SharePoint and CRM capabilities.

Design

Azure is designed in several layers, with different things going on under the hood.

Layer Zero

Layer Zero is Microsoft's Global Foundational Service. GFS is akin to the hardware abstraction layer (HAL) in Windows. It is the most basic level of the software that interfaces directly with the servers.

Layer One

Layer One is the base Azure operating system. It used to be code-named "Red Dog," and was designed by a team of operating system experts at Microsoft. Red Dog is the technology that networks and manages the Windows Server 2008 machines that form the Microsoft-hosted cloud.

Red Dog is made up of four pillars:

- Storage (a file system)
- The fabric controller, which is a management system for deploying and provisioning
- Virtualized computation/VM
- Development environment, which allows developers to emulate Red Dog on their desktops

Red Dog is designed by Microsoft such that it only has to be deployed on a single machine, and then multiple instances of it can be duplicated to the rest of the machines in the cloud.

Layer Two

Layer Two provides the building blocks that run on Azure. These services are the aforementioned Live Mesh platform. Developers build on top of these lower-level services when building cloud apps.

SharePoint Services and CRM Services are not the same as SharePoint Online and CRM Online. They are just the platform basics that do not include user interface elements.

Layer Three

At Layer Three exist the Azure-hosted applications. Some of the applications developed by Microsoft include SharePoint Online, Exchange Online, Dynamics CRM, and Online. Third parties will create other applications.

Intuit QuickBase

Cullen Coates, a management consultant from Larkspur, California–based Crystal Bay Solutions, is not a software engineer. But that didn't keep him from creating an entire suite of on-demand software applications to assist nonprofit organizations—everything from donor management to collaborative tools for workgroups—without writing a single line of code.

Coates is just one of a growing group of value-added resellers, or VARs, that are shifting their business models away from reselling and installing packaged solutions to take advantage of the implementation speed and cost-effectiveness of delivering SaaS.

To support this new generation of consultants, Intuit Inc.'s QuickBase launched its new QuickBase Business Consultant Program. The program allows members to use their expertise to create unique business applications tailored specifically to the industries they serve—without technical expertise or coding. This helps members expand their reach into industries formerly served only by IT experts. Using QuickBase, program members will be able to easily build new on-demand business applications from scratch or customize one of 200 available templates and resell them to their clients.

"SaaS implementations do not require highly technical people, although they may require consultants with data integration skills. Instead, seasoned business process management consultants will become the focus for successful project delivery," according to Forrester Research Inc.'s Oct. 29, 2008 report, "SaaS Economics Will Change ISVs' SI And VAR Channels."

"As a result, the technical integration and customization services revenues shift to process transformation projects—and into the coffers of system integrators and VARs that have these consulting skills," the report adds.

Before joining the QuickBase program, Coates' firm was limited to recommending off-the-shelf applications that cost more than $100,000 or custom-developed solutions built on other platforms.

"Today, I can deliver a QuickBase application customized specifically for a customer's business process in a quarter of the time, at half the cost and twice the margin," said Coates. "Plus, since it's a software-as-a-service application, the costs are lower for my customers and they can be up and running in weeks, rather than months."

To help members succeed, the program provides training, partner relationship management, and lead-generation tools to help them locate potential customers and maximize the power of QuickBase. QuickBase Business Consultants also receive a free version of QuickBooks Online to help them better manage and grow their own businesses.

"Until now, businesses had to choose either a tailor made solution that fit their process, or a SaaS solution that was fast, low risk and provided anytime, anywhere access. Now, creating a tailored solution for business on a SaaS platform is not only possible, it's easy," said Bill Lucchini, vice president and general manager of QuickBase. "Making software fit the business needs was formerly the exclusive territory of IT and engineers. With the QuickBase Business Consultant Program, the value shifts to the entrepreneurs and industry experts who can now solve real business problems without being a technical expert. Entrepreneurs and forward-thinking VARs will see huge benefits from this shift."

For more information on the QuickBase Business Consultant Program and to apply to the program, visit: http://quickbase.intuit.com/links/partners.asp.

Cast Iron Cloud

Cast Iron Systems introduced its development platform, the Cast Iron Cloud. Cast Iron offers the choice of a completely cloud-based integration service or an on-premise integration appliance as an organization's application ecosystem evolves. Any organization, regardless of size or resources, can connect SaaS solutions with other on-demand and on-premise applications, immediately boosting productivity.

"Productive SaaS deployments don't operate in a vacuum," said Ken Comée, CEO and president of Cast Iron Systems. "Companies must be able to efficiently integrate SaaS solutions with other enterprise systems to effectively orchestrate cross-functional business processes. By delivering our integration solution in the Cast Iron Cloud, or via our on-premise appliances, we can provide organizations with a seamless and secure transition between on-demand and on-premise environments."

As SaaS usage expands from departmental silos into the extended enterprise, integration of data and applications is even more critical to productivity and success. Cast Iron and its partners can deliver the most widely used solution for connecting SaaS and enterprise applications through the simplicity and speed of Integration as a Service (IaaS). The Cast Iron Cloud leverages the company's delivery of completed integration projects quickly and also eliminates the need for customers to invest in integration infrastructure or deep middleware expertise.

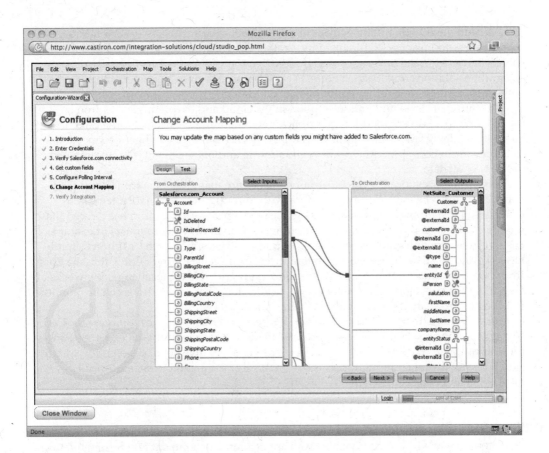

"Our customers have been very successful using Cast Iron to bring Force.com and Salesforce CRM into their IT environments," said Ariel Kelman, senior director of platform product marketing at Salesforce.com. "With Cast Iron integration solutions available on the Force.com AppExchange, small businesses and large enterprises alike tell us that Cast Iron gives them great time to value for their integration projects."

"Given the growing number of vertical solutions built on NS-BOS for NetSuite, as well as the increasing sophistication of our customer base, we wanted to provide our customers and partners options on how to connect to specific vertical and legacy systems," said Mini Peiris, NetSuite's vice president of product marketing. "With built-in connectivity to NetSuite solutions and the flexibility to deliver integration in the cloud or using an appliance, Cast Iron accelerates adoption of our ERP, ecommerce, and CRM suite."

Analyst firms Saugatuck Technology and Gartner explain the importance of this announcement for both SaaS users and providers.

Analyst Michael West of Saugatuck Technology summarizes: "To take advantage of SaaS at an enterprise level, users must have access to broad, deep, and sophisticated integration capabilities. Requirements for integration could stifle effective and efficient enterprise-wide deployment of SaaS unless SaaS providers commit to delivering more and better enterprise-ready integration solutions."

According to Gartner, "An analysis of a cross-section of successful SaaS vendors reveals that business-to-business (B2B) flexibility—rather than any one B2B standard or approach—lowers barriers to SaaS integration and helps drive SaaS adoption. The diversity of SaaS integration solutions from SaaS vendors is good because it gives customers more options to solve their diverse integration requirements."

By offering its SaaS integration solution in the cloud and on-premise, Cast Iron is anticipating these diverse end-to-end application integration needs, including data cleansing and migration, and application integration by offering intelligent connections, data transformations, process workflow, monitoring and management, plus guaranteed delivery of all data.

Cast Iron is transforming the integration experience using the Cast Iron Cloud. The company is introducing a cloud-based library of preconfigured Template Integration Processes (TIPs) for the most common SaaS business processes. Cast Iron has created these templates based on its experience with thousands of customer integrations. For example, if customers need to integrate two SaaS applications, they simply search Cast Iron's cloud-based library of TIPs, choose the TIP that matches their scenario, and deploy it to the Cast Iron Cloud. In minutes, their SaaS integration project goes live rather than taking weeks or even months to develop using custom code. In addition, SaaS integrations can be monitored from anywhere at any time using the Cast Iron Cloud.

For companies that want to customize TIPs based on their specific requirements, Cast Iron is providing a self-guided wizard similar to the simple wizard-based experience in popular products like Intuit TurboTax. Users answer a few questions based on the specific situation, and the integration process is automatically customized to expedite SaaS integration and adoption.

Bungee Connect

Bungee Labs offers its Bungee Connect web application development and hosting platform. Developers use Bungee Connect to build desktop-like web applications that leverage multiple web services and databases, and then deploy them on Bungee's multitenant grid infrastructure.

Bungee Connect provides development, testing, deployment, and hosting in a single, on-demand platform. The company claims that using their solution, significant time and cost are eliminated across the entire application life cycle—reducing time-to-market by as much as 80 percent.

Bungee Connect includes the following features:

- A single, on-demand environment for developing, testing, deploying, and hosting
- Interaction delivered entirely via browser with no download or plug-in for developers or end users
- Delivery of highly interactive user experience without compromising accessibility and security
- Automated integration of web services (SOAP/REST) and databases (MySQL/PostgreSQL)
- Built-in team collaboration and testing

- Built-in scalability, reliability, and security
- Deep instrumentation of end-user application utilization for analytics
- Utility pricing model based on end-user application use

Developers and IT managers can leverage a completely online platform to build and deliver powerful, AJAX-enabled, multiple data-source web applications. Applications may be embedded within other web applications and pages, Software as a Service (SaaS) solutions, or delivered as stand-alone web destinations.

"Cloud computing, internal-external mashups and online business services are hastening the need for new business models that can support entire application lifecycles," said Dana Gardner, principal analyst of Interarbor Solutions. "It's not enough to develop as a service, or to deploy as a service—the fuller cost-benefit payback comes from the application lifecycle as a service. All the better that costs to support the applications from inception to sunset are commensurate with use and demand. Enterprise IT innovators and efficiency-minded independent developers alike should view the Bungee Connect model as the platform and mashup approach of the future."

Development, team collaboration, and test deployment hosting on Bungee Connect are free of charge. Developers pay only when their applications are actually used by end users. Once a Bungee-powered application is deployed on the Bungee Grid infrastructure, end-user utilization of the application is deeply instrumented to provide developers with detailed insight into application performance and usage patterns, and to compute the application's utility bill.

Depending on the usage profile of an application, businesses can expect to pay between US$2 to US$5 per user per month for a heavily used business productivity application, or fractions of a cent per e-commerce transaction. All Bungee-powered applications are hosted for free during the Bungee Connect Public Beta.

For more information about Bungee Connect, visit http://www.bungeeconnect.com.

Development

As we have noted, there are many different places you can turn to develop your own applications. We don't have the space to cover each and every development platform, so we'll walk you through the development steps with three different, popular platforms: the Google App Engine, Salesforce.com, and Microsoft Azure.

Google App Engine

Google uses Python, so we'll use that script in this demonstration. Again, this is not meant to be a comprehensive explanation of Python. Indeed, entire books have been written about Python, but we're only going to use one Python command. We aren't going to make anything particularly robust (or useful for that matter), but it'll demonstrate the basics so you get an idea of how apps are developed.

Environment

To get started, you must first download the Google App Engine development kit, located at http://code.google.com/appengine/downloads.html. The SDK is available for Windows, Mac OS X, and Linux environments that also have Python 2.5.

The SDK includes a web server application that simulates the App Engine environment. It also includes a local version of datastore, Google Accounts, and the ability to get URLs and send email from your computer using the App Engine APIs.

NOTE *You will need Python 2.5 installed on your computer. Mac OS X Leopard users already have Python 2.5 installed. You can download Python from the Python web site at http://www.python.org/.*

Download and install the App Engine SDK. For this demonstration, you will use two commands from the SDK:

- `dev_appserver.py` The development web server
- `appcfg.py` Used to upload your app to App Engine

If you are using the Zip archive version of the SDK, those commands are located in the google_appengine directory.

The App

App Engine applications communicate with the web server using the CGI standard. When the server receives a request for your application, it runs the app with the request data in environment variables and on the input stream. When it responds, the app writes the response to the output stream and includes HTTP content.

Here's Johnny! The app we are going to make displays a little greeting. To get started, make a directory named heresjohnny. All the files for this app will be stored in this directory.

Inside that directory, create a file named heresjohnny.py to include this code:

```
print 'Content-Type: text/plain'
print ''
print 'Here's Johnny!'
```

What's going on here is that the Python script responds to the request with an HTTP header that describes content (HTTP), a blank line, and the message, "Here's Johnny!"

Configuration File Next, you need to have a configuration file called app.yaml. What this does is to describe—among other things—which handler scripts are to be used for which URLs.

Create a file in the directory called app.yaml and write it to read as follows:

```
application: heresjohnny
version: 1
runtime: python
api_version: 1

handlers:
- url: /.*
  script: heresjohnny.py
```

Here's what the code is doing, line by line:

- The application identifier is `heresjohnny`. When the application is registered with App Engine, you select a unique identifier, so this will change. It can be named whatever you want at this stage.

- Since this is the first version of this code, this is number 1. Use this field to keep track of different versions of your app's code.

- This code runs in the Python runtime environment, version 1.

- Every request to a URL whose path matches the regular expression /.* will be handled by the heresjohnny.py script.

Script Testing   Because the handler script and configuration file are mapping every URL to the handler, the application is done. That's it. Now you can test the app with the web server included with the App Engine SDK.

Start the web server with the following command (including the path to the heresjohnny directory):

```
google_appengine/dev_appserver.py heresjohnny/
```

Now that the web server is running, it is listening for requests on port 8080. Check to make sure it is using that port by entering this URL in a web browser:

```
http://localhost:8080/
```

You can leave the web server running, even if you make changes to the app. The web server knows to watch for changes in your source files and reload them if need be.

Test it out. Make a change to your heresjohnny.py file and then reload the page by entering http://localhost:8080.

Uploading the App

After creating and managing your app and registering it on Google, the next step is to upload the application using a command-line tool included in the SDK called appcfg.py.

Registration   After you've created your app using the Administration Console (found at http://appengine.google.com/), the next step is to register the application ID for your application. This is shown in Figure 11-3.

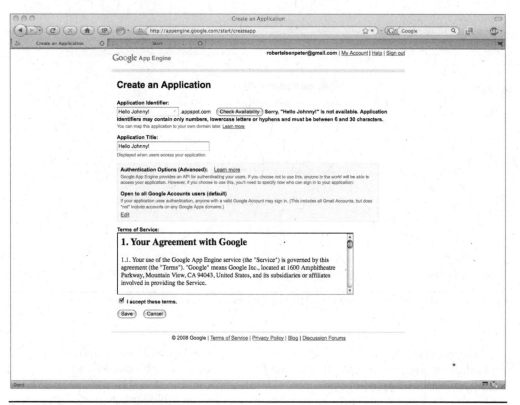

Figure 11-3   Use the Administration Console to register your apps on Google App Engine.

As you can see in Figure 11-3, the name we wanted—"Here's Johnny!"—has already been taken. We'll give it a more convoluted name. After trying several names (all of which were taken), we just threw in some random letters and numbers. What this does is register the app with Google. The app will still be called Here's Johnny. There can be a million apps named Here's Johnny, but they all need different registration codes. Once the registration is successful, you see a screen like the one in Figure 11-4 that lets you start managing your app on the Google Cloud.

Once the registration is completed, you access the application by going to http://application-id.appspot.com. In our case, it would be http://pos7412.appspot.com.

Next, you have to go back into your app.yaml file and change the value of the application: setting. In our case, it is being changed from heresjohnny to pos7412. This tells the system what the app is registered as.

Send It In   To upload your finished application to Google App Engine, run the following command:

```
appcfg.py update heresjohnny/
```

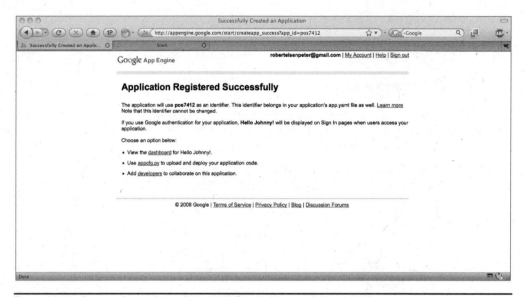

FIGURE 11-4   Once you've registered the app, Google lets you know that it's got a home.

Enter your Google username and password at the prompts. Now you can see your application on App Engine and all you need to do is open up a web browser and enter **http://application-id.appspot.com**.

Obviously, this is a very simple, very basic example. You can do much more with the Google App Engine SDK. You can find out more information on development from whatever vendor you get an SDK for.

Salesforce.com

Salesforce has two ways to create an application—using point-and-click methods or by using the command line. In this section, we'll examine the GUI method of application developing an application. In this example, we'll develop an application that tracks your lunch expenses.

Create an Account

The first step is to create your Salesforce account. This is a fairly straightforward affair and it's something you've probably already done on dozens of web sites. You need to go to http://developer.force.com/join. Simply follow the steps (you'll need to answer name, password, username, and so forth) and you'll be set up.

After a few minutes you'll get an email from Salesforce with a link to activate the account. Once you log in to your Developer Edition organization, then log in to https://login.salesforce.com.

Create an Object

The next step is to create an object that will hold the data—our lunch expenses. Salesforce applications already contain a lot of prebuilt objects—called standard objects—for the data your applications need. However, you can build custom applications. Those are called custom objects.

To create the object, log in to your Salesforce account at https:/login.salesforce.com and enter your username and password. Next, create the custom object by following these steps:

1. Select Setup in the upper-right corner of the page.

2. Click Create Objects in the sidebar menu to show the Custom Objects page.

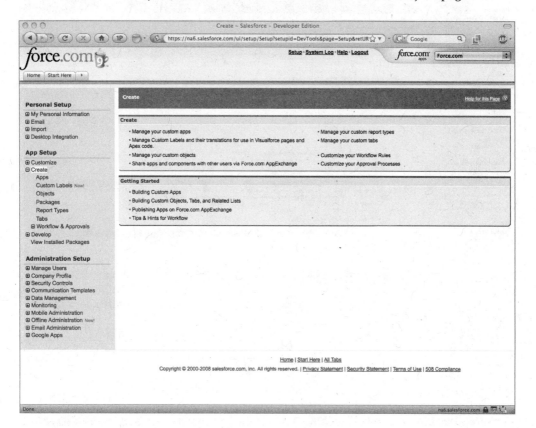

Fill in the custom object definition. This is shown in Figure 11-5:

3. Under Label, enter **Lunch**.

4. Under Plural Label, enter **Lunch**.

5. Under the Object Name, enter **Lunch**.

6. Under the Description, enter **Anobjectthatholdslunchexpenseinformation**.

7. Select the Allow Activities check box.

8. Select the Allow Reports check box.

9. Leave all the other values at their default levels.

10. Click Save to finish the custom object creation.

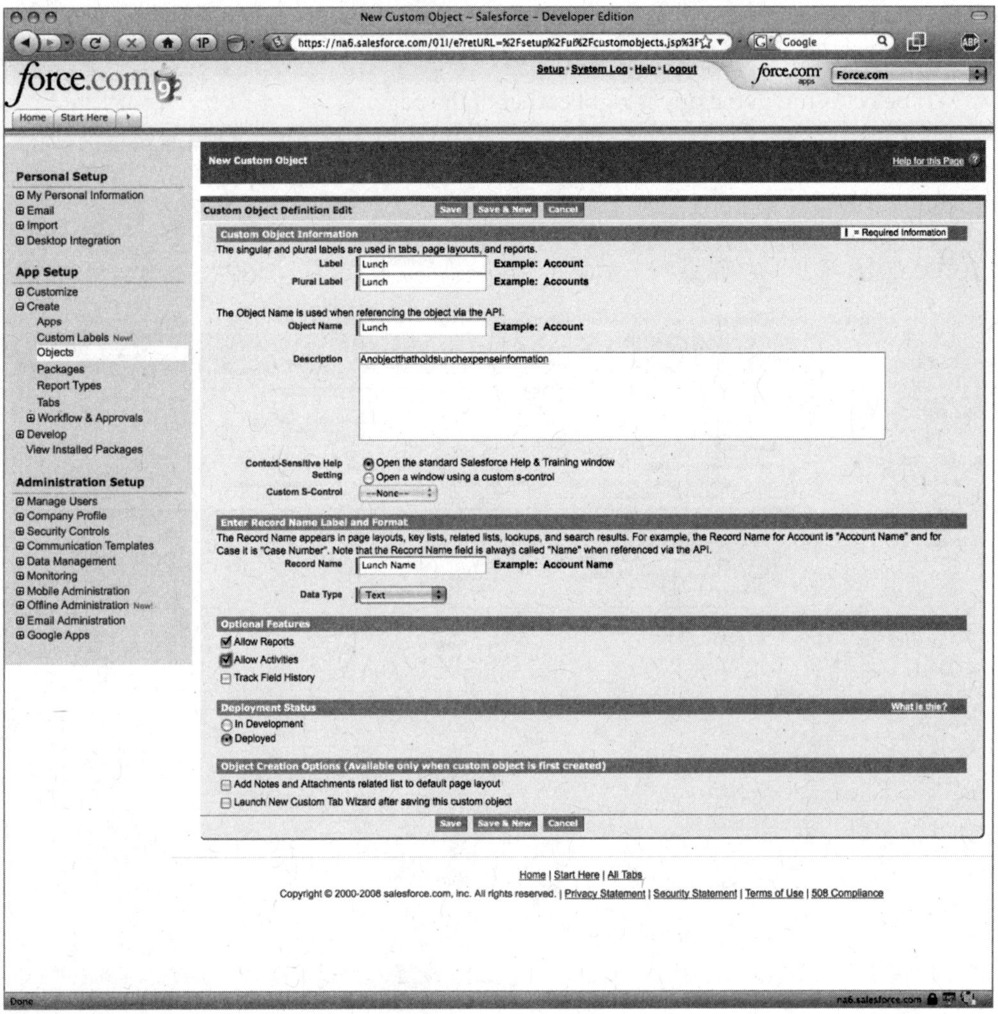

FIGURE 11-5   Start creating your app by defining a custom object.

Fields

After the custom object is made to hold your lunch expenses, the next step is to add fields that capture the date of your business lunch, how much you spent, and the person you entertained.

Date   First, create the Date field (shown in Figure 11-6).

1. Scroll down to the Custom Fields & Relationships related list.
2. Select New to start the New Custom Field Wizard.
3. Under Data Type, select Date and click Next.

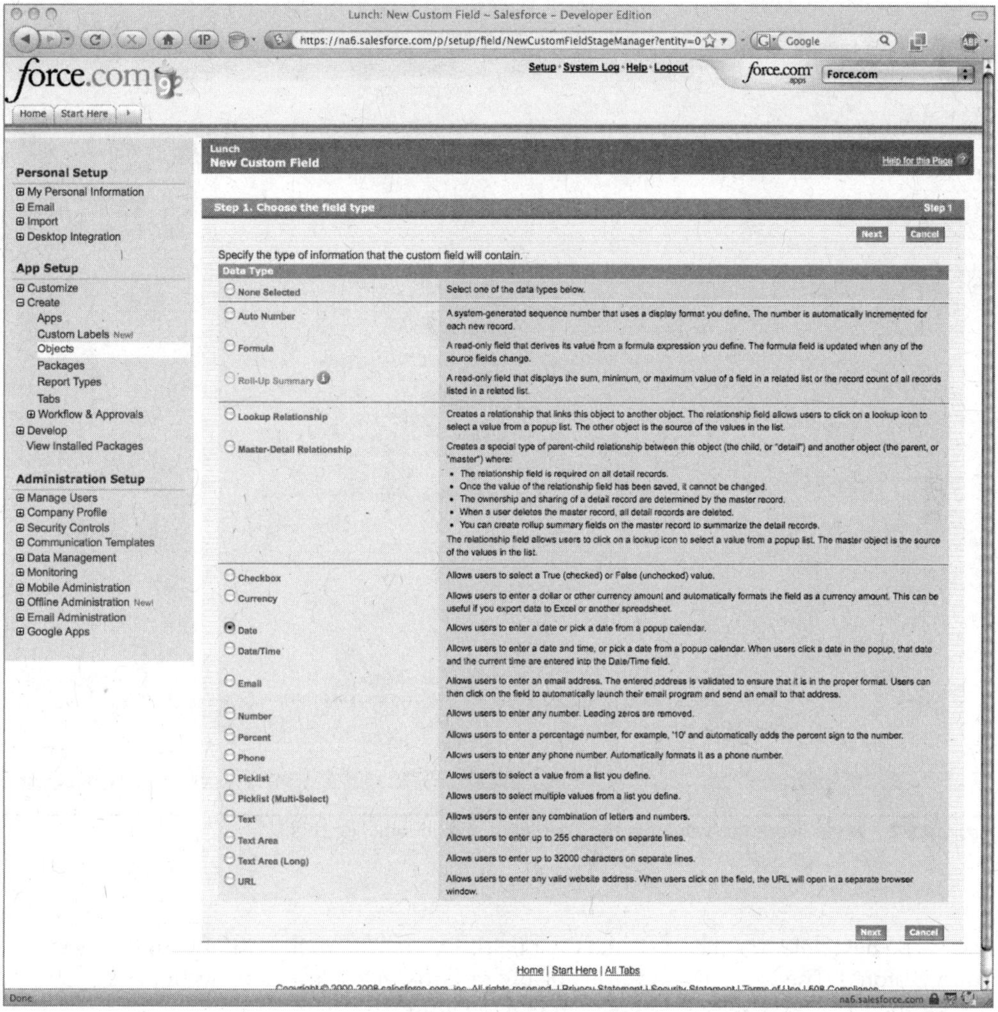

FIGURE 11-6   A key piece of data to be tracked by this app is the date.

4. Enter the following data (shown in Figure 11-7):

   - Under Field Label, enter **Date**.
   - Under Field Name, enter **Date**.
   - Under the Description, enter **Dateoflunch**.
   - Check the Required check box.
   - For the Default Value, enter **Today()**.

5. Click Next, accept the defaults, and click Next again.

6. Click Save & New to create the Date field and to restart the wizard for the next field.

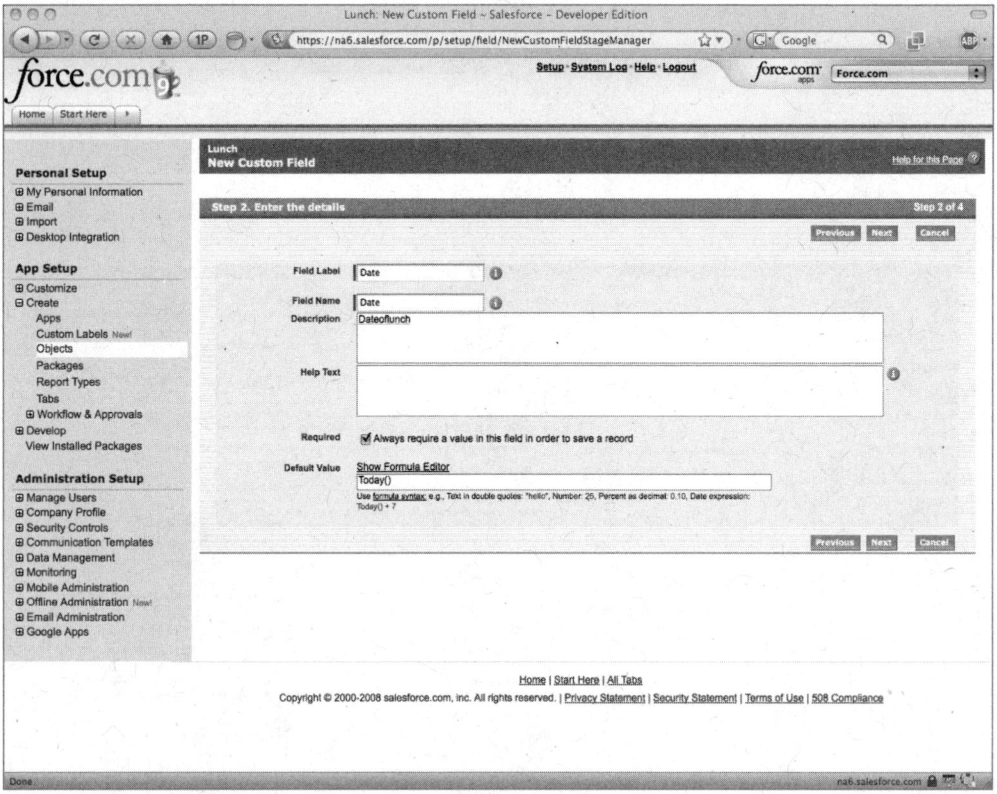

Figure 11-7   When filled, the values in the Date field should look like this.

Cost   The next field to generate is the Cost field. This is where the cost of your business lunch is stored. The wizard was automatically restarted in the previous section.

For the Data Type, select Number (shown in Figure 11-8).

Fill in the fields as follows (shown in Figure 11-9):

1. Under Field Label, enter **Cost**.

2. For the Length, enter **4**.

3. Under Decimal Places, enter **2**.

4. For the Field Name, enter **Cost**.

5. For the Description, enter **Costoflunch**.

6. Check the Required check box.

7. Click Next, accept the defaults, and click Save & New to create the next field.

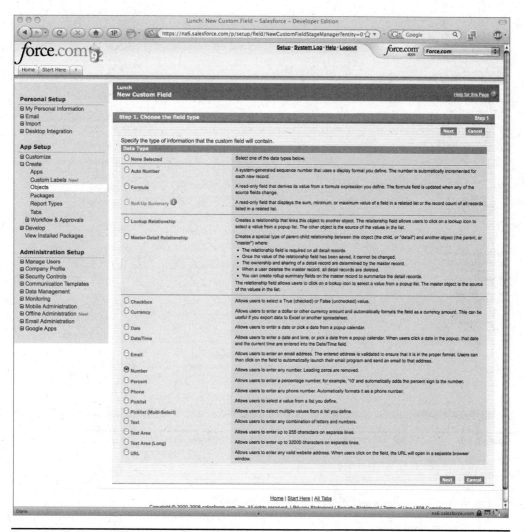

FIGURE 11-8   The next field to define is the Cost field.

Contact   The next field is the Contact field. This is the person with whom you had your business lunch. Again, if you clicked Save & New in the previous section, the field wizard restarts.

For the Data Type, select Lookup Relationship (shown in Figure 11-10) and click Next. The Lookup Relationship data type allows you to link two data objects. In this example, we'll connect the Cost object and the Contact object.

In the Related To drop-down list, select Contact and click Next.

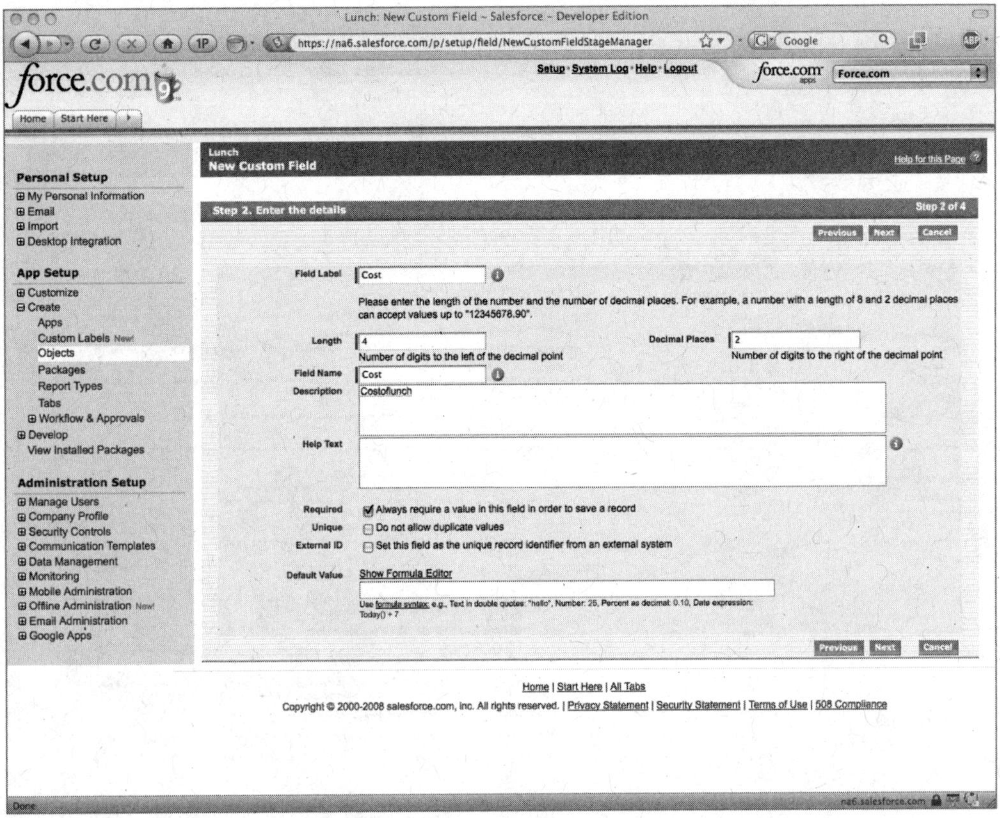

FIGURE 11-9 When filled, information in your Cost field will look like this.

Fill in the field details as follows (shown in Figure 11-11):

1. Under Field Label, enter **Contact**.

2. Under Field Name, enter **Contact**.

3. Under Description, enter **PersonIhadlunchwith**.

4. Leave the remaining defaults as they are, and then click Next.

5. Accept the defaults again and click Next.

6. Click Next two more times.

7. Click Save to finish up the field creation process.

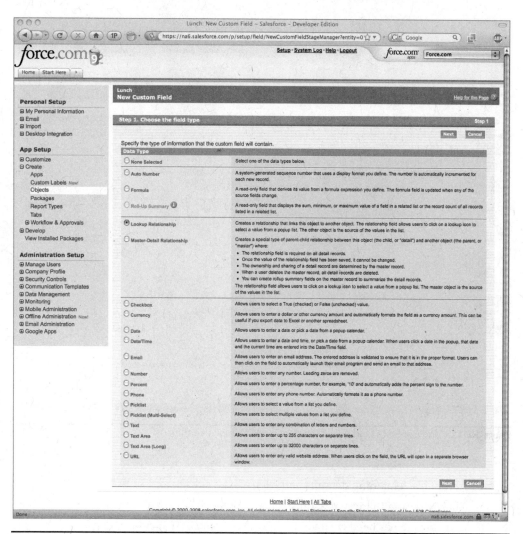

FIGURE 11-10   Selecting the Lookup Relationship data type allows you to link data for two objects.

Create a Tab

To show your application on the Salesforce web site, you need to create a tab to be added to the existing tabs. When users click this tab, they'll be able to track their lunch expenses.

1. On the startup page, click Create Tabs (this was the same screen where you created the object).

2. Click New in the Custom Objects tab list to launch the New Custom Tab wizard.

3. From the Object drop-down list, select Lunch.

4. For the Tab Style, click the lookup icon and select the apple, shown in Figure 11-12 (it was our only food option).

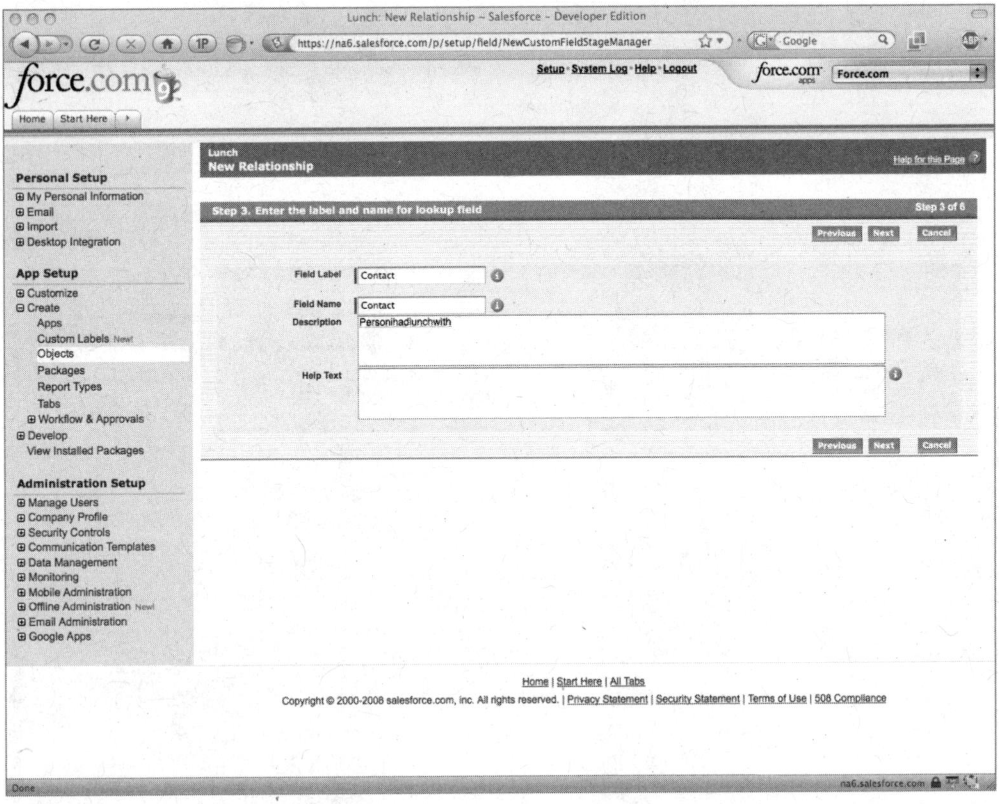

FIGURE 11-11 The Contacts field should be configured to look like this.

5. Accept the remaining defaults and click Next.

6. Click Next and then Save to finish creating the tab.

7. Once the tab has been created, it is added to your set of tabs.

Make the App

At this point, we have created three fields and a tab. These are all pulled together to create our app. You make the app by following these steps:

1. Go to Setup Create Apps.

2. Click New to launch the New Custom App Wizard.

Enter the following details (shown in Figure 11-13):

1. Under App Label, enter Lunch Tracker.

2. Under the App Name, enter Lunch_Tracker.

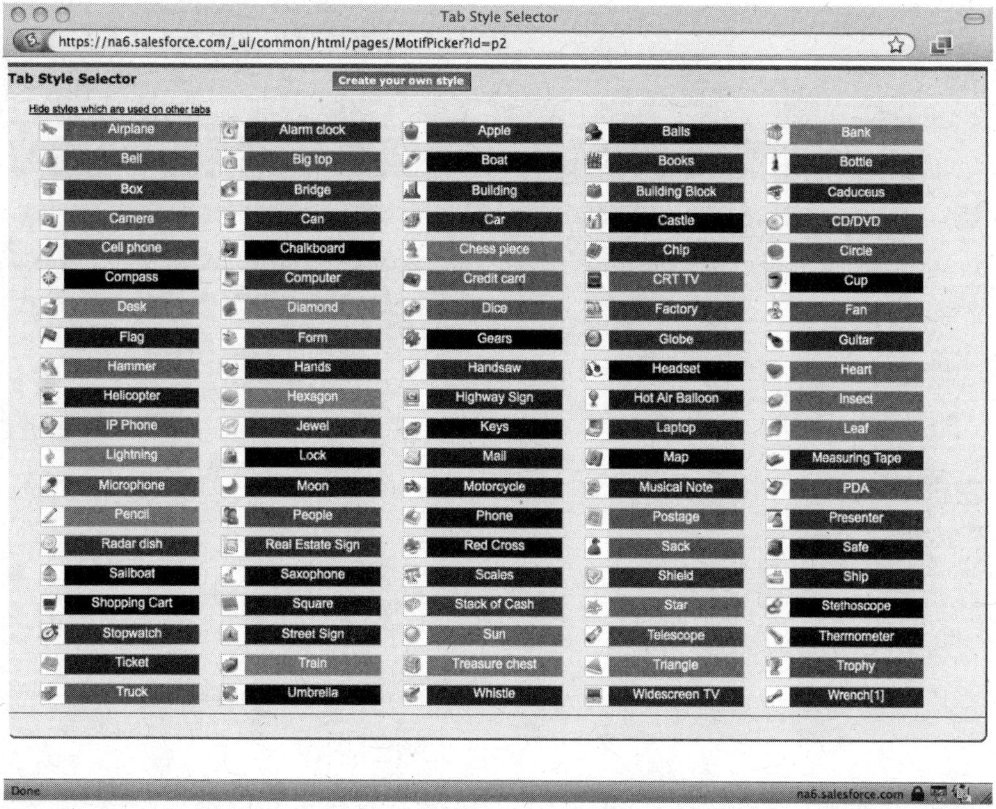

FIGURE 11-12 Start creating your app by defining a custom object.

3. Under the Description, enter **Thisapplicationtracksyourlunchexpenses**.

4. Click Next.

5. Accept the defaults and the default logo for the app, and then click Next.

6. In the Available Tabs box, locate the Lunch tab and click Add to add it to the selected tabs.

7. Leave the Default Landing tab set to the Home tab and click Next.

8. Select the Visible check box to make the app available to all users.

9. Click Save to create the Lunch Tracker app.

10. Repeat the steps 1–9, but this time select the Contacts tab. This is shown in Figure 11-14.

11. After the app is created, it is shown on the Force.com app menu in the upper right.

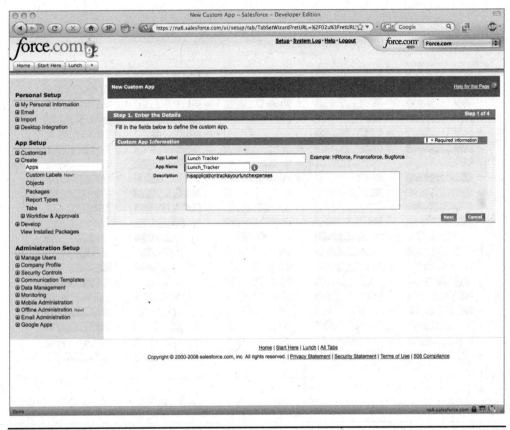

FIGURE 11-13   Configure your app to have settings like this one.

Test It Out

Now that your app has been created, let's take it for a spin.

1. Select the Lunch Tracker application from the Force.com app menu at the upper right of the screen.

2. Click on the Lunch Tracker tab and click New to create a new lunch expense entry.

3. Enter some test data (our example is shown in Figure 11-15).

4. For the Contact field, click the lookup icon, click New to create a new contact named BruceDickinson, and then click Save.

5. Click Save to save your record and to return to the detail page for the new record.

And there you have it. You were able to make your very own app on Salesforce quickly and easily, and you didn't need to use any coding—it was all point and click.

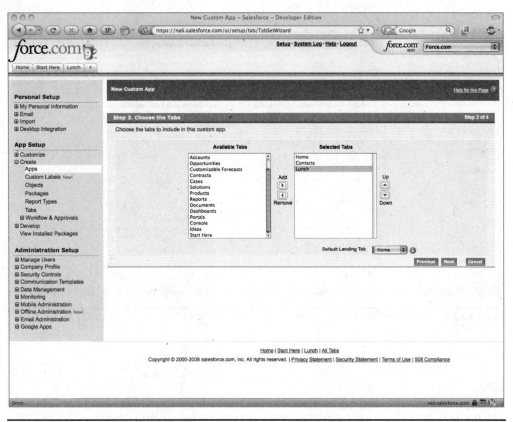

FIGURE 11-14   Choose Contacts and Lunch to be included in tabs.

Microsoft Windows Azure

Microsoft's Azure platform is a little different to develop apps for. It is similar to Google App Engine in that you have to download an SDK, but its features are a little more rich.

You develop applications within Visual Studio, which you then publish to the Windows cloud.

The Azure Services Platform is designed to help you quickly and easily create, deploy, manage, and distribute web services and applications on the Internet.

Windows Azure is an operating system for the cloud that serves as the development, run-time, and control environment for the Azure Services Platform. Windows Azure provides developers with on-demand compute and storage to host, scale, and manage web applications on the Internet through Microsoft datacenters.

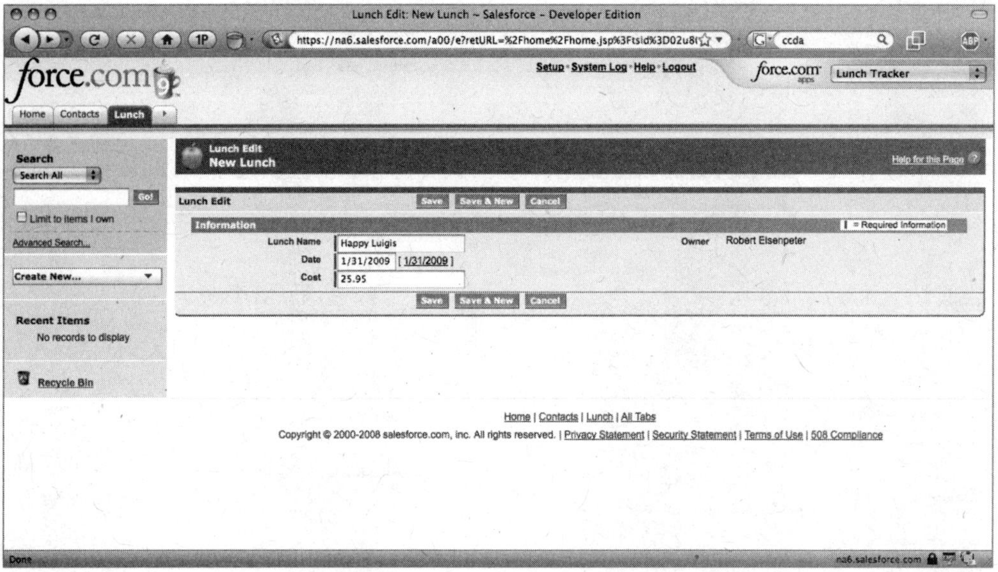

FIGURE 11-15   Start creating your app by defining a custom object.

SDK

To get started developing applications for Azure, you must first download the SDK. The January 2009 release is located at http://www.microsoft.com/downloads/details .aspx?FamilyID=80e3eabf-0507-4560-aeb6-d31e9a70a0a6&displaylang=en.

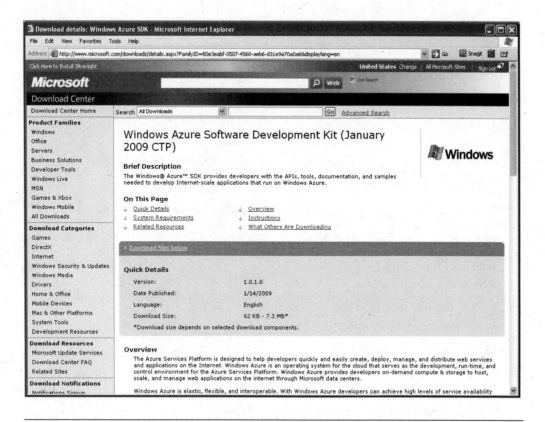

NOTE *There have been several different releases of the SDK. Check the Microsoft web site for the most current version.*

Unlike the Google App Engine, which has been written for Windows, Linux, and Mac OS X, Azure only operates on the latest Windows machines. Take a look at the system requirements to see if your machine is capable of running the SDK.

Supported operating systems include

- Windows Server 2008 Enterprise
- Windows Server 2008 Standard
- Windows Vista Business
- Windows Vista Business 64-bit edition
- Windows Vista Home Premium
- Windows Vista Home Premium 64-bit edition
- Windows Vista Ultimate
- Windows Vista Ultimate 64-bit edition

> **NOTE** *If you have a 64-bit machine, you need to use the 64-bit version of the SDK. The 32-bit version will not work.*

Other software requirements include

- Windows Vista SP1 (when installing on Windows Vista)
- .NET Framework 3.5 SP1
- IIS 7.0 (with ASP.NET and WCF HTTP Activation)
- Microsoft SQL Server Express 2005 or Microsoft SQL Server Express 2008
- Windows PowerShell (optional)

Microsoft also recommends that you have the Windows Azure Tools for Microsoft Visual Studio installed.

Once you install the Azure SDK, it will add new templates:

- Blank Cloud Service
- Web Cloud Service
- Web and Worker Cloud Service
- Worker Cloud Service

Windows Azure SDK includes two development utilities. This helps us develop our Windows Azure application in our local machine:

- **The Development Fabric**   This tool helps us to run and test Windows Azure application locally before deploying into Cloud.
- **The Development Storage**   This simulates the Blob, Queue, and Table Storage services available in the cloud.

Enabling IIS 7.0 on Windows Server 2008

You will need to enable IIS 7.0 with WCF HTTP Activation on Windows Server 2008. To do this, follow these steps:

1. Click the Start button and then point to All Programs.
2. Point to Administrative Tools and then click Server Manager.
3. In Server Manager under Features Summary, click Add Features.
4. In the resulting dialog box, under .NET Framework 3.0, click .NET Framework 3.0.
5. Under WCF Activation, click HTTP Activation.
6. Click Next to start HTTP Activation.
7. In Server Manager, under Roles Summary, verify that Web Server (IIS) is on the list of available roles. If it is not on the list, click Add Roles to install Internet Information Services.
8. In Server Manager, under Roles Summary, click Web Server (IIS).
9. In the resulting window, click Add Role Services.

10. In the next window, expand Web Server, expand Common HTTP Features, and then click Static Content.

11. In the Add Role Services dialog box, expand Web Server, expand Application Development, and then click ASP.NET.

12. Click Next to enable Static Content and ASP.NET.

Enabling IIS 7.0 on Windows Vista

To enable IIS 7.0 with ASP.NET and WCF HTTP Activation on Windows Vista, follow these steps:

1. Click the Start button, click Settings, click Control Panel, click Programs, and then click Programs and Features.

2. Click Turn Windows Features On or Off.

3. Under Microsoft .NET Framework 3.0, click Windows Communication Foundation HTTP Activation.

4. Under Internet Information Services, expand World Wide Web Services.

5. Under Application Development Features, click ASP.NET.

6. Under Common HTTP Features, click Static Content.

7. Install the selected features.

Install the Windows Azure SDK

If you have an old version of the Windows Azure SDK on your machine, you must remove it before installing the new version. Right-click the Microsoft Windows Installer file, and then click Uninstall to remove the previous version of the SDK.

Next, install the SDK on your computer by running the Windows Installer file. By default, the SDK is installed into the C:\Program Files\Windows Azure SDK\ directory.

Test the SDK

The SDK comes with a number of samples that you may find useful. Here, we're going to use them to test out the new installation.

Navigate to the aforementioned SDK directory and unzip the file to a directory where you have write access.

NOTE *You might not have write access to the directories under the Program Files directory, so it's advised to choose a different parent directory for the sample applications.*

To test the SDK installation, follow these steps:

1. Open the Windows Azure SDK command prompt by clicking the Start button, clicking Program Files, and then clicking Window Azure SDK (January 2009 CTP).

2. Navigate to the sample directory, and then run the RunDevStore.cmd utility to build the samples, create local tables required by the samples, and launch development storage. Running development storage starts the local Blob, Queue, and Table services.

3. Navigate to the HelloWorld application directory, and then run runme.cmd.

4. The development fabric icon will appear in the system tray after a moment. Running the sample automatically launches your web browser and points to the service's default web page.

The web interface for the Hello World sample will be displayed in the browser window.

NOTE *If you don't see anything, refresh the window.*

Creating the App

Creating cloud apps with Windows Azure is accomplished through Microsoft Visual Studio 2008. To start making your apps, follow these steps:

1. Run Visual Studio 2008 as an administrator. Click the Start button and then point to all programs.

2. Point to Microsoft Visual Studio 2008, right-click Microsoft Visual Studio 2008, and click Run as Administrator.

3. When the User Account Control box appears, click Continue.

4. From the File menu, click New, and then click Project.

5. In the resulting dialog box, select Cloud Services from the Visual C# project type.

6. In the Templates list, click Web Cloud Service. This creates a web role.

7. Enter the names for your project and solution, and make sure that the Create Directory for Solution box is checked.

8. In the Solution Explorer, you'll see that the solution structure was created. You'll see two projects, a Cloud Compute project and an ASP.NET project. The ASP.NET project will contain your code. The Cloud Compute project contains a reference to the ASP.NET project, as well as the service definition file (.csdef) and service configuration file (.cscfg).

9. Change the Default.aspx page to display some custom text for this example.

Running the App Locally

Next, test the application locally before publishing it to the Azure cloud. You can do that by following these steps:

1. Press F5. This starts the service in the development fabric.

2. Expand the tree on the left panel to see the service deployments.

3. Expand the HelloFabric node to see the web role and worker role that are running within the service.

4. Expand the node for the web role or worker role to view the running instances of the role.

5. Click on a numbered node to see the messages being written to the log for this role instance.

6. Click the Service Details node. This shows you the roles and ports that were requested and issued.

NOTE *If this is the first time you've run the app, the Services Details will show a service URL of http://*:80 and an IP address of 127.0.0.1:80. If port 80 is not available, it will pick the next available port.*

---

7. Switch back to Visual Studio, and press SHIFT+F5 to stop debugging.

Troubleshooting

Troubleshooting on the cloud is a different animal than in a traditional IT environment. Conventional troubleshooting tools and processes were developed around the hub-and-spoke concept, with remote applications being the spokes to the centralized datacenter being the hub. But applications delivered from an off-site provider's datacenter defy traditional monitoring and require a different way to troubleshoot.

At your organization, you have local visibility and control of applications. That control is much more limited with SaaS applications. In particular, it is difficult to distinguish SaaS traffic from other Internet usage going in and coming out of remote locations.

IT staff do not have the local ability to determine whether the service is running or if the client has connectivity to the hosted application. Deep packet inspection (DPI) can deliver this granularity, but this technology is expensive to deploy throughout the enterprise.

NOTE *According to Forrester Research, 40 percent of companies consider SaaS application performance a key concern.*

Another issue is that when users face performance problems or have other issues, they are not going to contact the SaaS provider. They're going to call the IT support desk. And before your IT department relays the problem to the SaaS provider, they must first pursue the problem on their end to rule out local problems. For instance, there could be a legitimate issue with Amazon, for which you need to invoke the service level agreement (SLA). On the other hand, the problem could simply be the result of contention for the Internet.

The problem could be exacerbated by SaaS users within the enterprise working from different remote sites, using different types of access and competing for resources. This can quickly eat up bandwidth.

Also, the user could be on a wireless LAN competing for shared bandwidth with other applications that have fluctuating usage needs, are experiencing slowdowns, or have issues with signal interference.

To troubleshoot SaaS problems, you must be able to understand the perspective of the application and the end user, and to see all the variations inside and outside the infrastructure. That visibility is not available with traditional management tools and technology, but new tools are available.

By using this tracking information, profiles are created for all applications and for the networked application experiences of each end user that allow IT to detect unusual behavior and figure out the root cause of the performance problems. This way, IT can discover hidden causes of SaaS performance problems by figuring out which applications are generating high bandwidth on the link or by finding applications that are causing congestion. When IT staff has this information, they can quickly shut down problematic users and alert SaaS providers about problems at their datacenter.

Application Management

Once you've got your application on the cloud, you need to be able to manage it. While the application isn't in your datacenter, there are still ways you can manage it. A lot will depend on the terms of service you have with your cloud provider. They may not allow for you to manage the applications at all. That's a little more draconian than it should be, but always check your terms of service so you know what you can and cannot manage.

When you do decide to manage your cloud application, you can use a product like Kaavo's (www.kaavo.com) cloud application management software: Infrastructure and Middleware on Demand (IMOD).

IMOD is the first solution with an application-focused approach to IT infrastructure management through public and private clouds. Companies traditionally manage their servers individually, which is complex and costly and impedes business growth across an enterprise. By tapping the capabilities of cloud computing, however, IMOD enables users to manage infrastructure as a unified system and provides the following benefits:

- **Application and service–centric n-tier configuration**   IMOD automatically brings online one or multiserver systems for running applications.
- **Business continuity**   An interface to schedule automatic data backups ensures business continuity.

- **Security and access control**   IMOD provides a point-and-click interface to secure data in the clouds through the National Security Association's recommended AES 256-bit data encryption. It allows users to easily and securely connect to servers, transfer data to and from internal datacenters, and configure custom firewall rules on cloud servers.

- **Effective monitoring and alerts**   Users can monitor resources used by their applications and set up alerts to proactively manage application service levels.

"Moving infrastructure to the cloud is gaining momentum. Kaavo will enable organizations to effectively reap the benefits of cloud computing and to maximize fewer resources. This is particularly critical given current economic conditions and the growing need for companies to reduce their carbon footprint," said Jamal Mazhar, founder and CEO of Kaavo. "Through patent-pending technology, we are pleased to launch IMOD and provide simplicity, flexibility, and security for users. This in turn, allows them to focus on innovation and core business activities necessary for business growth."

IMOD is available for a free 30-day trial at https://imod.kaavo.com.

Developing your own apps is definitely doable, and there is no lack of places that would welcome you to host your apps on their clouds. The differences come down to the features they offer and how much they charge, but if there is a specific function you want done, just point your programmers to the cloud and get them started.

In the next chapter, we'll change gears slightly and talk about the client machines you can use to connect your workers to the cloud—be it an internal or external cloud.

PART III

Local Clouds and Thin Clients

The cloud computing model doesn't always mean your clients have to traverse the Internet to get at content. A local cloud—also known as *presentation virtualization*— skips the service provider component, and allows you to manage all the content yourself in your own datacenter.

Most organizations will not jump to the cloud all at once. Most cases will start as a hybrid model, moving some business applications to the cloud while retaining a majority "in-house." One way to become familiar with cloud computing concepts and benefits without the outsourcing commitment is to bring the cloud as close as possible by building your own cloud for your business. With a local cloud, you keep your server in-house and clients connect to it. Doesn't sound too much different than what you have already, right? Well, you start to offer computing resources to your users as a utility. You provide flexible, low-cost business applications instead of "yet another server." You might also change the delivery of these applications by using presentation virtualization. That is, they are clients that don't use hard drives, DVD-ROM drives, or any other peripherals. Rather, they communicate with the server and it is the server performing all the processing and storage, only to pass the data back to be displayed on the thin client.

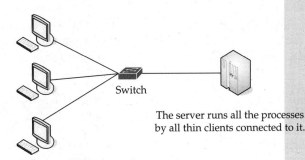

Switch

The server runs all the processes by all thin clients connected to it.

Thin clients display results of applications being run on the server.

In this chapter, we'll take a look at virtualization and its benefits. We'll also look at the leading technologies driving virtualization and talk about a company that decided to move from the conventional hub-and-spoke configuration to a virtualized environment.

Virtualization in Your Organization

There are pros and cons to going virtual. In this section, we'll take a closer look at the benefits and limitations of a virtualized solution. We'll also examine the issues surrounding making a virtualization move.

When we talk about presentation virtualization, we have to define a couple of extra terms. There are a lot of competing products out that do sort of the same thing, but they do it in different ways. Let's take a look at what some different terms mean:

- **Server virtualization**   This is a method of partitioning a physical server computer into multiple servers so that each has the appearance and capabilities of running on its own dedicated machine. An example of this is VMware or Hyper-V (which we'll talk about later in this chapter).

- **Application virtualization**   This is a method that describes software technologies that separate them from the underlying operating system on which they are executed. A fully virtualized application is not installed in the traditional sense, although it still executes as though it were. The application is tricked at run time to believe that it is directly interfacing with the original OS and the resources it manages.

- **Presentation virtualization**   This method isolates processing from the graphics and I/O, which makes it possible to run an application in one location (the server) but be controlled in another (the thin client). In this method, a virtual session is created and the applications project their interfaces onto the thin clients. It can either run a single application or present an entire desktop.

Why Virtualize?

Virtualization can help companies maximize the value of IT investments, decreasing the server hardware footprint, energy consumption, and cost and complexity of managing IT systems while increasing the flexibility of the overall environment.

Cost

Depending on your solution, you can have a cost-free datacenter. You do have to shell out the money for the physical server itself, but there are options for free virtualization software and free operating systems.

Microsoft's Virtual Server and VMware Server are free to download and install. If you use a licensed operating system, of course that will cost money. For instance, if you wanted five instances of Windows Server on that physical server, then you're going to have to pay for the licenses. That said, if you were to use a free version of Linux for the host and operating system, then all you've had to pay for is the physical server.

Naturally, there is an element of "you get what you pay for." There's a reason most organizations have paid to install an OS on their systems. When you install a free OS, there is often a higher total cost of operation, because it can be more labor intensive to manage the OS and apply patches.

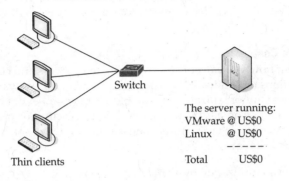

Virtualization can be cost-effective.

Switch

Thin clients

The server running:
VMware @ US$0
Linux   @ US$0
─────
Total   US$0

NOTE *If you repurpose an existing server, then the whole endeavor is free.*

Administration

Having all your servers in one place reduces your administrative burden. According to VMware, you can reduce your administrative burden from 1:10 to 1:30. What this means is that you can save time in your daily server administration or add more servers by having a virtualized environment. The following factors ease your administrative burdens:

- A centralized console allows quicker access to servers.
- CDs and DVDs can be quickly mounted using ISO files.
- New servers can be quickly deployed.
- New virtual servers can be deployed more inexpensively than physical servers.
- RAM can be quickly allocated for disk drives.
- Virtual servers can be moved from one server to another.

Fast Deployment

Because every virtual guest server is just a file on a disk, it's easy to copy (or clone) a system to create a new one. To copy an existing server, just copy the entire directory of the current virtual server.

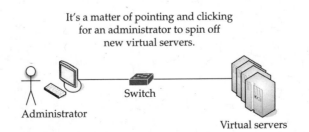

It's a matter of pointing and clicking
for an administrator to spin off
new virtual servers.

Administrator

Switch

Virtual servers

PART III

This can be used in the event the physical server fails, or if you want to test out a new application to ensure that it will work and play well with the other tools on your network.

Virtualization software allows you to make clones of your work environment for these endeavors. Also, not everyone in your organization is going to be doing the same tasks. As such, you may want different work environments for different users. Virtualization allows you to do this.

Reduced Infrastructure Costs

We already talked about how you can cut costs by using free servers and clients, like Linux, as well as free distributions of Windows Virtual Server, Hyper-V, or VMware. But there are also reduced costs across your organization. If you reduce the number of physical servers you use, then you save money on hardware, cooling, and electricity. You also reduce the number of network ports, console video ports, mouse ports, and rack space.

Some of the savings you realize include

- Increased hardware utilization by as much as 70 percent
- Decreased hardware and software capital costs by as much as 40 percent
- Decreased operating costs by as much as 70 percent

How to Virtualize

As with setting up a network security solution or figuring out the best wireless networking solution, the best way to implement a virtualization solution is to start by making sure you fully understand the issues surrounding virtualization.

Assessment

The first step is to conduct an environmental assessment of your organization to determine each department's server processing needs. Deploy custom configured resource and environment auditing agents to poll the servers to identify the current totals of

- CPU
- Memory
- Adapters
- File and system capacity
- Total used and unallocated disk space

Along with this assessment, you should also identify peaks in

- CPU
- Memory
- Adapter usage
- Read
- Write
- Wait cycles

Discover also data that has not been accessed over extended periods of time.

Analyze

Take a good hard look at your current server environment. Identify and consolidate processing-compatible applications to a single server, or you can virtualize your existing multiserver datacenter to share processing capabilities from a common pool.

Identify your mission-critical servers. Those might be good candidates to be left in place in a one-to-one relationship. Those are the servers that house SAP, PeopleSoft, and Siebel. But then consolidate the non-heavy-hitting applications (like file and print, Exchange, and so on) and virtualize the remaining servers to construct a common pool of hardware resources.

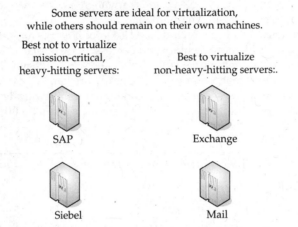

Some servers are ideal for virtualization, while others should remain on their own machines.

Best not to virtualize mission-critical, heavy-hitting servers:

SAP

Siebel

Best to virtualize non-heavy-hitting servers:.

Exchange

Mail

Then, configure the aforementioned consolidated servers so that their CPU, memory, and adapters can be shared with the heavy-hitting servers when needed. Most servers today hover around 10 to 15 percent utilization. When you are done with virtualization, the average CPU utilization is about 80 percent.

Save Your Money

Over the past 30 years or so we've gotten into the habit of buying more servers when we get new applications. That may have been the solution 25 years ago, but it isn't today. It's more than likely that you are not even tapping the resources of the equipment you have, so stop buying new stuff.

Tap into your existing hardware pool and reduce the number of servers you think you need, simply to increase on-demand processing capacity. If you virtualize the servers you have, you can save money (by not buying new equipment) and get the most out of the resources you already have.

You needn't buy new equipment. You can repurpose existing servers to perform your virtualization functions.

Old server

Now houses four virtualized servers.

Virtualizing your servers enables them to identify their own CPU, memory, and adapter requirements. They will be able to seek out resources on neighboring servers when more capacity is needed, and then surrender those resources when the demand has lessened.

Concerns

Sure, we've clapped virtualization's back and described how it can be helpful, but there are times when it is not ideal. For instance, graphics-intensive applications are not well suited for today's virtual environment. Video cards cannot handle the requirements of a high-performance graphics adapter. Gaming, CAD, and software requiring three-dimensional graphics are not ideal for a virtualized environment.

Databases and business intelligence software are also poor matches for virtualization, simply because they require a lot more memory and processor power than current virtualized servers can provide. Databases can be successful, if small enough, but they will scale poorly.

Further, server applications that require access to hardware like PCI cards and USB devices are difficult to virtualize. Also server virtualization doesn't typically play well with proprietary hardware, so applications that need the use of more than the Ethernet jack are not typically going to work.

NOTE *These are issues now, but expect virtualization software companies to figure it out in the near future.*

Security

When it comes to security, the same risks that exist for a physical server exist for a virtualized server. There is a misconception that virtual servers are somehow immune to these problems or that the host server acts as sort of a bodyguard, but that's not the case. Virtual machines need to have the same networking concerns dealt with and the same virus concerns addressed as a physical machine. You also need to protect against spyware and malware.

When configuring your servers, let your host server do just its job—don't add any extra applications that it doesn't need. It will be safer and perform its duties better when it just has one thing to do.

In fact, security is extra important on a virtualized server, because a virtualized host can potentially lead to the failure of other virtualized machines on the same physical server.

It's ideal to separate the virtualization host and virtualized machines and be extra cautious when setting up perimeter security to further protect host servers. It's also ideal to have strong, highly guarded passwords and run with the smallest number of privileges.

Server Solutions

There are two (major) components of a virtualized environment—clients and servers. While this sounds no different than the traditional server/client model, it is substantially different in a virtualized environment.

First, the server is different. Rather than housing shared files and performing specific tasks, in a virtualized environment the server does everything. Want to work on the third-quarter financial reports? You'll access and work on the spreadsheet on the server. Want to use a calculator to figure out some basic math problem? It, too, runs on the server. The client is simply used to display the results.

In this section, we'll take a close look at a couple of the more prevalent server virtualization products: Microsoft Server 2008 Hyper-V, VMware, and VMware ESX.

Microsoft Hyper-V

Microsoft Server 2008 Hyper-V (Hyper-V) is a hypervisor-based virtualization technology that is a feature of select versions of Windows Server 2008. Microsoft's strategy and investments in virtualization—which span from the desktop to the datacenter—help IT professionals and developers implement Microsoft's Dynamic IT initiative, whereby they can build systems with the flexibility and intelligence to automatically adjust to changing business conditions by aligning computing resources with strategic objectives.

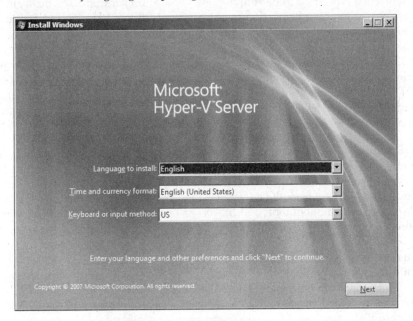

Hyper-V offers customers a scalable and high-performance virtualization platform that plugs into customers' existing IT infrastructures and enables them to consolidate some of the most demanding workloads. In addition, the Microsoft System Center product family gives customers a single set of integrated tools to manage physical and virtual resources, helping customers create a more agile and dynamic datacenter.

"Customers who buy Windows Server 2008 are not only getting the scalability benefits, the high performance and reliability, and all the great things that Windows Server is known for; as of today they can benefit from integrated virtualization with Hyper-V," said Bill Hilf, general manager of Windows Server Marketing and Platform Strategy at Microsoft.

Case Study

Take Minnesota-based Land O'Lakes, for example. They suffered from a common IT challenge resulting from tremendous growth through mergers and acquisitions. The agricultural cooperative's datacenter was packed with a compilation of aging servers running at an average utilization rate of just 3 percent, putting a considerable strain on IT resources.

IT pros call the condition "server sprawl," and Land O'Lakes had a bad case of it. "We faced a combination of underutilized and aging hardware, applications running on outdated operating systems, and rising datacenter power and cooling costs," said Jason Nord, the company's server administrator.

To counter the problem, Land O'Lakes did what an increasing number of similarly challenged companies are doing: It turned to a virtualization solution. Specifically, it became an early adopter of Microsoft virtualization technologies, including Windows Server 2008 Hyper-V.

The company's IT team initially rolled out a Microsoft Virtual Server 2005 R2 in its test and development environment, in which four physical servers each hosted 10 to 13 virtual machines, with each virtual machine running one application. During 2008, the team migrated this environment to Hyper-V and moved an additional 10 to 15 new applications directly into virtual machines in the production environment, thus saving the cost of hardware servers.

"Our Microsoft virtualization solution is a key part of a business strategy we have at Land O'Lakes called Best Cost Initiative," said Tony Taylor, the company's director of IT services. "It's not just about cutting costs, but about looking where our money is being spent and finding ways to leverage our investments across the company. Virtualization holds a lot of promise in helping us maximize the value of our IT investments."

Integrated Systems

To accompany Microsoft virtualization technologies such as Hyper-V, the System Center family of solutions delivers management tools to configure, operate, deploy, and back up physical and virtual servers from the datacenter to the desktop—all from a single pane of glass. With proper management tools and processes, customers can control the power of virtualization and become agile, while still maintaining control. This can help prevent such issues as "virtual server sprawl"—one of the challenges that can be introduced by the increased use of server virtualization.

Ironically, this virtual equivalent of physical server sprawl stems from the ease with which virtual machines can be created. Some IT teams have allowed multiple groups within the organization to create their own virtual machines, only to lose track of them later. This kind of uncontrolled usage can lead to legal and security concerns.

"To truly see the full benefits of virtualization, it is critical to have the right processes and tools in place," Hilf said. "That's why management tools are so important—they are the glue that holds it all together and helps deliver the real benefits of virtualization."

The ability to centralize server management was a key factor in The SCOOTER Store's quest to find the right virtualization solution. The New Braunfels, Texas–based company is a leading provider of power mobility devices such as power chairs to help people with mobility challenges lead full, self-sufficient lives.

To manage the recent rapid growth and stay in compliance with ever-changing government mandates for documentation, reporting, consumer safety, and patient privacy, the company must maintain agile and flexible IT systems.

To that end, The SCOOTER Store virtualized its server environment and centralized server management using Virtual Server 2005 R2 and System Center Virtual Machine Manager 2007. As part of its overall virtualization strategy, the company is evaluating Hyper-V to increase the performance of its existing environment.

"Hyper-V is very exciting for us because it is integrated and designed into the operating system," said Barrett Blake, The SCOOTER Store's infrastructure architect. "I expect Hyper-V to be even easier to use, faster, and more efficient."

Scalability and Other Benefits

Scalability and cost were prime considerations for Ray Pawlikowski as he sought a virtualization solution for his growing company, HotSchedules. The Austin, Texas–based company specializes in online labor scheduling, offering employees of clients such as The Cheesecake Factory, Outback Steakhouse, and P.F. Chang's access to their work schedules on the web, text messaging, email, and the ability to pick up and release shifts, among other benefits.

With nearly a quarter-million users and 4 million logins per month, the 10-year-old business has doubled in size each year for the past couple years and shows no sign of slowing down. Like Land O'Lakes' IT team, Pawlikowski signed up for the Microsoft Rapid Deployment Program (RDP) to test Windows Server 2008 Hyper-V. "By virtualizing everything, we have been able to increase our server utilization by a factor of 10, providing dramatic opportunities in consolidation and power savings," he said.

Hyper-V's scalability derives from its support for multiple processors and cores at the host level and improved memory limits at the host and guest level within virtual machines. This enables customers to scale their virtualization environment to support a large number of virtual machines within a given host and to take advantage of quick migration for high availability across multiple hosts.

HotSchedules is running 40 physical servers, and Pawlikowski wants to reduce that number by 50 to 75 percent. The IT organization is also running 14 virtual machines with applications running faster on the virtual servers than they did on the physical servers used previously. This is a critical benefit that keeps the company's web-based application responsive.

Customers are not the only ones benefiting from the increasing demand for virtualization. Microsoft storage partner QLogic published a benchmark for I/O throughput for storage devices going through Windows Server 2008 Hyper-V. At 180,000 I/Os per second on a system running Hyper-V, virtual machine connections are just 10 percent shy of native performance. This benchmark demonstrates Hyper-V's ability to bring the advantages of virtualization to the most demanding datacenter.

Meanwhile, Microsoft itself has been using Hyper-V in production environments, including heavy-traffic web properties such as MSDN, TechNet, and Microsoft.com. MSDN has more than 3 million average page views per day, TechNet averages more than 1 million per day, and Microsoft.com averages more than 38 million per day.

Familiarity

Microsoft touts the familiarity of the Windows platform as one of the benefits of Hyper-V. For example, HotSchedules' Pawlikowski looked at a number of other virtualization technologies, but his company has strong ties with Dell, which made a compelling case for Microsoft's early-adopter program.

"Not only is Hyper-V faster, it's also faster to get up to speed with," Pawlikowski said. "It's integrated with our existing platform and with the familiar roles in Windows Server 2008, so our knowledge base didn't have to change too much and I didn't have to retool our IT staff to move forward with virtualization."

Microsoft's Hilf says that's a particularly compelling reason for customers to choose Hyper-V. "It's been designed as a Windows feature, which our customers know, so those with Windows Server certification will be familiar with it; the people who have all the in-house skills on Windows Server will know how to use it."

To help both customers and partners assess whether their existing servers are good candidates for virtualization using Hyper-V, Microsoft has released the Microsoft Assessment and Planning (MAP) Toolkit 3.1 Beta to help accelerate virtualization planning and deployment. The final release of MAP 3.1 is expected in July and will be available for free at http://www.microsoft.com/MAP. MAP belongs to a family of Microsoft Virtualization Solution Accelerators including Infrastructure Planning and Design guides and the Offline Virtual Machine Servicing Tool.

In addition, more than 130 independent software vendors (ISVs) have certified a total of 150 applications on Windows Server 2008. This designation identifies applications that have been independently tested to exploit Hyper-V capabilities and meet mission-critical expectations in a virtualized environment.

Microsoft is working with its partners to meet customers' needs for interoperable solutions. The alliance with Citrix Systems in the areas of virtual desktop infrastructure (VDI) and virtual machine portability between the Xen Hypervisor and Hyper-V provides customers with broader deployment scenarios. Additionally, the extensive collaboration with Novell enables customers to take advantage of virtualization in mixed Microsoft and SuSE Linux environments.

Along the same lines, original equipment manufacturer (OEM) vendors such as Dell, Fujitsu-Siemens Corp., Fujitsu Ltd., HP, IBM, NEC, Sun Microsystems, and Unisys are qualified to ship and create systems with Hyper-V. In all, 250 systems from server and white-box vendors are already logo-qualified for Windows Server 2008 and Hyper-V. More information can be found at http://www.windowsservercatalog.com.

Get Your Own Copy

You can download your own copy of Windows Server 2008 Hyper-V to try it out.

"There have already been over 1 million evaluations of Hyper-V, and IT organizations everywhere can move it from the lab to production to fully experience the benefits that Hyper-V in Windows Server 2008 can bring," Hilf said. He added that customers can also use System Center Virtual Machine Manager 2008, to help them best configure and deploy their hypervisor-based environments.

New customers and partners can download Hyper-V at http://www.microsoft.com/Hyper-V. Customers who have deployed Windows Server 2008 can receive Hyper-V from Windows Update.

VMware

VMware offers its VMware Server, a free entry-level hosted virtualization product for Linux and Windows servers. The product is available for download at www.vmware.com/products/server/.

"Virtualization and VMware have become mainstream in the past year, and many customers have deployed thousands of VMware server environments across their enterprises. With VMware Server, we are ensuring that every company interested in, considering or evaluating server virtualization for the first time has access to the industry-leading virtualization technology," said Diane Greene, VMware president. "VMware Server makes it easy and compelling for companies new to virtualization to take the first step toward enterprise-wide virtual infrastructure."

Features

VMware Server, the successor to VMware GSX Server, enables users to quickly provision new server capacity by partitioning a physical server into multiple virtual machines, bringing the powerful benefits of virtualization to every server.

VMware Server is feature-packed with the following market-leading capabilities:

- Support for any standard x86 hardware
- Support for a wide variety of Linux and Windows host operating systems, including 64-bit operating systems
- Support for a wide variety of Linux, NetWare, Solaris x86, and Windows guest operating systems, including 64-bit operating systems
- Support for Virtual SMP, enabling a single virtual machine to span multiple physical processors
- Quick and easy, wizard-driven installation similar to any desktop software
- Quick and easy virtual machine creation with a virtual machine wizard
- Virtual machine monitoring and management with an intuitive, user-friendly remote console

VMware Server supports 64-bit virtual machines and Intel Virtualization Technology, a set of Intel hardware platform enhancements specifically designed to enhance virtualization solutions.

"Central Transport has saved hundreds of thousands of dollars with VMware virtual infrastructure," said Craig Liess, server administrator for Central Transport. "Introducing a new server virtualization product including Virtual SMP and support for 64-bit operating systems and Intel Virtualization Technology is a natural progression for VMware, furthering the company's leadership in the market. Offering VMware Server for free will bring VMware's proven virtualization technology to a wider audience, allowing companies to achieve the benefits of virtualization, such as cost reductions and flexible server provisioning."

VMware Server is a good starting point for users seeking to familiarize themselves with the concept of virtualization before progressing to the enterprise-class suite of VMware virtual infrastructure products that includes ESX Server with Virtual SMP and VirtualCenter with VMotion technology for large-scale production server consolidation, business continuity, and enterprise-hosted desktop solutions.

NOTE *We'll talk about VMware virtual infrastructure next.*

The suite is used by more than 20,000 companies worldwide today with more than 90 percent running VMware virtual infrastructure in production server environments and 25 percent choosing to standardize their industry-standard systems on VMware.

Teaming Up with Intel

Intel and VMware are launching a global marketing campaign to educate users on the value of virtualization on Intel platforms and to drive broader adoption of virtualization.

"VMware Server on Intel-based systems will allow customers from big IT to SMB to experiment with virtualization, understand its benefits and realize the value of Intel technologies such as Multi Core and Intel Virtualization Technology," said Diane Bryant, vice president and general manager, Intel Server Platforms Group.

VMware's leading OEM hardware partners welcome the introduction of VMware Server.

"Virtualization is a key enabling technology for our customers as they use scale out architectures for data center deployments," said Paul Gottsegen, vice president, Dell product group. "VMware Server is a great opportunity for our customer base to easily evaluate how the benefits of virtualization can help improve their server utilization rates."

"IBM xSeries delivers innovative virtualization solutions by leveraging our strong partnership with VMware and our industry leading X3 Architecture and BladeCenter platforms," said Leo Suarez, vice president and Business Line Executive, xSeries at IBM. "The new VMware Server offering will enable more xSeries and BladeCenter customers to experience the benefits of virtualization and see the value that virtualization can bring to their environment."

VMware Server is available for download at www.vmware.com/products/server/.

VMware Infrastructure

VMware is the biggest name in virtualization, and they offer VMware Infrastructure, which includes the latest version of VMware ESX Server 3.5 and VirtualCenter 2.5. VMware Infrastructure will allow VMware customers to streamline the management of IT environments

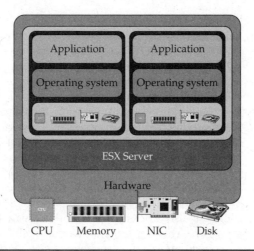

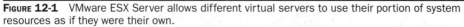

FIGURE 12-1   VMware ESX Server allows different virtual servers to use their portion of system resources as if they were their own.

through greater levels of automation, increase overall infrastructure availability, and boost performance for mission-critical workloads. The new release will also include updated packaging and pricing, including new offerings specifically targeted at midsize and smaller IT environments.

As Figure 12-1 shows, each virtualized server perceives the system resources as unique to them, and not shared with others.

"This release builds upon nearly a decade of continuous innovation," said Raghu Raghuram, vice president of products and solutions at VMware. "We continue to drive improvements across the VMware Infrastructure suite. The new features, such as the first solution to move virtual machine disks across data stores, provide compelling value to customers of all sizes, whether they are small businesses or large enterprises."

VMware Infrastructure is VMware's third-generation, production-ready virtualization suite. According to a study of VMware customers, 90 percent of companies surveyed use VMware Infrastructure in production environments. With more than 120 industry and technology awards, VMware provides a much-anticipated complete solution that meets customer demand for a next-generation firmware hypervisor, enhanced virtual infrastructure capabilities, and advanced management and automation solutions.

"Customers are continually looking for more ways to take advantage of their virtualized infrastructure and to maximize the ROI the software can deliver to their organization," said John Humphreys, program vice president at IDC. "With the announcement of VMware ESX Server 3.5 and VMware VirtualCenter 2.5, VMware is raising the bar by not only enhancing existing features but taking virtualization to the next level with new capabilities for increased mobility and service availability. These new features can enable new use cases which in turn will help to drive new customer adoption of virtualization within the industry."

The new features in VMware Infrastructure are targeted at a broad range of customers and IT environments—from midsize and small businesses to branch offices and corporate datacenters within global 100 corporations—and extend the value of all three layers of the virtualization suite.

"The new release will make our data center even more manageable and more flexible," said Kim Wisniewski, systems engineer at Curtin University of Technology. "For example, VMware Guided Consolidation will lower training costs for engineers new to VMware ESX Server and make it easier to extend virtualization throughout the organization. Also, VMware Storage VMotion will help us manage our virtual infrastructure storage lifecycles more effectively by giving us the ability to transparently move workloads away from storage needing downtime for maintenance, or dynamically rebalance storage workloads without affecting our virtual machines and the services they support."

"The VMware Update Manager addresses a process each virtual infrastructure administrator dreads facing: tracking patch levels, and applying current security patches and bug fixes across their environment," said Fazil Habibulla, vice president and systems engineer at Natixis. "VMware Update Manager allows for this through an automated update and remediation process within the entire virtual infrastructure environment—not only easier for administration, but also for ensuring that all VMware ESX Server hosts and guest operating systems are secure. This functionality works on all hosts, templates, and virtual machines, even those powered off or in a suspended state. From a risk control perspective, the ability to seamlessly automate patch management and security remediation from a centralized console is a huge value-add for us."

Features

Virtualization platform enhancements help deliver new levels of performance, scalability, and compatibility for running the most demanding workloads in virtual machines:

- Expanded storage and networking choices such as support for SATA local storage and 10 Gig Ethernet as well as enablement of Infiniband devices expand storage and networking choices for virtual infrastructure.

- Support for TCP Segment Offload and Jumbo frames reduces the CPU overhead associated with processing network I/O.

- Support for hardware-nested page tables such as in-processor assists for memory virtualization.

- Support for paravirtualized Linux guest operating systems enables higher levels of performance through virtualization-aware operating systems.

- Support for virtual machines with 64GB of RAM and physical machines with up to 128GB of memory.

Virtual infrastructure capabilities help deliver increased infrastructure availability and resilience:

- VMware Storage VMotion enables live migration of virtual machine disks from one data storage system to another with no disruption or downtime. VMware VMotion has become an indispensable tool for many infrastructure administrators to dynamically balance their server workloads and eliminate planned downtime for server maintenance. Storage VMotion extends VMotion to storage resources of a virtual machine, namely virtual disks. Using Storage VMotion, administrators can dynamically balance the storage workload and address performance bottlenecks by migrating virtual machine disks to the best available storage resource. Administrators

can minimize service disruption previously incurred for upgrading storage arrays
and free storage administrators to improve and manage the storage infrastructure
without having to coordinate extensively with application and server owners.

- VMware Update Manager automates patch and update management for VMware
  ESX Server hosts and virtual machines. Update Manager addresses one of the most
  significant pain points for every IT department: tracking patch levels and manually
  applying the latest security/bug fixes. Patching of offline virtual machines enforces
  higher levels of patch standards compliance than physical environments. Integration
  with VMware Distributed Resource Scheduler (DRS) enables zero-downtime
  VMware ESX Server host patching capabilities.

- VMware Distributed Power Management is an experimental feature that reduces
  power consumption in the datacenter through intelligent workload balancing.
  Working in conjunction with VMware DRS, Distributed Power Management is
  designed to automatically power off servers not currently needed in order to meet
  service levels, and automatically power on servers as demand for compute
  resources increases.

- VMware Guided Consolidation, a feature of VMware VirtualCenter, enables
  companies to get started with server consolidation in a step-by-step tutorial fashion.
  A wizard discovers physical servers, identifies consolidation candidates, converts
  them to virtual machines, and leveraging intelligently, places them onto the best
  VMware ESX Server or VMware Server hosts. Guided Consolidation helps to make
  the consolidation process quick and easy for users with little knowledge of
  virtualization.

Products
VMware Infrastructure is available for purchase in the following editions:

- VMware ESX Server 3i, providing single-server partitioning, is delivered embedded
  as firmware in server systems or as a stand-alone purchase for hard drive
  installation. If purchased stand-alone for hard drive installation, ESX Server 3i list
  price is US$495 per two processors.

- VMware Infrastructure 3 Foundation (previously called "Starter") includes VMware
  ESX Server, VMware ESX Server 3i, VMware Consolidated Backup, and the new
  VMware Update Manager. Unlike the previous VMware Infrastructure 3 Starter,
  VMware Infrastructure 3 Foundation has no restrictions on shared storage
  connectivity, memory utilization, or number of CPUs of the physical server.
  VMware Infrastructure Foundation list price is US$995 per two processors.

- VMware Infrastructure 3 Standard is designed to bring higher levels of resiliency to
  IT environments at greater value. In addition to the capabilities of VMware
  Infrastructure 3 Foundation, VMware Infrastructure 3 Standard includes VMware
  HA, which provides automated restart of virtual machines affected by hardware
  failure. VMware Infrastructure 3 Standard list price is US$2995 per two processors.

- VMware Infrastructure 3 Enterprise contains the entire array of virtual infrastructure
  capabilities for resource management, workload mobility, and high availability.
  In addition to the capabilities in VMware Infrastructure 3 Standard, it also includes

VMware VMotion, VMware Storage VMotion, and VMware DRS with Distributed Power Management (DPM). VMware Infrastructure 3 Enterprise list price is US$5750 per two processors.

- VMware VMotion, Storage VMotion, and DRS with DPM are available for stand-alone purchase with VMware Infrastructure 3 Foundation and Standard.

Thin Clients

Desktop and mobile thin clients are solid-state devices that connect over a network to a centralized server where all processing and storage takes place, providing reduced maintenance costs and minimal application updates, as well as higher levels of security and energy efficiency. In fact, thin clients can be up to 80 percent more power-efficient than traditional desktop PCs with similar capabilities.

Sun

Sun's thin client solution is called Sun Ray, and it is an extremely popular product. Contributing to the demand for it is further market demand for Sun Virtual Desktop Infrastructure (VDI) Software 2.0, which ships on approximately 25 percent of Sun Ray units since being introduced in March 2008. Further, Sun Ray machines are able to display Solaris, Windows, or Linux desktops on the same device.

Sun Ray virtual display clients, Sun Ray Software, and Sun VDI Software 2.0 are key components of Sun's desktop virtualization offering, which are a set of desktop technologies and solutions within Sun's vim virtualization portfolio.

NOTE *More information on the Sun Ray family of virtual display clients can be found at www.sun .com/sunray.*

"As an early innovator in the thin client market with nearly a decade of experience, we're pleased to see the growth Sun Ray clients have experienced during the past year and are encouraged by the growing appeal of desktop virtualization technologies industry-wide. Organizations have truly begun to realize the benefits that thin clients and virtual desktop solutions offer—with respect to cost savings, ease of management, eco advantages, and more—to their business," said Bob Gianni, senior engineering director of desktop systems, Sun. "Sun is investing heavily in desktop virtualization technologies and believes strongly in the market's potential for further growth."

Sun offers a comprehensive desktop-to-datacenter virtualization product portfolio and set of virtualization service offerings to help customers deploy new services faster, maximize the utilization of system resources, and more easily monitor and manage virtualized environments. Sun's virtualization products help to provide unified software management tools and virtualization capabilities across operating systems, servers, storage, desktops, and processors.

NOTE *For more information visit www.sun.com/xvm.*

Sun has seen a number of unique and compelling new deployments of Sun Ray technology by customers around the world. For example, Colorado State University (CSU) is a leading research university, dedicated to energy conservation by implementing programs that help reduce CO2 emissions and promote the use of solar technology and recycling. Through its Academic Village, Colorado State University uses Sun Ray virtual display clients in an innovative way to enhance learning and create an eco-friendly IT infrastructure.

"Sun Ray solutions fit in nicely with what we've done to build the green Academic Village. Not only do Sun Ray clients take up half the space of a PC, but we've also seen that they consume less than 10% of a typical PC's power. Sun is dedicated to providing eco-friendly solutions and that really matters to CSU," said Mark Ritschard, director of Engineering Network Service, College of Engineering at Colorado State University.

The U.S. Navy's Integrated Warfare Systems Lab (IWSL) is part of the Naval Surface Warfare Center (NSWC). The NSWC provides the right technology, capabilities, and specialized research to support all aspects of surface warfare. The IWSL chose the Sun Ray virtual display client solution running on Sun Fire V490 servers to provide access to a broad range of IT systems from a single device.

Hewlett Packard

Hewlett Packard (HP) is certainly a well-known technology company, and their products extend into the world of thin clients. In fact, HP is the leading manufacturer of thin clients. In this section we'll examine their thin clients in depth.

Offerings

In late 2008, HP introduced three thin client products, including the company's first mobile offering, that address business needs for a more simple, secure, and easily managed computing infrastructure.

According to researchers IDC, HP (including recently acquired Neoware) led the industry in thin client unit shipments with more than 34 percent market share worldwide in the third quarter of 2007.

Three months after closing its acquisition of Neoware, HP added to the industry's broad portfolio of thin clients with two flexible desk-based models as well as the first HP-branded mobile thin client—all of which combine notebook and thin client expertise from both HP and Neoware.

Thin clients are at the heart of HP's remote client portfolio of desktop virtualization solutions, which also include the blade PC-based HP Consolidated Client Infrastructure platform, HP Virtual Desktop Infrastructure (VDI), blade workstations, remote deployment, and management software and services.

"Customers have acknowledged our commitment to providing the most trusted and reliable business computing solutions by making HP the worldwide leader in the thin client market," said Klaus Besier, vice president, Thin Client Solutions, Personal Systems Group, HP. "HP recognizes thin clients play an integral role in driving next-generation business computing platforms, and we will continue innovating across our remote computing solutions portfolio to help customers achieve their business goals."

6720t Mobile Thin Client   6720t Mobile Thin Client is ideal for on-the-go professionals such as insurance claim processors, remote staff, warehouse and inventory managers, and office administrators.

It is based on Microsoft Windows XPe (embedded) and features a 15.4-inch display; solid-state design with no hard drive, fan, or other moving parts; enhanced security with no data residing on the notebook; Wi-Fi Certified WLAN along with support for 3G broadband wireless via PC memory card slot; and solid-state flash module for greater durability, faster data access, and quieter and cooler operation.

The 6720t also helps increase security by accessing software applications hosted on a server, virtual PC, or blade PC computing platform over a secure virtual private network Internet connection. Data files and software applications also are saved remotely on a secure server to help reduce the risk of data loss, viruses, and product theft.

Client management is simplified, as IT administrators are able to remotely install, manage, update, and execute application software simultaneously across an entire fleet of clients that are pushed to the mobile thin clients as soon as they are connected to the network.

"Together, HP and VMware deliver a comprehensive portfolio of solutions that leverage VMware's industry-leading virtualization solutions for simplifying and reducing costs in the data center," said Brian Byun, vice president, global partners and solutions, VMware. "HP's latest thin client offerings provide a compelling addition to the joint HP and VMware VDI solutions for our customers who look to secure their environments, reduce computing-related energy and management costs, and improve productivity."

HP Compaq t5730 and t5735 Desktop Clients   HP also offers its HP Compaq t5730 and t5735 Thin Clients. The HP Compaq t5730 is based on Microsoft Windows XPe, and select models include integrated WLAN. Based on Debian Linux, the HP Compaq t5735 supports a variety of open-source applications.

Both solutions include a combination of desktop-like features, high-end graphics, the HP Secure USB Compartment, and HP Quick Release support for business environments requiring a combination of simplicity, flexibility, power, and enhanced security.

"In today's world, the demand for reliable infrastructure becomes more prevalent and increasingly important to ensure solutions offer the best user experience," said Gordon Payne, senior vice president and general manager, Delivery Systems Division, Citrix Systems Inc. "Our strong relationship with HP and its extensive client product portfolio enable seamless interoperability with Citrix application delivery infrastructure. These new HP devices can be used as desktop appliances with Citrix's desktop virtualization solution, Citrix XenDesktop, providing unmatched performance required for the most demanding business environments."

In addition to centralized data storage for protection of business information and data integrity, the two thin clients provide controlled user access and support two-factor user authentication.

Every HP thin client also includes a full license of Altiris Deployment Solution and a free download of HP Client Automation Software to provide customers with their choice of an enterprise-level management solution for large deployments.

For customers who need an easy-to-use deployment tool with basic capabilities, exclusive HP ThinState Tools are included with every HP thin client. With this tool, the t5730, for example, can easily deploy images to other thin clients in the network with no need to buy, install, or learn any external deployment solution.

The HP Compaq 6720t Mobile Thin Client is available at a starting U.S. list price of US$725, while the HP Compaq t5730 and t5735 Thin Clients are available at a starting U.S. list price of US$499 and US$450, respectively.

NOTE *Those numbers were accurate at the time of writing, and likely they will become less expensive and/or be replaced by other HP offerings.*

More information about HP's current thin client offerings is available at www.hp.com/go/thinclient.

HP and VMware

HP made another effort to ensure they continue their thin client strides. In early 2009, HP announced that its entire line of thin clients is certified for VMware View, making the products even easier for customers to deploy in VMware environments.

The certification, which covers the Microsoft Windows CE, Windows XP Embedded, and Linux operating systems, includes rigorous testing and quality assurance with VMware View for enhanced reliability and ease of deployment.

HP is among the first in the industry to offer customers Linux thin clients certified for VMware View Manager, an enterprise desktop management server that enables IT administrators to quickly provision and tightly control user access. Additionally, HP is currently the only vendor to receive View Manager certification for Windows CE.

HP offers an extensive lineup of Windows and Linux-based thin clients that are ideally suited for VMware View deployments and deliver a range of performance and features to support a wide variety of user needs—from basic data entry to advanced 3-D imaging and remote collaboration. The HP t5135 and t5145 Thin Clients with simple HP ThinConnect operating system are HP's first Linux-based thin clients to be certified for View Manager.

Dell

Another well-known player in the world of client development is Dell, and they, too, offer a thin client (their first). But they are also touting environmental responsibility with a new line of PCs. Their most recent additions are a line of OptiPlex commercial desktops, Flexible Computing Solutions, and service offerings designed to reduce costs throughout the desktop life cycle.

NOTE *More information is available at www.dell.com/seriousbusiness.*

"As the world's leading supplier of desktops, Dell understands the importance of simplifying customers' IT environments and saving them money in every step of the desktop lifecycle," said Darrel Ward, director, Dell Product Group. "According to Gartner, a locked and well-managed system can be 42 percent less expensive to maintain than an unmanaged one. With today's product announcement, we are introducing end-to-end solutions that are more manageable and secure, while also giving customers the flexibility to deploy solutions outside of traditional computing models."

The OptiPlex systems feature new technologies in serviceability, manageability, security, and power consumption to help simplify day-to-day operations while reducing operating expenses. The OptiPlex portfolio is designed to reduce costs in four key areas:

- **Management**   Remote system maintenance; designed for easy serviceability; Dell ProSupport offerings.

- **Security**   Automated data security with full disk encryption and solid state drives for added data protection on select systems; improved chassis intrusion prevention; Dell Control Point security management, smart card authentication; remote patching and isolation.

- **Stability**   Factory-built, preconfigured, and delivered to customer specifications; up to 36-month product life cycle; global standard platforms available on select systems.

- **Environmental Responsibility**   Energy-efficient design; post-consumer recycled plastics on select systems; recyclable packaging; leading power-supply efficiency on select systems.

In total, the company introduced four new platforms in early 2009—including the flagship OptiPlex 960. It also delivers the most environmentally responsible features of any commercial desktop from any major vendor.

OptiPlex 960   The OptiPlex 960 offers these features:

- Up to 43 percent less power consumption to reduce energy costs over previous generation of OptiPlex desktops

- Up to 89 percent recyclable packaging

- At least 10 percent post-consumer recycled plastic on small form factor

- An average of 28 percent faster service time than a comparable system from HP and 43 percent faster than a Lenovo

- Optional QuietKit technology reduces noise by as much as 60 percent

- Available in three chassis styles (mini-tower, desktop, and small form factor), the OptiPlex 960 starts at US$863.

OptiPlex 760   The OptiPlex 760 offers mainstream security, productivity, and energy-efficient features with improved management capabilities. It requires an average of 22 percent less time to service than a comparable system from HP and an average of 38 percent less time than a Lenovo. The OptiPlex 760 starts at US$593.

OptiPlex 360   The OptiPlex 360 enables the performance needed to help customers build their business and drive essential office productivity. The OptiPlex 360 starts at US$476.

OptiPlex FX160   The OptiPlex FX160 is Dell's first thin client and supports embedded or streamed operating systems for virtual desktop implementations. The FX160 starts at US$399.

Flexible Computing Solutions

Dell is expanding its Flexible Computing Solutions (FCS) to include global availability of On-Demand Desktop Streaming and the company's new Virtual Remote Desktop offering available in the United States. Dell's range of Flexible Computing Solutions are network-based and use virtualization computing architectures to give customers unprecedented choice and flexibility, while enabling IT to retain full control of data and application management without sacrificing end-user performance or productivity. Details of Dell's FCS solutions include:

- **On-Demand Desktop Streaming**   Processing happens on the desktop where data is hosted on a partitioned server in the datacenter with processing happening on a local client for an uncompromised end-user experience.

- **Virtual Remote Desktop**   Datacenter processing and hosted virtual client desktops accessed from a variety of devices and locations.
- **Dedicated Remote Workstation**   PC-over-IP solution that connects to a Dell Precision R5400 rack-mount workstation in a datacenter for high-performance users in harsh or highly secure environments.

FCS offerings feature engineer-tested and optimized hardware—including desktops, server, storage, and networking, in addition to software and support for the complete solution. Dell Services will help customers assess, design, plan, and deploy the FCS solutions that meet their specific needs.

Remote Management and Personalization Services

Dell's Remote Management and Personalization services include:

- **ImageDirect**   Allows customers to securely create, load, and manage custom images onto the Dell desktop systems they purchase; it is fully integrated into Dell's production systems so images are applied during the manufacturing process.
- **Application Packaging**   Allows IT departments to efficiently manage, deploy, install, and uninstall applications; can significantly reduce portfolio management and application support costs.
- **Desktop Manager**   Automates asset management, software distribution and upgrades, patches, and antivirus and malware updates.
- **Software Inventory and Usage**   Automates applications monitoring and inventories and tracking software usage.
- **Back-up and Restore**   Automates desktop data backup to a secure, off-site datacenter using single instancing and data compression.
- **Email Management Services**   Automates email backup and archiving to help prevent downtime, at a fraction of the cost of typical on-premise solutions.
- **Crisis Management and Alerting**   Utilizes automation to provide continuous communication, reaching thousands of employees in minutes and keeping them updated during a crisis or disaster.
- **Dell Asset Recovery and Recycling Services**   Recycle systems; recover residual value for customers; dispose of older assets in an environmentally responsible manner.

Case Study: McNeilus Steel

Different companies chose virtualization for different reasons. For a steel distributor in Dodge Center, Minnesota, McNeilus Steel, the main reason for a 2006 change was reliability.

Benefits

"We did not want any downtime," observed IT Manager Darren Boeck. "The longest we wanted to be down for was three minutes."

PART III

Before deciding on virtualization, McNeilus considered eight-way servers. The problem with that solution was that every server had just one backup. By using blade servers, if the system fails, it is instantly switched over to a new blade. Workers don't notice that anything has changed, and Boeck gets a message to notify him of the failure. All he has to do is swap over a new blade. This is a huge benefit over the past where it could sometimes take an entire day of system downtime to repair a failed network.

Additionally, if he wants to spin off a server for a specific resource, VMware will tell him how many resources it will require.

"It's amazing because you always buy a new server and you wind up overbuying," said Boeck. "You never use all those resources."

Reliability was their key issue, but McNeilus faced other problems that virtualization helped with. The first was server sprawl. The company had maxed out the total number of servers it could house.

Boeck notes that when buying blade servers, make sure to get enough RAM. The processing power is not usually an issue.

"You'll run out of RAM before you run out of processor," observed Boeck.

Another benefit is in administration. Now that everything is centralized, it can be managed from one location, rather than scattered around the organization or at remote sites.

There were some benefits that the company didn't realize it would encounter. Moving to virtualization allowed the company to implement its own Green IT initiatives and reap the rewards. The company spends less money on electricity and cooling, and they are a more socially responsible corporate citizen.

"We were lucky to get that benefit," said Boeck.

Making the Sell

Changing over to a virtualized datacenter is not inexpensive. For Boeck, it was necessary to sell the company's CFO on the change.

Luckily, the company was moving to a new headquarters and Boeck and his team had the benefit of being able to design the new datacenter that they thought most appropriate. When he presented the idea to the CFO, he signed off on it.

"I just said, 'This is how I think we should do it,'" said Boeck, along with giving the CFO some good reasons why.

Equipment

In terms of hardware, McNeilus switched from Hewlett Packard servers to an IBM 4700 Fiber SAN with Expansion Bay, IBM Blade Center Chassis with HS20 and HS21 IBM Blade Server, and Cisco C9020 Fiber Switches.

While they liked the Hewlett Packard machines, there was more of a comfort level in using IBM's equipment because they have been in the blade market longer than Hewlett Packard or Dell.

"We've always been an HP shop. We loved them," observed Boeck. "But IBM has been in the game longer."

Also, there is an IBM headquarters in nearby Rochester, Minnesota. If there are problems, someone can get to them fast.

"They can have someone in our lobby in 30 minutes," said Boeck.

The company plans to develop a mirror imaging of this setup to one of their remote facilities and use the second site disaster recovery/high availability via SAN-to-SAN synchronization across a WAN link. They are also considering including FatPipe and Cisco's WAAS/RiverBed products. They are also considering putting their System I onto a Power 6 blade in the same timeframe.

McNeilus didn't have to spend much money on new clients—they repurposed the fat clients that were already in place. The old fat clients just need to be able to display the functions operating on the server.

On the software side, they are using VMware ESX Servers, which include high availability and VMotion options.

At the time, VMware was McNeilus' only option. VMware had a proven record. Microsoft was still developing its solution and if they had waited, Boeck feared adopting the brand new Microsoft solution had the potential to bring problems, since it would be so new and untested.

In the end, Boeck has nothing but praise for VMware.

"VMware wasn't cheap, but it is efficient," said Boeck.

Making the Move

When it came time to implement the move, Boeck said that they used a VMware tool called P2V (Physical-to-Virtual) that allowed them to copy their server images onto the blades. Then it was an issue of physically schlepping client computers to the new building.

"It's amazing that users don't want to pick up their own computers," said Boeck. "They think they'll break them."

They started moving the systems just after Thanksgiving in 2005 and were moved in by the first of the year.

Doing New Things

In addition to the benefits already mentioned, McNeilus has been able to change the way the company works—for the better. When they want to test a new application, it's simply a matter of spinning up an identical virtual server, installing the application there, and testing it. If there are problems, they don't deploy the application to the main image.

"We didn't have the money to build a test environment, but with the virtual server, we have it," said Boeck.

Also, it was not uncommon for them to be surprised by a mandated application. However, since they didn't know the application was coming, it would take weeks extra to find the correct server, order it, and install the application. Now it's just a matter of testing it on a copy of the work environment.

Patch management has also been simplified with VMware's snapshot feature. Now, when a new patch is issued, Boeck can test the patch to ensure it works. If it does work properly, he can simply approve the change and it will be applied to the work environment.

A local cloud is helpful for a number of reasons, not the least of which include reliability and centralized management. Being able to put your clients on a virtual cloud also has some great benefits for the environment. Whether or not virtualization is right for your organization is a case-by-case issue, but if you think it might be a good move for your organization, think about it before budget time.

If you are considering a move to the cloud, there are some considerations to keep in mind, not the least of which is migration, which we will talk about in the next chapter.

PART III

Migrating to the Cloud

Moving to the cloud is a lot like eating an elephant. Where do you start? It is such a big and unique thing that you might not even know where to take the first bite. But the fact of the matter is that you just need to study your organization, think about what can (and should) be moved to the cloud, and then just dig in.

Obviously you don't want to do it all at once. Besides, network administrators need something to do, and if you take away everything locally, there's only so much computer solitaire they can play.

In this chapter we'll look at migration tools and strategies for people at different levels—starting with individuals and small groups, then moving to mid-sized organizations, and then finally to considerations for enterprise-sized groups.

Cloud Services for Individuals

The most basic—and the easiest—way to move to the cloud is at an individual or small business level. There are a growing number of popular applications out there, and they tend to be free or offered at a very low cost. Let's take a look at some services that you may or may not have heard of, and talk about how they can help you.

Available Services

Chances are you have one of these services already. Take, for instance, Gmail. It's a free, online web mail application. And probably the reason you signed up for it is the reason many of us do—it's convenient to be able to check your email from any computer. And at an individual level, that's probably the most appealing part of web applications. You can check your email from work; work on a document during a boring family get-together; or synchronize files among your laptop, computer, and smartphone using cloud-based services.

Let's take a look at some of the most popular cloud applications out there.

- **Apple Mobile Me** (http://www.me.com/)   This service synchronizes emails, photos, and contacts among multiple devices. Your computer, laptop, and mobile devices can remain in sync as long as they have access to Apple's cloud servers.

- **Google Docs** (http://docs.google.com/)   Providing an intuitive interface, Google Docs provides applications that you normally associate with the desktop—a word processor, spreadsheet, and presentation designer. Documents can be saved to the cloud or locally. Multiple users can collaborate on the same document from different computers with changes taking effect instantly.

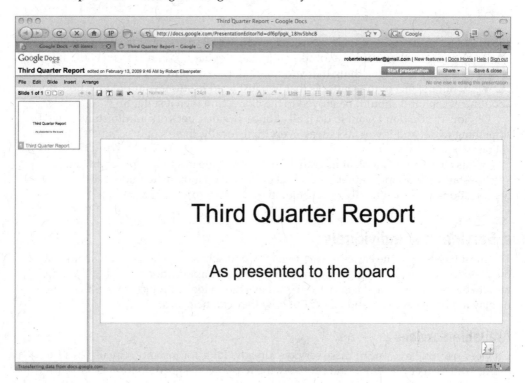

- **Adobe Acrobat** (http://www.acrobat.com/) Known for its free PDF reader (among other tools), Adobe provides its own online word processor and cloud storage space for your documents. It also includes collaboration tools and an online PDF converter.

- **Jooce** (http://www.jooce.com/) Jooce is a Flash-based desktop environment, mostly for users of Internet cafés. Dragging a file onto the desktop uploads it to the cloud, giving you access to your files from any Internet-connected computer.

- **Evernote** (http://www.evernote.com/) Evernote allows you to save photos, screenshots, or files to their servers in the cloud. If the images contain text, they are scanned and indexed to create a virtual database. Various client software packages allow PCs, Macs, iPhones, and other endpoints to synchronize Evernote data with the cloud.

- **Microsoft Live Search** (http://www.live.com/) Microsoft's mobile phone search engine uses heavy cloud processing to bring detailed searches to handheld devices.

- **Twitterfone** (http://www.twitterfone.com/) Twitterfone uses speech recognition in the cloud to transcribe voice messages into "tweets" on the Twitter social network.

- **Blist/Socrata** (http://www.socratablist.com/)   Blist, now called Socrata, is a database with an eye-catching interface, how-to videos, and a drag-and-drop design. After it's been created, the database can be shared with other users of the site.

- **Picnik** (http://www.picnik.com/)   This service provides photo editing in the cloud. You upload pictures from your local machine or import them from another site—like Flickr or Facebook. The site has powerful photo editing tools and it is also possible to add text, shapes, or a frame to your photos.
- **Adobe Photoshop Express** (http://www.photoshop.com/express)   This is another editor by the creators of the powerful Photoshop application. You can store your photos on the cloud and edit them with the same tools that you would use with a desktop version of Photoshop. Once your photo editing is done, you can add your photos to the site's gallery.

- **G.ho.st** (http://g.ho.st/)   Standing for Global Hosted Operating System, G.ho.st is a Flash-based virtual operating system. The site has the feel of a computer desktop and offers up to 5GB of free storage (you can earn more storage space by referring others to the site) and 3GB for email, web, and office applications (they use one named Zoho).

Skytap Solution

Skytap offers a virtual lab in the cloud. And to help you move your efforts from your local environment, they offer an API to help mount a solid migration. Let's take a look, first, at what the Virtual Lab is, and then we'll look under the hood of their API and talk about what it does.

Skytap Virtual Lab

Cloud-based virtualization solution company Skytap (formerly known as illumita) offers Skytap Virtual Lab, a virtual lab automation solution available as an on-demand service over the Web.

"Skytap provides customers with cloud-based services that enable them to capitalize on the wave of virtualization technology sweeping the industry," said Scott Roza, CEO of Skytap. "Cloud computing is gaining traction because a growing percentage of companies are demanding solutions that deliver value quickly, scale with business need, and don't have the risk of an in-house implementation. Skytap Virtual Lab, which combines cloud-based virtualized infrastructure with an industry leading lab automation application, has tremendous potential to improve the timely delivery of quality applications to the business while increasing lab efficiency and lowering cost."

Skytap Virtual Lab is a virtual lab solution available as a service over the Web. It enables application development and test teams to provision lab infrastructure on demand (including servers, software, networking, and storage) and utilize a powerful virtual lab management application to automate the setup, testing, and tear-down of complex, multitiered environments. It also gives distributed teams the capability to collaborate and rapidly resolve software defects using a virtual lab and virtual project environment.

"Virtualization is poised to become the defining technology of the 21st century," said Theresa Lanowitz, founder of analyst firm voke. "The market opportunity of virtualized solutions is enormous, as are the benefits virtualization delivers to an organization. Skytap's introduction of virtual lab automation as a SaaS [Software as a Service] offering provides a flexible entry point to the exciting world of virtualization."

Skytap's customers include Independent Software Vendors (ISVs), Systems Integrators (SIs), and test outsourcing firms, mid-size companies, and departments within global enterprises that want the benefits that Skytap's virtual lab service provides.

"We've been using Skytap's service for several months and have been impressed with its capabilities and the significant productivity gains our team has experienced from Skytap's virtual lab technology," said Eric Blankenburg, CTO of Resolute. "The Skytap solution enables us to quickly scale up our lab infrastructure to meet our tight development deadlines and provides our global application development team with the tools and platform they need to test and ship our products on time."

"As a company that delivers both software products and consulting services to clients, we are constantly facing situations where we need dynamic lab environments that we can spin up quickly," said Clay Roach, president of J9 Technologies, another early customer of the Skytap solution. "Skytap Virtual Lab has given us the capability to rapidly bring lab resources online regardless of whether the team is working on-site or off-site. This has given us a significant competitive advantage and an ability to expand our business with new customer solutions and services."

Customers using Skytap are able to access the following:

- **Virtual infrastructure on-demand**   Virtually unlimited hardware, software, and storage available from any location and any browser. Skytap Virtual Lab scales up and down with software project demands and requires no upfront investment.

- **Automated setup and tear-down of environments**   A web-based virtual lab automation application that eliminates manual setup and tear-down tasks and enables the rapid provisioning and replication of multimachine production environments for development and testing.

- **Skytap Library**   A prepopulated software library that includes major operating systems, databases, and applications in multiple languages that dramatically reduces media installation tasks and enables construction of lab environments by dragging and dropping preconfigured virtual machines.

- **Collaboration in a virtual environment**   The capability to instantly collaborate on software issues and defects in a virtualized environment. Entire multimachine lab environments can be suspended and shared with distributed, global team members to enable reproduction and diagnosis of software bugs and issues.

Skytap Migration API

The Skytap API enables customers to blend Skytap's cloud-based Virtual Lab platform with their existing on-site IT infrastructure. Rather than using cloud resources in a silo, Skytap's Web Services API and one-click VPN functionality allows organizations to create a "hybrid" IT model whereby cloud resources can be used as an extension of existing on-site IT environments.

"A common misconception people have about cloud computing is that it has to be an all or nothing decision," said Theresa Lanowitz, founder of analyst firm voke. "Skytap's API and advanced networking features allow companies to progressively adopt cloud resources without completely abandoning the business processes and applications they've already established in their onsite environment."

Unlike most cloud computing offerings where applications must be specifically rewritten for the cloud, Skytap allows companies to run their existing applications, virtual machines, and systems unchanged on industry-standard platforms. Skytap cloud infrastructure supports the leading hypervisors, including VMware and Citrix Xen, and support is planned for Microsoft Hyper-V, and operating systems, such as Microsoft Windows, Linux, and Solaris.

The Skytap solution involves accessing their cloud and running lab services at your own site.

Using a hybrid cloud computing model, organizations have a way to realize the benefits of cloud economics. Migrating high-cost, dynamic environments, such as application development and QA, IT ops testing, training and demo environments, provides a low-risk adoption path to cloud computing. It also delivers a high ROI as dynamic environments fluctuate dramatically and are often the most expensive to administer. In a hybrid model, companies can maintain production applications on-site while conducting all their testing in the cloud. This enables on-demand scaling of test environments as needed and eliminates the cost of underutilized hardware. This approach also allows organizations to benefit from the management and automation capabilities of a fully automated virtual lab solution, leading to huge productivity increases.

The API and advanced networking features that are now in Skytap Virtual Lab include

- A REST-based Web Service interface that enables cloud resources to be controlled programmatically
- Public/static IP addresses to provide seamless access to Skytap environments
- One-click VPN for easy connection back to the onsite IT environments
- Automated upload of existing virtual machines and software to run in Skytap Virtual Lab

Skytap Virtual Lab provides virtualized infrastructure, including hardware, storage, and networking resources that can be accessed on demand. When Skytap's Virtual Lab management application is combined with the Skytap Library, a prepopulated virtual machine library that includes major operating systems, databases, and other application software, customers get access to a complete virtual lab solution on demand.

"As a provider of the industry's leading cloud application platform, our consulting organization works with enterprises to deliver applications on large-scale private clouds," said Mark Sundt, vice president of professional services, Appistry. "The Skytap environment allows us to help our customers get cloud applications to market more quickly by adopting a 'hybrid' model for development and large scale testing. The ability to automatically scale up lab infrastructure using the Skytap API complements our clients' on-site infrastructure and gives us tremendous business flexibility."

For more information on this release of Skytap Virtual Lab visit www.skytap.com.

Cloud Services Aimed at the Mid-Market

At a mid-market level, it's likely that there are things you want to keep locally, but other applications and storage that you want to do on the cloud. This is where you can try some things out and make sure they're right for your organization.

NOTE   *At this level you might also consider a policy for your workers about what they can or cannot keep on their own private cloud solutions. For instance, Shelly in accounting might want to do some work at home, so she stores the spreadsheet on Google Docs. However, since she's doing work with sensitive data, you might not want it on the cloud. It's best to lay down some rules right up front so that nothing bad happens to that sensitive data and Shelly's chances for continued employment.*

Force.com

The Force.com Migration Tool is more of a roll-up-your-sleeves-because-you're-going-to-get-your-hands-dirty thing, compared to being able to point and click your way through a GUI. The Force.com Migration Tool is an Ant library that lets you migrate metadata (code and settings) from your organization to Force.com's cloud.

The Force.com platform holds your application as metadata on the platform, and you can access this metadata. That is how the Force.com IDE works—it uses the metadata to get your code, your packages, your triggers, and edit them locally. Each time you edit an Apex page, it sends the code back to the Force.com servers where it is compiled.

The Force.com Migration Tool is a Java/Ant-based command-line utility for moving metadata between a local directory and Force.com. The Force.com Migration Tool is especially useful in these scenarios:

- **Development projects**   When you need to populate a test environment with large amounts of setup changes. If you were to make these changes using a web interface, it would take a large amount of time.

- **Multistage release processes**   Most development processes run in iterative cycles of building, testing, and staging before they are released to a production environment. Scripted retrieval and deployment of your components makes this process easier and cleaner.

- **Repetitive deployment using the same parameters**   You can retrieve all your organization's metadata, make changes as needed, and deploy that metadata. If you need to do it again, you just have to call the same deployment target.

In Action

Let's look at an example script to see how to use Apex to migrate data.

There are some prerequisites. You should ensure you have the latest version of Java JDK. You can get it at http://java.sun.com/javase/downloads/index.jsp. You need at least version 6.1.

You also need Ant version 1.6 or greater on the deployment machine. It can be found at http://ant.apache.org/.

Next, set up the environment variables (like ANT_HOME, JAVA_HOME, and PATH) as instructed in the Ant Installation Guide (this can be downloaded at http://ant.apache.org/manual/install.html).

Ensure that everything is installed correctly by opening a command prompt and entering

```
ant -version
```

Your output should look like this:

```
Apache Ant version 1.7.0 compiled on December 13, 2006
```

You get started by following these basic steps:

1. On your deployment machine, log in to your Salesforce.com account.

2. Follow Setup | Develop | Tools, and then click Force.com Migration Tool.

3. Unzip the downloaded file. The Zip file contains the following:

   - A Readme.html file that explains how to use the tools

   - A Jar file containing the Ant task: ant-salesforce.jar

   - A sample folder containing

     - A codepkg\classes folder that contains SampleDeployClass.cls and SampleFailingTestClass.cls

     - A codepkg\triggers folder that contains SampleAccountTrigger.trigger

     - A mypkg\objects folder that contains the custom objects used in the examples

     - A removecodepkg folder that contains XML files for removing the examples from your organization

     - A sample build.properties file that you must edit, specifying your credentials, in order to run the sample Ant tasks in build.xml

     - A sample build.xml file that exercises the deploy and retrieve API calls

4. Copy the ant-salesforce.jar file from the unzipped file into the ant lib directory. The ant lib directory is found in the root folder of your Ant installation.

5. Open the sample subdirectory in the unzipped file.

6. Edit the build.properties file:

   a. Enter your Salesforce production organization username and password for the sf.user and sf.password fields, respectively.

NOTE *The username you use should have the permission to edit Apex.*

---

   b. If you are deploying to a sandbox organization, change the sf.serverurl field to https://test.salesforce.com.

7. Open a command window in the sample directory.

8. Enter the following:

   ```
   ant deployCode.
   ```

   This runs the deployAPI call, using the sample class and Account trigger provided with the Force.com Migration Tool.

   The ant deployCode calls the Ant target named deploy in the build.xml file.

   ```
   <!-- Shows deploying code & running tests for package 'codepkg' -->
       <target name="deployCode">
           <!-- Upload the contents of the "codepkg" package,
           running the tests for just 1 class -->
           <sf:deploy username="${sf.username}"
           password="${sf.password}" serverurl="${sf.serverurl}"
           deployroot="codepkg">
           <runTest>SampleDeployClass</runTest>
           </sf:deploy>
       </target>
   ```

9. Remove the test class and trigger added as part of the execution of ant deployCode. To do this, enter the following in the command window:

   ```
   ant undeployCode.
   ```

   ant undeployCode calls the Ant target named undeployCode in the build.xml file.

   ```
   <target name="undeployCode">
       <sf:deploy username="${sf.username}"
       password="${sf.password}" serverurl=
       "${sf.serverurl}" deployroot="removecodepkg"/>
   </target>
   ```

Force.com Apps

As you consider migrating your organization to the cloud—and if Force.com is appealing to you—the following are some of the most popular applications on Force.com. Most of these applications are free of charge, but others require a subscription. And remember, this is just a sampling of the applications on Force.com. There are hundreds more for your use.

The following are some of the (currently) most popular apps on Force.com:

- **Appirio Calendar Sync for Salesforce.com and Google Apps**   Appirio Calendar Sync for Salesforce.com and Google Apps is a simple tool to sync your Salesforce.com calendar with your Google Calendar. With Appirio Calendar Sync, it is easy to automatically keep your Salesforce Calendar in sync with your Google Calendar. You can share customer-related events across company boundaries through an easy-to-use online calendar. And it is easy to associate every event in your calendar with the right account, opportunity, lead, case, or any other custom object.

- **Gmail to Salesforce.com browser button for Firefox**   Browser buttons can easily be added to your browser's toolbar. When using Gmail, simply click the Gmail to Salesforce.com browser button to send the email and automatically copy it as an activity on related lead and contact records inside Salesforce.com.

- **Lead and opportunity management dashboards**   Install lead-tracking and opportunity management dashboards instantly within your Salesforce.com account. These dashboards only use standard fields and objects from within Salesforce.com; therefore, there is no configuration to be done, just a simple download.

- **Appirio CRM Dashboards for Salesforce.com & Google Apps**   Appirio CRM Dashboards for Salesforce.com & Google Apps allows you to put Salesforce data into graphs and tables on your Google Start Page, Google Document, or Google Site.

- **Sales Activity Dashboard**   This Dashboard is important to sales professionals who want to have visibility of the types of Activity their sales teams are engaging in on Opportunities. This is particularly helpful in team selling environments where, together with account executives, the Opportunity may have Activities from sales consulting, engineering, and professional services teams.

- **VerticalResponse for AppExchange**   VerticalResponse for AppExchange provides self-service email and direct mail solutions. Create custom mailing lists of any size, design professional sales and marketing campaigns, and track post-launch statistics.

- **Appirio Search for Salesforce.com & Google Apps**   Appirio Search for Salesforce .com & Google Apps allows you to find and add Google Docs to any Salesforce object as you work—without switching screens or copying URLs. An extension to "Salesforce.com for Google Apps."

- **Salesforce.com for Google AdWords**   Salesforce.com for Google AdWords allows online marketers to track the effectiveness of Google advertising campaigns and web site lead-generation activity.

- **Astadia Report Collaboration for Google Spreadsheets**   Astadia Report Collaboration for Google Spreadsheets allows a Salesforce subscriber to export any reportable information in Salesforce to Google Spreadsheets for further analysis and share the report with both Salesforce and non-Salesforce users.

- **Conga Merge**   Create content-rich output from Word/Excel templates or PDF forms. Custom quotes, proposals, account plans, and more from any custom object and related lists—as little as one click to print, attachment, or email.

PART III

Enterprise-Class Cloud Offerings

Moving to the cloud gets more complex as your organization grows in size. Enterprise-class organizations should follow the same sorts of guidelines as the mid-market group—that is, try out new things, figure out what to move, and then move over time—but their scope is entirely different. For instance, part of your migration might include moving a branch office's application to the cloud. In this section, we'll talk about how enterprise-class organizations can make a migration.

MS Exchange

A cornerstone of most enterprises is the Microsoft Exchange service for email. Microsoft now offers Exchange Online and Microsoft SharePoint Online for businesses of all sizes. These subscription services offer businesses a new way to purchase, deploy, and manage the industry-leading email and calendaring solution, and the industry-leading solution for portals and collaboration.

And since Exchange is so prevalent, it is an easy tool to migrate to the cloud, especially given that the cloud offering is an online version of the traditional server and client application.

"Customers are embracing Microsoft's software and services strategy en masse because of the choice and flexibility it gives them," said Stephen Elop, president of the Microsoft Business Division. "Today, we bring business-class communications and collaboration technologies to the cloud, and we are committed to delivering more capabilities in the months ahead. No one has done what we are doing at this scale, and I'm certain that our customers will continue to take on these solutions as our offerings grow."

The service can be tried at http://www.microsoft.com/online. As part of the Microsoft Online Services product family, Exchange Online and SharePoint Online are available separately or as a suite together with Office Live Meeting for conferencing and Microsoft Exchange Hosted Services and Microsoft Office Communications Online for instant messaging and presence.

A growing number of companies, from small businesses to large enterprises, are adopting Microsoft Online Services. In 2008, Microsoft sold more than a half million seats for Microsoft Online Services, including Exchange Online, SharePoint Online, and Office Communications Online. New customers include Pitney Bowes Inc.; CG Healthcare Solutions LLC, an affiliate of Cowan, Gunteski & Co., P.A.; Clean Power Research LLC; Corefino Inc.; and Fair Isaac Corp.

To help businesses plan, deploy, and operate the services, Microsoft released Microsoft Solution Accelerators for Microsoft Online Services. These include automated tools and guidance, such as the Microsoft Assessment and Planning Toolkit, the Infrastructure Planning and Design Guide, and the Microsoft Operations Framework Companion Guide. More information about Microsoft Solution Accelerators for Microsoft Online Services is online at http://technet.microsoft.com/en-us/solutionaccelerators/dd277934.aspx.

"With Microsoft Online Services, Eddie Bauer was able to improve associate productivity in a cost-effective manner—and that translates to a high return on our IT investment," said Rich Mozack, CIO at Eddie Bauer Inc. "The online aspect of the solution enabled us to transition from our old environment to the Microsoft tools very quickly and smoothly. On a Friday, 1,400 of Eddie Bauer's associates went home as Lotus Notes users, and on Monday they came to work as Outlook users with Microsoft Online Services."

Between July 2008 and November 2008, more than 1,500 companies have enrolled in the Microsoft Partner Program for Microsoft Online Services, with 100 more joining every week. These companies are realizing a wide range of revenue opportunity that spans reselling, migration, customization, consulting, training, support and application development, and integration services.

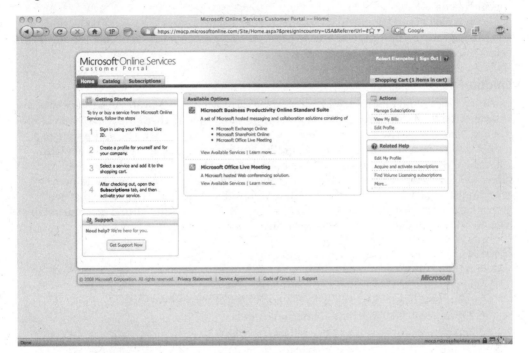

Many partners are delivering customized capabilities for Microsoft Online Services. To increase awareness of these solutions, Microsoft also introduces the Partner Solutions Showcase Program for Microsoft Online Services, and a Partner Solutions Showcase Program Award that is given to two partners annually. This award is designed to recognize outstanding application and integration work on the part of partners. Microsoft presented the first Partner Solutions Showcase Program Award to ThoughtBridge, which has built a human resources application on top of SharePoint Online. Partners can learn more about the showcase and award at http://www.microsoft.com/online/partner/solutions-showcase.mspx.

"ThoughtBridge recognized an immediate opportunity for building unique, vertical capabilities on top of Microsoft SharePoint Online, and we see tremendous opportunity to grow our business around this model," said Tim Tisdale, CTO and cofounder of ThoughtBridge. "Already, we're seeing strong customer demand for migration, customization and integration services. Microsoft Online Services give us the agility to address this demand with fewer resources. We think this opportunity will bring us the bulk of our revenue moving forward."

Microsoft also has other online services in the pipeline. In addition to Office Communications Online, Microsoft is planning to offer a Microsoft Online Services solution that will provide IT management and security capabilities for businesses, enabling IT managers to secure and manage desktops using a web-based subscription service. These online services will be based on components from existing systems management, identity, and security offerings, and will complement Microsoft's on-premise solutions, as customers begin to adopt cloud-based computing to address specific needs.

It's not likely that you are going to put all your email on the cloud at the same time. But you can take advantage of the service to phase in a few users or satellite branches at a time before moving everyone over.

VMotion

The main tool for migrations in VMware's arsenal is VMotion. VMware says that VMotion leverages the complete virtualization of servers, storage, and networking to move an entire running virtual machine instantaneously from one server to another. The entire state of a virtual machine is encapsulated by a set of files stored on shared storage, and VMware's vStorage VMFS cluster file system allows both the source and the target VMware ESX server to access these virtual machine files concurrently. The active memory and precise execution state of a virtual machine can then be rapidly transmitted over a high-speed network. Since the network is also virtualized by VMware ESX, the virtual machine retains its network identity and connections, ensuring a seamless migration process.

Features

VMotion offers these capabilities:

- Perform migrations with no downtime, undetectable by your users.
- Optimize virtual machines in resource pools.
- Perform hardware maintenance without downtime and disrupting operations.
- Move virtual machines from poorly performing or failing physical servers onto new machines.
- Multiple concurrent migrations can optimize a virtual IT environment.
- A migration wizard can provide real-time availability information to identify the optimal placement of a virtual machine.
- Migrate any virtual machine running any operating system across hardware supported by VMware ESX, including Fibre Channel SAN, NAS, and iSCSI SAN.
- Prioritize live migrations to ensure that mission-critical virtual machines maintain access to the resources they need.
- Schedule migrations to happen at predefined times, and without an administrator's presence.
- Maintain an audit trail with a detailed record of migrations.

VMware VMotion is included in the VMware Infrastructure Enterprise edition. VMware VMotion and VMware Storage VMotion are available as an add-on product to VMware Infrastructure Foundation and Standard editions.

VMware vCenter Converter

VMware offers its vCenter Converter to migrate physical servers to virtual servers. The application can be run on a number of different types of hardware and supports most versions of Microsoft Windows operating systems.

With this enterprise-class migration tool, you can

- Quickly convert local and remote physical machines into virtual machines with no downtime.
- Simultaneously convert multiple servers with a centralized management console and conversion wizard.
- Convert other virtual machine formats (like Microsoft Virtual PC and Microsoft Virtual Server) or back up images of physical machines to VMware virtual machines.
- Restore VMware Consolidated Backup (VCB) images onto running virtual machines.
- Clone and back up physical machines to virtual machines, as part of a disaster recovery plan.

Among its features, VMware Converter includes these attributes:

- The ability to perform simultaneous conversions, enabling large-scale virtualization projects.
- Quiescing and snapshotting of the guest OS on the source machine before migrating. This ensures the data is migrated reliably.
- Hot cloning allows for non-disruptive conversions.
- Sector-based copying to enhance cloning and conversion speed.
- Use of a centralized management console that allows users to queue up and monitor multiple simultaneous remote locations, as well as local conversions.
- Wizards minimize the number of steps in a conversion.
- The ability to clone both local and remote servers allows conversions in remote locations.

VMware vCenter Converter can import virtual machines created in

- Workstation 5.x and Workstation 4.x
- VMware Player 1.x
- VMware ESX 3.x
- ESX Server 2.5.x (if the virtual machine is managed by VirtualCenter 2.x)
- GSX Server 3.x
- VMware Server 1.x
- VirtualCenter 2.x
- Microsoft Virtual PC version 7 and later
- Any version of Microsoft Virtual Server

There are two versions of VMware Converter:

- **VMware vCenter Converter Starter**   A free download (located at http://www .vmware.com/download/converter/), used for single conversions.
- **VMware vCenter Converter Enterprise**   An enterprise-class product for managing and automating large-scale conversions.

Hyper-V Live Migration

Microsoft Server 2008 Hyper-V makes migration a very clean affair, although it is used for moving virtual servers around to different machines. That said, it is extremely simple to use. It is a matter of pointing and clicking on a management console.

Migration is accomplished through Live Migration, a tool part of Windows Server 2008 R2. Live migration utilizes the integrated hypervisor technology and high-availability features of the server operating system so that customers can move running applications between servers to accommodate changing, dynamic computing needs across a datacenter. In addition to other features, the next version of Microsoft Hyper-V Server will have live migration capabilities.

Microsoft is pushing its new virtualization products including System Center Virtual Machine Manager 2008, Microsoft Application Virtualization 4.5, and Microsoft Hyper-V Server 2008, which is a no-cost download.

"Now is the time for customers to get virtual," said Bob Kelly, corporate vice president of infrastructure server marketing within Microsoft's Server and Tools Business. "With desktop and datacenter virtualization offerings available from Microsoft and its partners, customers are adopting Microsoft solutions because they have better value and will make IT operations more dynamic. At a lower cost than other datacenter virtualization solutions, Microsoft software meets customers' needs from the desktop to the datacenter in an integrated offering on the platform they know."

Web-based human resource, payroll, and employment verification services provider TALX is now in the process of developing a new, advanced datacenter to service its 9,000 clients. By using Windows Server 2008 Hyper-V to enhance virtualization performance and host more virtual machines per physical server, TALX will be able to further consolidate its server environment, reduce hardware costs, save on power and cooling costs, and conserve datacenter space. TALX expects to save another $1,000 in software licensing costs per each physical server it can replace with a virtual machine. The company also expects to save approximately 50 percent in annual power and cooling costs by consolidating its server environment with Windows Server 2008 Hyper-V.

"In the employer and verifier marketplace, a lot of our competitive advantage is related to time to market. If we can shave days or weeks off our cycle, that's a big plus," said Bryan Garcia, vice president of technology at TALX. "With Hyper-V and Virtual Machine Manager, we're going to make the infrastructure a lot more flexible and agile. We expect to save at least $5,000 per year per installed virtual host machine, directly out of infrastructure costs for energy, hardware acquisition, and hardware maintenance."

Microsoft's virtual products include

- Microsoft Hyper-V Server 2008, a hypervisor-based server virtualization product, that is available at no cost via the Web. Microsoft Hyper-V Server 2008 provides an optimized virtualization solution that allows customers to consolidate Windows or

Linux workloads onto a single physical server. Hyper-V Server 2008 allows customers to leverage their existing patching, provisioning, management and support tools, processes and skills.

- System Center Virtual Machine Manager 2008 enables customers to configure and deploy new virtual machines and centrally manage their virtualized infrastructure, whether running on Windows Server 2008 Hyper-V, Microsoft Virtual Server 2005 R2, Microsoft Hyper-V Server 2008, or VMware Virtual Infrastructure 3. System Center Virtual Machine Manager is part of the System Center suite of products, which provides centralized, enterprise-class management of physical and virtual resources across desktops and datacenters.

- Microsoft Application Virtualization 4.5 gives desktop users a boost in fully harnessing the power of Windows Vista by streaming resource-heavy applications to the desktop. This helps eliminate potential software conflicts driving desktop stability and performance, while simultaneously enabling IT managers to centrally control key applications and their use. Application Virtualization 4.5 is included as part of Microsoft Desktop Optimization Pack 2008 R2.

Migration

The preceding sections of this chapter discussed specific sizes of organizations. But there are some general considerations for any organization that you should keep in mind when considering a move. Let's talk about them in more detail.

Which Applications Do You Need?

Deciding what you should migrate to the cloud really comes down to figuring out what you want out of the cloud. That is, are you looking to store data on someone else's servers? If that's the case, it's simply a matter of deciding which data you want to send (and pay for) and what data doesn't need to be sent.

If you are using the cloud for SaaS or PaaS, you have to look at which applications are most appropriate for maintenance on the cloud. It will obviously differ from organization to organization, but you likely won't move your key mission-critical tasks to the cloud. For instance, a company that develops software for healthcare providers is going to have different needs than a financial advisor, for instance. But even within the same industry, different organizations will get different things out of the cloud.

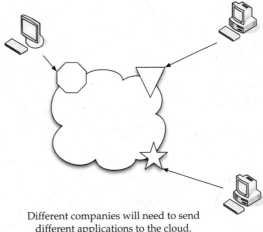

Different companies will need to send different applications to the cloud. Even companies in the same industry will perform different work on the cloud.

But when you do decide to move to the cloud, make sure the applications you are going to use don't consume too many network resources. This is something to figure out before you've committed and started migrating data.

One regional bank decided to go forward with a Salesforce.com solution, but even after they successfully piloted the program, they had not planned for the bandwidth that it would need. Not only did it affect the speed of their cloud use, but it also slowed down employees' Internet access.

Also, if the application you want to use on the cloud demands high performance and low latency, make sure that the provider you've elected to go with can deliver on your needs. Companies like Amazon have built their content delivery network with data centers at points all around the world. You won't have to try and access your servers in Los Angeles if you are in Washington, D.C.

NOTE *We're not pushing Amazon here. Just be sure to ask your vendors what they're doing to reduce latency.*

Sending Your Existing Data to the Cloud

There are all sorts of data that you can send to the cloud. You can store specific files, you can run applications online—you name it. But let's take a look at Symantec's solution and what one of their customers gets out of sending their data to the Symantec cloud.

Symantec Online Backup is used to protect business records while reducing the time and money spent managing backups. With Symantec's Software-as-a-Service (SaaS) online backup application, small and mid-sized businesses can ensure their data is protected against catastrophic loss while remaining easily recoverable.

Symantec Online Backup provides businesses with backup and recovery for PCs and servers over the Internet. Businesses using Symantec Online Backup eliminate the need to purchase and manage on-site hardware and receive increased protection from theft and disasters. Data is automatically stored off-site in multiple geographically distributed datacenters and can be restored to any location using a supported web browser. The service is hosted in the cloud by Symantec, eliminating the need for businesses to devote resources to managing patches and upgrades. The customer subscription includes 24/7 support, delivered by a team of SaaS specialists at no extra cost.

Cameron Consultation, based outside Boston, provides intensive therapeutic intervention to children with autism and other special needs. Cameron recently lived the nightmare of discovering that 20 years' worth of its intellectual property and client records were lost after two hard drives failed and the supposed automatic nightly backups had not been performed for more than a year. The company spent six weeks and thousands of dollars to recover some—but not all—of its lost records, and has since turned to Symantec Online Backup to create dependable backups while reducing the time and cost spent doing so.

"Knowing that Symantec is storing my data in more than one location makes me confident it will be there if I ever need it," said Susan Shea Cameron, clinical director and partner, Cameron Consultation. "The plan I'm using is not much more expensive than buying an external hard drive that has only a 30-day warranty and backup software. Symantec Online Backup gives me much more peace of mind. The system sends me an email to confirm that a backup was successful, and when I get the alert I feel relieved that there is one less thing for me to worry about."

An independent study finds that small and medium businesses (SMB) rate backup as their second-highest computing priority, after defense against viruses and other malware, and ahead of issues such as reducing costs and deploying new computers. However, the survey sponsored by Symantec and conducted by Rubicon Consulting found that 50 percent of small and mid-sized businesses have still experienced data loss and more than half do not store backup data off-site.

"There are a number of online backup applications in the market now, and moving sensitive business records online creates security concerns an organization must be aware of before partnering with a provider," said Darren Niller, group product manager, Symantec. "Failure to provide adequate levels of security enables attackers to read and even change the data being backed up or restored when it's transmitted over the Internet. As a market leader in security, disaster recovery and data protection, we've focused intensively on making sure our online backup service is highly reliable and secure."

Use the Wave Approach

The best way to migrate your data to the cloud is by following the same steps you would when rolling out a new operating system to your organization. Use the wave approach and release your data in waves. At first, you're testing the waters. You're finding out if the solution was what you expected. You're finding out if your vendor is the right one to work with.

Start with small data that is of low importance. Then, as you add more data, send more important stuff. Now, if you start with the data of least importance, you aren't going to see the performance that you will when more important data moves to the cloud. That just makes sense, because the low-priority data isn't accessed all that much to test the cloud. But, starting small gives you a place to start.

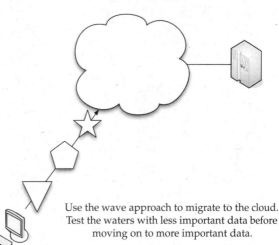

Use the wave approach to migrate to the cloud. Test the waters with less important data before moving on to more important data.

When you use a phased-in approach, it gives you a chance to see how the data fits on the cloud. Rather than throw everything over at once, you get a chance to see how things are going. If it turns out things aren't going well, you can take corrective action to fix it, or just pull the plug and walk away.

As we said at the outset, moving to the cloud is like eating an elephant. It's a daunting task and you just don't know where to begin. But with a little planning and effort, starting small will polish off your cloud efforts in a methodical manner. Now that we've covered migration, the next and final chapter will cover best practices and the future of cloud computing.

Best Practices and the Future of Cloud Computing

So now you've moved to the cloud, and you want to ensure a continued good experience. There are a myriad of things you should address when seeking to optimize your cloud efforts, ranging from the technical side to the human side. In this final chapter, we'll look at optimizing your cloud experience and talk about what things you can adjust and what tools you can use to tweak them.

Analyze Your Service

Once you've selected a cloud vendor, you should perform some tests and make sure you're still getting what you are paying for. In this section, we'll talk about some tips and techniques for checking up on your vendor to make sure everything is still up to par.

Not only will we be talking about checking statistics, but we'll also talk about some tools that will help you gather those statistics.

Establishing a Baseline and Metrics

There's some research you should do before signing on with a vendor, and that you should regularly perform once subscribed. There are a number of variables that you should use as a baseline, and then check back with frequently. Here are some variables to check:

- **Connection speed**   The speed at which you connect to the vendor's cloud.
- **Datastore delete time**   How long it takes to delete the datastore.
- **Datastore read time**   How long it takes to read data.
- **Deployment latency**   The amount of latency between when an application is posted and ready to use.
- **Lag time**   How slow the system is.

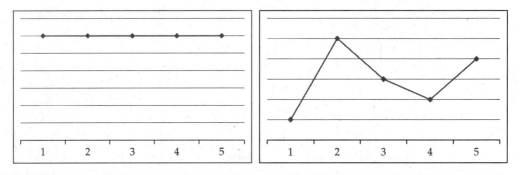

Figure 14-1   Consistency is essential when evaluating performance.

The first stat—connection speed—has nothing to do with your cloud vendor. It's your ISP's issue. What you are looking for is consistency. You don't want to see huge spikes in performance over time. A graph of your connection speed should look like the one on the left of Figure 14-1, not the one on the right.

There is no shortage of tools you can use to check your speed. Sites like www .myconnection.com offer a speed-testing tool that you can use to make sure you're getting consistent speeds from your ISP. An example of the tool is shown in Figure 14-2.

Tools

The market hasn't been saturated with performance monitoring tools for cloud computing yet. There are only a couple, but look for the market to broaden in the months and years to come. Here is a rundown of some tools you can use to check your cloud performance.

Hyperic HQ

Hyperic Inc offers its Hyperic HQ 4.0, the latest version of its systems monitoring and management application. The release addresses the needs of businesses embracing Amazon cloud services to create scalable IT deployment strategies. Hyperic HQ enables the modern enterprises to monitor their Amazon Web Services securely alongside internal infrastructure. It is also the first enterprise-class monitoring and management software offered for deployment and payment directly through Amazon Web Services.

"Cloud computing and virtualization technologies are making it easier, cheaper and faster to deliver scalable web applications. However, this has made the job of managing these web applications significantly harder. Administrators who are used to managing anywhere from 15 to 50 servers in a single datacenter can now be responsible for 500 or more servers sprawled across their datacenter and beyond the firewall," explained Javier Soltero, CEO, Hyperic. "With Hyperic HQ 4.0, we've delivered the tool web operations teams need to maintain service levels in these environments of massive scale and complexity, allowing them to embrace virtualization and cloud computing with confidence."

Hyperic HQ is poised to grow as cloud computing continues its development. IDC senior vice president and chief analyst, Frank Gens said that "a recent IDC survey of IT

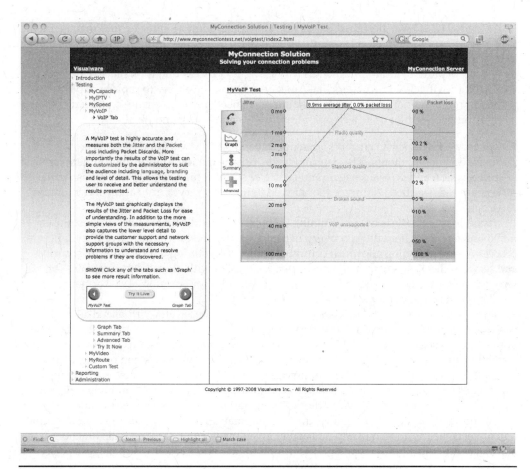

FIGURE 14-2   MyConnection.com allows you to monitor your connection speeds.

executives, CIOs, and their line of business (LOB) colleagues shows that cloud services are 'crossing the chasm' and entering a period of widespread adoption." Further, the analyst firm predicts that spending on cloud services will reach $42 billion in the next five years, and will capture 25 percent of IT spending growth in 2012.

To meet these growth expectations, adopters of cloud services need additional tools and updated deployment strategies to succeed. According to the survey respondents, top concerns for adoption include performance level assurances, supporting the need for new monitoring and management tools to help ensure the success of these deployments.

Datacenters have a fixed capacity for handling application traffic at any given time, and they distribute resources to match average peak capacity. Businesses deploying in Amazon's cloud now have access to an unlimited number of resources, and pay only for the services they need at any given time. To remain cost-effective, operations teams need to frequently tune web and application server capacity to match fluctuations in demand.

Hyperic HQ 4.0 was designed to address next-generation monitoring and management to help enterprises adopt cloud computing strategies, by better equipping operations teams to perform repetitive management tasks more efficiently. Traditionally, installing a new server and deploying it into production was a lengthy process that took place over days or weeks. Now, with cloud providers like Amazon offering the ability to rapidly deploy servers in minutes and pay by the hour, companies need a way to ensure consistent monitoring oversight of their web operations that is just as fast and flexible.

Performance   Hyperic HQ currently manages over 3,500 VMware and XenServer virtualization deployments. Also referred to as "private clouds," these environments consist of both physical and virtual servers, and typically support high rates of change as virtual servers are easily added, subtracted, or moved to improve server utilization and maintain service levels.

Hyperic HQ 4.0 starts by streamlining the process of adding new software resources into management. After auto-discovery registers the new resources into inventory, a new process of server cloning allows all configuration profiles for log data collection, security, and services checks to be immediately applied. Coupled with global alert templates for resource types, the entire system of monitoring and rules for warning of performance problems can be incorporated in under a minute.

Further, the release also addresses additional areas of concern for virtualized and cloud-based deployment including security, application management, and capacity planning. A new server communication protocol allows agents monitoring external resources to always initiate communication with the HQ Server in order to meet security protocols and operate across firewalls. HQ uses unidirectional communication, but the agent still maintains a full range of capabilities including the ability to update and run diagnostics remotely, and issue corrective control actions such as a service restart or running garbage collection to free memory.

Additionally, a capacity planning function automatically analyzes historical performance and projects the future resource trends of any given management metric. This function allows users to quickly assess and predict future trends, and proactively manage capacity needs to anticipate demand or conserve costs.

Hyperic HQ for EC2   Also part of the 4.0 release Hyperic HQ Enterprise 4.0 is available as a fully configured system on Amazon Web Services. An Amazon Machine Image (AMI) preconfigured for Amazon's Elastic Block Storage (EBS) is available. The distribution will be available directly on Amazon's DevPay service for an initiation fee and a monthly charge based on the amount of management data being collected to the HQ Server. This is a familiar arrangement to businesses looking to embrace the cloud; there will be no contract term and users will simply pay for how much value they are deriving from the Hyperic HQ Enterprise application.

Hyperic HQ 4.0 is available at www.hyperic.com. Hyperic HQ for EC2 is available through Amazon.

CloudStatus

Hyperic also offers a free cloud monitoring tool, CloudStatus. Their most recent addition to the tool is continuous monitoring of Google. Google App Engine is the second significant cloud service to be monitored by CloudStatus, which launched in June 2008 with support for Amazon Web Services.

NOTE *Support for additional cloud providers is planned in the near future.*

Hyperic's free CloudStatus service delivers real-time, independent insight into the health and performance of the App Engine, giving users a greater level of confidence in the reliability, availability, and scalability of web applications running on Google's infrastructure. CloudStatus is shown in Figure 14-3.

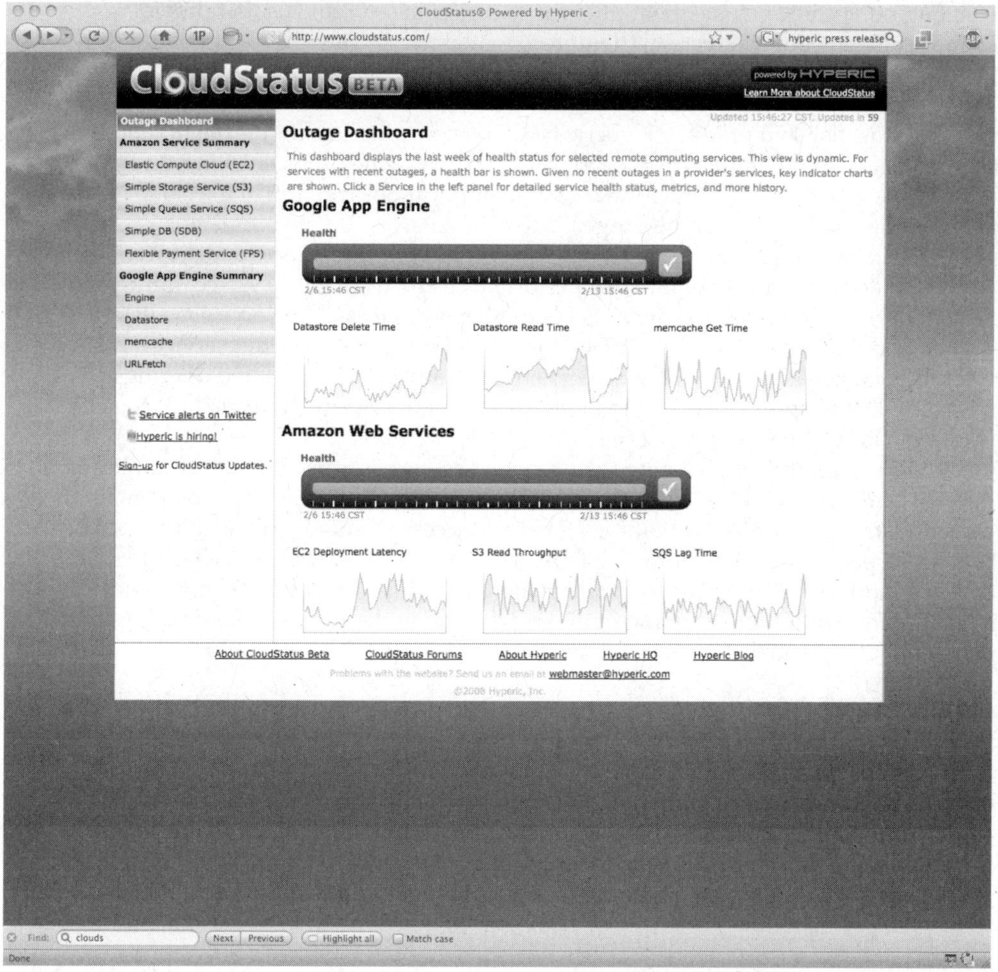

FIGURE 14-3   CloudStatus shows the internal performance of vendors like Amazon and Google.

"Monitoring helps maintain the health and performance of any application, including those powered by App Engine," said Paul McDonald, an App Engine product manager at Google. "We are excited to work with Hyperic to provide additional transparency to our service's real-time performance."

The addition of App Engine monitoring is designed to provide customers with the ability to obtain up-to-the-second perspectives on performance and network connectivity from both inside and outside the App Engine platform. The initial release will allow for continuous monitoring of the health and performance of major App Engine infrastructure, including the DataStore, Memcache, and global network connectivity. CloudStatus uses App Engine–specific management plug-ins to collect measurements that provide administrators and developers with unprecedented insight into the health of the App Engine platform.

As part of this development, Hyperic also offers the first cloud-specific management plug-in for its flagship product, Hyperic HQ. The new plug-in extends the full monitoring and management capabilities of Hyperic HQ to App Engine users, enabling them to examine the performance of their own custom applications running in the cloud. This plug-in is free for download on HyperForge.

To ensure reliability and more completely understand and trust cloud service stability, customers need transparency into real performance and availability. A free, third-party hosted service, CloudStatus provides a comprehensive measure of service availability, latency, and throughput for cloud-based infrastructure and application services. It allows users to obtain detailed, service-specific metrics on any of the monitored offerings, providing the perspective needed to determine the cause of any performance changes within their cloud-based applications.

"Cloud computing is changing the way businesses consume and deliver applications. Internet leaders like Google allow these businesses to eliminate the need to maintain their own infrastructure while also gaining affordable access to unlimited scalability," said Javier Soltero, Hyperic CEO. "We're thrilled to be working with vendors like Google to define the next generation of monitoring and management tools needed to assure performance and reliability for applications running in the cloud—and in the process help cloud computing realize its full potential."

CollabNet CUBiT 2.0

CollabNet's CUBiT 2.0 strives to eliminate the time-intensive process of configuring servers for build and test by managing those configurations as "profiles" across the application life cycle. Applying the cloud computing model to distributed development, CollabNet CUBiT 2.0 enables teams to access on-demand servers from private corporate datacenters or public clouds, to significantly reduce development cycles and hardware expenses.

⊠ CLOSE or Esc Key

Developers spend a great deal of time configuring servers and aligning the software stacks throughout the application life cycle—an arduous task for server-intensive methodologies such as agile, scrum, and continuous integration. CUBiT eases these pain points by enabling code, build, and test teams to accelerate development cycles, eliminate build and test errors, and gain flexibility in utilizing machines. It provides a secure way to reuse build and test profiles, reducing the likelihood of configuration errors that can delay software projects by months. In addition, CUBiT's self-service dynamic provisioning capabilities automate labor-intensive server provisioning and configuration that can take weeks. A financial services customer has decreased their time to build by 400 percent—from months to days.

CUBiT 2.0 allows teams to group and manage their computing resources as clouds. It enables development teams to access a global pool of on-demand build and test services. Teams manage their own library of software profiles and quickly can apply a configuration onto a machine, and control the version control profile throughout development, build, and QA.

Clouds in CUBiT are groups of server pools from a corporate datacenter or from public clouds like Amazon EC2. Amazon EC2 is the public cloud initially supported by CUBiT 2.0 and can be used, for example, to extend resources temporarily and at a very low cost.

Other new features in CUBiT 2.0 include support for LDAP/Active Directory, and advanced accounting and chargeback capabilities tied to role-based access control for allocating costs per server and profile type.

"CollabNet CUBiT reduces Ford's testing cycles by up to 50 percent. Because CUBiT virtualizes our test environment and manages ever-changing configurations, our release cycles have gone from four–six weeks to one week," said Marc Fecker, director of technology at FordDirect.com, a joint venture between Ford Motor Company and Ford Dealers. "CUBiT is critical because it enables our internal and external QA team worldwide to securely manage and track standardized sets of build and test services. We not only have complete traceability of the configuration changes being made, anyone has the ability to grab servers for running tests on-demand, as they need them, which saves us on hardware costs as well."

"At CollabNet, we're dedicated to easing the critical pain points of software development by helping teams to be more productive and responsive," said Tony de la Lama, CollabNet vice president of worldwide marketing and corporate strategy. "Teams are faced with increasingly complex software development cycles that require more flexible solutions. CUBiT 2.0 is specifically designed to meet these needs by bringing build and test operations to the cloud for fast, easy, self-service access."

CollabNet CUBiT 2.0 is available as a managed service or as an on-site license, starting at US $1,000 per node. A free trial is available at http://www.collab.net/trycubit.

Cassatt

Cassatt Corporation offers several products to help internal cloud computing—an IT approach that delivers the benefits of cloud computing using the resources that organizations already have inside their datacenters.

"Cloud computing offers great promise by having third parties deliver the computing resources needed to run applications as an on-demand service, with a lot of the IT infrastructure invisible to the user," said Bill Coleman, chairman and CEO of Cassatt Corp. "However, at this point most IT professionals are not comfortable outsourcing the mission-critical parts of their sensitive internal applications to an external cloud provider. They are concerned about availability, vendor lock-in, not having the control they need, and having to rebuild these applications from scratch with proprietary tools running on provider-specific platforms."

To address these problems, the Cassatt offerings help customers implement cloud-style computing environments using their existing systems, inside the firewalls of their datacenters without having to modify their current hardware or software. The resulting "internal cloud" can provide the same operational efficiency, fault tolerance, and energy savings promised by external clouds, but without the worries over security, compliance, lack of control, or the need or delay required to change or replace their current applications.

Benefits   The Cassatt software and services provide organizations with initial steps toward realizing the benefits of cloud computing. The Cassatt Active Profiling Service gives companies a head start on establishing internal clouds by tackling a major problem facing corporate IT—a lack of information and understanding about the assets, interrelationships, and dynamic, real-time usage patterns within datacenters.

Through the control capabilities of Cassatt Active Response 5.2, Cassatt can help customers improve energy efficiency, application availability, and enable the best use of computing resources—across the diverse hardware, software, and virtualization technologies already running in a datacenter.

"Cassatt gives organizations the ability to run their data centers like Amazon or Google, but using the IT infrastructure they already have in-house," said Coleman. "We think internal cloud computing is the key to data center efficiency. And, because of that, internal clouds can't be limited to only one type of virtualization or operating system. With Cassatt, customers can control and optimize the many types of hardware, operating systems, virtualization, and network resources that they already have—and they can start today."

The Cassatt Active Profiling Service gathers information about servers and their configurations, server usage patterns, utilization, energy consumption, server interdependencies, and other key details. Then, Cassatt experts analyze the data to help companies make the best decisions on ways to improve datacenter efficiency and operations—including recommendations such as finding "orphan" or unused servers, identifying candidate servers for virtualization and consolidation, suggesting policies to save on datacenter energy costs, and mapping out the steps to move toward an internal cloud-style IT infrastructure that could provide utility-style computing.

Use   Example recommendations could include using active power management technology to curb energy waste from idle servers; automating failover to provide improved application availability, regardless of platform; implementing dynamic resource repurposing to make better use of every server while preserving availability and service levels; or coupling policy-based management with resource repurposing, allowing datacenter infrastructure to respond quickly to changes in business demand.

Cassatt also offers broadened operating system, virtualization, and networking support for Cassatt Active Response 5.2. This latest revision extends Cassatt's existing, broad operating system, virtualization, and networking support to include the IBM AIX operating system and Force10 network switches, with forthcoming support for Parallels Virtuozzo Containers OS-level server virtualization solutions.

Active Response   Cassatt Active Response enables datacenter managers to use policies to control and optimize the multiple diverse components of their IT infrastructure. Cassatt Active Response can monitor and automatically provision or decommission physical and virtual server, software, and network resources as appropriate to meet the application demand.

This means that with Cassatt Active Response customers can break down the static silos of hardware and software that sit mostly idle in datacenters today, overprovisioned in anticipation of the largest expected spikes in demand. Instead, customers can pool their hardware and software into a cloud of computing resources shared across applications, and use only the amount of computing capacity needed at any one time. This approach frees up previously unusable compute capacity, increases control, and can reduce traditional IT operations costs for datacenters by as much as 50 percent, fundamentally altering the calculations for what could or should be outsourced.

"As organizations become aware of the potential cost benefits and flexibility associated with cloud computing, they are going to look for ways to get these same benefits in their internal data centers," said Al Gillen, program vice president, system software at IDC. "Cassatt recognized the benefit of building a management system that could deliver services using a cloud-like paradigm long before the term 'cloud' was in everyday use. Cassatt continues to expand its support for the hardware, software, virtualization, and networking resources that customers use in their data centers today."

"We are pleased that the combination of IBM AIX systems, with the latest version of Cassatt Active Response, will result in further energy efficiency in the data center," said Jay Kruemcke, AIX offering manager, IBM Systems and Technology Group. "Through the application of utility computing principles including resource repurposing and power management, the AIX platform can be one of the most power-efficient compute platforms on the market today."

"With Cassatt's newly added support of Force10 Networks data center switching solutions, customers can automatically optimize the configuration of network infrastructure, guaranteeing the quality of service and bandwidth required by applications, based on policies they set, to deliver cloud-style optimization and agility," said Steve Garrison, vice president of marketing, Force10 Networks. "Customers can save on space, power, cooling, and cabling, while using our agile, robust switch infrastructure to provide the best network configuration to support their business needs at any given time."

Cassatt Active Response 5.2 provides

- Platform support for Linux, Sun Solaris, Microsoft Windows, and IBM AIX.
- Support for virtualization from VMware, Citrix (Xen), with Parallels Virtuozzo Containers coming in the first quarter of 2009. Microsoft Hyper-V will be supported as customer demand warrants.
- Networking support for equipment from Cisco, Dell, Extreme Networks, Nortel Networks, F5, and Force10 Networks.

Cassatt Active Response 5.2 is available in a Standard Edition, Premium Edition, and Data Center Edition. Cassatt Active Response, Standard Edition, starts at US$200 per managed machine. Cassatt Active Response, Premium Edition, starts at US$1,250 per managed machine. Cassatt Active Response, Data Center Edition, starts at US$2,500 per managed machine.

The Cassatt Active Profiling Service is priced based upon the number of servers to be profiled, the number of days of profiling, plus the cost of professional services personnel. The minimum starting point is profiling 150 servers for 30 days, plus one consultant, which starts at US$40,500.

Best Practices

When you plan to move to a cloud solution, there are good ways to go about making the change to ensure an optimal experience while paying less than a colossal price. It starts with your analysis and selection of a vendor, and continues with your day-to-day usage of that service.

Finding the Right Vendor

We've been touting the cost-effectiveness of cloud computing in some way, shape, or form in nearly every chapter of this book. And it's true—it's less costly to go with a cloud model than to buy. However, that doesn't mean it's cheap. With prices as high as $300 per user per month, it's important to be able to measure your options. You have to weigh such issues as:

- Does the provider support me the way I need support?
- Are they easy to work with?
- Will they charge me a crippling amount of money?
- What is their support like?
- What is their track record for uptime?
- Can they give me some references?

There are a lot of issues to weigh. Let's take a closer look at some issues.

Read the Fine Print

Make sure you don't just sign a contract without understanding it. Check the fine print to see if there is a user limit cap on your software. Sometime vendors will allow a low number of users. Then, as your business grows, you get hit with awful penalty charges—even if your software needs haven't changed.

Small businesses are especially at risk here. They are often lured to the cloud with the promise of being able to use enterprise-class software. They sign on for the least expensive package, and then once they hire a few more employees, the monthly bill goes through the roof. It is not uncommon to see the price jump five or six times the starting cost.

Performance

A key thing to consider is assessing the maturity of the cloud service and what is acceptable—to you—from a service delivery standpoint. Since you and your organization will be affected by any outages, it's important to get a service level agreement (SLA) in place, but also to check on past performance. That is, what is their percent uptime guarantee. For example, Amazon has a 99.5 percent uptime guarantee—less than four and a half hours of downtime per year.

Spread Your Services

You may find a vendor who is a perfect match for what you want to do, and you can't wait to get started. But it is a good idea to keep your eyes on what other vendors are offering. To be truly redundant and downtime-proof, you shouldn't have your services on just one cloud. You could have one server on Amazon and another on Azure, for instance.

Data

Make sure your vendor(s) provide customizable data views and reporting. This allows you to get to the data you need quickly. Also, make sure you can get your data back from the vendor. Many vendors make it difficult to export data from the system by only allowing it to be extracted in a proprietary format. Make sure you can export in a common format, like comma-separated-value (CSV).

It is not uncommon during free, trial periods for data to be kept in a proprietary format. However, once you sign the dotted line, you want to be able to take your toys and leave if you wish. The issue is not always brought up, and once you are hip deep into a vendor's services, it isn't the time to find out whether your data is exportable or not.

Data Flow

Automating your processes comes from workflow rules that control where and how data flows through your organization. Data security rules, bound to the workflow, not only automate where the data goes, but also who gets to look at it. Be sure to get a definitive price on how much it will cost to create customized workflow rules and real-time alerts, as well as what effort is required to customize user profiles and role hierarchies to secure your data.

Phased-in vs. Flash-cut Approaches

IT administrators tend to be control freaks, and the thought of giving control of their systems to someone else is difficult. One of the mental hurdles to overcome is being willing to give up physical control of some of your systems. And while you don't need to put everything on the cloud (nor should you), use a phased-in approach, rather than moving everything, all at once.

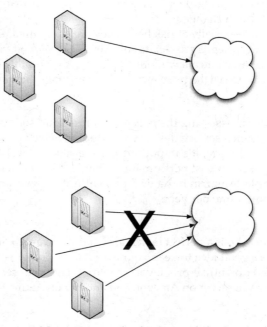

Move services to the cloud as needed rather than
moving everything en masse.

The best way is to do it organically. If a server is failing or not performing up to par, can its duties be offloaded to a cloud vendor? You won't have to buy a new server, and it makes the move to the cloud less frightening.

Be Creative in Your Approach

Just because a cloud is normally used one way, doesn't mean you can't think outside the box. For example, S3 is normally considered a way to store server data, but there's nothing saying you can't use it for general backup purposes.

Also, if your organization has busy times during the year, you can use the cloud to supplement your need. For example, if you get really busy during Christmas, using cloud computing means not having to buy servers to simply deal with demand. Have prebuilt image instances that you can use whenever you want to add capacity.

How Cloud Computing Might Evolve

Cloud computing takes its knocks from opponents who see it as an overused phrase with no real meaning. On the other side of the coin, there are plenty of professionals who see the cloud as not only a useful thing, but also an evolving beast. We are on the verge of Cloud 2.0.

As cloud computing changes, so must your relationship with it. In this section we'll look into our crystal balls and see where it might go. We'll also look at the opinions of researchers who get paid lots of money to make the right predictions.

Researcher Predictions

Researchers love to tell us what's going to happen next with cloud computing. Are they right? We don't know, but it's worth sharing their views. Gartner has been especially diligent in figuring out what's going to happen with cloud computing. Salesforce.com—while not researchers—has given its own prediction of the future, and it's interesting because they're not looking at hardware and software; they're looking at how customers will be affected by the cloud.

Gartner

Gartner sees cloud computing as an evolution of business that is no less influential than e-business. Gartner maintains that the very confusion and contradiction that surrounds the term "cloud computing" signifies its potential to change the status quo in the IT market.

Gartner defines cloud computing as a style of computing where massively scalable IT-related capabilities are provided "as a service" using Internet technologies to multiple external customers.

"During the past 15 years, a continuing trend toward IT industrialization has grown in popularity as IT services delivered via hardware, software and people are becoming repeatable and usable by a wide range of customers and service providers," said Daryl Plummer, managing vice president and Gartner Fellow. "This is due, in part to the commoditization and standardization of technologies, in part to virtualization and the rise of service-oriented software architectures, and most importantly, to the dramatic growth in popularity of the Internet."

Plummer said that taken together, these three major trends constitute the basis of a discontinuity that will create a new opportunity to shape the relationship between those who use IT services and those who sell them. Essentially it will mean that users of IT-related services will be able to focus on what the service provides them rather than how the services are implemented or hosted. Gartner maintains that although names for this type of operation have come into vogue at different times—utility computing, Software as a Service (SaaS), and application service providers—none has garnered widespread acceptance as the central theme for how IT-related services can be delivered globally.

The types of IT services that can be provided through a cloud are wide-reaching. Compute facilities provide computational services so that users can use central processing unit (CPU) cycles without buying computers. Storage services provide a way to store data and documents without having to continually grow farms of storage networks and servers. SaaS companies offer CRM services through their multitenant shared facilities so clients can manage their customers without buying software. These represent only the beginning of options for delivering all kinds of complex capabilities to both businesses and individuals.

"The focus has moved up from the infrastructure implementations and onto the services that allow for access to the capabilities provided," said David Mitchell Smith, vice president and Gartner Fellow. "Although many companies will argue how the cloud services are implemented, the ultimate measure of success will be how the services are consumed and whether that leads to new business opportunities."

Gartner predicts that the impact of cloud computing on IT vendors will be huge. Established vendors have a great presence in traditional software markets, and as new Web 2.0 and cloud business models evolve and expand outside of consumer markets, a great deal could change.

"The vendors are at very different levels of maturity," said David Cearley, vice president and Gartner Fellow. "The consumer-focused vendors are the most mature in delivering what Gartner calls a 'cloud/Web platform' from technology and community perspectives, but the business-focused vendors have rich business services and, at times, are very adept at selling business services."

Branding is a powerful and revenue-generating asset for potential vendors. Gartner analysts cited Wal-Mart as an example of a company that has two brands—one with consumers for its low prices and one in the business world for its supply chain expertise, its core competency, which it capitalizes on to support its consumer-facing brand.

"Companies invest billions of dollars in building up their core competencies, much of which goes into IT," Smith said. "If companies could lease their core competencies to other companies then they would capitalize on both brands, driving revenue both in the consumer-facing market and the business service market in the way that Amazon has done with technology."

Gartner maintains that cloud computing is very much an evolving concept that will take many years to fully mature. It also underlines the fact that the cloud-computing model is not simply the next generation of the Internet.

"When organizations cross the threshold between the Internet as a communications channel and the deliberate delivery of service over the Internet, then we truly start to head for an economy based on consumption of everything from storage to computation to video to finance deduction management," said Plummer.

Three Stages

Gartner also observes that while the cloud computing market is in a period of excitement, growth, and high potential, it will still require several years and many changes in the market before cloud computing—or service-enabled application platforms (SEAPs)—is a mainstream IT effort.

Gartner said that technologically aggressive application development organizations should look to cloud computing for tactical projects through 2011, during which time the market will begin to mature and be dominated by a select group of vendors. Following this period, Gartner predicts that the market will see a surge of new vendors and subsequent consolidation as cloud computing becomes appealing to more mainstream application development organizations. By 2015, cloud computing will have been commoditized and will be the preferred solution for many application development projects.

"SEAPs are the foundation on which software-as-a-service solutions are built," said Mark Driver, research vice president at Gartner. "As SEAP technologies mature during the next several years, Gartner foresees three distinct, but slightly overlapping, phases of evolution. The first phase, through 2011, will be that of the pioneers and trailblazers; the second, running from 2010 through 2013, will be all about market consolidation; while the third phase, from 2012 through 2015, will see mainstream critical mass and commoditization."

Phase 1: 2007 to 2011 — Pioneers and Trailblazers   This will largely be a market development phase. Through 2011, given the natural immaturity of SEAP solutions, compounded by their proprietary nature, Gartner advises most SEAP adopters to focus on opportunistic solutions— quick-hit, tactical opportunities where time to market and developer productivity outweigh long-term technical viability. Although some rare exceptions will exist, mainstream IT developers should focus primarily on SEAP investments where return on investment can be acquired within 18 to 24 months.

As a result of a focus on technical merit over investment protection, technology providers with the strongest market "vision" will garner the most success among early adopters. Building on this trend, many early SEAP vendors will focus on rapid-application-development-oriented tools and deployment features, making their solutions particularly attractive among end-user computing efforts and social-computing projects.

Phase 2: 2010 to 2013 — Market Consolidation   Gartner predicts that by 2012, the SEAP market will become overcrowded with a broad range of solutions from large and small vendors, and competitive pressure will drive many weaker players from the market, resulting in acquisition activity. During this consolidation phase, SEAP infrastructure will become increasingly attractive to a broader range of potential adopters, resulting in a more mainstream and conservative user base. Consequently, the "ability to execute" will become equally as important as technical innovation and market vision among most mainstream adopters. Return-on-investment time frames will be extended from tactical short-term opportunities to longer, strategic time frames of three to five years.

By 2013, Gartner expects SEAP technology to be the preferred, but not the exclusive, choice for the majority of opportunistic and architecturally simple application development efforts among Global 2000 enterprises, and as a result, some will seek to expand their reliance on SEAP platforms to include longer-term strategic (systematic) investments.

Phase 3: 2012 to 2015 and Beyond — Mainstream Critical Mass and Commoditization   In 2013, a small number of large SEAP providers will dominate the market, providing de facto standards. These vendors will primarily leverage proprietary technologies developed during the previous five years, but they will also widely support intracloud application programming interfaces to establish a SEAP technology "fabric," linking cloud-based solutions across vendor platforms.

Market expansion into increasingly conservative user bases will further shift market emphasis from innovation to stability, cost, and investment protection. Competition between proprietary lock-in and open-SEAP technologies will increase and, by 2014, concern over lock-in will lead to critical-mass support for one or more open-source SEAP software stacks. These open-SEAP stacks will begin to compete with proprietary solutions and slowly growing portions of the SEAP market beyond the 2015 time frame.

Salesforce.com and Customer Service

Cloud evolution will not just take place in a technical realm. Also affecting how cloud services will change is how customers interact with the cloud. Salesforce.com is addressing customer service needs with its Service Cloud program.

Built on the Force.com platform, the Service Cloud transforms customer service through the power of cloud computing, and brings together industry-leading cloud computing platforms like Google, Facebook, and Amazon.com to capture every conversation and leverage every community expert in the cloud.

By capturing these conversations, the Service Cloud empowers companies to deliver the expertise of the community to customers, agents, and partners regardless of location or device—ensuring that the quality of customer service is consistent across every channel. The Service Cloud represents the future of customer service, where more than two-thirds of all service conversations will take place in the cloud.

"The Service Cloud is the first customer service solution that empowers companies to join and manage all service conversations happening in the cloud," said Marc Benioff, chairman and CEO of Salesforce.com. "This has been made possible through the emergence of native cloud computing platforms like Force.com that are built to harness the power of other clouds like Facebook, Google, and Amazon.com."

According to Gartner analyst Michael Maoz, vice president and research fellow, Gartner, Inc., "The new generation of consumers trusts content created by peers. This consumer expectation that they can create answers and content as part of a community will lead businesses and other organizations to adopt similar techniques to succeed. Ultimately, organizations will have to change their singular emphasis on tools for agents, to a broader strategy that also supports the role of community experts."

"Increasingly, people connect with organizations and products through the trusted friends and communities of experts that are part of their online social network," said Elliot Schrage, vice president, communications, public policy and platform marketing, Facebook. "Organizations need a powerful way to become part of the conversations about their products, and we believe Force.com for Facebook and Facebook Pages enable companies to engage with customers on a more personal level."

Traditionally, contact center technologies have been removed from the experts and knowledge found in the cloud. Yet already 50 percent of all service conversations are taking place in the cloud. The Service Cloud unites these two disconnected, yet important, worlds to establish the new model for customer service. Capturing and funneling information from inside the enterprise and in the cloud into the knowledge base is at the heart of the Service Cloud. The Service Cloud is made up of six main components around the knowledge base to gather, distill, and disseminate the expert knowledge found in the cloud to customers, agents, and partners:

- **Community**   Developing an online customer community is an integral part of the Service Cloud. The Service Cloud represents a fundamental shift in how companies approach their online presence—it's not just a place to post information, but a community where customers can interact with each other and have conversations with the company at large. Companies can easily set up and maintain an interactive cloud community for their customers by leveraging new Salesforce.com technologies such as Salesforce CRM Ideas and Force.com Sites as building blocks.

- **Social**   The Force.com platform enables the Service Cloud to connect to leading social networking sites such as Facebook, community forums, blogs, and more. Through these connections, companies will be able to funnel this information directly into their knowledge base. The Service Cloud ensures that the company's knowledge base has the most up-to-date support information sourced from community experts.

- **Search**   More times than not, customers begin with a Google search to find answers to their questions. By creating an active online community with the Service Cloud, companies can ensure that their site is one of the top results returned in a customer's search. It is through the power of Force.com Sites that the expert knowledge of the community is made available in search engine results.

- **Partners**   Using the Service Cloud, companies can now share all of the information in the knowledge base quickly and easily with their partners. Cloud computing's unique model has enabled Salesforce.com to easily and securely connect separate Salesforce CRM deployments, allowing companies to share cases, contacts, and company information, without the need for complex integration software.

- **Phone, email, and chat**   The Service Cloud will give agents access to knowledge in the cloud, regardless if they use phones, email, or chat to service customers. By providing the contact center with the same knowledge found in the community, the Service Cloud ensures that the quality and cost of service across every channel is strengthened by the expertise of the community.

- **Force.com**   The Service Cloud utilizes the latest Force.com capabilities, including Force.com Sites, Force.com for Facebook, and more to uniquely join together knowledge and conversations regardless of where they take place online. The Service Cloud also taps into the power of more than 100 customer service extensions on the Force.com AppExchange for areas like chat, field service, and CTI. Additionally, customers using the Service Cloud gain all the benefits of the proven security, reliability, and scalability of Salesforce.com's trusted global infrastructure.

Responding to Change

Keep up on apps. You have the ones that you want, and they were serving your organization well, but it's worth it to see what others are developing. For instance, if you go to Force.com, you can search through apps that others have shared. You may find one that does the job better than the one you're using now, or you may discover an application that does the job in a different way.

On a deeper level, analyze the applications to see if there is some fundamental, philosophical change to understand how apps are revolutionizing your industry.

Keep up on vendors—not just your current ones, but new players. There may be a new vendor who is a better match for you, but unless you keep your ear to the ground, you won't know about them. Also, read what others are saying about their vendors. If you're hearing good buzz about a vendor, and if you are in the market to switch vendors, they should be at the top of your list.

Also, you can use a tool like CloudStatus to see how different cloud providers are doing in overall performance.

Get Ready

As we mentioned in the previous section, understanding how applications are evolving can help you be ready for Cloud 2.0. That said, you should also stay on top of changes to the world of cloud computing, in general. Is there a new cloud provider offering something more unique than anyone else? Is there a new company using cloud computing in a unique way?

Cloud computing is in its infancy. Think of it like the Internet back in 1995—it wasn't very glamorous, somewhat clunky, but still useful. As more people have gotten their hands into it, it has evolved and changed (and will continue to do so). Look for more evolution of cloud computing and look for more ways that it can benefit your organization.

Glossary, Vendors, and Resources

E ven though you're looking at the last few pages of an entire book on cloud computing, it's really just the tip of the iceberg. Cloud computing is a very large subject that is evolving at a rapid pace. In this appendix, you'll see a glossary of terms, and you'll find some excellent places to bone up on cloud computing, learn more about the services out there, and perhaps discover a few new things. The first part of this appendix is a glossary of cloud computing terms. It's all the jargon you're likely to hear that pertains to cloud computing. Next, we'll talk about some of the companies that offer their own cloud services. Finally, we'll offer some resources for you to find out more information.

Glossary

The more you're exposed to the world of cloud computing, the more cloud jargon you'll hear. There is no lack of web sites and blogs out there that rail on cloud jargon. We're not going to take a stance either way, but for the sake of understanding what everyone means when they use a cloud term, here's a glossary of some of the more commonly spoken (and written) cloud terms.

application virtualization　The separation of the application from the OS. This applies to applications at all tiers, from servers to desktops. Normally, this is achieved using encapsulation. Encapsulating and isolating the application from the OS changes the way applications can install and interact with the OS. This makes it possible for the application to be moved from one system to another, patched, and updated without interactions with other applications or OSes. Application virtualization also allows applications to be copied or backed up as a single file.

capsules　Capsules embody an isolated application and its dependencies so that an application in a capsule can run on any host OS. With encapsulation, the application's OS dependency has been broken.

cloud app   A software application that is not installed on a local machine. It is accessible via the Internet.

cloud arcs   An abbreviation for cloud architectures, which are designs for software applications that can be accessed over the Internet.

cloud bridge   Running an application so that its components are integrated within multiple cloud environments. This could be a combination of internal or private or public clouds.

cloud client   A computing device for cloud computing. Also known as a thin client.

cloud envy   A vendor who rebrands an existing service to jump on the cloud computing bandwagon.

cloud lock-in   The level of difficulty associated with moving an application or data from one cloud provider to anywhere else—to another provider or back to your organization. Cost, time, level of difficulty, and portability are all variables in determining cloud lock-in.

cloud OS   Another way to describe Platform as a Service (PaaS) like Google App Engine or Salesforce.com

cloud portability   The ability to move applications and data between several cloud computing vendors.

cloud provider   A provider that makes storage, software, or an operating system available to others over a private or public network.

cloud service architecture (CSA)   An architecture in which applications and application components act as services on the Internet.

cloud storage   Storing data on a cloud provider's storage infrastructure. Data you generate is housed off-site with a third party.

NOTE *Cloud storage is often compared to leasing a car—you always have the latest and greatest technology, but you pay for it each month and never own it.*

cloudburst   A euphemism used when your cloud service has a security breach or you are unable to access your data.

cloudcenter   A large service provider (like Google) that rents its infrastructure.

cloud-oriented architecture (COA)   An architecture that lends itself to incorporating cloud computing components.

cloudsourcing   Making use of any type of cloud service.

cloudstorm   Occurs when multiple cloud computing environments are tied together. Also called cloud network.

cloudware   Software that allows building, deploying, running, or managing applications in a cloud computing environment.

cloudwashing   Putting the word "cloud" on products and services you already have.

encapsulation   Defining an application and all of its dependencies, and then locating them in a physical, isolated folder.

external cloud   A cloud computing environment that is external to the organization.

funnel cloud   Dialogue about cloud computing that goes round and round, yet never touches the ground (that is, comes to fruition).

grid computing   A technique in which disparate computing and storage resources are organized to perform a specific task. The resources are brought together through the Internet or more secure private networks.

hardware virtualization   A technology that emulates hardware to allow multiple OSes, multiple instances of a single OS, or any combination thereof to coexist on the same machine.

hypervisor   Software that controls the layer between the hardware operating systems. It allows multiple operating systems to run on the same physical hardware. There are two types of hypervisors:

- Bare metal, which allows the hypervisor to run directly on the hardware
- Hosted architecture, in which the hypervisor runs on top of an existing operating system

hybrid cloud   A computing environment in which both public and private cloud computing environments are present.

internal cloud   Sometimes called a *private cloud*. This type of cloud exists within the boundaries of an organization.

network virtualization   Mapping two disparate networks into a single, unified network. This makes it look as if all remote networks are in a single place.

OS virtualization   The creation of a separate run-time environment within the same operating system. Applications are installed and interaction with the operating system is not changed, so there are no substantial changes occurring to the host operating system.

paravirtualization   A virtual server technique that emulates hardware for a guest operating system. Paravirtualized servers are modified guest operating systems existing on top of the hypervisor. The chief difference between a virtual machine and a paravirtualized machine is that the guest OS on a virtual machine is unmodified, while the OS in a paravirtualized environment is modified to work more directly with the hypervisor.

personal cloud   Sometimes known as MiFi (pronounced "me fi"). This is a portable, personal router that allows multiple users to connect by taking mobile wireless signals and translating them to WiFi.

Physical-to-Physical migration (P2P)   Moving a complete OS environment and installed applications from one physical server to another. This is done either by cloning drives and putting the cloned drive into a new server, or by using application virtualization to control the transfer from server to server.

Physical-to-Virtual migration (P2V)   The process of capturing and migrating a complete OS environment and applications from a physical to a virtual environment.

private cloud   *See* internal cloud.

public cloud   Cloud computing environments that are open for use to the public.

server virtualization   The ability to host multiple OS images on a single hardware platform.

storage virtualization   The abstraction of physical storage from logical storage. Storage may consist of storage pools and devices in different physical locations, but the end user would only see it as one, centrally managed pool.

utility computing   A metered service in which computing or storage is provided on a needed basis, much like the way public utilities (water, gas, and so on) are provided to homes and paid for on a similar basis. Utility customers pay for the service they use, rather than specific equipment.

virtual appliance   A minimalist virtual machine image designed to run a virtualization technology (like VMware). Virtual appliances aim to eliminate the installation, configuration, and maintenance costs associated with running complicated software. The difference between a virtual machine and a virtual appliance is that a virtual appliance is fully preinstalled and preconfigured, while a virtual machine is ready for software to be installed.

vertical cloud   A cloud computing environment that is optimized for a particular vertical industry.

virtual machine   A server emulating real or fictional hardware for an unmodified guest OS. It is installed as an application on a host OS. Applications installed on the virtual machine are not aware that they exist on a virtual machine.

Virtual-to-Physical migration (V2P)   The process of installing a virtual environment onto a physical server.

virtual private cloud (VPC)   Akin to a virtual private network (VPN), but the cloud version of it. It is often used to bridge private clouds to a public cloud.

Cloud Vendors

While we talked about some of the big names in cloud computing in Chapter 3, they aren't the only ones. Not by a long shot. Table A-1 lists some other cloud vendors. The list is not exhaustive, and there are dozens more out there; this is just a little look at the rest of the iceberg.

Name	URL	Description
3PAR	www.3par.com	Offers adaptive provisioning for organizations needing dynamic resources.
3Tera	www.3tera.com	Allows for the provisioning and deployment of "scalable clustered applications in minutes from anywhere in the world."
10Gen Agathon Group	www.agathongroup.com	Offers nonprofits and charitable groups the ability to scale on demand.
Amazon	www.amazon.com	Amazon introduced Elastic Compute Cloud (EC2) by saying, "to enable you to increase or decrease capacity within minutes, not hours or days." They also brought the topic to the forefront of public awareness.
Apache Hadoop Core	Hadoop.apache.org	Apache Hadoop Core is a software platform that makes it easy to write and run applications that process vast amounts of data.
Appirio	www.appirio.com	Offers services and products to help accelerate the adoption of on-demand solutions.
Appistry	www.appistry.com	Offers a grid-based application platform that makes it easy to scale out CPU- and data-intensive applications across a virtualized grid.
Apprenda	www.apprenda.com	Offers an operating system for building and deploying SaaS applications and a platform for conducting SaaS business.
Aptana	www.aptana.com/cloud	Aptana bills its cloud as follows: "[It] is architected to complement cloud infrastructure providers like Amazon, Google, Joyent, and others."
Arjuna	www.arjuna.com	Arjuna describes its Agility service as an "on-ramp to the cloud [that] allows the IT department to begin to experiment with cloud computing in a gradual, incremental way, without any need for disruption to existing service."

TABLE A-1   Several Cloud Computing Vendors

Name	URL	Description
AT&T	www.att.com	Entered the cloud business in August 2008 with the launch of its AT&T Synaptic Hosting service, which it describes as "a next-generation utility computing service with managed networking, security and storage for businesses."
Bluewolf	www.bluewolf.com	Provides on-demand software deployment services and remote database management. Its Arcade cloud offering allows users to store unlimited files through a Salesforce interface.
Cassatt	www.cassatt.com	Developers of internal cloud computing solutions, reasoning that issues like service level agreements and compliance are too difficult to manage.
Cisco	www.cisco.com	No formal offerings (as of this writing), but with the acquisition of WebEx and PostPath, they seem headed to the cloud.
Citrix	www.citrix.com Select Products and then CloudCenter	Citrix Cloud Center is a set of Citrix products intended to be part of a cloud solution. Intended primarily for service providers but enterprise organizations already use components directly.
Cloud 9 Analytics	www.cloud9analytics.com	Offers "the industry's first truly on-demand analytics platform."
Cloudera	www.cloudera.com	Helps customers install, configure, and run Hadoop for large-scale data processing and analysis.
Cloudscale	www.cloudscale.com	The company says, of its patent-pending technology, "[It] automatically provides the parallelism and scalability required to handle anything from one-off personal analytics agents up to the most demanding live analytics applications required by the world's leading organizations in business, web, science and government."
Cloudworks	www.cloudworks.com	Helps small and mid-market companies outsource computers, software, and data. Users can log in and access everything via the cloud.
CohesiveFT	www.cohesiveft.com	Provides what it calls "Elastic Server On-Demand." The platform allows users to assemble and deploy servers to the cloud in minutes.
Cordys	www.theprocessfactory.com	The Process Factory is a simple solution for creating MashApps business processes from the cloud. Simply mix and match standard business applications to create the customized app you need.

TABLE A-1   Several Cloud Computing Vendors *(continued)*

Name	URL	Description
Dataline	www.dataline.com	Provides large Federal System Integration (FSI) organizations (like Northrop Grumman and Lockheed Martin) with cloud advice and expertise.
Dell Desktoptwo	www.desktoptwo.com	Bills itself as "your home in the cloud." Allows you to store documents and other information on the cloud and also offers opportunities to develop applications and share them with others.
Elastra	www.elastra.com	Elastra offers to "design, deploy and manage database and application infrastructure in the cloud in minutes—all with the click of a button."
EMC	www.emc.com	Helps manage client data on the cloud.
Engine Yard	www.engineyard.com	On-demand deployment and management of Ruby on Rails applications on Amazon EC2.
Enomalism	www.enomalism.com	Says they focus on "solving the cost and complexity for enterprises that run large technical server infrastructures."
eVapt	www.evapt.com	Promises to enable "usage based monetization (instant SaaS metering) for SaaS and Cloud Computing vendors."
FlexiScale	www.flexiscale.com	A flexible, scalable, automated hosting platform.
G.ho.st	g.ho.st	An online desktop complete with standard office applications.
GigaSpaces	www.gigaspaces.com	Allows businesses and developers "to predictably scale on-line systems under any peak demand, guarantee real-time performance under any data processing load and seamlessly leverage the economies of scale offered by virtual computing environments such as clouds and grids."
GoGrid	www.gogrid.com	GoGrid offers customers the ability to grow production servers in real time to meet demand without affecting uptime.
Google	www.google.com	Google is the hands-down leader in cloud computing, offering everything from online applications to a development platform for creating custom apps.
Hyperic	www.hyperic.com	Provides monitoring and management applications for all types of web tools.
IBM	www.ibm.com	IBM is focused on helping organizations build secure and efficient infrastructures with cloud computing as part of the solution.

TABLE A-1   Several Cloud Computing Vendors

Name	URL	Description
Interoute	www.interoute.com	Europe's largest fibre optic network and largest privately owned cloud.
Joyent	www.joyent.com	Serves billions of web pages each month and is an on-demand computing provider.
Kaavo	www.kaavo.com	Kaavo's main product, Infrastructure and Middleware on Demand (IMOD), promises to "make it easier for individuals and businesses to implement on-demand infrastructure and middleware and run secure and scalable web services and applications."
Keynote Systems	Kite.keynote.com	Has long been a SaaS provider and recently added cloud infrastructure to its offerings.
Layered Technologies	www.layeredtech.com	Offers virtual private datacenters, virtual machines, virtual containers, and virtual storage.
LongJump	www.longjump.com	Offers Platform as a Service, which it describes as "an on-demand platform for creating and delivering business applications to manage data, streamline collaborative processes and provide actionable analysis."
Meeza	www.meeza.com.qa	Qatar-based Meeza is currently the only cloud provider in the Middle East/North Africa region.
Nirvanix	www.nirvanix.com	Offers companies more than 5TB of data with a scalable storage and delivery platform.
OpenNebula	www.opennebula.org	OpenNebula is an open source tool for virtual machines within datacenters. It supports on-demand access to Amazon EC2.
OpSource	www.opsource.net	Delivers web operations tool for SaaS and web companies.
Parallels	www.parallels.com	Provides virtualization and automation software to businesses and service providers. Their technology is also used by large businesses to create their own, in-house clouds.
ParaScale	www.parascale.com	ParaScale says its solution "enables the enterprise or service provider to build enormous storage pools on commodity hardware at an affordable cost."
Platform Computing	www.platform.com	Believes there is crossover between grid and cloud computing in that both clouds and grids mask the complexity of management tasks from the end user.

TABLE A-1 Several Cloud Computing Vendors (continued)

Name	URL	Description
Quantivo	www.quantivo.com	Says they are "revolutionizing the Business Intelligence (BI) world by combining Cloud Computing with an innovative and patented 'Affinity Analytics' technology."
Rackspace	www.rackspace.com	Offers cloud storage and Linux-based cloud servers.
RightScale	www.rightscale.com	RightScale's main offering is an automated cloud management tool that helps create scalable web applications running on EC2 and Amazon Web Services (AWS).
rPath	www.rpath.com	The company says of their virtual appliances: "Virtual appliances eliminate the hassles of the general purpose operating system and free vendors and customers to focus on application value instead of technology management."
Salesforce.com	www.salesforce.com	A leader in customer relationship management tools and a huge name in cloud computing circles. Their toolkit for cloud development is Force.com.
SIMtone	www.simtone.net	Commercialized their Universal Cloud Computing Platform, which allows network operators and businesses to host, manage, and provision any cloud-hosted services.
Skytap	www.skytap.com	Skytap Virtual Lab is a hosted, on-demand service for virtual lab automation and management.
SLA@SOI	www.sla-at-soi.eu	The European company's vision is "to create a business-ready service-oriented infrastructure that will empower the service economy in a flexible and dependable way."
SmugMug	www.smugmug.com	Offers unlimited storage and stores backups of stored photos in multiple datacenters.
SOASTA	www.soasta.com	Web testing is at the heart of SOASTA's CloudTest offering.
Sun	www.sun.com	Network.com is Sun's cloud offering and is based on the Sun Grid project.
Terremark	www.theenterprisecloud.com	Offers enterprise cloud services that allow organizations to control a resource pool of processing, storage, and networking.
VMware	www.vmware.com	VMware is nearly synonymous with virtualization and the technology that makes today's clouds possible.
Zuora	www.zuora.com	The leader in cloud billing technology. The company calls its Z-Commerce platform "the first commerce platform for cloud developers."

PART III

TABLE A-1 Several Cloud Computing Vendors

Resources

Cloud computing is constantly evolving, so keeping up on what's new is essential. Table A-2 contains a list of cloud computing resources available on the World Wide Web.

Name	URL
3TERA—Grid Operating System for Web Applications	http://www.3tera.com/
Access Grid Project	http://www.AccessGrid.org/
Amazon Elastic Computer Cloud (Amazon EC2)	http://aws.amazon.com/ec2/
CenterGate Research Group LLC	http://www.centergate.com/
CloudBuddy—Your Virtual Desktop	http://www.mycloudbuddy.com/
Cloud Computing and Emerging IT Platforms: Vision, Hype, and Reality for Delivering Computing as the 5th Utility	http://www.gridbus.org/reports/CloudITPlatforms2008.pdf
Cloud Computing and High-Performance Computing	http://search.techrepublic.com.com/search/cloud+computing+and+high-performance+computing.html
Cloud Computing Expo	http://cloudcomputingexpo.com/
Cloud Computing Journal	http://cloudcomputing.sys-con.com/
Cloud Computing Resource Center	http://www.deitel.com/ResourceCenters/Programming/CloudComputing/tabid/3057/Default.aspx
Cloud Computing Resource, News and Support	http://www.dabcc.com/section.aspx?sectionid=12
Cloud Computing—Wikipedia	http://en.wikipedia.org/wiki/Cloud_computing
Cloudo—The Computer Evolved	http://www.cloudo.com/
CloudSim: A Novel Framework for Modeling and Simulation of Cloud Computing Infrastructures and Services by Rodrigo N. Calheiros, Rajiv Ranjan, César A. F. De Rose, and Rajkumar Buyya	http://www.gridbus.org/reports/CloudSim-ICPP2009.pdf
Condor Project—High Throughput Computing	http://www.cs.wisc.edu/condor/
DataMiningGrid Consortium	http://www.datamininggrid.org/
Digipede Technologies—Distributed Computing Solutions on Microsoft.NET Platform	http://www.digipede.net/
Distributed.net—Node Zero	http://www.distributed.net/

TABLE A-2   Cloud Computing Resources

Name	URL
Distributed Computing Resources	http://www.jamesthornton.com/hotlist/distcomp.html
Distributed Generic Information Retrieval (DiGIR)	http://digir.sourceforge.net/
Distributed Search Engines	http://www.openp2p.com/pub/t/74
Distributed Systems—Google Code University	http://code.google.com/edu/parallel/index.html
Distributed Systems Laboratory at University of Chicago	http://dsl.cs.uchicago.edu/
eyeOS—Cloud Computing Operating System	http://eyeos.org/
Force.com—Cloud Computing for the Enterprise	http://www.Force.com/
Ganglia—Distributed Monitoring System for Clusters and Grids	http://www.ganglia.info/
Google App Engine—Run Your Web Apps on Google's Infrastructure	http://code.google.com/appengine/
Google Apps—Software-As-a-Service for Business Email, and Information Sharing	http://www.google.com/apps/intl/en/business/index.html
IBM Cloud Computing	http://www.ibm.com/ibm/cloud/
IEEE Task Force on Cluster Computing	http://www.ieeetfcc.org/
Internet-based Distributed Computing Projects	http://distributedcomputing.info
IRIS: Infrastructure for Resilient Internet Systems	http://iris.lcs.mit.edu/
Lawrence Berkeley National Laboratory—Above the Clouds: A Berkeley View of Cloud Computing	http://www.lbl.gov/CS/
Manjrasoft—Innovative Cloud and Grid Computing Technologies	http://www.manjrasoft.com/
Microsoft Cloud Computing Tools	http://msdn.microsoft.com/en
Mithral—Client-Server Software Development Kit (CSSDK)	http://www.mithral.com/products/cs
MysterNetworks—The Evolution of Peer-to-Peer	http://www.mysternetworks.com/
Network World Fusion	http://www.nwfusion.com/
NeuroGrid—P2P Search	http://www.neurogrid.net/
NSF Middleware Initiative	http://www.nsf-middleware.org/
NVIDIA Tesla Personal Supercomputer	http://www.nvidia.com/object/personal_supercomputing.html
Open Cluster Group	http://www.openclustergroup.org/
OpenP2P.com	http://www.openp2p.com/

TABLE A-2 Cloud Computing Resources

Name	URL
OSCAR: Open Source Cluster Application Resources	http://www.csm.ornl.gov/oscar/
Parabon Computation—Internet Computing Is Computing Outside the Box	http://www.parabon.com/
Peer to Peer Working Group—P2P WG—Internet2	http://p2p.internet2.edu/
PlanetLab	http://www.planet-lab.org/
Public Data Sets on AWS	http://aws.amazon.com/publicdatasets/
PVM: Parallel Virtual Machine	http://www.csm.ornl.gov/pvm/
QADPZ—Quite Advanced Distributed Parallel Zystem	http://qadpz.sourceforge.net/
Reservoir—Infrastructure for Cloud Computing	http://www.reservoir-fp7.eu/
rPath—A Pragmatic, Incremental Approach to Cloud Computing	http://www.rpath.com/corp/cloud-adoption-model?pi_ad_id=2947665472&gclid=CLzfgpmhk5kCFQITswodsmUaZw
SmartFrog—Smart Framework for Object Groups	http://www.hpl.hp.com/research/smartfrog/
The Cloud, Cloud Computing, Cloud Hosting, and Cloud Services	http://www.mosso.com/
TOP500 Supercomputer Sites	http://www.top500.org/
UNICORE Distributed Computing and Data Resources	http://www.unicore.eu/
UPnP Forum	http://www.upnp.org/
WaveMaker—Open Source Development Platform	http://www.WaveMaker.com/
Worldwide Virtual Computer—Legion	http://www.cs.virginia.edu/~legion/
Yahoo! Directory Computer Science > Distributed Computing	http://dir.yahoo.com/Science/Computer_Science/Distributed_Computing/

TABLE A-2   Cloud Computing Resources (continued)

Index